Linn's

U.S. STAMP YEARBOOK 1992

A comprehensive record of technical data, design development and stories behind all of the stamps, stamped envelopes, postal cards and souvenir cards issued by the United States Postal Service in 1992.

By
George Amick

Published by *Linn's Stamp News*, the largest and most informative stamp newspaper in the world. *Linn's* is owned by Amos Press, 911 Vandemark Road, Sidney, Ohio 45365. Amos Press also publishes *Scott Stamp Monthly* and the Scott line of catalogs.

ISSN 0748-996X

With gratitude . . .

It would be impossible to produce the *Linn's U.S. Stamp Yearbook* series without the help of dozens of people. My associates at *Linn's* and I deeply appreciate the generosity with which they give of their time and information.

For the concept sketches and other art-in-progress developed by the U.S. Postal Service in the creation of 1992's stamp and stationery designs, and for many hours of recollections as to how the stamps and the designs came about, we thank Donald M. McDowell, former director, Office of Stamp and Philatelic Marketing; Jack Williams, Joe Brockert, Terrence McCaffrey and Elizabeth A. Altobell of the Design Section, and Bradbury Thompson, Howard Paine, Richard Sheaff, Derry Noyes and Jerry Pinkney, design coordinators who worked with the Citizens' Stamp Advisory Committee.

Information on production and other details were furnished by Richard H. Arvonio, manager, Stamp Acquisition, and Kathy Caggiano, Al Fatah, Frank Farrell, Sonya Mae, Robin Minard, Jim Murphy, Mike O'Hara, Kim Parks and Frank Thomas of USPS; Leah Akbar, Thomas K. Brown, Leonard Buckley, Cecilia Hatfield, Maureen McGuinness and Norma Opgrand of the Bureau of Engraving and Printing; Paul Martein of the Government Printing Office; Richard Sennett, Sandra Lane and Lynda Tilton of Sennett Enterprises; Alan Green of Avery Dennison; Thomas C. Harris and Kelly Keough of the American Bank Note Company; Richard Salois and Barry Levenson of Westvaco-USEnvelope Division; Benny Rich and Roy Hogshed of Dittler Brothers; Hugh Ashton and Barry Switzer of Ashton-Potter America; Sidney R. Goodman and Julie Kay Anderson of Postal Buddy; and Phil Hurowitz of Banknote Corporation of America.

Time, artwork and information were also generously shared by former CSAC chairman Jack Rosenthal and CSAC members C. Douglas Lewis and Mary Ann Owens, and stamp designers Byron Birdsall, Higgins Bond, William Bond, Christopher Calle, Anthony DeLuz, Steff Geissbuhler, Robert Giusti, Michael Hagel, Joe Hautman, Howard Koslow, Karen Mallary, Robert T. McCall, Lou Nolan, Chuck Ripper, M. Gregory Rudd, Dennis Simon and Ren Wicks.

Requests for specific details and collateral material were willingly answered by Ann Bagne of the Jet Propulsion Laboratory library, Pasadena, California; Kineret Jaffe of the University of Chicago; William Sharon Farr Jr. of Washington, D.C.; John Hotchner of the U.S. State Department; Alan A. Reich and Mark Lewis of the National Organization on Disability; John W. Patten, publisher of *Business Week*; Anne Serio, museum specialist, National Museum of American History, Smithsonian Institution; Gus Salinas of San Diego; Michael W. Bennett of Willamette University; Jennifer Huget and Linda Ayres of the Wadsworth Atheneum; Elizabeth Parker Rafferty of the Rosenfeld Collection at Mystic Seaport; Teri Strauss, postmaster, Stevenson, Washington; Andrew Epstein, attorney-at-law, Boston, Massachusetts; and stamp dealers Lowell Newman and Jacques C. Schiff Jr.

For sharing their philatelic expertise, thanks to Ken Lawrence, Robert Kitson, George Godin, George Brett, Kim Johnson, Richard C. Schulman, Michael Schreiber, Dan Myers and Wayne Youngblood.

Finally, my personal thanks, as always, go to Donna O'Keefe, my editor at *Linn's*, who each year skillfully transforms my words and pictures into a book, and to my wife and resident computer expert, Donna Amick, for her patience and expert assistance.

— George Amick

Contents

INTRODUCTION

The year 1992 was one of transition for the U.S. Postal Service and its stamp program.

Projects set in motion by the administration of Postmaster General Anthony M. Frank produced a single-year record number of collectible varieties of stamps and postal stationery. But during 1992, Frank resigned and was replaced by a different kind of postmaster general — one who was less interested in stamps and more interested in slashing the Postal Service's costs and collateral enterprises.

The new chief, Marvin T. Runyon Jr., decimated what had been the Department of Philatelic and Retail Services and replaced most of its key decision-makers. People of different professional backgrounds, abilities and outlook were assigned to shape the U.S. stamp program of the future. Among other things, this meant that 1992 was probably the last year for the sheer numbers of stamps that collectors had become accustomed to in recent years.

By the *Yearbook's* count, 181 distinctively new philatelic items, including tagging changes, were placed on sale during the year. The total included an unannounced new variety of the Fishing Boat coil that wasn't spotted until early 1993. Add the Interior Department's duck stamp to the list, and the total reaches 182.

That easily topped the previous record of 140 set in 1991, a year when an overhaul of postal rates provided at least a plausible practical reason for many of the new items.

In 1992 USPS continued to follow two significant stamp-related policies. Postmaster General Runyon has vowed to stick with at least one of these policies — diversification of source of supply — because it has proved to be cost-effective. Two new prime contractors, Bank Note Corporation of America and Dittler Brothers, produced stamps for USPS in 1992, and an established supplier, Stamp Venturers, acquired an intaglio-printing capability.

The other policy is a push for technical innovation, and its future under Runyon is less clear. Once again in 1992, however, this policy made life interesting (and in some cases complicated) for collectors.

An experimental machine called a Postage and Mailing Center, dispensing variable-rate stamps, was introduced (and quickly encountered numerous breaking-in problems). Pressure-sensitive stamps for over-the-counter sale emerged from the experimental category and were distributed nationwide. The Postal Buddy computerized address-change and postal card printing system got a new look and new refinements. For the first time in the modern era, general-use stamps were printed by offset lithography with no intaglio element added for security. In place of intaglio, special printing innovations were developed to make the stamps photocopy-resistant.

But the biggest story of the year in U.S. stamps revolved around a stamp that wouldn't even be issued until 1993. It was the announcement that rock music legend Elvis Presley would be pictured on a commemorative, followed by a nationwide postcard poll to determine the design. Conceived and directed by Anthony Frank with the touch of a public-relations genius, Operation Elvis gave stamps and stamp collecting unprecedented publicity — and ended up being a strange but profitable legacy from Frank to his successor.

In this, the tenth annual edition of *Linn's U.S. Stamp Yearbook*, we tell that story in detail, along with the story behind each of those 182 collectible stamp varieties. We hope you enjoy reading the book as much as we at *Linn's Stamp News* have enjoyed putting it together.

COMMEMORATIVES

In 1992 the U.S. Postal Service issued the astonishing total of 118 commemorative stamps. That number was easily a record; in fact, it was far higher than the total number of commemoratives, definitives, special stamps and postal stationery items that appear in most years.

Of the 118, 76 were accounted for by just three multiple issues. The biggest of these was a 50-variety pane depicting American wildflowers, the fourth such mega-set in USPS history. Next was the 16-stamp recreation of the first U.S. commemoratives, the 1893 Columbian Exposition set. The third item was the World War II sheetlet containing 10 stamps. This sheetlet, the second in a projected five-year series marking the war's 50th anniversary, recalled key events of 1942.

Several other multiple issues helped swell the commemorative total. For instance, two se-tenant strips of five publicized the Olympic Games — and the Olympic sponsor's role played by USPS. Two topical booklets, each of five varieties, depicted hummingbirds (American) and wild animals (mostly non-American). Three se-tenant blocks of four marked the 500th anniversary of Christopher Columbus' first voyage, displayed the beauty of American minerals and saluted American and Russian space exploits.

The year also saw the customary additions to two long-running series: Black Heritage and Literary Arts.

29¢ OLYMPIC WINTER GAMES (STRIP OF FIVE)

Date of Issue: January 11, 1992

Catalog Numbers: Scott 2611-2615 (stamps); Scott 2615a (strip of 5)

Colors: magenta, yellow, cyan, black

First-Day Cancel: Orlando, Florida

FDCs Canceled: 1,062,048

Format: Panes of 35, horizontal, 5 across, 7 down. Gravure printing cylinders of 140 (10 across, 14 around) manufactured by Armotek Industries Inc., Palmyra, New Jersey.

Perf: 10.9 (L perforator)

Selvage Inscription: "The 1980 U.S. Ice Hockey/Team's history-making/gold medal performance/remains one of the/country's most emotional/and meaningful Olympic/Winter Games triumphs." "Figure skaters combine/the strength of gymnastics/with the grace of dancing/in one of the most beautiful/and expressive athletic/competitions of the/Olympic Winter Games." "Speed skaters, dressed to/reduce wind resistance,/slice around an oval track/in races from 500 to 10,000/meters in length, pushing/themselves to speeds of up/to 30 miles per hour." "Challenging to the beginner/and expert, slalom skiing/puts a premium on style and/speed. It requires great skill/as athletes race around flags,/called gates, on a zigzag,/downhill course." "Bobsled competition may be/between teams of two or four/and may reach speeds close/to 90 miles per hour down an/artificial run coated with ice/and snow. It is fast, thrilling/and dangerous." "The XVI/Olympic/Winter/Games will/be held in/Albertville,/France,/Feb. 8-25,/1992."

Selvage Markings: "©/United States/Postal Service/1991." "Use Correct/ZIP Code/®/36 USC 380." USPS Olympic logo.

Designer: Lon Busch of Ellisville, Missouri

Art Director and Typographer: Richard Sheaff

Project Manager: Joe Brockert (USPS)

Printing: Stamps printed by Stamp Venturers on a Champlain gravure press in Richmond, Virginia. Stamps perforated, processed and shipped by Stamp Venturers in Milwaukee, Wisconsin.

Quantity Ordered: 160,000,000

Quantity Distributed: 160,000,000

Cylinder Number Detail: 1 group of 4 gravure cylinder numbers preceded by the letter S alongside corner stamp

Cylinder Number Combinations: S1111

Tagging: overall

The Stamps

In 1992 the United States issued a total of 11 stamps to commemorate the Olympic Games, thus continuing a tradition that has lasted 60 years. No other regularly recurring event has had so long a history of U.S. postal recognition. The first U.S. Olympic stamp was a 2¢ value that was issued for the 1932 Winter Games in Lake Placid, New York. It was followed later that year by 3¢ and 5¢ stamps honoring the Summer Games in Los Angeles, California.

A long hiatus followed. Then, in 1960, the Winter Games returned to the United States — to Squaw Valley, California — and the U.S. Post Office Department welcomed them with a 4¢ commemorative stamp.

Twelve years later the U.S. Postal Service had taken over the mail, and began what has become a practice of issuing stamps for every Olympic Games, Winter and Summer, regardless of the country of location.

For the Games of 1992, of which it was an official sponsor, USPS began the postal publicity two years ahead of time. Its 1990 issue was a set of five stamps, arranged in horizontal strips on the pane, honoring past Olympic gold medalists from the United States. This same pane layout — five different stamps in horizontal strips — was used in 1991 for a series paying tribute to Olympic track and field sports.

And on January 11, 1992, the Postal Service issued a third set of stamps in this format, this time in a salute to the 16th Winter Olympic Games that were scheduled for Albertville, France, the following month. The five stamps of the strip featured ice hockey, figure skating, speed skating, skiing and bobsledding.

The 1992 Winter Olympics stamps, like the stamps in the 1990 and 1991 sets, were semijumbos. Like the 1990 set, they were printed 35 stamps to the pane instead of 40, which is the usual number for that size.

The panes contained only seven horizontal rows; USPS used the

The wrong date for the Olympics was printed in the selvage of the panes. The Games ended February 23, not February 25.

eighth-row space for an extra-deep selvage, or series of tabs, at the top or bottom of the pane. On this selvage was printed descriptive paragraphs about the winter sports depicted in the adjacent vertical row of stamps. "The tabs will not be tagged with phosphor ink so that they cannot be used as stamps," USPS advised would-be postage cheats in its press release.

The narrower selvage at the side of the pane was used for an additional message, placed next to the top or bottom horizontal row of stamps: "The XVI Olympic Winter Games will be held in Albertville, France, Feb. 8-25, 1992." Unfortunately, those dates were wrong. The Games actually were scheduled to end February 23.

Asked how the mistake happened, Kim Parks of the USPS Office of Olympic Marketing said: "It was just one of those things. Somebody wrote something down and didn't check it. What was really strange was that after it was written we had to submit all the marginal information to the U.S. Olympic Committee, and they approved it. Then the Postal Service had an independent researcher look at it. The researcher knew the USOC had checked it and assumed that it was right.

"It was just carelessness."

USPS discovered its mistake after the stamps were printed, but before they were placed on sale. No consideration was given to reprinting the sheets, and for a good reason.

A year earlier, when the Hubert Humphrey Great Americans definitive was printed with the wrong dates of Humphrey's vice presidential term in the selvage, an announced decision to reprint at a cost of $580,000 had drawn so much criticism from Congress and the public that Postmaster General Anthony M. Frank rescinded it. So the new commemoratives, like the Humphrey stamp, were issued, wrong date and all. However, USPS did call attention to the Winter Olympics mistake with a brief footnote on the press release that described the stamps.

USPS also used direct-mail advertising and ads in national publications to market an "Official Limited Edition Souvenir Series" consisting of six cacheted covers bearing the Winter Olympics stamps and special pictorial U.S. postmarks from Albertville. (The postmarks themselves were an anomaly, inasmuch as the covers never actually went through the French mail system.) The covers sold for $29.95 per set; 3,000 individu-

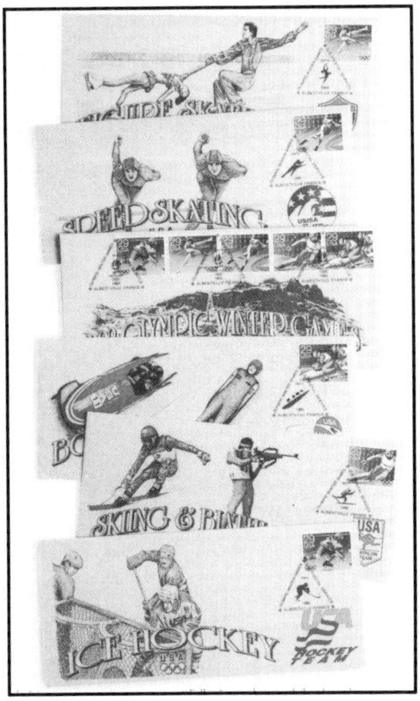

These are the six foil-embossed covers the Postal Service sold as "official souvenirs" of the 1992 Olympic Winter Games.

ally numbered sets autographed by members of the U.S. team were priced at $59.95 each. Proceeds went to the Postal Service's "Celebrate the Dream" program, which helped pay housing costs in Albertville for relatives of participating Olympians.

The same triangular special postmarks used on the souvenir covers were also made available to collectors for 90 days after the dates on them, which ranged from February 8 to February 21. They could be obtained by sending stamped, addressed covers to the postmaster in Silver Spring, Maryland. As *Linn's Stamp News* columnist Fred W. Baumann asked

These are the six pictorial postmarks with themes from the Olympic Winter Games that USPS introduced in Albertville, France, and later offered to collectors in the United States.

rhetorically, "What kind of Winter Olympic souvenir is a cover canceled in May (the wrong season) in Maryland (the wrong continent)?"

A record number of athletes, 2,174, took part in the 16 days of competition in the French Alps. The 64 participating teams also represented a record, and this list included some strange new names: the Unified Team, a combination of athletes from five former Soviet republics; separate teams from three other former Soviet republics, independent Estonia, Latvia and Lithuania; separate teams from Slovenia, Croatia and Yugoslavia; and a reunited Germany.

The German team won the most medals, 26, with the Unified Team next with 23. The United States placed fifth with 11 medals. Individual stars of the Games included Alberto Tomba of Italy, whose gold medal in the giant slalom made him the first Alpine skier to win two gold medals in different Olympics in the same event; Toni Nieminen, a 16-year-old Finn who won two golds and a bronze in ski jumping and became the youngest male gold medalist in Winter Olympic history; Bonnie Blair of the United States, who added two speed-skating gold medals to the one she won in 1988; and Kristi Yamaguchi of the United States, winner of the gold in women's figure skating.

The interval between the 16th and 17th Winter Games — and the stamps that commemorate them — will be only two years instead of the customary four. In order to put the Winter and Summer Games on different quadrennial cycles, the next Winter Games, in Lillehammer, Norway, will be held in 1994.

The Designs

The stamps were designed by Lon Busch of Ellisville, Missouri, an artist specializing in airbrush painting. Busch had previously designed the Pan-American Games commemorative of 1987 and the Basketball Centennial commemorative of 1991.

His Winter Olympics designs consisted of dramatic, stylized depictions of a hockey player, a figure skater, a speed skater, a skier and a pair of bobsledders, each placed against an abstract patterned backdrop. To create the impression of grace, speed and power, Busch laid the athletes' bodies diagonally across the designs and filled his pictures with curves: curved torsos and limbs; extravagant curved stripes and slashes on the costumes; arcs and circles and loops on the ice and snow.

Lon Busch won the job of designing the 1992 Olympic Winter Games stamps with this airbrush concept sketch of a speed skater, done in glowing shades of blue, green, red, orange, yellow and lavender. CSAC asked that the background of this and the other stamps be made somewhat less abstract.

Because of Olympic Committee requirements, art director Richard Sheaff had to revise his planned typography, shown here. He moved the five interlocked Olympic rings to a lower corner of each stamp and made them black rather than dropout white.

The artist used the bold, almost fluorescent colors fancied by modern-day international athletes. These competitors could never be mistaken for Olympians of the 1950s. Despite the limitations of the four standard process colors used in gravure printing, the effect Busch sought came through to a substantial degree on the finished stamps.

CSAC had chosen Busch for the job on the basis of a concept sketch of a speed skater that he submitted. The committee liked the style, and asked only that the finished painting and the other four designs be slightly less abstract than the original submission.

Richard Sheaff, the art director for the stamps, created the typography, a clean Helvetica typeface that dropped out of the background color in the stamps' upper-left corners. Sheaff's original intention had been to drop out the five linked Olympic rings immediately below the "29 USA" logo, creating one compact graphic unit. This plan was forestalled, however, by the rigid guidelines of the U.S. Olympic Committee, which prescribed a specific, block-letter typeface for "USA" when those initials were used in combination with the rings.

"Rather than do that, I said I'd put the rings somewhere else," Sheaff said. That turned out to be a lower corner — right or left, depending on which space was most open — and the rings were printed in black.

First-Day Facts

The stamps were issued in Orlando, Florida, in conjunction with the 1992 U.S. Figure Skating Championships in the Orlando Arena. There was no traditional first-day ceremony, but Postmaster General Anthony M. Frank was joined at center ice by pairs champions Calla Urbanski and Rocky Marvel to officially dedicate the stamps before the finals of the women's figure skating event.

The dedication was followed by an appearance by the Haydenettes, world precision skating champions, carrying 30 flags in formation around the ice, each flag bearing one of the five stamp designs.

No special ceremony program was produced, but the Postal Service distributed an official souvenir that resembled a program and a first-day canceled card, each with the Olympics strip.

Stamps and first-day cancellations were available at the Orlando General Mail Facility.

29¢ WORLD COLUMBIAN STAMP EXPO 92

Date of Issue: January 24, 1992

Catalog Number: Scott 2616

Colors: yellow, red, black (offset); brown, blue (intaglio)

First-Day Cancel: Rosemont, Illinois

FDCs Canceled: 309,729

Format: Panes of 50, vertical, 10 across, 5 down. Offset printing plates of 200 subjects (10 across, 20 around); intaglio printing sleeve of 400 subjects (10 across, 40 around).

Perf: 11.1 (Eureka off-line perforator)

Selvage Markings: "©/United States/Postal Service/1991/36 USC 380." "Use Correct/ZIP Code/®." USPS Olympic logo.

Designer, Typographer and Art Director: Richard Sheaff of Needham Heights, Massachusetts

Project Manager: Jack Williams (USPS)

Engravers: Thomas Hipschen (BEP), vignette; Deborah Alexander (BEP), frame

Printing: printed by BEP on 4-color offset, 3-color intaglio F press

Quantity Ordered: 148,685,000

Quantity Distributed: 148,665,000

Plate/Sleeve Number Detail: 1 brown intaglio sleeve number and 1 group of 3 offset plate numbers in selvage of adjacent corner stamps.

Plate/Sleeve Number Combinations: 111-1, 211-1, 212-1, 322-1, 423-1

Tagging: phosphor-coated paper

The Stamp

The major philatelic event of 1992 in the United States was World Columbian Stamp Expo 92 (WCSE), an international stamp show held in suburban Chicago May 22-31 in conjunction with the 500th anniversary of Christopher Columbus' discovery of the New World.

To give advance publicity to the show, USPS issued a 29¢ commemorative stamp that was placed on sale January 24 in Rosemont, Illinois, site of WCSE.

Even before WCSE opened, several other Chicago-area stamp shows figured in the stamp's history.

The first was the Compex 91 stamp show at the Rosemont-O'Hare Exposition Center in Rosemont, where the stamp's design was unveiled May 24, 1991. Speakers at this event were Illinois Governor Jim Edgar; John G. Mulligan, Central Regional postmaster general; and Charles Berg, president of both WCSE and Compex.

At that time, USPS said the stamp would be issued November 1, 1991, at another stamp show, Chicagopex. But in August the Postal Service announced that the stamp would be delayed until 1992 because of uncertainty over what the first-class postal rate would be on or shortly after the scheduled issue date.

Finally, with the rate firmly set at 29¢, the stamp made its debut. It was placed on sale January 24, 1992, at yet another stamp show, the 15th annual Chicago Philatelic Fair, at the Ramada Hotel O'Hare in Rosemont.

The commemorative featured a stamp-on-stamp design. The item that it partially depicted was a classic of American philately — the 15¢ value of the 1869 pictorial series, a bicolor reproducing John Vanderlyn's painting of the *Landing of Columbus*, which hangs in the U.S. Capitol.

The designer was Richard Sheaff, a U.S. Postal Service design coordinator from Needham Heights, Massachusetts, who had previously designed the stamp-on-stamp commemoratives for Ameripex 86 (showing the 1¢ Franklin of 1870-71) and World Stamp Expo 89 (showing the 90¢ Lincoln of 1869).

The idea of using the 15¢ 1869 in a stamp-on-stamp design to announce WCSE was first proposed by Charles Berg in a letter to Assistant Postmaster General Gordon C. Morison February 20, 1990.

"One of the most attractive stamps issued in 1989 was the 25¢ stamp for World Stamp Expo, which reproduced the 90¢ definitive of 1869," Berg wrote. "I think a similar stamp could be designed for WCSE 92." He enclosed a rough sketch in colored pencil and press-on lettering prepared by his daughter Bridget, who would later be a student at the Maryland Institute College of Art, and himself. In their concept, a simulated cork cancel obliterated a corner of the 1869 stamp design.

Morison wrote back to Berg April 18, promising to bring the proposals before the Citizens' Stamp Advisory Committee at its next meeting. CSAC approved both the stamp and the design concept.

The stamp was printed by the Bureau of Engraving and Printing on its combination offset-intaglio F press. The portion of the design showing the 1869 stamp was engraved, like the original on which it was based.

This was the first stamp printed on the F press. The press was operated by German engineers as part of acceptance trials.

A constant variety was found in the offset portion on five stamps from left-side panes of 50. The variety was a circular area at the back of the letter "a'' in the word "May'' at the top of the stamp where the dates of the show were given.

The affected stamps were the five in the second vertical column from the left on upper-left or lower-left-side panes. Ira Polikoff, spokesman for BEP, told *Linn's Stamp News* that the flaw that created the variety was on the film used to create the offset plate for that part of the stamp.

The 1869s were the first series of U.S. stamps with pictorial designs and the first to include bicolors. Printed by the National Bank Note Company of New York, they were smaller than the previous issue of portrait stamps, had an unfamiliar square shape and were grilled as a protection against cancellation removal and reuse.

The *American Journal of Philately* of May 1869 had this comment about the design of the original stamp:

"Fifteen Cents. — Landing of Columbus, blue and brown, reminds us somewhat of the dollar jewelry store, too much fancy work crowded together, still we consider it decidedly the best of the two-colored ones.''

WCSE 92 president Charles Berg and his daughter Bridget prepared this sketch of a stamp-on-stamp design to promote World Columbian Stamp Expo 92, using colored pencils and press-on lettering. They "canceled" the 15¢ 1869 stamp with a cork cancel on its upper-right corner. Their proposed design correctly identified the location of WCSE 92 as Rosemont, Illinois, rather than Chicago, which was the location given on the stamp as issued.

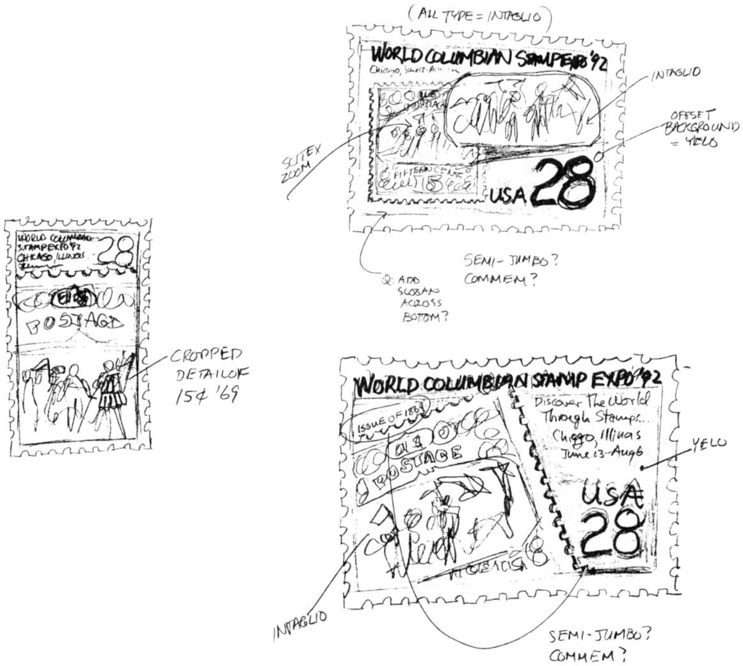

Richard Sheaff began the design process with these rough sketches of three alternative treatments of the stamp-on-stamp idea.

And the September 1869 issue of *Mason's Coin and Stamp Collector's Magazine* added this more critical appraisal:

"Either the stamp is too small for the picture, or the latter too large for the stamp. As a postage stamp we consider the 15¢ article a failure; as a pretty picture for an illuminated ABC book, a decided success.''

The 29¢ WCSE commemorative wasn't the only 1992 item with which BEP pictorially recalled the 15¢ 1869. BEP also printed full reproductions of three different versions of the stamp, including one with an inverted center, on the two philatelic souvenir cards it issued in 1992, for WCSE and the American Philatelic Society show (see separate chapters).

WCSE, with the theme "Exploring the World Through Philately," ran 10 days, from May 22 to May 31. Although it was the biggest stamp show of the year in the United States, it was not an internationally sanctioned exhibition (like Ameripex 86) nor was it sponsored by USPS (like World

Arrow points to the offset black constant plate variety in the letter "a" of the word "May."

Stamp Expo 89). It was organized by a group of Chicago collectors and dealers. As such, it was the first private, non-sanctioned stamp exhibition to be commemorated by a U.S. stamp.

USPS did cooperate, however, by issuing the WCSE commemorative stamp, and also by holding first-day ceremonies at the show for a series of souvenir sheets reproducing the 1893 World's Columbian Exposition commemorative stamps and a joint issue of space stamps with Russia (see separate chapters).

USPS also produced a new set of covers for the $2.90 Flag With Olympic Rings stamp booklet that was originally issued in 1991. The new covers contained a complimentary pass to WCSE, with this wording on the outside back cover: "FREE PASS INSIDE! Come to this world-class philatelic event at the Rosemont-O'Hare Exposition Center! The U.S. Postal Service will reissue the philatelically famous Columbian Series stamps of 1893 in souvenir sheet formats."

The Postal Service's advance promotion efforts proved disappointing to WCSE officials in several ways, beginning with the late appearance of the commemorative stamp.

"The late release date meant that the stamp had only four months of use prior to the opening of WCSE 92, as opposed to the eight months for the World Stamp Expo 89 stamp and 12 months for the Ameripex 86 stamp," Berg wrote in a letter to the *Yearbook*. "This may have contributed to the diminished publicity WCSE 92 achieved in the general population, which was the USPS' responsibility for the show.

"In addition, since October 1991 we had been promised that the selvage of the WCSE 92 sheets would bear information on the show. This was partly to 'make up' for the late release of the stamp; it was doubly important, however, since the stamp (and, later, the cancels at WCSE 92) indicated that the show was being held in Chicago, when it was actually being staged in Rosemont.

"We were very disappointed to discover that the promised information was not printed on the sheet margins, which bore the USPS Olympic logo instead. When we asked what had happened, we were told that the Olympic marketing program had the greatest pull at USPS headquarters those days!"

Berg said the Postal Service's decision to use Chicago, not Rosemont, in the stamp's design was partly based on the fact that the Columbian Exposition of 1893 had been held in Chicago, and partly because Chicago had a worldwide name recognition that Rosemont didn't. He noted that the Ameripex 86 stamp had carried similar misinformation.

The Postal Service's booklet-cover promotion for the show was also disappointing to the sponsors.

"Following discussions of more than a year, WCSE 92 was told in August 1991 that USPS would prepare a booklet cover with a free pass and promotion for the show, to be released around the beginning of February 1992," Berg wrote.

"In October 1991 we were told that this would involve a revised cover for the 29¢ Wood Duck stamp booklet, since no new booklets were planned prior to the intended date. In response to a request from Dickey Rustin, I prepared a mockup of the information to be included on the booklet cover, with alternate possibilities for the inside text. USPS had not entirely decided whether they wanted people to send a self-addressed stamped envelope, or names and addresses to be 'captured' for later USPS promotional mailings.

"In preparing the mockup, I used the booklet for Ameripex 86 as a guide to both content and layout. My layout involved reducing the image of the stamp on the front of the existing booklet to permit the front of the booklet to give some indication of the information to be found inside, as had been done on the Ameripex 86 booklet.

"In the end, USPS decided to prepare a revised cover for a different stamp booklet: the 29¢ Flag With Olympic Rings. The press release stated that the booklet would be released the first week of February 1992, as was subsequently reported in the press." However, shipment of the booklets containing WCSE passes were delayed until March, and the Philatelic Sales Division didn't receive a supply until April 3, according to a letter Berg received from Barry Wells, manager of the Stamp Distribution Branch.

Stocks of the booklets were still being released to local post offices in 1993, at least seven months after WCSE closed, Berg wrote, adding: "We continue to receive spurts of requests for information on the show!"

Despite its lack of endorsement by the International Federation of

The ribbon-cutting ceremony at World Columbian Stamp Expo 92 included, from left to right, Rich Drews, WCSE executive director; Catalina Vasquez Villalpando, treasurer of the United States; John Sununu, former White House chief of staff; Gordon Morison, assistant postmaster general; Governor Jim Edgar of Illinois; and Charles Berg, WCSE president.

Richard Sheaff used a computer to develop these preliminary layouts of two different horizontal designs.

Philately (FIP), the show had hundreds of frames of exhibits. The American Philatelic Society held its 1992 spring meeting during the show, with all of the 42 exhibits in the APS competitive section winning either gold or vermeil awards.

The Design

Richard Sheaff prepared preliminary designs for a World Columbian Stamp Expo commemorative in a horizontal arrangement. One showed a partial view of the 1869 stamp, tilted to the left, which was similar to his treatment of the 1¢ Franklin stamp on the Ameripex 86 commemorative. Too similar, Sheaff ultimately concluded.

The other employed a zoom effect to pull the central vignette out of the 1869 stamp and into the foreground in a series of step enlargements. This was done by a private firm in the Boston area, using a powerful Scitex electronic design modification system. "The idea was to give you something that made it clear at a glance that you're supposed to be seeing that vignette enlarged,'' Sheaff explained.

Though the second idea was novel, it didn't appeal to the CSAC. One obvious problem with the concept was that it prominently displayed two different denominations. CSAC's final choice, made early in 1991, was a vertical design that took from the 1869 stamp a top-down bite consisting of simulated top perforations, the words "U.S. Postage'' and the central part of the blue vignette.

"The committee and I felt that this one allowed the stamp-on-stamp image to be bigger and clearer and simpler,'' Sheaff said, "and that people

A powerful Scitex computer system was employed to achieve the zoom effect on this finished version of one of Richard Sheaff's horizontal layout sketches.

would be able to understand a little more easily what was going on.''

To make "what was going on'' even more apparent to the public, the words "Detail of U.S. 1869 Stamp'' in tiny white dropout letters were added at the bottom of the stamp.

The outline around the blue vignette that exists on the original stamp was eliminated in the reproduction. This gave a cleaner look and also provided a break between the brown and blue intaglio portions to minimize ink contamination.

George Brett, one of philately's leading experts on stamp printing, praised the finished stamp in an article in *The United States Specialist.* "I believe the sparkling, clean-cut detail of the new issue should make more people realize that production today, using 'dry' printing as against the prior 'wet' printing of the 1869 originals, is a different ball game for engravings,'' he wrote.

First-Day Facts

Although USPS some time earlier had stopped holding full-fledged first-day ceremonies at stamp shows, it temporarily abandoned the policy for the World Columbian Stamp Expo commemorative. USPS was fully present at the Chicago Philatelic Fair on opening day. Assistant Postmaster General Gordon C. Morison dedicated the stamp, and USPS prepared

These 10 pictorial cancellations were offered on the 10 days of World Columbian Stamp Expo 92.

a special souvenir program for distribution at the event.

The main address was given by Illinois Governor Jim Edgar, honorary chairman of WCSE 92. Arthur Morowitz, president of the American Stamp Dealers Association, gave the welcome, and Charles Berg, president of WCSE 92, also spoke briefly. A special guest was "Christopher Columbus," played by Larry Bell.

Also making its debut at the Philatelic Fair January 24 was a set of six United Nations stamps picturing some of the world's shared wonders and titled "World Heritage — UNESCO."

29¢ W.E.B. DU BOIS
BLACK HERITAGE SERIES

Date of Issue: January 31, 1992

Catalog Number: Scott 2617

Colors: brown, yellow, magenta, cyan, black, dark brown (offset); blue (intaglio)

First-Day Cancel: Atlanta, Georgia

FDCs Canceled: 196,219

Format: Panes of 50, vertical, 10 across, 5 down. Offset printing plates of 200 subjects (10 across, 20 around); intaglio printing sleeve of 400 subjects (10 across, 40 around).

Perf: 11.1 (Eureka off-line perforator)

Selvage Inscription: "Civil rights advocate/W.E.B. Du Bois/(1868-1963) was/one of the founders/of the NAACP." "Du Bois was a noted/writer, historian,/scholar, educator/and sociologist."

Selvage Markings: "Use Correct/ZIP Code ®." "©/United States/Postal Service/1991/36 USC 380." USPS Olympic logo.

Designer: Higgins Bond of Teaneck, New Jersey

Art Director: Jerry Pinkney (CSAC)

Project Manager: Terrence McCaffrey (USPS)

Typographer: John Boyd of Anagraphics, Inc., New York, New York

Engraver: Richard Everett, lettering (BEP)

Modeler: Clarence Holbert (BEP)

Printing: printed by BEP on 6-color offset, 3-color intaglio D press (902)

Quantity Ordered: 150,000,000

Quantity Distributed:	149,990,000
Plate/Sleeve Number Detail:	1 intaglio sleeve number and 1 group of 6 offset plate numbers in selvage of adjacent corner stamps.
Plate/Sleeve Number Combinations:	111122-1, 112322-1, 113222-1, 113422-1, 233433-1, 234433-1
Tagging:	overall

The Stamp

For much of this century, the notion of a U.S. stamp depicting a member of the Communist Party would have been unthinkable. The postal establishment, as much as any American institution, has always been aware of and guided by what was politically correct. It was the Post Office Department, after all, at the onset of the Cold War, that abandoned a stylized symbol it had been using as a "cents" sign because some people thought it looked too much like the Communist hammer and sickle.

But in 1992 the Cold War was over. And when the U.S. Postal Service decided to issue a Black Heritage series stamp honoring William Edward Burghardt (W.E.B.) Du Bois, an achiever in several fields who near the end of a long life joined the U.S. Communist Party and renounced his American citizenship, there were no investigations in Congress, no calls for the postmaster general's resignation. Only a flurry of letters, pro and con, to the philatelic press indicated that the choice of Du Bois was in any way controversial.

Postmaster General Anthony M. Frank said when he unveiled the stamp December 11, 1991, that he knew "there was some opportunity for controversy." But with the collapse of Communism abroad, Frank said, he believed Americans were "beyond" worrying about Du Bois' political views and would realize that USPS was honoring him for creating the intellectual framework for what would become the civil rights movement of the 1950s and 1960s.

Donald M. McDowell, director of the Office of Stamp and Philatelic Marketing, told *Linn's Stamp News* that members of the Citizens' Stamp Advisory Committee had discussed the pros and cons of honoring Du Bois. "They looked at the whole of his life," McDowell said, "and found there was much more to Du Bois than that bitter chapter."

Even so, the USPS announcement of the stamp made no mention of his late conversion to Communism, but focused on his years as an author, historian, educator and crusading editor. The same was true of the thumbnail biography of Du Bois that appeared in the first-day ceremony program. And in preparing the stamp design, the Postal Service turned down a proposed portrait based on a photograph made in Du Bois' old age, after his politics had turned more radical. A younger portrait would be more suitable, USPS said.

The stamp, 15th in the Black Heritage series, was issued on January 31, in conjunction with Black History Month, which the nation observes every February. It was printed by the Bureau of Engraving and Printing

These four pencil sketches show various portraits of Du Bois and various miniature vignettes as Higgins Bond and Jerry Pinkney tried to hit on the best combination. Bond preferred the portrait of the older Du Bois, but USPS officials turned it down because it was in old age that Du Bois joined the Communist Party. One of the miniatures represents the Niagara Movement, with Niagara Falls in the background. Another depicts an NAACP march staged in New York City in 1917 to protest lynching and mob violence (Du Bois is the second marcher from the right in the second row).

on its D press in a combination of offset lithography and intaglio. All previous Black Heritage stamps, whether done by BEP or private contractors, had been printed by gravure.

"The decision to do that stamp by that process had as much to do with the most efficient scheduling of equipment at the Bureau as anything else,'' said McDowell. "I'm not predicting the demise of the Andreotti (gravure) press, but they've got exactly half as many gravure presses at the Bureau as they had a few years ago, and so that's obviously a factor.

"I think it was a piece of art that could have been done quite effectively either way. But Joe Peng (head of the Stamp Manufacturing Division) and his people are doing much more and closer work with the Bureau in planning production well in advance — what it's going to be, and on which press, and how to maintain the optimum work flow going through the Bureau — because, among other things, it helps them control their costs, and that benefits us in the Postal Service. So I think it's all tied up in that, more than in a conscious decision to get away from gravure.''

Du Bois was born in Great Barrington, Massachusetts, February 23, 1868, of mixed French, Dutch and African parentage. He earned an A.B. at Fisk University in 1888, and subsequently, at Harvard University, he received an A.B. (1890), M.A. (1891) and Ph.D. (1895). He was the first black to receive a Harvard graduate degree. After teaching Latin and Greek at Wilberforce College, he became a professor of economics and history and head of the sociology department at Atlanta University, now Clark Atlanta University.

Du Bois' views clashed with those of another noted black leader,

In these two pencil sketches, the portrait and the subject of the small vignette have been decided upon and the artist is developing her final approach to the details.

Booker T. Washington. Washington, who stressed the importance of self-help and economic empowerment for African-Americans, was criticized by Du Bois for being too willing to endure the wrongs inflicted by white segregationists — a charge that Washington's modern-day defenders deny.

Du Bois argued that basic legal rights for minorities were essential. In 1905 he organized a conference of like-minded writers and activists who inaugurated the Niagara Movement, with the goal of winning the abolition of all forms of segregation and other racial injustice. The Niagara Movement later merged into the National Association for the Advancement of Colored People. Du Bois was a co-founder of this new group, which first convened in 1909 and incorporated in 1911.

In 1919 Du Bois organized the first Pan-African Conference, which expressed opposition to the colonial rule of Africa by Europeans. For 22 years he edited the NAACP's periodical, *The Crisis*. In *The Crisis* and in speeches, he itemized other aspects of his vision: a complete end to segregation in public accommodations and public transportation, equal protection of the laws for blacks, the right of access to public education and higher education, the nullification of laws outlawing intermarriage, anti-lynching laws and equal rights for all races in the armed services. With the NAACP as a catalyst, all these aims were eventually achieved.

But in 1934 Du Bois resigned from the NAACP in a policy dispute. Though no longer editor of *The Crisis*, he continued to produce large numbers of articles and books. With advancing age, he became more strongly committed to socialist solutions. In 1961 he joined the Communist Party, and a few days later moved permanently to Ghana, in Africa, where he died August 27, 1963, at the age of 95.

Arnold Rampersad, in *The Dictionary of American Biography*, wrote: "In his combination of excellent academic training and political activism on behalf of blacks, Du Bois had virtually no superior among his fellow Americans . . . In his best work, such as *The Souls of Black Folk*, Du Bois established himself firmly among the major interpreters of American history and culture and at the very center of the Afro-American intellectual tradition."

Critics of the Du Bois stamp, in letters to *Linn's* and *Stamp Collector*, stressed his membership in the Communist Party, a group "advocating the violent overthrow of the United States." Defenders of Du Bois emphasized his great contributions to the cause of equal rights. Besides, as one letter writer pointed out, Du Bois never actually went to war against his country, unlike several other men who had previously been pictured on U.S. stamps, including Robert E. Lee, "Stonewall" Jackson, Jefferson Davis, members of the United Confederate Veterans, Crazy Horse, Red Cloud, Sitting Bull — and even the fictional Scarlett O'Hara!

In conjunction with the issuance of the Du Bois stamp, USPS marketed a book and stamp collection titled *I Have a Dream*. The book featured 28 portraits of African-Americans, including Du Bois, who had appeared on U.S. stamps. These were painted by Thomas Blackshear, who had designed four previous Black Heritage stamps.

The Design

For the Du Bois stamp design, USPS turned to Barbara Higgins Bond of Teaneck, New Jersey, an artist and illustrator who uses the name Higgins Bond professionally. She had designed the previous year's Black Heritage stamp, which honored Jan Matzeliger, inventor of the first practical shoe lasting machine.

Bond painted her finished picture for the stamp in acrylic on illustration board. As mentioned previously, USPS officials demurred when she suggested that her portrait of Du Bois be modeled on a photograph showing the civil rights leader in old age. The photo she finally used was of indeterminate origin, although a very similar photograph appears on a Tuskegee Institute postcard in the collection of Milton Meltzer and is reproduced in *The Correspondence of W.E.B. Du Bois*, a three-volume work edited by Herbert Aptheker. It was a full-face portrait depicting Du Bois somewhere in his middle years, virtually bald, with the neat mustache and Vandyke beard that were his trademarks.

Because the photo was black and white, Bond said, she had to guess at the appropriate skin tones. (She had had the same problem with Matzeliger, of whom only one old photograph existed.) In the Du Bois photograph, the subject was wearing a tweed jacket, but Bond changed it to a pinstripe in her painting. She had painted Matzeliger in a tweed jacket, she explained, and wanted to do something different this time.

For the smaller secondary vignette that is a standard part of Black Heritage designs, Bond showed Du Bois in his role as editor of *The Crisis*, seated at an old-fashioned manual typewriter. Before arriving at that solution, however, she and her art director, Jerry Pinkney, had experimented with other ideas. One was a group of people, with Niagara Falls in the background, to represent the Niagara Movement. Another was a civil rights march, taken from a photo of a 1917 NAACP march in New York City held to protest lynching and mob violence. A third possibility was the logo of *The Crisis*. After they had settled on the typewriter picture, they experimented with combining it with the logo, but decided that it would crowd the design too much.

The hardest part of that phase of the job, Bond said, was finding an authentic 1930s typewriter for a model. Eventually she located a photograph of the African-American writer Langston Hughes at a typewriter — its make unknown — and used that, but the image was small and she had to fill in the details of the machine as best she could. She made the typewriter black, but at Pinkney's suggestion changed the color to green to make it show up better when the picture was reduced to stamp size.

"After I had done the stamp, when I went down to Atlanta for the first-day ceremony, they had Du Bois' own typewriter there," she laughed. "I said, 'Why didn't somebody show me this months ago? I would have killed to have found a picture of his actual typewriter!' "

Bond based her picture of the seated Du Bois on photographs that

This is the original version of Bond's painting. She later removed the coat on the smaller figure, changed the tie from plaid to solid color, and widened the figures so they overlapped the border on the left. Also, the colors of the typewriter and the border were altered.

showed him working with papers at a desk. In these pictures, he was wearing a suit coat, and she painted him that way at first. But in her final painting she removed the coat and pictured him in a vest and shirtsleeves, which lightened up that corner of the stamp.

The cufflink in the visible sleeve was an authentic touch, verified by the photographs, she said. His tie, as shown, was a solid green. Bond originally made it plaid — "He loved plaid ties, and I hated to make the change,'' she said — but a pattern would have been invisible in the tiny space occupied by the tie on the finished stamp.

Bond placed a border around the stamp, thus restoring a design practice that USPS had followed with its first nine Black Heritage stamps but abandoned for the next five. She originally made the border a bluish gray, the same color as Du Bois' coat, but at Pinkney's suggestion she changed it to a darker shade of the brownish pink she had used as the background color. She also widened her painting so that the Du Bois figures overlapped the border on the left side.

Higgins Bond had painted Du Bois before. In 1980 she created a montage for the cover of the 70th anniversary issue of *The Crisis* that showed the five editors of the magazine from Du Bois, the founder, to the present. It proved popular and was made into a poster.

This poster by Bond was based on a cover she painted for the 70th anniversary of The Crisis *in 1980. It depicts the magazine's editors, beginning with the founding editor, W.E.B. Du Bois (center front) and followed by (shown clockwise from the bottom, but not in chronological order) James W. Ivy, Henry Lee Moon, Roy Wilkins and Warren Marr II.*

First-Day Facts

The first-day ceremony for the Du Bois stamp was held at the Woodruff Library on the campus of Clark Atlanta University. Joseph J. Mahon, senior assistant postmaster general, dedicated the stamp. Speakers included LeGree S. Daniels, a member of the USPS Board of Governors, and David G. Du Bois, the son of the civil rights leader's second wife, Shirley Graham Du Bois. W.E.B. Du Bois' granddaughter, Dr. Du Bois Williams, was among the honored guests.

29¢ OLYMPIC BASEBALL

Date of Issue: April 3, 1992

Catalog Number: Scott 2619

Colors: magenta, cyan, yellow, black, blue (PMS 282C)

First-Day Cancel: Atlanta, Georgia

FDCs Canceled: 105,996

Format: Panes of 50, horizontal, 5 across, 10 down. Gravure printing cylinders of 200 subjects (10 across, 20 around).

Perf: 11.1 (Eureka off-line perforator)

Selvage Markings: "©/United States/Postal Service/1991/36 USC 380." "Use Correct/ZIP Code/®." USPS Olympic logo.

Designer: Anthony DeLuz of Boston, Massachusetts

Art Director and Typographer: Richard Sheaff

Project Manager: Joe Brockert (USPS)

Printing: printed by BEP on 7-color Andreotti gravure press (601)

Quantity Ordered: 160,000,000

Quantity Distributed: 170,865,000

Cylinder Number Detail: 1 group of 5 gravure cylinder numbers alongside corner stamps

Cylinder Number Combination: 11111

Tagging: overall

The Stamp

Baseball, America's self-proclaimed national pastime and a demonstration sport in seven Olympic Games since 1912, became an official event at the 1992 Summer Olympics in Barcelona, Spain. To commemorate the game's forthcoming new status, the Postal Service issued a 29¢ stamp April 3 in Atlanta, Georgia.

The stamp's design, showing a dramatic play at home plate, was chosen in a USPS-sponsored competition among artists. The Postal Service promoted the stamp widely. Unknown to postal officials, however, the image was strikingly similar to a photograph that had been published five years earlier in *Sports Illustrated* magazine.

On January 8, 1993, nine months after the stamp's issuance, USPS pulled it from sale without prior notice. There was published speculation that the action had been taken because the Postal Service's role as an official sponsor of the Olympic Games had expired, and with it the right to use the five interlocking Olympic rings in the baseball stamp's design. That didn't make much sense, however, because other stamps displaying the Olympic rings continued to be available.

A few weeks later, however, the real reason suddenly seemed clear. *Linn's Stamp News* disclosed that the photographer who had made the *Sports Illustrated* photograph had filed suit against the Postal Service for copyright infringement. As of this writing, the outcome of the suit has not been determined.

The design contest had been announced in 1990. USPS said that the United States and "30 partner postal administrations from around the world" would each conduct a competition, select a single design to be developed as a finished postage stamp and issue the stamp. These stamps would commemorate the Olympic Games and be jointly issued during worldwide dedication ceremonies in 1992, in the interval between the Winter and Summer Games.

In the United States, the contest was open to all, including professional artists and employees of the Postal Service and their families. A $100 entry fee was charged to cover the cost of administering the program and "to encourage serious artists to enter," USPS said. The theme was Olympic baseball. Any art medium was permitted, but the design had to be in full color. "No identifiable person or team can be represented in the design," the rules specified.

Potential contestants were told that their entries would be given preliminary judging by a panel of printing, art and philatelic experts. The top 100 designs would be forwarded to the Citizens' Stamp Advisory Committee, with the postmaster general having ultimate approval of the winning design.

As it turned out, only 80 entries were received, and so there was no screening by a "panel of experts." The Postal Service's Office of Olympic Marketing, which organized and ran the contest, sent all the artwork along to CSAC.

The committee narrowed the field to three designs and then each

Bart Forbes prepared this painting as an entry in the Olympic Baseball stamp design competition. It was purchased by Jack Rosenthal, chairman of CSAC, and hangs on the wall of Rosenthal's home in Casper, Wyoming.

member voted, assigning three points to his or her first choice, two to the second and one to the third. The winning entry would be the one with the highest total. In August 1991, the winner's name was announced: He was Anthony DeLuz, a professional illustrator from Boston, Massachusetts.

USPS said nine other countries — not 30 — completed similar contests, and it identified them as Australia, Brazil, Cyprus, France, Greece, Kenya, Korea, Mexico and New Zealand. Of these, all but Australia issued stamps. With one exception, all the foreign stamps were issued April 3, the day the U.S. stamp appeared. South Korea issued its two stamps July 25, the opening day of the Olympic Games.

DeLuz received the standard $3,000 fee that USPS pays for a stamp design. As the contest winner, he was also offered an expenses-paid trip to Barcelona for the Olympics, but didn't go. The timing was wrong, he said. He and his wife had a new baby, and were also engaged in house hunting and trying to rent a condo they owned.

The contest produced a second "winner" in addition to DeLuz. CSAC chairman Jack Rosenthal, whose collecting interests include not only stamps but art, was so impressed by one of the runner-up entries — a painting of a catcher and umpire seen from the pitcher's mound — that he bought the original from the artist, Bart Forbes of Dallas, Texas, and hung it in his home in Casper, Wyoming. Forbes had previously designed U.S. stamps relating to the Olympic Games (1988, Winter and Summer) and baseball (1989, Lou Gehrig).

DeLuz' winning watercolor painting showed a base runner sliding home, as the catcher, mask in place, ball in his mitt, attempted to tag him out. It was a nicely balanced composition, with the runner's outstretched left arm creating a horizontal base, his head and upraised right arm establishing a diagonal, and the bulky vertical figure of the catcher anchoring the design on the left. The empty space at the upper right was the logical place for the Olympic rings and the typography.

The Postal Service promoted the stamp with full-page magazine ads that displayed a blowup of the design with the caption "Don't let this one slide by." A Philatelic Sales Division coupon was attached, with which one could obtain for $16 a pane of 50 of the stamps (face value $14.50) along with a "commemorative saver page."

And on the day the stamp was dedicated in Atlanta, a photograph of DeLuz holding a blowup of the design was published in the sports section of *The San Diego Union-Tribune*. A former *Sports Illustrated* staff photographer and San Diegan named Andy Hayt saw the picture in the paper and thought he recognized the scene on the stamp as one of his photographs.

The color photograph had been published as a double-page spread in the July 6, 1987, issue of *Sports Illustrated*, an issue devoted to baseball. It was captioned: "In San Diego: Chris Brown slides, Benito Santiago makes the tag . . . he's out!" Santiago was a catcher for the San Diego Padres, and Brown was a third baseman for the San Francisco Giants.

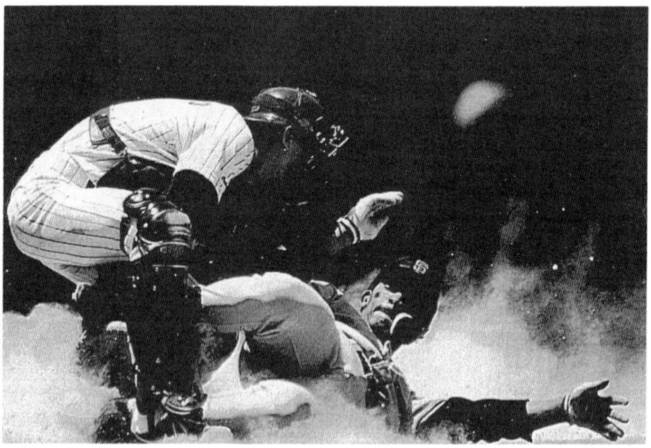

This is a print of the Andy Hayt color photograph that occupied two pages of Sports Illustrated's July 6, 1987, issue. The magazine's caption read: "In San Diego: Chris Brown slides, Benito Santiago makes the tag... he's out!" (Copyright 1987 Andy Hayt)

Hayt retained Anthony D. Epstein, a Boston lawyer whose clients included several commercial photographers. Epstein investigated, and on December 17, 1992, on behalf of Hayt, he filed a suit against the Postal Service in the U.S. Court of Federal Claims in Washington, D.C., seeking unspecified damages and court costs. The action was brought under U.S. copyright laws "to redress the infringement of a copyrighted photograph which was used without permission by the United States Postal Service, its agents, servants or employees, as the basis for a commemorative postage stamp."

According to the complaint, Time, Inc., which had copyrighted the photo for *Sports Illustrated*, had assigned the copyright to Hayt. The Postal Service had used the picture on the stamp, and for advertising and promotional purposes, without the permission or authority of either the magazine or the photographer, the complaint said.

Moreover, it continued, USPS, in its official rules for the stamp design contest, "was to be the 'author' of the winning stamp art, was to be the owner of all of the copyrights therein and was to have full rights to use and exploit the illustration for any purposes whatsoever." This made the rules a "work for hire agreement," as defined in the Copyright Act, and made USPS responsible for "any and all acts of infringement performed by or for the Postal Service or by any of its agents, servants or employees, including DeLuz," the complaint stated.

Postal Service spokeswoman Robin Minard told *Linn's* that USPS wouldn't comment on the situation until it was resolved.

Anthony DeLuz, interviewed by *The Yearbook* in November 1992, said he had based his painting — with some changes — on a photograph he had found in a sports magazine, but declined to identify the source. Later, when *Linn's* reporter Michael Schreiber asked him about the lawsuit, he said he had chosen the photograph concerned as his reference, but he believed he made substantial changes in the scene that became the accepted design. "I thought I changed it enough," DeLuz told Schreiber, "even though I didn't change the overall shape." He said USPS had never asked him for his source material.

A comparison of the stamp design and the Hayt photograph (see illustration) shows the similarities. The uniforms are different, but the positions of the ballplayers are nearly identical. The only significant difference is that the catcher on the stamp is holding the ball in his glove, which is visible prominently in front of the runner, while in the photograph the catcher's hands are mostly concealed by his right leg.

Open competition among artists is the standard way the Department of Interior obtains its annual duck stamp designs. But relatively few U.S. postage stamp designs have been selected that way.

One of the best-known examples was the 1938 series of definitives known as the Presidentials, which was based on a prototype designed by free-lance artist Elaine Rawlinson of New York in a contest sponsored by the Treasury Department. Other designs chosen through competition included the Children's stamp (Scott 1085) of 1956, the Battle of

Gettysburg centennial (Scott 1180) and Sciences (Scott 1237) commemoratives of 1963, and the Family Unity (Scott 2104) and Christmas Santa Claus (Scott 2108) stamps of 1984, the latter two designed by schoolchildren.

Baseball has been a topic to which U.S. stamps have periodically turned since 1939, when a commemorative was issued in Cooperstown, New York, to mark the centennial of the "invention" of the game by Abner Doubleday — an honor most authorities now think belongs elsewhere. However, baseball and the Olympics hadn't been combined in a U.S. stamp before.

Olympic baseball was also the theme of one of three Olympic Games coins issued by the U.S. Mint in 1992. The silver dollar, designed by John R. Deecken of Fairfield, Connecticut, showed a pitcher in action.

The U.S. baseball team made a disappointing showing in the Barcelona Games. Unlike the U.S. men's basketball team, which easily won the gold medal with a lineup consisting mostly of all-stars from the professional National Basketball Association, the baseball team was made up of amateurs and was assembled only a few weeks before the Olympics began. The Americans lost their last three games, including a 6-1 setback to Cuba in the semifinals. Cuba took the championship by beating Taiwan 11-1.

The Design

Anthony DeLuz said his first sketch for the contest was altogether different from the finished product.

"I did a tight horizontal illustration of a batter, very focused in on his head, hands and the barrel of his bat," he said. "I decided it looked boring. It kind of looked like the Major League Baseball logo. There wasn't action in it. I wanted to do something that had action. My next idea was to do a close play at the plate, showing a guy sliding into home, that dramatic kind of a moment, which is what I ended up doing. I could have done an outfielder making a leaping catch, or a pitcher throwing the ball, or a first baseman making the stretch, or a batter. I figured that just about every baseball scene is something that's been done before. It was hard to come up with something unique, so I didn't really try.

"I did something that you've seen many times, a guy sliding into home, and being either safe or out. And I leave that up to people who look at it,

A pitcher preparing to fire the ball toward home plate was featured on this obverse design for the Olympic silver dollar coin produced by the U.S. Mint. The design was by illustrator John Deecken.

whether he's safe or out." (As was pointed out previously, however, *Sports Illustrated* had made it exclamation-point emphatic that the runner in its photograph was out.)

DeLuz took pains to make the uniforms and equipment authentic and up-to-date. "You have to be on the ball technically," he said. "The equipment has to look right. You can't show a 1970 mask in a 1992 scene.

"Nowadays, guys have bright, colorful equipment, like the catcher's shin pads on the stamp. When I did those, I thought of the catcher on the Milwaukee Brewers, B.J. Surhoff, who has these horrendous-looking blue and gold knee-and-shin pads. I made them red and blue, not blue and gold, but that was the kind of bright look I wanted to get.

"At the same time, when I did the uniforms, I tried to make them look like amateur baseball uniforms, the way Olympic baseball uniforms might look — even though I didn't know at the time what the Olympic team's uniforms were going to look like. I just did something with a red jersey with a white and blue stripe, which fit the bill."

Collectors, unaware that the design was based on a real photograph, attempted to analyze it in letters to stamp publications. One noted that the catcher hadn't shed his mask, as many catchers do to improve their view when they expect a play at the plate, and speculated that the base runner was attempting the unexpected: a theft of home. Asked about this in the earlier interview, DeLuz said:

"At the dedication of the stamp, I was talking to Steve Yeager (a former Los Angeles Dodgers catcher) and that subject came up, because someone had asked why the mask was still on. And Yeager said, 'I always left my mask on!' A lot of guys will leave them on, unless they're going for a pop-up, of course, because they don't want to get nailed by someone barreling into home; they don't want to get their noses broken." Moreover, DeLuz volunteered, the catcher in the photograph from which he had worked had his mask on.

DeLuz did his finished painting in gouache, an opaque watercolor, on watercolor paper. He observed that the painting was "the largest-scale thing I've ever done in terms of distribution, but the smallest, obviously, in terms of illustration size."

First-Day Facts

Atlanta was chosen for the first-day sale of the stamp because it is the site of the next Summer Games, in 1996. It is also the home of the Atlanta Braves, who had won the National League pennant in 1991 and would do so again in 1992.

USPS held no formal first-day ceremony April 3. However, a media event, closed to the public, was staged at Atlanta's Fulton County Stadium, home of the Braves, to publicize the new commemorative.

Jerry Lee, regional postmaster general, unveiled a blown-up picture of the stamp. He was helped by Henry Aaron, a Braves official who, as an outfielder with the team, had broken Babe Ruth's record for career home runs and went on to set the record that still stands. Aaron then engaged in a bit of byplay over whether the runner on the stamp was safe or out with Maury Wills, one-time holder of the career base-stealing record; Steve Yeager, former catcher with the Los Angeles Dodgers; and Ron Luciano, a major-league umpire.

Others who spoke briefly were Creighton Hale, president of Little League International; Peter O'Malley, president of the Dodgers; Richard Case, executive director of the U.S. Baseball Federation; and Robert Smith, president of the International Baseball Association.

29¢ FIRST VOYAGE OF CHRISTOPHER COLUMBUS BLOCK OF FOUR (JOINT ISSUE)

Date of Issue: April 24, 1992

Catalog Numbers: Scott 2620-2623 (single stamps); 2623a (block of 4)

Colors: magenta, yellow, cyan, black (offset); black (intaglio)

First-Day Cancel: Christiansted, Virgin Islands, and Granada, Spain

FDCs Canceled: 509,170

Format: Panes of 40, horizontal, 5 across, 8 down. Offset printing plates of 160 subjects (10 across, 16 around); intaglio printing sleeves of 320 subjects (10 across, 32 around).

Perf: 11 by 10.9 (Eureka off-line perforator)

Selvage Markings: "Use Correct/ZIP Code/®." "© United States/Postal Service/1991/36 USC 380." USPS Olympic logo.

Designer: Richard Schlecht of Arlington, Virginia

Art Director and Typographer: Richard Sheaff

Project Manager: Jack Williams (USPS)

Engraver: Richard Everett (BEP)

Modeler: Peter Cocci (BEP)

Printing: printed by BEP on 6-color offset, 3-color intaglio D press (902)

Quantity Ordered: 160,020,000

Quantity Distributed: 160,020,000

Plate/Sleeve Number Detail: 1 group of 4 offset plate numbers alongside corner stamps; 1 intaglio sleeve number in selvage of adjacent stamps.

Plate/Sleeve Number Combinations: 1111-1, 2111-1, 2122-1, 2222-1, 2232-1, 2242-1, 3242-1, 3252-1, 4463-1

Tagging: overall

The Stamps

On April 24, USPS and the Italian Ministry of Posts and Telecommunications jointly issued blocks of four se-tenant stamps to commemorate the 500th anniversary of the first voyage of Christopher Columbus to the New World in 1492. It was the third joint issue between the United States and Italy, following the Philip Mazzei stamps of 1980 (U.S. stamp, Scott C98) and the Francis Vigo postal cards of 1986 (U.S. card, Scott UX111).

Both countries used identical designs for the 1992 stamps, created by U.S. stamp designer Richard Schlecht of Arlington, Virginia. Inscriptions on the U.S. stamps were in English; on the Italian stamps, in Italian. The designs, as identified on the U.S. versions, showed Columbus "Seeking Queen Isabella's Support," and his expedition "Crossing The Atlantic," "Approaching Land" and "Coming Ashore."

The U.S. stamps bore the 29¢ first-class rate. The Italian stamps were valued at 500 lire, and were available through the USPS Philatelic Sales Division until September 27. The cost was 45¢ each, $1.80 for a block of four designs or $18 for a pane of 40.

A first-day ceremony for the two blocks was held on the island of St. Croix in the U.S.-owned Virgin Islands. St. Croix was first visited by the Columbus expedition during his second voyage, on November 14, 1493.

"That is the only site in United States territory on which historians agree that Columbus landed," Dickey Rustin, manager of the USPS Stamp Product Development Branch, told *Linn's Stamp News*.

The stamps also were placed on sale April 24 in Italy and in Granada, Spain, at Granada 92, the international stamp show.

The U.S. stamps were printed by a combination of offset and intaglio on the Bureau of Engraving and Printing's D press. The typography was the only engraved element on the stamps. The Italian stamps were printed by photogravure at Instituto Poligrafico e Zecca dello Stato.

The first announcement of the joint issue came not from USPS but in press releases from the Italian government and the organizers of the World Exhibition of Thematic Philately (Genova 92), which was held September 18-22, 1992, in Genoa, Italy. The releases, distributed in the summer of 1991, disclosed that the two countries' four-stamp sets would be issued in April in conjunction with Granada 92.

In one sense, the U.S. block was the culmination of a four-year postal project undertaken in cooperation with the Postal Union of the Americas, Spain and Portugal (PUASP). PUASP had called on its member postal administrations to produce a series of annual America issues leading up to the 500th anniversary of the first Columbus voyage. These were assigned a common theme: pre-Columbian peoples and their artifacts (1989), natural wonders that the early European explorers might have seen (1990), voyages of exploration (1991) and, of course, the Columbus voyage itself in 1992.

But the Postal Service's enthusiasm for the project, which was never great, diminished markedly over the four-year period. In each of the first two years, USPS issued two stamps, a regular commemorative and an airmail. These bore the PUASP logo, as per the organization's instructions, although the odd-looking device was totally unfamiliar to U.S. postal customers. In 1991, however, the Postal Service settled for a single America stamp, an airmail, and relegated the PUASP logo to the selvage. And the 1992 block of four, while its issuance conformed to the PUASP master plan, contained no reference to either the America series or the hemispheric organization.

Columbus' voyage of 1492 was also commemorated by the U.S. Mint with a set of three commemorative coins. The $5 gold coin showed Columbus facing a map of the New World, and, on the reverse, the crest of Admiral of the Oceans, an honor the explorer received. The $1 silver coin carried a full figure of Columbus beside a globe and in front of his three ships, the *Nina*, *Pinta* and *Santa Maria*. Its reverse was described by the Mint as "a dramatic split image of the *Santa Maria* and the U.S. Space Shuttle *Discovery*." The copper-nickel half-dollar showed on its two sides Columbus coming ashore, and the three ships. The three-coin sets were offered in proof condition for $220, with the surcharge earmarked for a newly created Christopher Columbus Fellowship Foundation, to finance postgraduate research.

In planning the stamps and their designs, the Postal Service consulted the log kept by Columbus himself, as translated by Robert H. Fuson. In it, Columbus described the first landfall and the coming ashore on the Bahamian island that he named San Salvador.

During the day of October 11, 1492, Columbus wrote, he and his crew saw several signs of land nearby, including a large flock of sea birds flying overhead and floating plants, a small plank, and a stick that appeared to have been carved with a tool. That night he doubled the lookout, and reminded his men that the first to sight land "would be given a silk doublet as a personal token from me" and, in addition, would receive "an annuity of 10,000 maravedies from the Sovereigns."

At 10 p.m. Columbus, aboard the *Santa Maria*, thought he saw a light to the west, looking like "a little wax candle bobbing up and down." Though one of his crewmen professed to see it too, others did not. "It was such an uncertain thing," the explorer wrote, "that I did not feel it was adequate proof of land." However, at two hours past midnight, the *Pinta* fired a cannon, Columbus' prearranged signal for a landfall. "When we

This concept sketch for a single Columbus quincentennial commemorative, by Robert Brangwynne, was based on the Lotto portrait of the explorer.

caught up with the *Pinta*, which was always running ahead because she was a swift sailer, I learned that the first man to sight land was Rodrigo de Triana, a seaman from Lepe," he wrote.

Columbus ordered all sails but the mainsail hauled in and lay to until daylight. "At dawn we saw naked people, and I went ashore in the ship's boat, armed, followed by Martin Alonso Pinzon, captain of the *Nina*," Columbus wrote. "I unfurled the royal banner." The rest is history — as well as philatelic history.

The Designs

One of the early design concepts for the block employed the familiar stamp-on-stamp approach. Richard Sheaff, art director for the block of four and the man who designed all the Postal Service's stamp-on-stamp commemoratives of recent years, explained why.

"During this period the Postal Service wasn't sure if it was going to reissue the original Columbians," Sheaff said. "And they weren't sure, if they did, whether they might redo them rather than use the original dies.

"They weren't sure whether, in addition, they were going to issue these other four stamps, sort of for public use, if you will — on the assumption that, really, only stamp collectors would take the souvenir sheets, and they wouldn't get a lot of play in the mailstream. If they were interested in promoting the discovery of America in the mailstream, they ought to have another block of four.

"So one of the things I did was lay out a block of four commemorative stamps with stamp-on-stamp designs. Basically, each one said 'Discovery of the New World,' and each stamp would have reproduced one of the 1893 Columbians. This would, in a way, have accomplished both of those things — reproducing some of the original Columbians, and having stamps in the mailstream."

The decision to reissue the original stamps in souvenir sheet form made the stamp-on-stamp proposal for the block of four unusable, and Richard Schlecht, an Arlington, Virginia, artist who had designed several previous stamps for USPS, was commissioned to create four appropriate paintings that could be reproduced in the desired semijumbo format.

The first of Schlecht's four watercolor designs showed Columbus explaining his plans to Queen Isabella as other members of the court looked on. The second showed the three ships of the expedition on the

bus. Sheaff used it as the side visual for the souvenir sheet titled "Claiming a New World."

This painting, which hangs in the U.S. Capitol, has been a rich source for U.S. stamps. It was the basis for the design of the 2¢ Columbian commemorative of 1893 — and, of course, its 1992 reproduction. Even earlier, it had been shown on the 15¢ stamp of 1869. This stamp, in turn, was partially depicted on the 29¢ commemorative of January 1992 saluting World Columbian Stamp Expo 92.

The background image of Columbus on the $5 sheet, "Christopher Columbus," was taken from an old engraving by one T. Johnson. It was based on an image described as "the Lotto portrait," and was provided by The Granger Collection, New York.

The "Royal Favor Restored" background image was a different depiction of the scene featured on the 8¢ Columbian stamp. It was taken from a wood engraving inscribed "Reception of Columbus by Ferdinand and Isabella," signed by "A. Laby" and furnished by Culver Pictures Inc., New York.

The sheet titled "Reporting Discoveries" was a different depiction of the scene shown on the 15¢ Columbian stamp. It was taken from an old illustration inscribed "Columbus at the Court of Barcelona," attributed to Victor A. Searles and furnished by Culver Pictures.

The "First Sighting of Land" sheet had a background image based on an old engraving inscribed "Columbus — Discovery of Land," attributed to a "Ch. Rubens" and furnished by The Granger Collection. It was a different depiction of the scene featured on the 1¢ Columbian stamp.

On the sheet titled "Seeking Royal Support," the background image and the vignette of the 5¢ Columbian stamp both came from the same source, an 1884 painting by the Bohemian artist Vaczlav Van Brozik titled *Columbus at the Court of Ferdinand and Isabella*. The version of the picture on the sheet was taken from a mezzotint, *Columbus Before Isabella*, provided by Culver Pictures Inc.

The art director suggested that all the side visuals be printed in black, for maximum contrast with the color of the stamps, but the committee opted for colors, albeit dark ones.

Sheaff prepared the screened negatives, complete with captions, on a Scitex electronic image modification system at a Boston area firm. In the process, in order to give all six images approximately the same visual weight, it was necessary to electronically lighten some of them and make others heavier. The finished negatives were then sent to the American Bank Note Company for making the offset plates.

As his final contribution to the project, Sheaff designed the envelopes in which the sheets were packaged and sold. The envelopes reproduced in color a set of the sheets, and for this purpose the artist borrowed an early set of proofs from ABNC and had them photographed. He also wrote the text for the envelope, which read in part:

"In 1492, Christopher Columbus made the first of his four voyages to the New World. In 1892, as America awaited the World Columbian

Exposition, the Post Office prepared its first commemorative format stamps. In 1992, the U.S. Postal Service released these six souvenir sheets, featuring the 1893 Columbian stamp designs — slightly modified — printed from plates made from the original dies.''

Included in the envelope with each set of sheets was a brochure describing the Smithsonian Institution's National Postal Museum and soliciting contributions of money to the museum.

First-Day Facts

More than 1,500 persons attended the 11 a.m. dedication ceremony for the souvenir sheets, held at the Rosemont-O'Hare Exhibition Center one hour after the opening of World Columbian Stamp Expo 92. It was standing room only in the large hall where the ceremony was held. USPS brought 2,000 first-day programs, each bearing one of the souvenir sheets tied by the first-day handstamp, but these ran out before the event began.

Richard J. Strasser Jr., senior assistant postmaster general, dedicated the U.S. sheets. The Italian sheets were dedicated by Enrico Veschi, director general, Ministry of Posts and Telecommunications; the Portuguese sheets by Dr. Carlos Reinaldo Pinheiro da Silva, president of the Portuguese Postal Services; and the Spanish sheets by Manuel Gonzalez Garcia of the Spanish Postal Administration.

Honored guests included other officials from the three European postal agencies, as well as John Sununu, former White House chief of staff. Jack Rosenthal, chairman of CSAC, made the principal address, and the welcome was extended by Charles Berg, president of WCSE 92. Actors played Columbus, King Ferdinand and Queen Isabella. Columbus quipped, to the delight of the audience, that the ceremony was taking longer than one of his voyages.

The night before WCSE 92 opened, cachetmakers were busy preparing for a midnight visit to the main post office in Chicago, where they could buy the sheets at 12:01 a.m. They spent the pre-dawn hours affixing stamps to envelopes, and by the time the show opened at 10 a.m., several of them had left on long road trips to create unofficial first-day covers.

Customers ordering first-day covers by mail were required to affix their own sheets. To give them time to obtain the sheets at local Philatelic Centers or through the Philatelic Sales Division, the Postal Service allowed a 90-day grace period for submitting the stamped covers.

Foreign and combination first-day postmarks could also be obtained by mail. For combination covers, USPS stressed that each country's postmark would be applied only to the stamps of that country, and that sufficient blank space on the envelopes — at least one inch to the left of each sheet — had to be allowed for the cancellations to be applied without touching the stamps of the other countries.

In an unusual waiver of its rules, USPS announced that it would provide the first-day postmark to individual U.S. Columbian stamps of less than the 29¢ first-class rate even if they were placed alone on envelopes. However, customers were required to submit complete sets of

Columbian souvenir sheets from Spain and Portugal.

16 covers, one for each of the Columbian stamps, to receive this special service. Mail orders had to include an addressed stamped envelope with sufficient first-class postage for the return of the sets of covers.

29¢ SPACE (BLOCK OF FOUR) (JOINT ISSUE)

Date of Issue: May 29, 1992

Catalog Numbers: Scott 2631-2634 (single stamps); 2634a (block of 4)

Colors: magenta, cyan, yellow, black

First-Day Cancel: Chicago, Illinois

FDCs Canceled: 277,853

Format: Panes of 50, vertical, 10 across, 5 down. Gravure printing cylinders of 200 subjects (10 across, 20 around).

Perf: 11.1 (Eureka off-line perforator)

Selvage Inscription: "This is a joint stamp/issue by the United/States and Russia." "The designs portray/past space achievements/ and envision possible/future cooperation/in space exploration." "A designer from each/of the two countries/ worked together to create/the unique painting/for the four stamp designs."

Selvage Markings: "Use Correct/ZIP Code/®." "©/United States/Postal Service/1991/36 USC 380." USPS Olympic logo.

Designer: Robert T. McCall of Paradise Valley, Arizona, and Vladimir Beilin of Moscow, Russia

Art Director and Project Manager: Jack Williams (USPS)

Typographer: John Boyd, of New York, New York

Printing: printed by BEP on 7-color Andreotti gravure press (601)

Quantity Ordered: 150,000,000

Quantity Distributed: 149,260,000

Cylinder Number Detail: 1 group of 4 gravure cylinder numbers alongside corner stamps

Cylinder Number Combination: 1111

Tagging: overall

The Stamps

It's not every year that the United States sets up a joint stamp issue with another country — and then sees that country disappear from the political map before the stamps are printed. But it happened with a joint issue scheduled for 1992.

Somehow, despite much confusion and uncertainty, the stamps came out, and on schedule — but with a new partner for the United States. The original party of the second part, the Union of Soviet Socialist Republics, was replaced by Russia.

There were other changes, both planned and unplanned. For instance, because of a communications failure within USPS, the U.S. stamps were smaller than the Russian stamps, contrary to the terms of the two countries' agreement. And the Russian stamps' color fidelity to the original artwork turned out to be unexpectedly poor.

As conceived, the stamps were to comprise a se-tenant block of four celebrating the space achievements of the United States and the U.S.S.R. The dedication ceremony would be a showcase event at World Columbian Stamp Expo 92, the big stamp show set for May 1992 in Chicago.

Two earlier U.S.-U.S.S.R. joint issues were produced according to plan: a Creatures of the Sea block of four in 1990, and a single stamp honoring Armenian-American author William Saroyan in 1991. When the Creatures of the Sea block was dedicated, Soviet and U.S. postal officials, who had come to Baltimore, Maryland, for the ceremony, met and worked out the terms for a third joint issue — the Space block.

Their memorandum of understanding called for an artist from each country to co-design the block, with each artist producing an identical painting that his postal agency would use to prepare the finished stamps. Other details, such as the stamps' size and format, were also covered.

But a funny thing happened on the way to the joint issue.

The Soviet Union broke up, and its former component republics became sovereign countries, loosely associated in a Commonwealth of Independent States. That left USPS — at least for a while — uncertain as to what entity, if any, would constitute the other half of the partnership.

The upheaval also made instantly obsolete the stamp design, which by then had been completed. A cosmonaut depicted on one of the four stamps wore a space suit with the letters "CCCP," which represented, in the Cyrillic alphabet, the initials "U.S.S.R."

Planning for the joint issue was in its final stages when, on November 1, 1991, the Ministry of Communications of the U.S.S.R., along with other Soviet ministries, ceased to exist. On the same day, new ministries of the Russian Federation, including the Ministry of Communications, Informatics and Space, officially came into being.

Arguably, the new postal ministry was the legal successor to the obligations of its outgoing Soviet counterpart insofar as international affairs were concerned. Assumptions, however, weren't certainties. In the weeks that followed, probably nobody inside Russia — and certainly nobody on the outside, including the U.S. Postal Service — fully understood what was going on in the disintegrating U.S.S.R., or could predict what events might flow from it.

Thus, when USPS unveiled its four stamps on December 11, 1991, along with the designs of other stamps scheduled for issue in 1992, Postmaster General Anthony M. Frank told reporters that he wasn't sure what other country would be issuing the Space block. However, he said,

Except for the missing denominations, this artwork for the U.S. stamps is identical to the pictures released to the public December 11, 1991. It shows the markings on the space suits as they were originally approved and painted when the Soviet Union (represented by the CCCP on the cosmonaut's uniform) still was a political entity. Subsequently, the uniform insignia were changed.

the United States intended to issue it.

USPS had conducted its joint-issue negotiations through the U.S.S.R. Stamp Agency in North America (later to become the Russian Stamp Agency), a division of Unicover World Trade Corporation of Cheyenne, Wyoming. The agency was familiar with the Soviet postal establishment, its personnel, its requirements and its predilections. It was James A. Helzer, chairman of Unicover, who now assumed a central role in working out the many new problems that threatened to abort the project.

On December 12, the day after the USPS stamp unveiling, Helzer sent a telex message to the Russian Ministry of Communications. He reported that Americans were wondering whether the stamps would still be issued on the other side, and by whom. He had told people, Helzer said, that "it was understood that the agreement would be assumed by Russia." He had also pointed out to USPS officials that the "CCCP" on the cosmonaut's space suit was no longer appropriate, he added, and he asked for a quick decision on what to do about it so that necessary changes could be made in the artwork.

Five days later Moscow sent an answer. "As you know, the situation in our country is very difficult, unexpected, and unfortunately, nobody knows anything," the message said. However, it confirmed that Russia would issue the stamps as per the memorandum of understanding. It also agreed that the "CCCP" on the space suit would have to come out, and suggested that blank chest panels on the uniforms and a "small red stripe" on the cosmonaut's arm would suffice.

Helzer telephoned Jack Williams, the USPS project manager, to tell him of this communication. Williams proposed that the "USA" be removed from the space suit of the American astronaut in the design for consistency, and that the two space suits bear replicas of the U.S. and Russian flags. This would help identify the two space explorers at stamp size and would add some color to the design, Williams said. Helzer agreed to relay this suggestion to the Russians.

Williams then telephoned the U.S. artist, Robert McCall, about the changes under discussion. McCall had no artistic objection to replacing lettering with flags, if that was the decision. He would like to do the repainting himself on his version of the design, McCall said, but because of deadline pressures and the fact that both his painting and the painting prepared by the Russian artist, Vladimir Beilin, were then in Moscow, the two men agreed that it might not be feasible.

Then, on Christmas day, in a faxed message to Helzer, Moscow turned down the flag proposal. "As you suppose, the future space flights will be fulfilled under projects of the Commonwealth and from the territory of (the Republic of) Kazakhstan," the message explained. The clear implication was that use of a Russian flag on the cosmonaut's uniform would offend the other republics. The message reiterated the earlier proposal that a simple red stripe be added to the uniform instead, and asked that the idea be put again to USPS.

(In the same message, in answer to a query from USPS, Moscow said it would be "practically impossible to settle the face value of the Russian stamps because nobody knows what the currency will be." "As you see," the message continued, "the whole situation is very uncertain. The only thing we can say for sure is that everything will be changed!")

Helzer telephoned USPS December 26, but found nobody at home in the stamps section. All the key officials were on Christmas holiday or year-end annual leave. Then, on December 29, came another telex from Moscow, with a new proposal: to replace the "CCCP" and "USA" on the uniforms with the emblems of Glavkosmos, which had become the Commonwealth's space agency, and the National Aeronautics and Space Administration (NASA).

"This idea seems to be interesting for us from our point of view and it helps to settle the problem with flags," the message said. It asked Helzer to consult USPS and reply, but added that the Russian ministry was about to close down until January 4. "Happy New Year!" it concluded.

On December 31, Helzer finally managed to reach a decision-maker at USPS headquarters: It was Joe Brockert, design section manager. Speaking for the Postal Service, Brockert authorized Helzer to approve the use of the space-agency emblems in the design. Helzer relayed this information to Russia by fax. With time slipping by rapidly, the Russian artist would have to make the changes on both paintings. Helzer included a copy of the NASA logo for Beilin to use as reference. "Please urge Beilin to work quickly, as the Postal Service is under much pressure to get the art for these stamps in production," Helzer wrote. "Artwork must be in Cheyenne prior to January 10."

On January 5, the Russian ministry, back at work, notified Helzer by telex that Beilin had "started to create a new version" of the space suits. The work wouldn't be finished until January 15, the ministry said, but it promised that the paintings would then be delivered "by the fastest usual means." After adding that the Russian Orthodox Christmas was two days away, the message ended with a cheery: "Merry Christmas!"

On January 15 another telex message to Cheyenne advised that the revised designs had been sent on their way. "Please deliver to the Postal Service . . . and return the appropriate materials and artworks by the end of January," it said. For some reason, the Russians sent not only Robert McCall's painting, which BEP would need to print the U.S. stamps, but also Beilin's painting, which Gosnak, the Russian security printer back in Moscow, would have to have for its version. Unicover quickly repackaged the Beilin artwork and returned it to Moscow.

There ensued a quiet period while both sides attended to details. Then came the big surprise.

The Baltimore agreement between the two postal agencies had specified that both countries' stamps would be of the same size, 1.23 inches across and 1.94 inches deep, and would be issued in panes of 32. The Soviets had asked for this specification so that the panes would contain an equal number of full blocks of four — eight — with no individual stamps left over.

The purpose of this was to avoid complaints like those they had heard from Russian collectors who had bought panes of the previous multiple-stamp joint issue, Creatures of the Sea. Both countries' Creatures panes had contained 40 stamps, but the U.S. panes were laid out five stamps across by eight down, which yielded only eight complete blocks instead of 10. The Soviet panes, on the other hand, were four across and 10 down, producing a full 10 blocks.

But USPS failed to follow this part of the agreement. The Stamp Manufacturing Division, which somehow hadn't been informed of it, directed the Bureau of Engraving and Printing to make the U.S. Space stamps standard commemorative size — 0.99 inches wide by 1.56 inches deep — and print them 50 to a pane. BEP proceeded with the prepress work, and, late in February, USPS sent a set of color separations to Cheyenne to be relayed to Russia. This was the Russian representatives' first inkling that the U.S. stamps were being prepared in the wrong size.

Helzer phoned USPS officials to try to find out what was going on. They conceded that the Postal Service had made a mistake. They were willing to stop the press at BEP and start over, they said, but they warned that this would push the stamps' issue date back to August. On behalf of the Russians, Helzer said a delay would be unacceptable; the Russians had already made plans to send a delegation headed by the pioneering Soviet cosmonaut Gherman S. Titov to Chicago for the May 29 joint first-day ceremony. During the conversation, USPS threw out an alternative suggestion: Might the Russians want to stop their stamp production and redo their stamps in smaller size to match the U.S. block?

On March 4 Helzer faxed a lengthy message to Moscow outlining the

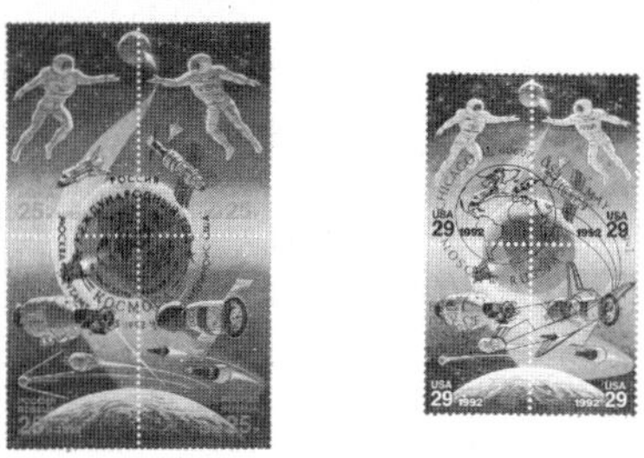
Challenging the infinite ocean of space, we confront the most awesome of all frontiers. In the first three decades of the space age, courage and technology have taken us away from our home planet toward the supreme adventure.

On the eve of the 21st century, we face this final frontier with confidence. Space presents limitless future and a limitless challenge; the only ingredients needed to meet the challenge are imagination, desire, and inventiveness. The world of space is a world we have only begun to explore.

The Space stamps encompass the whole thrilling pageant: from Sputnik, the first simple satellite beeping its message home, to the complex giant space shuttles of today and tomorrow .

The U.S. Postal Service and the Russian Ministry of Communications proudly issue the Space stamps in tribute to the cooperative exploration of space between the two countries. The design is a joint collaboration between Robert T. McCall of Paradise Valley, Arizona, and Vladimir Beilin of Moscow, Russia.

This page from the U.S. Postal Service souvenir program shows the difference in size between the Russian stamps, at left, and the U.S. stamps. The agreement between the two countries had called for both sets of stamps to be the same size, but the word didn't get to the right people within the USPS.

problem. The Russian ministry replied in a two-page telex March 17.

The ministry officials' first reaction upon learning of the size differential, they said, "was so dramatic that it is difficult to describe.'' They had been discussing the situation for three days. Destroying the Russian stamps already in production was out of the question. The press run was 80 percent complete, and it would be "impossible'' to find ink and paper for a new printing in the chaotic conditions that had gripped Russia's economy. There was "no other alternative,'' the ministry conceded, but to proceed with the issuance of stamps of different sizes.

Two days later, on March 19, the Russians had regained their equanimity. "In any event,'' they messaged Helzer, "from our side, we will do the utmost to finish the project successfully.''

The combination of relentless deadlines and a swiftly changing political situation also affected so prosaic a detail as the selvage inscriptions. On February 19, 1992, USPS sent Helzer a draft of the inscription that was to appear in the selvage of both countries' stamp panes. Helzer and the Postal Service's Jack Williams conferred by telephone and agreed on some editing changes. For example, the original draft read: "'This is a joint stamp issue by the United States and the Commonwealth of Independent States, once the Union of Soviet Socialist Republics.'' Since that was obviously a misstatement, they changed it to " . . . the United States and Russia.''

Helzer then sent the new wording to Moscow, asking for a quick yes or no, but this time he got no response. Hearing no demurrer, USPS proceeded to use the inscription as Williams and Helzer had revised it. In the end, the Russians placed no marginal inscription at all on their panes (which was, in fact, also an oversight under the Baltimore agreement).

The Russian stamps, as issued, were less faithful in color to the original paintings than were the U.S. versions. They had a brownish cast, and the areas meant to be blue came out closer to purple. On the other hand, the larger Russian stamps, printed by offset lithography, presented a clearer image than did the smaller, gravure-printed U.S. stamps. The word "Glavkosmos'' on the cosmonaut's space suit is legible on the Russian stamp but is only a blur of gravure dots on its U.S. counterpart.

The face value that was ultimately set for the Russian stamps was 25 rubles. The stamps were available in the United States at World Columbian Stamp Expo 92, at the Philatelic Center at USPS headquarters in Washington, and by mail order from the Philatelic Sales Division. The stamps cost 47¢ each, $1.88 for a block of four and $15.04 for the complete pane of 32.

The Designs

The block of Space stamps had the kind of se-tenant arrangement that some specialists call "confluent,'' meaning flowing together. The stamps form one continuous picture, although each individual stamp has its own center of focus and can stand alone artistically. Previous U.S. space-related stamps that featured confluent designs included the Accomplish-

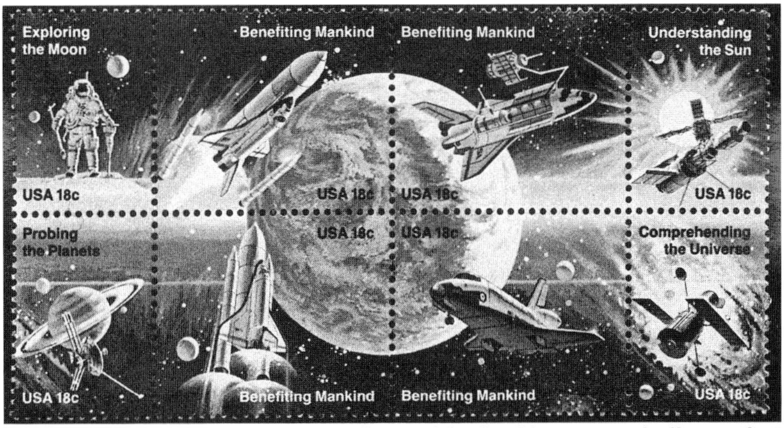

The design concept of the 1992 Space block of four was similar to that used by Robert McCall in his design for the 1981 Space Achievement block of eight (Scott 1912-1919).

ments in Space pair ("Space Twins'') of 1967 (Scott 1331-1332), the Space Achievement Decade pair of 1971 (Scott 1434-1435), and the issue that was most similar to the new block, the Space Achievement block of eight of 1981 (Scott 1912-1919).

The man who designed the 1971 pair and the 1981 block, space artist Robert T. McCall of Paradise Valley, Arizona, was called on by USPS to co-design the new joint issue. His partner for the project, Vladimir Beilin (pronounced Bay-lin), had designed two of the four stamps in the Creatures of the Sea block that the United States and the U.S.S.R. had issued jointly in 1990.

Working in partnership with a Russian artist was nothing new for McCall. In 1975 he and the U.S.S.R.'s Anatoly M. Aksamit had each designed one of the two stamps comprising the first U.S.-Soviet joint issue, the se-tenant pair of 1975 (Scott 1569-1570) that commemorated the historic linkup of the U.S. spacecraft *Apollo* and the Soviet *Soyuz*. And in 1989 and 1990 McCall and Soviet space artist Andrey Sokolov had painted together in McCall's Arizona studio to produce a huge triptych, 11 feet long by 6 feet deep, representing the vast sweep of space exploration from its origins into the future.

The design that McCall and Beilin produced for the new block of stamps was a busy little mural in which the space exploits of the two countries were carefully balanced. The rim of the Earth peeps above the bottom edge of the block. The moon is seen at dead center. The planet Mars hangs at the top, in the far distance. Two humans clad in space suits float in the top half of the design, a Russian at the left, an American at the right; they reach out toward each other in friendship.

The lower stamps feature the *Apollo-Soyuz* mission, with *Apollo* on the left, *Soyuz* on the right. Other historic spacecraft of both countries are also shown. In a nod to the future, a distant space ship leaves a luminous path across the block as it heads for Mars, representing a possible U.S.-

Russian manned mission to that planet.

USPS yielded to the Soviet/Russian practice of placing the year of issue in the design, as it had done with the Creatures of the Sea joint-issue stamps. Thus "1992" appears beside "USA 29" on each stamp.

The design concept was worked out in April 1991 in Moscow in a series of meetings between McCall and Beilin, after McCall had presented some preliminary sketches he had made on the plane from New York to Moscow. The two artists' discussions were conducted through an interpreter, since Beilin spoke only a little English.

Soviet postal officials approved the artists' concept drawings, and McCall returned home. In late June Beilin visited McCall in Arizona, and here the final details were agreed upon. Eventually, each man painted his own version of the block and sent it to the other for examination.

By mutual agreement, McCall's version was chosen to be the basis for both countries' stamps. Beilin, who was considerably younger than the 72-year-old McCall, had had little experience in painting space subjects, and readily deferred to his American partner's expertise in depicting space hardware and planetary bodies. He considered it a privilege, he told acquaintances, to learn from the American.

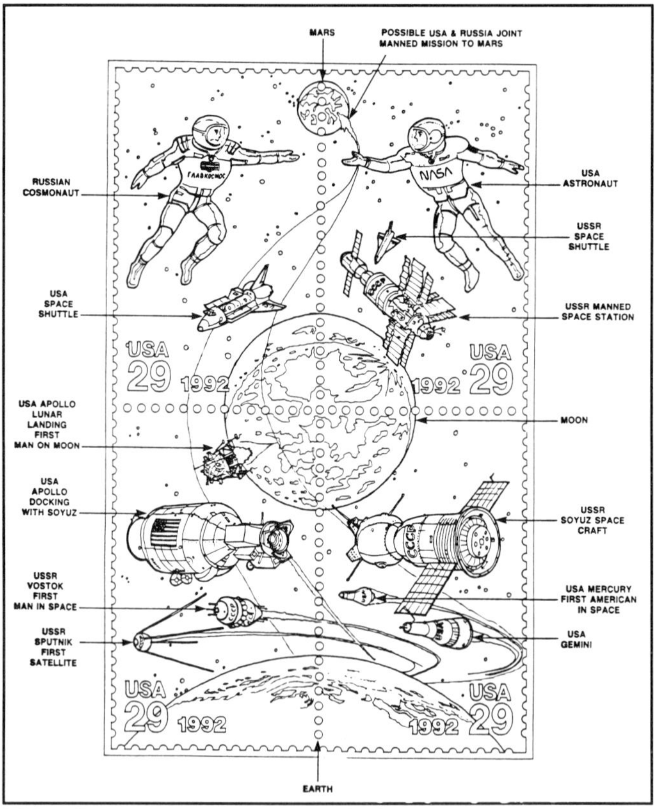

This diagram, prepared by USPS, identifies the various design components of the Space block.

McCall's painting was shipped to Moscow, and Beilin made his own exact copy — so exact, McCall said, that "when I saw it I had to take a magnifying glass and look very, very carefully to realize that it was a separate painting. It was so near in every detail to mine that I could hardly realize it myself.''

First-Day Facts

The dedication ceremony for the U.S. Space block of four was part of the closing weekend's activities at World Columbian Stamp Expo 92. The ceremony was held May 29 at the Rosemont/O'Hare Exhibition Center in Rosemont, Illinois, a suburb of Chicago.

John G. Mulligan, Central Region postmaster general, dedicated the U.S. stamps, and Viatcheslav A. Poliakov, chief of posts for the Russian Ministry of Communications, dedicated the Russian block. The speakers were three members of one of the world's most exclusive societies, the Association of Space Explorers, membership in which is limited to individuals who have flown in outer space. They were Gherman Titov, who as pilot-cosmonaut of the Soviet spacecraft *Vostok 2* in 1961 was the second human to orbit the earth; *Mercury*, *Apollo* and *Apollo-Soyuz* Astronaut Donald K. "Deke'' Slayton, and Henry W. Hartsfield Jr., an astronaut (and stamp collector) who had flown on the space shuttles *Columbia, Discovery* and *Challenger*. Another *Apollo* astronaut, Scott Carpenter, had been scheduled to speak, but was unable to attend.

The space explorers received a standing ovation from an audience estimated at 1,000 or more. Titov, in his remarks, drew a cheer when he said he would like to see a Soviet rocket go into space with an international crew and land in the United States, and that the cargo should

Among the guests at the May 29 first-day ceremony for the U.S. and Russian Space stamps were (left to right) astronaut Henry Hartsfield, cosmonaut Gherman Titov, U.S. designer Robert T. McCall and astronaut "Deke" Slayton.

contain postal artifacts for collectors. After the ceremony, participants signed autographs for more than two hours.

On the same day, Jerry K. Lee Sr., Southern Region postmaster general, and Michael O'Hara of USPS headquarters staff joined officials from the Russian Ministry of Communications at dedication ceremonies for the Russian version of the Space stamps in Star City, the cosmonaut training center near Moscow, Russia.

Both countries provided special handstamped pictorial cancellations. First-day covers could be obtained in several variations, including combination covers bearing a single or block of each country's stamps. For these, collectors were instructed to leave sufficient space on the envelopes so that each country's cancellation could be applied without touching the other country's stamps.

29¢ ALASKA HIGHWAY

Date of Issue: May 30, 1992

Catalog Number: Scott 2635

Colors: magenta, yellow, cyan, black, brown (offset); black (intaglio)

First-Day Cancel: Fairbanks, Alaska

FDCs Canceled: 186,791

Format: Panes of 50, vertical, 10 across, 5 down. Offset printing plates of 200 subjects (20 across, 10 around); intaglio printing sleeve of 400 subjects (20 across, 20 around).

Perf: 11.1 (Eureka off-line perforator)

Selvage Inscription: "Known first as the/Alcan Highway, the/Alaska Highway was/completed in 1942." "The 1500-mile road/through Northwest/Canada is the major/land route to Alaska." "Today the highway/remains a symbol of/cooperation between/the U.S. and Canada."

Selvage Markings: "©/United States/Postal Service/1991/36 USC 380." "Use Correct/ZIP Code ®." USPS Olympic logo.

Designer: Byron Birdsall of Anchorage, Alaska

Art Director and Project Manager: Jack Williams (USPS)

Typographer: Bradbury Thompson (CSAC)

Engraver: Gary Slaght (BEP)

Printing: printed by BEP on 6-color offset, 3-color intaglio D press (902)

Quantity Ordered: 146,610,000

Quantity Distributed: 146,610,000

Plate/Sleeve Number Detail: 1 group of 5 offset plate numbers alongside corner stamp; 1 intaglio sleeve number in selvage of adjacent stamp.

Plate/Sleeve Number Combinations: 11111-1, 11211-1, 22211-1, 22311-1

Tagging: overall

The Stamp

On May 30, USPS issued a stamp to commemorate the 50th anniversary of one of the great hurry-up engineering feats in U.S. history — the construction of the Alaska Highway. The 1,520-mile road that winds through Canada into central Alaska was built in less than nine months in 1942 by the Army Corps of Engineers as a World War II military route.

The principal advocates of the stamp were members of the Anchorage Philatelic Society. They first proposed that it be included in the series being planned to commemorate U.S. participation in World War II.

"It didn't fit, really, into the (World War II) souvenir sheets," said Jack Williams, project manager for the stamp. "But the Citizens' Stamp Advisory Committee thought it was a subject worth doing. It would call attention to the connection between the United States and Canada, the good relationship we've had for so long and the common border."

Belmont Faries, former chairman of CSAC, said the committee was well aware of the highway and its significance and would have approved the stamp without any outside pressure. "It's the type of thing we like to do," Faries told Bill McAllister of *The Washington Post.*

Nevertheless, the Anchorage philatelists did no harm to their cause when they enlisted the help of Senator Ted Stevens, R-Alaska, to lobby the Postal Service. Stevens was a man to whom USPS paid attention. As ranking minority member of the Senate Subcommittee on Federal Services, Post Office and Civil Service, he had worked assiduously to make sure that mail service in his huge state was no less accessible nor more expensive than it is in the "lower 48."

After Postmaster General Anthony M. Frank had approved the CSAC recommendation for an Alaska Highway stamp, Frank wasted no time getting the word out. On June 4, 1990, while in Anchorage for a meeting of the USPS Board of Governors, he announced to the Anchorage Chamber of Commerce that the stamp was in the works. It was almost two years before the issue date.

The design was first shown to the public December 6, 1991, at a brief ceremony in Fairbanks, with Senator Stevens and Representative Don Young, R-Alaska, joining Robert J. Opinsky, general manager/postmaster of the Anchorage Division, to do the honors. The unveiling took place five days before USPS was scheduled to display its full lineup of designs for the 1992 stamp program. "Senator Stevens asked if he could do it at an event in advance," Robin Minard, a spokeswoman for the Postal Service, told *Linn's Stamp News*.

Canada, which paid the United States $108 million in 1946 and took over its portion of the highway, also marked the 50th anniversary with a commemorative stamp. The 42¢ stamp, issued May 15, depicted a map with the location of the road, plus scenes from its construction. Canada had previously shown a scene on the Alaska Highway on an 8¢ definitive stamp of 1967 (Scott 461).

The idea of a highway across western Canada to link the United States with the Alaska Territory had been discussed for decades. But the Japanese attack on Pearl Harbor in December 1941 suddenly made such an artery an urgent necessity. U.S. military leaders feared that a blockade of Alaskan seaports, followed by an invasion, might be imminent.

Two months later, the U.S. and Canadian governments agreed on a plan to build the road, from Dawson Creek in British Columbia to Delta Junction south of Fairbanks. It would cross five mountain ranges and numerous rivers. Survey crews, guided by trappers, set out in March. By June, some 10,000 GIs had begun to push a ragged track through dense spruce forests and across seemingly bottomless muskeg bogs.

The growing workforce was a mixture of servicemen and civilian contractors. A famous advertisement warned would-be civilian workers that employment would be "NO PICNIC." "Men hired for this job will be required to work and live under the most extreme conditions imaginable," the ad continued. "Temperatures will range from 90 degrees above zero to 70 degrees below zero. Men will have to fight swamps, rivers, ice and cold. Mosquitoes, flies and gnats will not only be annoying but will cause bodily harm. If you are not prepared to work under these and similar conditions DO NOT APPLY."

The GIs, of course, had no choice. Three of the seven Army regiments sent north were segregated units made up of black troops commanded by white officers. They were assigned to the most remote, least populated areas, and for many of these soldiers, who hailed from the deep South, the

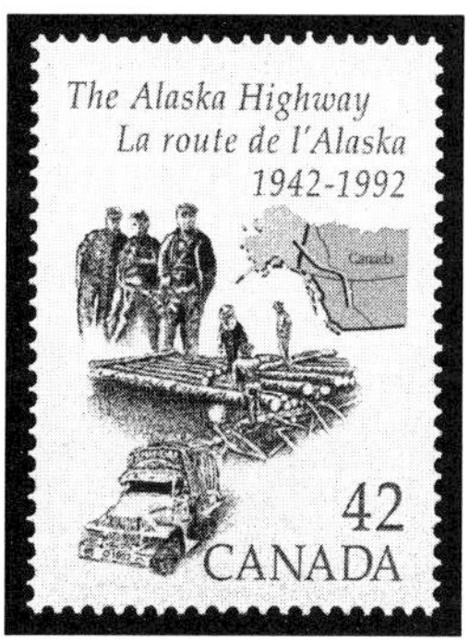

This is the Canadian stamp issued May 15, 1992, to mark the 50th anniversary of the Alaska Highway.

encounter with 70-below weather was especially punishing.

The engineers had to improvise a way to build over muskeg, which was spongy, peatlike organic matter overlying a permanently frozen bog. They laid down layers of corduroy and gravel; the corduroy was made from thousands of logs laid crosswise atop the muskeg and beneath the roadbed, each of which had to be hand-cut from the surrounding forests.

The road was built along a meandering path because of the need to avoid muskeg where possible. "The emphasis was on speed, so we followed the path of least resistance," Walter Mason, then an officer with the 97th Engineering Regiment, told Jon Krakauer, a writer for *Smithsonian* magazine. "We tried to stay as close as we could to the men out front blazing the trail. Often our Caterpillars were right on top of the people setting the survey stakes. Once we crossed the Tanana River, we were putting in better than five miles of road a day."

On November 20, just eight months and 12 days after building began, the road was officially opened. Another 11 months of work were required before it was passable year-round, and for many years thereafter bridges would regularly wash out in the spring and summer floods. "But however much it may have been subject to the caprices of nature, the fact that it had been built at all — to say nothing of the incredible speed involved — made the Alaska Highway one of the engineering marvels of the century," Krakauer wrote.

At first, the road was called the Alaska-Canadian Military Highway, or "Alcan Highway" for short. That name occasionally still is used, but the designation has been officially changed to the Alaska Highway, which is how it is generally known today.

The dirt surface has mostly given way to paving, and each year construction crews modify a few more of the more hazardous hairpin turns and steep hills. Some 40,000 civilian vehicles a year use the Alaska Highway. Still, *The New York Times*, in an anniversary article, said it remains "the last great driving adventure in North America."

"Sure, there are other places to routinely spot moose, wolves and even bears wandering across your path amid majestic mountain scenery and pristine lakes," *Times* writer Robert D. Hershey Jr. continued. "But probably nowhere else do you get these in half-continent dimension and with the sense of isolation provided (by the Alaska Highway) . . . Much of the time you're not within earshot of any radio station and the next gasoline may be as much as 100 miles ahead."

The Design

Byron Birdsall of Anchorage, Alaska, is a watercolor painter who specializes in landscapes. On the advice of a friend who handled public relations for the local post office, he sent samples of his work to USPS and asked to be considered for a future stamp design project. A few months later, when USPS was looking for someone to design the Alaska Highway stamp, the idea of using an Alaska artist proved irresistible. Birdsall was asked to submit some sketches for the design.

Birdsall assembled his research material, which included photographs that the USPS researcher, Susan Robb, had found in Washington, D.C., and that he had located in such places as the Yukon Territory Archives in Whitehorse and the Public Archives of British Columbia in Victoria. He then prepared color renderings in horizontal and vertical formats.

CSAC chose a vertical sketch showing an Army vehicle cresting a hill in the foreground, with the road stretching off straight in the distance toward a massive mountain range. Birdsall had based the picture on a 1942 U.S. Army photograph from the Library of Congress. The vehicle was identifiable — a Dodge 4 by 4 quarter-ton carryall truck, called a command car — but, unfortunately, the location of the scene wasn't. However, the committee members felt the picture had all the elements they wanted in a harmonious combination: primitive road, mountainous

This is the U.S. Army photograph from the Library of Congress on which the final design for the Alaska Highway stamp was based. It shows a Dodge 4 by 4 quarter-ton carryall truck that was used as a command car. The location of this mountain scene wasn't given on the photograph, and the artist was unable to supply it.

terrain, and an authentic and recognizable vehicle.

On CSAC's instructions, relayed through art director Jack Williams, Birdsall repainted the picture four times.

"The road just went to nowhere," Williams said. "It stopped as if it had dropped over a cliff. And an area at the center, no matter how lightly he was painting it, was clogging up when we tried to take the design down to stamp size. We kept going back and saying, 'lighter, lighter.'

"Finally, we told him the solution, we thought, was to make the road more serpentine, make it twist, take artistic liberties and get it moving into the center. That's exactly what he did. Then we said we needed more color; this was already a dark stamp. So he put some fireweed into the

Byron Birdsall prepared these color sketches of various scenes along the highway. Sources for the photographs on which the sketches were based are given in parentheses. The jeep is driving over the rough corduroy road during the early construction stage (Library of Congress). The truck is making the first cargo shipment to Fairbanks (Yukon Archives, Whitehorse). The night scene shows the moon hanging low over Kluane Lake at the base of the St. Elias Range (Public Archives of British Columbia, Victoria). Another scene shows the highway in early winter with mountains in the background (National Archives and artist's own experience). The view of a winding road with fireweed in the foreground is also from the artist's own experience. The captions on these sketches read "The Alcan Highway," which was the original name for the road.

This is one of Byron Birdsall's intermediate versions of the design, before he made the road angle across the background in a series of curves to create greater visual interest.

picture, touches of it in front and along the road, which brightened it up."

The idea of curving the road "was something I should have probably figured out, because it bothered me a little bit," Birdsall said. "The road in my original painting looked like a pillar of salt. By curving it, it assumed a more realistic configuration."

CSAC's Bradbury Thompson provided the typography, consisting of the logo "USA 29" in the lower-right corner and the words "Alaska Highway 1942" across the bottom. The Bureau of Engraving and Printing printed the stamp by a combination process, with the basic stamp done by offset lithography and the black "USA 29" in intaglio.

Birdsall said he was pleased with the end product. He and his family were enjoying a sabbatical in Stratford, Ontario, when the stamp came out, and when they moved back to Anchorage, Birdsall had 40 boxes of art supplies and personal effects to send home. "Rather than ship them from Canada," he said, "I drove across the border to the post office in Port Huron, Michigan, and said 'I'd like to send these airmail to Anchorage, and I want to use the Highway stamp.' So I have 5,000 of them, all with a Port Huron cancellation! They were a little miffed that I didn't want to use the meter."

Varieties

A collector in Colorado, buying stamps from a USPS vending machine, found two horizontal strips of 10 Alaska Highway commemoratives that were missing the black intaglio logo "29 USA." One was a top margin row, and the other was the second row. Martin Wilkinson of the Colorado Stamp Company in Boulder told *Linn's Stamp News* that the collector originally purchased one package, noticed the error, then continued buying packages until the supply was exhausted. Only one other package with the error was found.

In November, a single specimen of the error was auctioned by Lowell S. Newman and Company for $1,100.

The 29¢ black intaglio denomination and "USA" are missing from this Alaska Highway stamp, one of 20 discovered in Colorado.

First-Day Facts

Susan E. Alvarado, a member of the USPS Board of Governors, dedicated the stamp in a ceremony at Alaskaland Civic Center in Fairbanks May 30. Senator Stevens was the principal speaker. Other speakers included Colonel John W. Pierce, Alaska district engineer for the U.S. Army Corps of Engineers; designer Byron Birdsall; and Wayne Nelson, mayor of Fairbanks, who gave the welcome. Among the items on display was an Army Dodge command car like the one Birdsall had included in his stamp design.

The people of Delta Junction, where the highway actually terminates, protested at being snubbed in favor of the larger city 95 miles to the north. To satisfy them, USPS scheduled a second-day ceremony — a rerun of the first — and provided an official second-day postmark. "We all went to Delta Junction the next day and gave the same speeches we had given in Fairbanks," Birdsall said.

The first-day ceremony program produced by USPS carried the wrong abbreviation for Alaska on the cover. It referred to Fairbanks AL instead of the correct AK. The postmark inside the program was right, however.

29¢ KENTUCKY STATEHOOD

Date of Issue: June 1, 1992

Catalog Number: Scott 2636

Colors: magenta, yellow, cyan, black, line blue

First-Day Cancel: Danville, Kentucky

FDCs Canceled: 251,153

Format: Panes of 50, horizontal, 5 across, 10 down. Gravure printing cylinders of 200 subjects (20 across, 10 around) manufactured by Armotek Industries Inc., Palmyra, New Jersey.

Perf: 10.9 (L perforator)

Selvage Markings: "Use Correct/ZIP Code/®/36 USC 380." "©/United States/Postal Service/1991." USPS Olympic logo.

Designer: Joseph Petro of Lexington, Kentucky

Art Director and Project Manager: Jack Williams (USPS)

Typographer: Bradbury Thompson (CSAC)

Printing: Printed by Stamp Venturers on a Champlain gravure press in Richmond, Virginia. Perforated, processed and shipped by Stamp Venturers in Milwaukee, Wisconsin.

Quantity Ordered: 160,000,000

Quantity Distributed: 160,000,000

Cylinder Number Detail: 1 group of 5 gravure cylinder numbers preceded by the letter S alongside corner stamp

Cylinder Number Combination: S11111

Tagging: phosphor-coated paper

The Stamp

The Postal Service commemorated Kentucky's 200th anniversary of statehood with a stamp issued June 1 in Danville, Kentucky. The stamp pictured Federal Hill, the brick mansion in Bardstown that was immortalized as My Old Kentucky Home in the Stephen Collins Foster song that has been adopted as the official state song.

The stamp was the second to celebrate a Kentucky statehood anniversary. Exactly 50 years earlier, on June 1, 1942, the U.S. Post Office Department had issued a 3¢ commemorative (Scott 904) to mark the state's sesquicentennial. The stamp depicted Daniel Boone, a pioneer closely identified with the exploration and settlement of Kentucky. It was one of only three U.S. stamps issued in that wartime year, and the only one without a war-related theme.

The design of the 1992 stamp was revealed without advance notice to the philatelic press. On October 16, 1991, James D. Syers, field division general manager/postmaster of the Louisville Division of USPS, and Ron Gentry, secretary of the Kentucky Tourism Cabinet, unveiled the stamp in a special ceremony at Federal Hill. This was nearly two months before the Postal Service would officially release pictures of its planned 1992 stamps in Washington.

The Postal Service's Louisville Division and the Kentucky Department of Travel Development co-sponsored the Bardstown event, which philatelic reporters learned about only after an account was published in a Hopkinsville, Kentucky, newspaper, *The Kentucky New Era*. USPS "later admitted that it knew of the unveiling, but it had simply missed releasing the information at that time," *Linn's Stamp News* reported.

According to another newspaper that covered the event, *The Kentucky Standard* of Bardstown, the prime mover of a stamp picturing My Old Kentucky Home was Bardstown's Catherine Conner, who began her campaign in 1985. Mimi Lewis, commissioner of the Kentucky Department of Travel Development, credited Conner for "getting the ball rolling," the newspaper said, and Alice Heaton, manager of My Old Kentucky Home State Park, said Conner "called people and did a lot of legwork when people just laughed."

"She persevered, and she got her dream today," Heaton said.

There was little disagreement among Kentucky officials over the design subject. Both the state Bicentennial Commission and the governor wrote letters asking that My Old Kentucky Home be depicted.

"Federal Hill's familiarity and sense of home was the force behind the commission's decision to encourage the stamp design," said Senator David K. Karem, the chairman. "It is such a well-known symbol of Kentucky hospitality. People all over the country identify with this landmark, which will spur nationwide interest in our celebration."

Kentucky and Kentuckians have been featured on many U.S. stamps besides the 1942 Statehood commemorative. Natives of the state who have been postally depicted include Abraham Lincoln, 16th president of the United States; Jefferson Davis, president of the Confederate States of

The design of the 1942 stamp commemorating Kentucky's sesquicentennial (Scott 904) features a mural by Gilbert White depicting Daniel Boone and three frontiersmen. The mural is in the capitol at Frankfort.

America, whose image was shown on the 6¢ Stone Mountain Memorial stamp (Scott 1408) with other Confederate leaders; Montgomery Blair, Lincoln's postmaster general; Whitney Young, long-time president of the Urban League; D.W. Griffith, pioneer motion-picture director; and John Luther "Casey" Jones, who was nicknamed for the town of Cayce, Kentucky, where he worked as a young man. The flag-raising Marines who were shown on the 3¢ Marine Corps stamp of 1945 (Scott 929) included Franklin R. Sousley, who was born in Kentucky.

Two Kentucky anniversaries were marked by stamps in 1974. One was the 200th anniversary of Fort Harrod, the first settlement in Kentucky (Scott 1542), and the other was the centennial of the state's most famous sporting event, the Kentucky Derby (Scott 1528). Horse breeding, the major industry in Kentucky's bluegrass region, was commemorated with a block of four (Scott 2155-2158) that had its first-day sale in Lexington, Kentucky, in 1985.

Kentucky was the second state to be added to the Union after the original 13, and the first to be organized west of the Appalachian Mountains. Its territory, which was part of Virginia, had been extensively explored by Daniel Boone and others in the years preceding the Revolutionary War. In 1774 James Harrod founded Harrodstown, now Harrodsburg, the first permanent settlement in Kentucky. Boonesboro, named for the famous pioneer, was established the following year. The two rival settlements united in fighting off Indian attacks.

In December 1784, after the colonies had won independence from Great Britain, Kentuckians met at Danville, and asked to be separated from Virginia. This was the first of 10 conventions that prepared the way for statehood. On June 1, 1792, Kentucky was admitted to the Union.

Federal Hill, the 2½-story brick mansion depicted on the stamp, is one of the best examples of Georgian Colonial architecture in Kentucky. It is located some 30 miles south of Louisville. Completed in 1818 by John Rowan, a member of Congress and a future U.S. senator, it became the manor house of a great plantation. Rowan's son, John Jr., became master of Federal Hill after his father's death in 1843, and tradition has it that young Rowan's cousin, Stephen Collins Foster, wrote the ballad *My Old Kentucky Home* while on a visit there in 1852. Foster was depicted on a Famous Americans stamp of 1940 (Scott 879).

The Design

The Citizens' Stamp Advisory Committee "was not exactly wildly enthusiastic" about depicting My Old Kentucky Home in the stamp design, said Jack Williams of USPS, art director and project manager for the stamp, "but they agreed that if this was what the state wanted, they would go along with it." The stamp as issued bore a strong similarity to a typical indicium in the Historic Preservation postal card series.

From an agent in New York, Williams sought the name of a Kentucky artist who could design the stamp, and was referred to Joseph V. Petro of Lexington. Petro, a professional painter for some 40 years, had created a variety of artwork, including murals, horse paintings, portraits and medical illustrations, but this was his first stamp assignment. "It's the pinnacle of my career," he told *The Kentucky Standard.*

He was awarded the job in December 1990, and went to Bardstown in January to sketch the home from every angle while the trees were bare. For the stamp design, however, he planned to include trees in full leaf.

Because state officials had asked that the stamp design show people in antebellum costumes, Petro prepared two different versions containing people. The committee reviewed his first version and asked for some revisions. Accordingly, the artist took out some of the foliage that partially concealed the building and sky, and grouped the people rather than spread them out across the lawn.

Meanwhile, the Kentucky officials were having second thoughts. They decided that to show only white people, who would have comprised the guests at Federal Hill before the Civil War, wouldn't be representative of the current ethnic makeup of Kentucky. But historical accuracy would require that any African Americans who were included in the design would be servants or slaves. So the final request made to the Postal Service was to omit people and show just the building.

The wording on the stamp was "My Old Kentucky Home State Park" rather than "My Old Kentucky Home." "That was done deliberately," said Williams, "because otherwise we would have gotten into questions of rights — who owns the rights to the song — and of how we would treat the title, whether we would put it in quotation marks or italics.

"There actually is My Old Kentucky Home State Park there, of course, and wording it that way was OK with the state of Kentucky."

Shown here are Joseph V. Petro's concept sketch and revised version of a design showing Federal Hill with guests gathered on the lawn as it might have appeared before the Civil War. Kentucky officials ultimately decided they wanted the home shown without people.

First-Day Facts

The Kentucky stamp was dedicated by Samuel Green Jr., regional postmaster general, in an outdoor ceremony at Constitution Square State Historic Site in Danville, where the first capitol stood. Danville is in central Kentucky, a few miles southwest of Lexington.

Speakers included Governor Brereton C. Jones; Senator Karem, the Bicentennial Commission chairman; and Dr. Thomas D. Clarke, Kentucky historian laureate. Among the musical selections, of course, was *My Old Kentucky Home*, by the Stephen Foster Story Singers.

The 1790 Danville post office, which USPS says was the first post office west of the Alleghenies, stands on the square, and was open to provide first-day postmarks on a handback basis. Stamps were also sold at Danville's main post office and from mobile units.

Unfortunately, wrote Allison Cusick, *Linn's Stamp News* first-day cover columnist, "The Danville post office provided the worst canceling services of any first-day ceremony I've attended in many years."

"The postal people apparently were wholly untrained on how to cancel first-day covers," Cusick wrote. "Sloppy, dirty postmarks with smears of ink were commonplace. The killer bars often missed the stamp entirely."

29¢ OLYMPIC SUMMER GAMES (STRIP OF FIVE)

Date of Issue: June 11, 1992

Catalog Numbers: Scott 2637-2641 (single stamps); 2641a (strip of 5)

Colors: magenta, yellow, cyan, black, red

First-Day Cancel: Baltimore, Maryland

FDCs Canceled: 713,942

Format: Panes of 35, horizontal, 5 across, 7 down. Gravure printing cylinders of 140 (10 across, 14 around) manufactured by Armotek Industries Inc., Palmyra, New Jersey.

Perf: 10.9 (L perforator)

Selvage Inscription: "The popularity of soccer/in the U.S. has grown/tremendously in recent/years, and the improved/quality of play has enabled/U.S. teams to become more/competitive than ever before/in the world soccer arena." "Many believe that gymnastics/may be the toughest of all/Olympic Summer Games/sports. The rigid competitive/standards for the sport require/that the gymnast be as agile/as a ballerina, as quick as a/sprinter and as strong as a/ weightlifter." "The U.S. men's volleyball/team goes to the 1992 Olympic/Summer Games in search of a/third consecutive gold medal./This truly American sport began/in Holyoke, Massachusetts,/and gained global popularity/ during World Wars I and II." "Cleverness, speed, defensive/skills and the ability to/score points on one's opponent/all outweigh the measure of/how much physical punishment/an athlete can absorb in the/sport of boxing." "U.S. men's and women's/swimming teams have won a/ significant number of medals in/Olympic Games competition./American swimmers and divers/are expected to be showcased/again in the 1992 Olympic/Summer Games at Barcelona,/Spain." "The XXV/Olympic/Summer/Games will/be held in/Barcelona,/Spain, July/25-August/9, 1992."

Selvage Markings: "©/United States/Postal Service/1991." "Use Correct/ZIP Code/®/38 USC 380." USPS Olympic logo.

Designer: Richard Waldrep of Baltimore, Maryland

Art Director and Typographer: Howard Paine (CSAC)

Project Manager: Jack Williams (USPS)

Modeler: Richard Sennett (Sennett Enterprises)

Printing: Stamps printed by Stamp Venturers on a Champlain gravure press in Richmond, Virginia. Stamps perforated, processed and shipped by Stamp Venturers in Milwaukee, Wisconsin.

Quantity Ordered: 160,000,000

Quantity Distributed: 160,000,000

Cylinder Number Detail: 1 group of 5 gravure cylinder numbers preceded by the letter S alongside corner stamp.

Cylinder Number Combination: S11111

Tagging: phosphor-coated paper with phosphor-blocking lacquer in margins

The Stamps

The Games of the 25th Olympiad were held in Barcelona, Spain, from July 25 to August 9, 1992, with 15,000 athletes from 170 nations participating. They were the first post-Cold War Summer Games, and in a welcome change from recent history, no nation boycotted them or was banned for political reasons. Although commercialism and professionalism reigned as never before, the Games were played in peace, relative harmony and in the spirit of their motto, "Friends for Life."

The U.S. Postal Service commemorated the Summer Games with five 29¢ stamps depicting five Olympic sporting events: soccer, gymnastics, volleyball, boxing and swimming. This was the fourth — and final — five-stamp commemorative set to be issued by USPS in its role as an official sponsor of the 1992 Games, Winter and Summer.

Like the other sets, which began in 1990, the stamps were semijumbo in size, issued in sheet form, and so laid out that each horizontal row in a pane contained five different varieties and each vertical row was made up of stamps of the same variety. Like two of the previous sets, the Summer Games stamps were issued in panes of 35 rather than the 40-stamp panes that are standard for semijumbos. This allowed use of an extra-wide selvage strip above or below each pane. The selvage, or tabs, carried text describing each of the five sports in the space adjacent to that sport's strip of stamps.

The Summer Games stamps were first placed on sale June 11 in Baltimore, Maryland, in conjunction with the opening ceremonies of the U.S. Gymnastics championships in the Baltimore Arena. Later in the

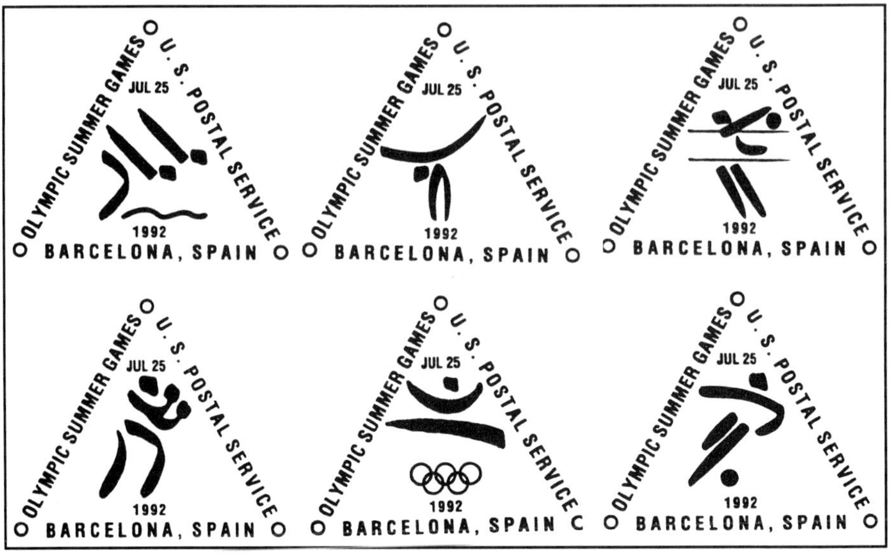

USPS introduced these six pictorial postmarks in Barcelona beginning July 25. They showed the Barcelona Olympic logo and pictograms of boxing, gymnastics, soccer, swimming and volleyball competition.

summer, USPS offered six pictorial postmarks saluting the Summer Games and a seventh honoring OLYMPHILEX 92, a stamp show that ran concurrently in Barcelona. The postmarks were introduced in Barcelona but also were available in the United States.

The 1992 Games also were the subject of U.S. commemorative coins that were sold to raise money for the U.S. Olympic Committee to use training American athletes. They consisted of a half dollar, silver dollar and $5 gold piece. The obverse of the $5 coin, depicting a sprinter

These two U.S. Olympic commemorative coins were issued by the U.S. Mint in 1992. The copper half dollar had on its obverse a pony-tailed gymnast in full leap, with a horizontal American flag in the background. The designer was William Cousins, a sculptor and engraver at the Mint. The gold $5 coin showed on its obverse a sprinter against a backdrop of a hanging American flag. Illustrator and stamp designer James C. Sharpe created this design.

superimposed over a vertically hanging U.S. flag, was designed by Jim Sharpe of Westport, Connecticut. Sharpe was better known to stamp collectors as the designer of all the stamps in the Postal Service's Performing Arts series, including the Cole Porter stamp of 1991.

Various artists, at the Postal Service's request, prepared these concept sketches for 1992 Summer Olympic Games stamps. They included realistic as well as highly stylized treatments of athletes, and two woodblock-type designs with artwork reminiscent of ancient Greece, where the Games originated.

Athletes representing the 12 former republics of the Soviet Union competed as teammates for the final time at the 1992 Summer Olympics. Their Unified Team won the most total medals, 112, including 45 golds. The United States was second, with 108 medals (37 golds), and Germany, participating as one nation for the first time since 1936, was third with 82 (33 golds). Among the star performers of the Games were:

• The players of the U.S. men's basketball team, recruited for the first time from the ranks of the professional National Basketball Association in a successful bid to restore U.S. basketball dominance in the Olympics. This so-called "Dream Team" won its eight games by average margins of 43.8 points.

• The U.S. men's 4- by 100-meter and 4- by 400-meter relay teams, which won their events in world record time. The 4- by 100-meter team was anchored by Carl Lewis, who also won the men's long jump, adding those two gold medals to six others he had won in the Summer Olympics

One artist prepared this proposed set of five designs showing a sprinter, pole vaulter, hurdler, javelin thrower and shot putter. The treatment was similar to Richard Waldrep's designs on the finished stamps but were much less tightly cropped.

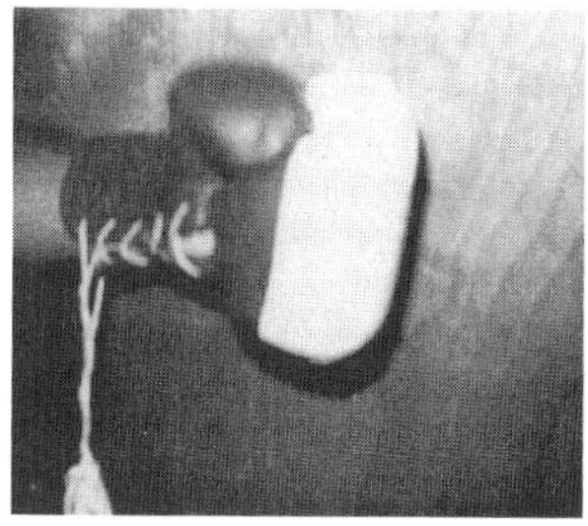

This is Richard Waldrep's first version of the boxer. On the advice of Bruce Mathis of USA Amateur Boxing, Waldrep gave the boxer headgear and made the thumb of the left glove more prominent, using as a model a Polaroid photo of a boxing glove.

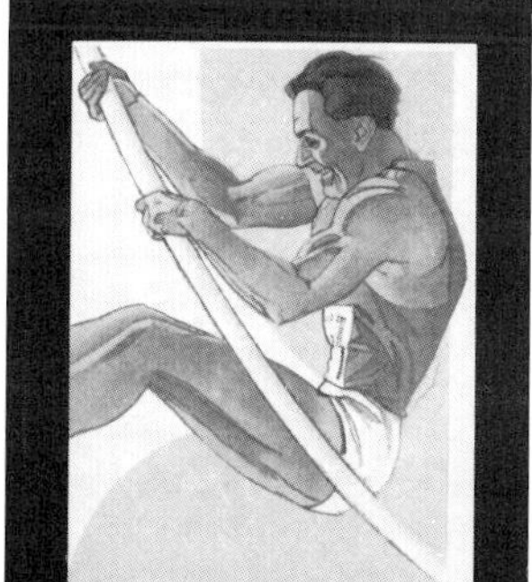

These are additional proposed stamp designs by Richard Waldrep that weren't included in his finished strip of five.

of 1984 and 1988.

• Vitaly Shcherbo and Tatiana Gutsu of the Unified Team, who won the individual all-around titles in men's and women's gymnastics, respectively.

• Cuba's boxers, who won seven of the 12 gold medals and two silvers.

• Robert Zmelik of Czechoslovakia, who captured the men's decathlon and with it the traditional title of "world's greatest athlete."

• Jackie Joyner-Kersee of the United States, who successfully defended her women's heptathlon gold medal, which she had won in 1988.

• Kevin Young of the United States, who set a world record in winning the 400-meter hurdles.

The Designs

Because of the importance of the Olympics stamps to USPS as a sponsor, several artists were asked to submit concept sketches for the Summer Games. These ranged in style from woodblock-type representations of two-dimensional drawings of ancient Greece to ultra-modern images depicting athletes as patterns of planes, angles and circles.

In the end, the Citizens' Stamp Advisory Committee chose five of the designs of Richard Waldrep, a first-time stamp designer from Baltimore, Maryland. They were realistic representations of a male kicking a soccer ball; a female gymnast in mid-leap; a male about to set a volleyball for a teammate to spike; a male boxer with fists raised, and a female swimmer diving into the water. Waldrep also submitted several other concept sketches that weren't chosen to be turned into final art.

Working with art director Howard Paine, the artist set his figures against flat single-color backgrounds and cropped them more tightly than had been done in any previous U.S. stamp art that showed human forms. In four of the five designs, the top frameline cut through the athlete's head; on the stamp depicting the swimmer, the outstretched arms and legs were cropped off. This technique was chosen, Paine explained, "to show the stress on the body, the unique posture or pose that each game forces the body into."

"We have a strange problem with Olympics stamps," Paine said. "We can't show real people, living people. We can't show the uniform or the tunic with the number on it. Over the years we've done Olympic art that has been more and more abstract, where there's a stroboscopic effect, or where the figure looks as if it's made of paper cutouts. In 1991 we had Joni Carter do those figures on a computer . . .

"I personally was sick of the abstractions, the blurs and the things that looked like no-parking signs, where you abstracted a bicyclist or a ballplayer in some kind of international code emblem . . . I argued for getting some realism, and getting an artist who does ads, like Arrow Shirt ads, that are really crisp and shiny and well rendered."

The use of extreme closeups made the Citizens' Stamp Advisory Committee and USPS staff especially conscious of the need for accuracy in the artwork. (As one example of realistic detail, Waldrep gave the swimmer a tan-line below the edge of her suit.) In the case of the boxer, several design alterations were made after Kim Parks of the USPS Office of Olympic Marketing had consulted Bruce Mathis, associate executive director of the USA Amateur Boxing Federation.

In Waldrep's first version, the boxer wore no headgear, was bare-chested and had no thumb showing on his left glove. Mathis informed Parks the boxer should have headgear, which could be either blue or white to correspond to the colors that the 1992 U.S. Olympic boxers would use. (Waldrep made it blue.) Mathis also recommended that the left glove be modified to more clearly indicate the thumb, and sent Parks some Polaroid photos of a glove on a boxer's hand to illustrate his point. While making these changes, the artist also gave the boxer a white tank top, as much to create color contrast as for accuracy.

In the case of the volleyball player, one CSAC member wondered whether the position of the hands was right; it looked awkward, with the fingers down and away and the wrists thrust forward. "We showed it to the Olympic volleyball people," said Jack Williams, the project manager. "They said the artwork was correct."

The text for the stamp tabs, which described each of the five featured sports, was written in the Office of Olympic Marketing. It was then edited and tightened by Williams and Donald M. McDowell, the director of the Office of Stamps and Philatelic Marketing, and then sent to the U.S. Olympic Committee for final review.

First-Day Facts

No traditional first-day ceremony was held for the Summer Games stamps in Baltimore June 11. However, the stamps and first-day cancellations were available at the Baltimore Arena, where the U.S. Gymnastics championships were being staged, and at Baltimore's main post office.

For covers sent by mail for the first-day cancellation, USPS would affix only strips of five or random singles. Requests for a specific single stamp weren't honored.

$5.80 HUMMINGBIRDS BOOKLET

Date of Issue: June 15, 1992

Catalog Numbers: Scott 2642-2646 (single stamps); 2646a (booklet pane of 5)

Colors: yellow, magenta, cyan, dark brown, light brown, special green, special orange

First-Day Cancel: Washington, D.C.

FDCs Canceled: 995,278

Format: 4 panes of 5 vertical stamps each, arranged horizontally. Gravure printing cylinders of 220 subjects (11 across, 20 around).

Perf: 10.9 (L perforator)

Selvage Markings: cylinder numbers printed on each pane binding stub.

Cover Markings: "© United States Postal Service 1991" and mailing information on inside of front cover. Universal Product Code (UPC) and promotion for personalized envelopes on outside of back cover. Coupon for personalized envelopes on inside of back cover.

Designer: Chuck Ripper of Huntington, West Virginia

Art Director and Project Manager: Jack Williams (USPS)

Typographer: Bradbury Thompson (CSAC)

Printing: Printed by Multi-Color Corporation, Scottsburg, Indiana, for American Bank Note Company on a Schiavi 10-color webfed gravure press. Perforated and formed into booklets at ABNC, Bedford Park, Illinois. Color separations by Intaglio Corporation, Chicago, Illinois. Cylinders by Intaglio Corporation.

Quantity Ordered: 400,000,000 stamps (19,523,000 booklets; 1,908,000 unfolded panes) plus additional order for 38,640,000 stamps (1,932,000 booklets)

Quantity Distributed: 438,640,000 stamps (21,455,000 booklets; 1,908,000 unfolded panes)

Cylinder Number Detail: 1 group of 7 gravure cylinder numbers preceded by the letter A on each pane binding stub

Cylinder Number Combinations: A1111111, A2212112, A2212122, A2212222, A2222222

Tagging: phosphor-coated paper

The stamps

Birds have become a favorite topical stamp subject of the U.S. Postal Service. They're bright, they're colorful and they're popular with postal customers. And one of the Postal Service's favorite bird artists is Chuck Ripper of Huntington, West Virginia, who has painted many of the feathered creatures that have shown up on U.S. sheet, coil and booklet stamps in the past few years.

Late in 1988 Jack Williams of USPS called Ripper and asked him to submit color roughs of four species of American hummingbird for a se-tenant block of four that the Citizens' Stamp Advisory Committee had approved. The choice of species was up to the artist, Williams said.

"I went through the books," Ripper recalled. "In the Eastern half of the United States, you only have one species, the ruby-throated hummingbird. West of the Mississippi River, particularly in the Southwest, the list grows considerably; there are a lot of things to pick from. What I did was pick species that covered the most ground geographically and also offered color variety. I didn't want all the birds looking alike.

"One of the hummingbirds I did not include was the broad-tailed hummingbird, which is very common in the Rockies. But it looks a lot like the ruby-throat, and I thought that since we had others to pick from, I wouldn't use it, even though it is well known." Another reason was that he had included a broad-tailed hummingbird among the 50 animals he had painted for the American Wildlife stamp pane of 1987, and he didn't want to repeat himself.

After CSAC saw Ripper's color roughs for the block of four, it decided to make the project into a booklet, which meant a fifth species of bird would be needed. Ripper's choice for the extra species was the calliope hummingbird.

Hummingbirds, from a family that includes the world's smallest birds, are found only in the Western Hemisphere. Numbering more than 300 species, they range from Alaska to southern South America.

Almost everything about hummingbirds is unusual. Their dazzling iridescent colors prompted John James Audubon to call them "glittering fragments of the rainbow." Their slender, pointed bills, straight or curved, are adapted especially to probing flowers for nectar and insects. Unique among birds, they can hover like helicopters, their rapidly beating wings imparting the droning sound that gives them their name. They can also fly backward, shift sideways, and fly straight up or down.

Because of their tiny size, hummingbirds have the highest metabolism of any warm-blooded vertebrate animal in the world, possibly excepting shrews, the smallest of the mammals. They must feed almost continuously all day to remain alive. Their tiny crops can store food for sustenance overnight, and they can endure temporary nighttime cold weather by becoming dormant.

The species shown on the booklet stamps were:

RUBY-THROATED HUMMINGBIRD. This bird ranges in summer over the eastern two-thirds of the United States from southern Canada south to Florida. It is metallic green above and gray below, and the adult male has a gorget — throat feathers — that appears black but flashes deep fiery red or orange in sunlight. Up to a dozen or more may swarm about a large flowering tree or bush, darting about, probing flowers, chasing each other and uttering bursts of sharp, jerky notes.

BROAD-BILLED HUMMINGBIRD. Named for its broad, red, black-tipped bill, which is unique among North American hummingbirds, this bird is metallic bronze-green above and has a metallic blue throat. It winters in Mexico and in summer ranges north to southern Arizona and New Mexico. The broad-bill is fond of nectar from red blossoms such as ocotillo and paintbrush. The female sometimes chases large butterflies from her feeding territory.

COSTA'S HUMMINGBIRD. Costa's appears twice in the booklet: on a stamp and (unidentified) on the cover. It was named in 1839 for Louis Marie Pantaleon Costa, Marquis de Beau-Regard in 19th-century France, the owner of a large collection of hummingbirds. At 3 to 3½

A broad-tailed hummingbird was one of 50 subjects painted by Chuck Ripper for the 1987 American Wildlife pane. The flower on the stamp is a Colorado columbine.

inches long, it is the smallest North American hummingbird, next to the calliope. The male has a purple crown and purple gorget, with prominent purple streamers down the sides of the neck. It nests in the southwestern United States and Mexico.

RUFOUS HUMMINGBIRD. The rufous summers farther north than any other hummingbird, reaching as far as Alaska. The male has reddish brown on the back, base of the crown and most of the tail. It has a brilliantly scarlet gorget that shines like burnished gold in certain light. The bird is strongly attracted to red flowers. Both sexes aggressively defend feeding and nesting areas, driving away other hummingbirds as well as larger birds and even chipmunks.

CALLIOPE HUMMINGBIRD. Adults are 2¾ inches to 3½ inches long, making this the smallest hummingbird in North America. Calliope, in Greek, means beautiful of voice. The bird is metallic green above and white below. The male has long, spreading, metallic purple feathers under the chin and overlaying the white throat, which gives a peppermint-candy effect. The calliope nests in the Cascade, Sierra and Rocky mountains north into Canada, nesting as high as 11,500 feet.

The design of the five booklet stamps was unveiled with the rest of the USPS 1992 stamp program December 11, 1992. The booklet was issued June 15 in Washington, D.C. The stamps were gravure printed by Multi-Color Corporation for the American Bank Note Company.

USPS promoted the stamps with four-color advertisements showing a booklet pane against a cloud-flecked sky with the message: "BUY BUY BIRDIES." "Hurry. Before they get away," the ad copy said. "Five exquisite hummingbird stamps from the Postal Service that capture all the vibrant color and beauty of the real things. But they're available for a limited time only . . . get a hummingbird for a song."

The Designs

As issued, the stamps were vertical and showed each bird in flight, with an appropriate flower nearby, against a white background.

Ripper's first color sketches showed one bird, the rufous, perched on a branch and the others in flight. Alongside the extended wings of the birds, the artist placed motion lines, to suggest their rapid beating. The committee members asked for revisions. They wanted all the birds to be shown flying, the way hummingbirds are most commonly seen, and they wanted the wings to be sharply defined, as if caught by a high-speed camera. They also specified that the backgrounds should be white instead of the yellow that Ripper had provided.

Ripper, who had painted many hummingbirds in his career, said the question of how to show the wings posed a continuing "dilemma" for the artist. "It's the old question of intellectual realism versus objective realism," he said. "Intellectual realism says you paint the wings sharp, because that's the way they are. Objective realism says you don't necessarily see the wings sharply, so you don't paint them that way."

Ripper included on each stamp and the booklet cover a red flower found in the area frequented by the depicted bird. Adding the flowers helped him meet the challenge of painting his five birds in different positions and wing configurations. For instance, he showed two of the birds, the broad-billed and calliope, sipping nectar from their blossoms.

As he does with all his wildlife artwork, Ripper strove for absolute anatomical accuracy. He has access to a wide selection of wildlife photographs, but he likes to back these up with actual specimens that can reveal details not seen in the pictures.

The ruby-throated hummingbird wasn't a problem; in fact, Ripper once held in his hand a ruby-throat that had flown into a windowpane near where he was sitting and was momentarily stunned. To get a close look at the Western species, he called on an old friend from West Virginia, Lloyd Kiff, director of the Western Foundation of Vertebrate Zoology in Los Angeles. Kiff sent him preserved, unmounted study skins of the other hummingbirds Ripper planned to paint.

"Study skins are a great resource,'' Ripper said. "However, their color does tend to fade over time, so they don't give you the whole story. But you can count the feathers and make sure you've got all your anatomical details correct. For instance, did you know that all songbirds have 12 feathers in their tails, but hummingbirds have only 10? That's one of the

These are Chuck Ripper's original concept sketches for a block of four hummingbird stamps. Note the motion lines around the wings of the birds in flight, lines that were eliminated in the finished designs.

This is Chuck Ripper's original concept sketch for the Hummingbirds booklet cover.

little sandtraps that can bury you as you go along if you're not careful.''

The flowers on the stamps, which were shown without identification, were: bee balm, also known as Oswego tea (Monarda didyma), with the ruby-throated hummingbird; ocotillo (Fouquieria splendens), broad-billed hummingbird; Eaton's firecracker (Penstemon eatonii), Costa's hummingbird (on the cover as well as on the stamp); Suksdorf's paintbrush (Castilleja suksdorfii), rufous hummingbird, and crimson columbine (Aquilegia formosa), calliope hummingbird. Ripper had originally shown the broad-billed hummingbird sipping from a thistle, but he was unable to confirm to his satisfaction that this was true to nature, so he changed the flower to an ocotillo.

To print the stamps, Multi-Color Corporation used the standard process colors of yellow, cyan, magenta and dark brown, plus three self-colors: orange and green, which were used alternately on the booklet pane as the frame colors for the stamps, and brown, which was used for the "USA 29'' and the bird names. The typeface was Galliard, one of typographer Bradbury Thompson's favorites.

First-Day Facts

The first-day ceremony for the Hummingbirds booklet was held at 9 a.m. at American University in Washington, D.C., in conjunction with the National Audubon Society's convention. The on-campus site was originally announced as the Bender Arena of Butler Pavilion, but was later moved to the Ward Circle Building.

Senior Assistant Postmaster General Comer S. Coppie and Audubon Society President Peter A.A. Berle dedicated the stamps.

29¢ AMERICAN WILDFLOWERS (PANE OF 50)

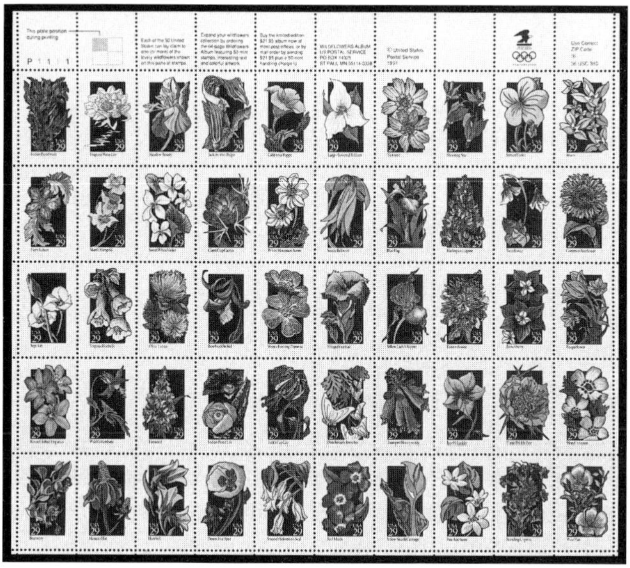

Date of Issue: July 24, 1992

Catalog Numbers: Scott 2647-2693 (single stamps); 2693a (pane of 50)

Colors: cyan, magenta, yellow, black

First-Day Cancel: Columbus, Ohio

FDCs Canceled: 3,693,972

Format: Panes of 50, vertical, 10 across, 5 down. Offset printing plates of 300 subjects (30 across, 10 around) and 200 subjects (20 across, 10 around).

Perf: 11.1 (stroke perforator)

Selvage Inscription: "Each of the 50 United/States can lay claim to/one (or more) of the/lovely wildflowers shown/on this pane of stamps." "Expand your wildflowers/collection by ordering/the 64-page Wildflowers/Album featuring 50 mint/stamps, interesting text/and colorful artwork." "Buy the limited-edition/$21.95 album now at/most post offices, or by/mail order by sending/$21.95 plus a 50-cent/handling charge to:" "WILDFLOWERS ALBUM/US POSTAL SERVICE/PO BOX 14328/ST PAUL MN 55114-0328."

Selvage Markings: "© United States/Postal Service/1991." "Use Correct/ZIP Code/®/36 USC 380." USPS Olympic logo. Plate-position diagram with "This plate position during printing."

Designer: Karen Mallary of Anacortes, Washington

Art Director: Derry Noyes (CSAC)

Project Manager: Joe Brockert (USPS)

Typographer: Bradbury Thompson (CSAC)

Printing: printed by Ashton-Potter America Inc., Amherst, New York, on 5-color sheetfed offset press

Quantity Ordered: 550,000,000

Quantity Distributed: 550,000,000

Plate Number Detail: 1 group of 4 offset plate numbers preceded by letter P alongside corner stamp

Tagging: phosphor-coated paper

The Stamps

The Wildflowers pane was the fourth pane of 50 different stamps to be issued by the U.S. Postal Service. Previous panes had depicted the 50 state flags (1976), the 50 state birds and flowers (1982) and American wild animal life (1987). But this one was unique in several ways.

It was the first 50-stamp pane to be printed by a private contractor. The previous ones had been products of the Bureau of Engraving and Printing (BEP) in Washington.

It was the first U.S. commemorative stamp issue — and the first first-class-rate issue in modern times — to be produced completely by offset lithography. Before, the Postal Service had felt that offset alone, despite its many advantages in terms of quality and cost, didn't provide sufficient security against counterfeiting. However, USPS has concluded that other materials and techniques used in stamp manufacture can provide the necessary security for offset-printed products.

The Wildflowers pane was the first U.S. issue to be printed on both 200-subject plates, divided into four 50-subject panes, and 300-subject plates, divided into six panes. This in turn led to another innovation: the provision of a small diagram, printed in the selvage of each pane next to the plate number, that showed from which position, on which size plate, the pane came.

Unlike the first three 50-stamp panes issued by USPS, the Wildflowers pane wasn't originally planned in that format. In fact, the subject matter wasn't even defined as wildflowers at first.

The first seeds were planted in 1986 when Karen Mallary, an Anchorage, Alaska, artist and illustrator, submitted some samples of her work to USPS and asked to be considered for future stamp design assignments.

Mallary moved to Alaska in 1965 with her husband, an oil industry engineer. Here they raised their two children and she pursued her career in art, specializing in flowers done in watercolor. She paints originals by commission, and her published works include limited-edition prints, posters and book covers.

Although USPS didn't respond immediately, Mallary's work went into a bank of unsolicited art samples that the Citizens' Stamp Advisory Committee's Quality Assurance Subcommittee considered promising. She didn't know it, but the fact she was a female artist would work in her favor; only a small percentage of U.S. stamp designers are women, a situation USPS was working to change.

On January 19, 1988, Joe Brockert, then a philatelic design program manager for USPS, forwarded the Mallary samples to Derry Noyes, a design coordinator for CSAC. At that time, CSAC had on its list of possible future topical issues a multiple featuring garden flowers, either in block of four or booklet format. Brockert suggested to Noyes that Karen Mallary might be a candidate for the assignment — although he had some reservations about whether her watercolor work ("a risky medium") would translate effectively to stamp design.

Noyes liked the samples, too, and told Mallary about the potential flower-stamp assignment. She also told the artist of the problems USPS had encountered in translating the delicate work of watercolorists into postage stamps.

"I think what saved me," said Mallary, "was the fact that I like 'hard edge' and I like bright colors, and the material that I sent them showed that my originals reproduce quite well. At the time I was publishing myself, and with each limited-edition print I created a small promotional card that reproduced the flower image, reduced way down." These cards, she said, demonstrated that her work held its effectiveness in reduction.

In April 1988, USPS asked Mallary to prepare concept sketches for a block of four garden flowers of her choice. As it happened, she had just finished a commission for the Sohio oil company to paint 16 wildflowers found on the north slope of Alaska. She had wildflowers on her mind and had assembled a file of information. So, instead of garden flowers, she decided to do wildflowers. To cover the continental United States, she chose Jacob's ladder, for the North; fragrant water lily, for the South; large flowered trillium, for the East, and California poppy, for the West.

Mallary submitted these four sketches, in colored pencil on paper. CSAC had no objection to her proposed switch from cultivated plants to wildflowers, and gave its approval for her to do finished artwork. At about the same time, the committee began thinking in larger terms.

The coincidental fact that there are 50 states in the United States and 50 stamps on a standard pane of commemorative-size stamps has led CSAC to look for subjects that can be assigned to 50-variety panes in such a way that every state can identify with at least one stamp. The committee has considered such state-specific subjects as state capitols, state seals and automobile license plates, along with more general subjects such as the fauna that graced the 1987 American Wildlife pane. Fifty-variety panes appropriately can be issued every four or five years, the committee believes. Its search for subjects is one of its higher priorities — so much so that Dr. C. Douglas Lewis, CSAC vice chairman, told a forum at World Columbian Stamp Expo 92: "We're desperate for things that come in multiples of 50."

"It turned out," said Joe Brockert, "that wildflowers were on a list of things that the committee's Topical Subcommittee had approved as possible subjects for a multiple — a block or a booklet or even a pane of 50. But we hadn't gone very far because we didn't know whether it was a practical possibility."

Brockert telephoned Mallary and asked a hypothetical question: If CSAC decided to do a pane of 50 wildflowers, could she fill it with attractive varieties, covering the color spectrum and giving each of the 50 states some representation?

Mallary was certain she could. On the understanding that the 50-stamp pane was still only a tentative project, she was told to begin compiling a list. At the same time, she was asked to do concept sketches, followed by finished art, for six more stamps. These she delivered in September 1988. The additional flowers she chose were columbine, chicory, plumeria, fireweed, marsh marigold and shooting stars.

Meanwhile, CSAC, a bit wary of assigning a 50-stamp pane to an untried artist, asked a second artist to submit some wildflower illustrations as well, for comparison purposes. But after looking over the additional submissions and giving the matter further thought, the committee decided to stay with Mallary.

To guard against a possible marketing fiasco, the Stamps Division asked the USPS Market Research Division to add Wildflowers to a list of proposed stamp designs that it was planning to test in a series of consumer focus groups. For this purpose, Total Research Corporation of Princeton, New Jersey, convened six groups in three cities, Washington, D.C., Chicago and Seattle, on August 30, 31 and September 1, 1988. Each city had two groups, consisting of 10 or 11 people each, one made up of casual stamp collectors and the other consisting of non-collectors. Mallary's 10 flower images, pasted up as a five-by-two block, were among the designs shown to these groups. Afterward, the company reported to USPS that of all the proposed stamps, the multiple issues had received the most positive responses. Stamps showing wildflowers were "regarded favorably" and viewed by the groups as "educational as well as attractive." "Appeal for these designs is broad-based," the company concluded, "and is considered to be appropriate for both business and personal correspondence."

Thus reassured, in late March of 1989 CSAC gave its formal approval to the project. By now Mallary had produced a list of 50 flowers as candidates to be on the pane. CSAC proposed the pane for the 1991 stamp program, and it was approved as part of that program by Postmaster General Anthony M. Frank.

Thereafter, Mallary did her artwork in groups of 10 stamps, submitting concept sketches, getting approval of the sketches by CSAC with, in some cases, requests for revisions, then sending the finished artwork back to Washington.

As it had done with the American Wildlife pane of 1987, CSAC specified that at least one flower on the pane must be an identifiable inhabitant of each of the 50 states. However, as with the 1987 pane, CSAC decided that state names wouldn't be used on the stamps. Wildflowers don't respect arbitrary boundaries such as state lines, and many of the flowers that would appear on the pane grow over wide portions of the country. The committee felt that nothing would be gained by labeling each flower with the name of a state in which it grows.

Among the reference works Mallary used in developing her list of proposed flowers were the Audubon Society's field guides to North American wildflowers ("lifesavers," she called them); the Smithsonian Institution's *Wildflowers of America*; *Wildflowers Across America*, published by the National Wildflower Research Center; and a wide assortment of nature and horticultural magazines.

"Color wasn't a problem here," Mallary said of the selection process. "It doesn't matter which flower you're looking at; the color is always exquisite. So first I looked for shapes. I wanted to make sure I had rounds and oblongs and so on. Then I broke it down into colors and groups of colors. I knew I had 50 stamps to work with, so I wanted a range of pinks and reds, and I wanted some yellows and oranges and purples and blues and whites, to cover all the bases.

"And, of course, the geography was essential. All 50 states had to be represented. I decided I wanted as few flowers that grew throughout the entire nation as possible. Those I would keep in reserve, because I knew that as I proceeded and got down to the last few selections I was going to have the problem of running out of certain shapes or colors. So I would need some flowers that grew nationwide that I could turn to if I had to."

The selection process took many days. To facilitate it, Mallary developed a cross-filing system, using index cards and listing her floral candidates by state, color and shape.

As the project developed, CSAC decided that all 50 flowers should be indisputably native to the United States. So now it became necessary to re-examine Mallary's preliminary list and, in some cases, drop flowers for which she had already done finished artwork. Not having the technical knowledge necessary to know the origin of each plant, she turned for help to the National Wildflower Research Center (NWRC), near Austin, Texas, of which she had been a member for several years.

NWRC is a non-profit corporation whose mission is to stimulate and carry out research on the propagation, cultivation, conservation and preservation of wildflowers and to serve as a clearinghouse to spread the resulting knowledge to developers, park managers and private citizens. It was founded December 22, 1982, by Lady Bird Johnson, widow of President Lyndon B. Johnson. Mrs. Johnson celebrated her 70th birthday on that date by giving 60 acres of land on the Colorado River outside Austin and $125,000 in seed money to establish the Research Center.

In seeking NWRC's help, Mallary was under the constraint USPS imposes on all its stamp artists. No stamp project may be disclosed before the Postal Service is ready to announce it. This requirement prevented her from telling NWRC staffers whom she was working for or why she needed the information. Nevertheless, they agreed to review her list.

Among the flowers that were ruled out as not native American wildflowers — or as having at least questionable status — were two that the artist had painted among her first 10. One was the plumeria, which would have represented Hawaii on the pane. Mallary was disappointed — plumeria was "one of my favorites, and such fun to design," she said — but it was obliged to yield to the ohi'a lehua, a tree-borne Hawaiian flower. The other dropout from the original 10 was chicory, replaced by Jack-in-the-pulpit. In other changes, salsify was traded in for scarlet gilia, which in the end would be identified on the pane by its other name, standing cypress; day lily was dropped in favor of Indian pond lily, and rose mallow was replaced by passionflower.

CSAC played a much less active role in the development of the list of subjects for the Wildflowers pane than it had assumed in determining what creatures would be shown on the American Wildlife pane of 1987. Mary Ann Owens, chairman of the committee's Topical Subcommittee, explained why:

"The feeling among committee members had been much stronger toward the animals. With the animals, we all had our little pets that we wanted; I insisted on the ladybug, for instance, and other members worked to get their own favorites onto stamps. There were also creatures on that original list of 50 wild animals that some members didn't particularly care for.

"So we were much more vocal then. With the wildflowers, there was no such passion. All we wanted this time was a lovely pane of 50, and most of the committee members couldn't have cared less which specific flowers were on it."

One of the final changes came after Postmaster General Anthony M. Frank had reviewed the finished artwork. He asked for replacement of the Indian pipe, a mostly white plant that Mallary had placed in the center of the pane. Indian pipe is a member of the heath family, related to the blueberry and the rhododendron. It has no chlorophyll and obtains all its nutrients from the forest floor rather than through its leaves. The postmaster general thought its odd appearance and lack of color made it an aberration.

Its departure was another disappointment to Mallary, who had chosen the plant precisely because it represented such a contrast to the others. "It had such an interesting shape, and an interesting color," she said. "It wasn't completely white — it had rust stains; it was fun to research and to paint. But we went with something else."

That something else was Dutchman's breeches, an Eastern woodland flower with small, white, pantaloon-shaped blossoms. "It was easy, because I knew I needed something basically white, and I was thumbing through the book and saw these," Mallary said. "They're charming and

The Indian pipe, one of the artist's favorites, was vetoed by Postmaster General Frank as too unusual and "unflowerlike." It was replaced by Dutchman's breeches.

delightful little flowers, and they do look exactly like what they're called, so I chose them."

The final list, as it appeared on the pane of 50, was as follows:

INDIAN PAINTBRUSH (Castilleja coccinea). This member of the snapdragon family, with small greenish-yellow flowers hidden in the axils of scarlet-tipped bracts, is found in meadows and prairies. Legend has it that the Great Spirit gave an Indian brave brushes dripping with the colors of the setting sun. The brave painted a picture of the sunset, then threw the brushes away. In every place they landed, this plant grows.

FRAGRANT WATER LILY (Nymphaea odorata). Like other water lilies whose flowers and leaves float on the surface of ponds, this plant has its leaf pores that absorb carbon dioxide on the upper surface rather than on the underside, as on most land-based plants. The white-to-rose-colored, sweetly fragrant flowers bloom in the morning hours. It is native to the eastern United States, but is now also found in the West.

MEADOW BEAUTY (Rhexia aristosa). This plant, with four pink petals and eight prominent yellow stamens, is found in damp areas along the Eastern seaboard. Henry David Thoreau wrote of the meadow beauty: "The scarlet leaves and stems of the rhexia, some time out of flower, make almost as bright a patch in the meadows now as the flowers did. Its seed-vessels are perfect little cream-pitchers of graceful form."

JACK-IN-THE-PULPIT (Arisaema triphyllum). An inhabitant of swamps and wet woodlands of the East, this plant features a hood of green or brown bracts (the "pulpit") enclosing a cylindrical structure called the spadix (the "jack"). Indians rid the turnip-shaped roots of a bitter taste by roasting them to serve with venison and drying and powdering them to make a flour; hence its other name, Indian turnip.

CALIFORNIA POPPY (Eschscholzia californica). The four-petaled California or golden poppy crowds roadsides, mountain slopes and clifftops, turning the landscape gold when the sun shines and closing its light-sensitive petals at night and on cloudy days. Poppies were imported to England and Europe in the 19th century and quickly became popular in gardens and spread wide to the countryside.

LARGE-FLOWERED TRILLIUM (Trillium grandiflorum). The trillium has three leaves, three sepals, and three petals atop an erect stem a foot or more long. This species, also called white wake robin, has showy white flowers that turn rosy-pink with age and is found in wooded areas from the Appalachians north through New England and eastern Canada. Overpicking has made it an endangered species.

TICKSEED (Coreopsis lanceolata). Like other members of the sunflower family, the tickseed is a composite, with six to eight bright yellow rays surrounding a flat disk. The disk soon turns brown and produces seeds that resemble small ticks, hence the name. Another common name, lanceleaf coreopsis, comes from the plant's narrow, lance-shaped leaves. Tickseed is found in open woods, fields and along roads in most of the eastern United States.

SHOOTING STAR (Dodecatheon meadia). This member of the primrose family gets its name from its swept-back pink petals trailing the "star," or cluster of yellow stamens. USPS writer Sara Day likens it to a jet-propelled missile with a nosecone. Clusters of these flowers nod at the top of tall stems. Shooting star can be found in open woods and meadows south of a line from northern Virginia to Wisconsin.

STREAM VIOLET (Viola glabella). Also known as pioneer violet or smooth yellow violet, this western flower is common along the banks of streams and in moist, shady woodland spots. The stream violet can be recognized by the spur or pouch behind the lower petal of the flower. The maroon lines at the base of the lower three petals guide bees and other insects toward the pouch, which contains the nectar.

BLUETS (Houstonia caerulea). These tiny, low-growing members of the madder or bedstraw family are predominantly white with light-blue edges and a bright yellow center, although the name bluets means "small blues" in French. They close and nod at night and open and bloom upright the next day, and are found in fields and open woodland areas from eastern Canada to Wisconsin, south to Georgia and Arkansas.

HERB ROBERT (Geranium robertianum). The namesake of this plant with its paired pink-to-lavender flowers is either St. Robert of Molesme or Robert Goodfellow, better known as Robin Hood. Herb Robert is one of the latest-blooming geraniums in the Northeast and often remains green quite late. As autumn nights grow cold, however, its hairy stems and fern-like leaves turn bright red.

MARSH MARIGOLD (Caltha palustris). Marsh marigold, with its bright, shiny-yellow flowers, is a member of the buttercup family. The plants often grow in masses, particularly along streams and in wet spring meadows. Its name could be related to the Anglo-Saxon word mere or marsh but is probably derived from the use of the flowers during medieval festivals dedicated to the Virgin Mary.

SWEET WHITE VIOLET (Viola blanda). Some 900 species of violets are found throughout the world, and because they hybridize easily it is often difficult to tell them apart. Sweet white violet, found in woods from New England south to Georgia and west to Minnesota, is very similar to the northern white violet (Viola pallens). It has a purple veined lower petal and backward-twisting upper petals.

CLARET CUP CACTUS (Echinocereus triglochidiatus). Because its three-barbed fruits are plump, red and tasty, the claret cup is also called the strawberry cactus. Its scarlet, cup-shaped flowers, sitting amid a web of white, feltlike hairs, bloom in early spring and remain open for three days. It is found in dry areas from southeastern California, east to Texas and north to southern Utah and Colorado.

WHITE MOUNTAIN AVENS (Dryas octopetala). This hardy member of the rose family grows on high ridges and peaks in the Northwest. The large, single, cream or white, hairy flowers open wide like miniature roses on numerous erect, leafless stalks above dense mats of leaves. Its many-branching stems take root in gravelly soils. The seeds travel long distances on the wind, suspended from feathery plumes.

SESSILE BELLWORT (Uvularia sessilifolia). A member of the lily family, sessile bellwort has yellow, drooping, narrowly bell-shaped flowers. Sessile means attached directly to the stalk and refers in this case to the leaves. The Latin name comes from the resemblance of the flowers to the uvula, the soft lobe hanging from the throat at the back of the mouth. It is also called little merrybells and wild oats.

BLUE FLAG (Iris versicolor). This is the common blue iris, which is also widely cultivated in gardens. It grows three feet tall, with three-foot-long leaves. At least 200 species of the iris genus are found in the northern hemisphere. Blue flag's striking violet-blue flowers with yellow markings are found in damp areas across the northern United States as far west as Minnesota.

HARLEQUIN LUPINE (Lupinus stiversii). This member of the pea family grows from the western slope of the Sierra Nevada mountains to southern California. Its harlequin name refers to the coloration of its petals, rose, yellow and white. "Lupine" derives from the Latin lupus, or wolf, and alludes to an old belief that lupines were predators, robbing the soil of minerals; actually, they put nitrogen into the soil.

TWINFLOWER (Linnaea borealis). A member of the honeysuckle family, the twinflower is a dainty, creeping plant with nodding, fragrant, funnel-shaped pink or white flowers that are borne in pairs atop slender stems. It is found in cool bogs across the northern half of the United States. Carolus Linnaeus, Swedish father of systematic botany, called twinflower his favorite flower.

COMMON SUNFLOWER (Helianthus annuus). There are 60 or more species of sunflower, a tall, striking member of the daisy family, and all are native to the Americas. The common sunflower, an annual (unlike the majority of sunflowers), is especially common alongside roads and the edges of fields. Flower heads consist of tubelike disc flowers and 10 to 25 yellow ray flowers; they follow the path of the sun each day.

SEGO LILY (Calochortus nuttallii). This exotic flower, with its showy, white, bell-shaped blossoms atop stalks up to 18 inches tall, thrives only in its native dry high country east of the Sierra Nevada, in Utah, Montana and North Dakota, and resists cultivation in gardens. The Ute Indians called the plant sago, and taught early Mormon settlers to add its nourishing bulbs to their diet in times of scarcity.

VIRGINIA BLUEBELLS (Mertensia virginica). The Virginia bluebell is a member of the forget-me-not family. Its blue flowers tinged with pink are delicate and shaped like wide flaring bells, and from March to May it forms colorful carpets in woods and on floodplains from Virginia through the Midwest. It is also called cowslip. Another name, oysterleaf, refers to the taste of its leaves when chewed.

OHI'A LEHUA (Metrosideros polymorpha). The ohi'a (lehua means blossom) is probably the most abundant of all the native Hawaiian plants and can be found from near sea level to 8,000-foot elevations. A flowering tree that grows up to 80 feet tall, ohi'a bears blossoms that consist mainly of clusters of red stamens, although they do have small petals. The flowers are often woven into leis.

ROSEBUD ORCHID (Cleistes divaricata). The rosebud orchid needs very acid soil and is most abundant in bogs from North Carolina south to Florida and west to Texas. It grows as tall as 30 inches. Unlike most orchids, it has a tubular (pink) flower rather than an open and spreading one; its Greek genus name, cleistes, means "shut." It has a crown of three long, narrow, brownish-green sepals.

SHOWY EVENING PRIMROSE (Oenothera speciosa). Lady Bird Johnson termed this "one of the most exquisite and feminine of all wildflowers." Its delicate, pink blossom with a yellowish center opens in the evening, releasing a strong fragrance that draws moths and other pollen-carrying insects. Drought-resistant and hardy, the showy evening primrose is found all across the southern United States.

FRINGED GENTIAN (Gentiana crinita). The blue, late-blooming fringed gentian is found in damp, secluded spots in woods and meadows of the North and East. Its great beauty makes it so vulnerable to picking that it is at risk of extinction in some areas. "Fringed" refers to the delicate structure of its petal, which collapses at a touch and thus prevents crawling insects from disturbing the flower.

YELLOW LADY'S SLIPPER (Cypripedium calceolus). This lovely orchid is found over wide areas of the United States and Canada. It has a large, pouch-shaped, yellow lip petal, or "slipper." Its two other petals, like the large sepal, are greenish-yellow to brownish-purple and are long, narrow and spirally twisted, like a slipper's shoelace. One or two of the fragrant flowers appear on the end of a leafy stalk.

PASSIONFLOWER (Passiflora incarnata). This strange-looking southern flower gets its name from the perception that its parts are related to the crucifixion story: a crown of thorns; hammer and nails (ovary and stigmas); wounds (stamens), and 10 of the 12 disciples (five sepals, five petals). Jesuit explorers believed it to be the flower that grew on the Cross in a vision of St. Francis.

BUNCHBERRY (Cornus canadensis). The bunchberry's flower is really a set of four white bracts surrounding a dense head of tiny yellow flowerlets. A six-inch-high circle of broad leaves supports a single bloom. The flowerlets are followed in the fall by bunches of edible red berries and the leaves turn purplish-red. The only dogwood that is an herb, bunchberry is found in woods across Northern North America.

PASQUEFLOWER (Pulsatilla patens). The pasqueflower, a member of the buttercup family, is found in prairies and alpine meadows. Its five to seven oval sepals of lavender, purple or blue color are covered with a silver hair and surround a yellow-orange disk, forming a cup shape. The leaves grow around the base. An early bloomer, its common name comes from the old French "pasque," meaning Easter.

ROUND-LOBED HEPATICA (Hepatica americana). Hepatica means "liver" in Latin, and the plant owes this name to its three-lobed leaf's resemblance to that organ. Even before the leaves unfold in the early spring, this low-growing perennial's fragile pink, lavender or white flowers have opened. A member of the buttercup family, it grows in woodlands in much of the eastern United States and Canada.

WILD COLUMBINE (Aquilegia canadensis). The five spurred red petals of the wild columbine alternate with spreading colored sepals, below which hang a column of numerous yellow stamens. The effect is of a circle of doves drinking at a dish, which inspired its name, derived from the Latin columba, or "dove." Another member of the buttercup family, this eastern flower is found in woods and on rocky slopes.

FIREWEED (Epilobium angustifolium). Sunlight-loving fireweed, a member of the evening primrose family, got its name from its tendency to move quickly into areas cleared by fire. Its four-petaled pink flowers can be found across northern North America. The blossoms open successively going up the stem so that at any one time there may be buds at the top, open flowers in the middle and seed pods beneath.

INDIAN POND LILY (Nuphar polysepala). The Indian pond lily of the West is odorless and less showy than its eastern cousin, the fragrant water lily. Its bright yellow, cuplike sepals surround a large, buttonlike central head and rows of small petals; the flowers and heart-shaped, leathery leaves float on the surface of ponds and quiet streams, attached by long stalks to stems buried in the mud at the bottom.

TURK'S CAP LILY (Lilium superbum). The largest and most spectacular of North America's 20 native lilies, turk's cap grows as tall as eight feet and can have up to 40 nodding orange flowers on one stem. The spotted petals curl back, creating the visual image that gives the plant its name, and revealing its six long stamens and pistil. An endangered species, it grows from southern New England south to Georgia.

DUTCHMAN'S BREECHES (Dicentra cucullaria). The name that has clung most firmly to this perennial member of the poppy family refers to its fragrant flowers' resemblance to baggy white bloomers with yellow belts hanging upside down on a clothesline. Other appellations are butterfly banners and white hearts. It is found throughout the eastern United States and Canada and as far west as North Dakota.

TRUMPET HONEYSUCKLE (Lonicera sempervirens). These beautiful scarlet tubular flowers, with yellow interiors, have no scent, which is unusual for a honeysuckle. However, their color and shape make them attractive to hummingbirds and long-tongued insects. They are found in woods and thickets across the East. Indians ate the plant's berries and relieved coughs with an extract made from the leaves.

JACOB'S LADDER (Polemonium vanbruntiae). This is one of only two species of the phlox family native to the East. Its five-lobed bell-shaped bluish-purple flowers with their long, protruding anthers grow in clusters among large compound leaves with paired leaflets arranged opposite each other like rungs. The perceived resemblance to the ladder to heaven of Jacob's biblical dream gave the plant its name.

PLAINS PRICKLY PEAR (Opuntia polyacantha). Although the prickly pear is thought of as a native of hot, dry, desert regions, it ranges widely over North America and as far north as Canada. Its stems are flat, pear-shaped and covered with formidable spines. Solitary, waxy, yellow or magenta flowers with reddish centers appear in late spring. They develop into small reddish-purple edible fruits known as Indian figs.

MOSS CAMPION (Silene acaulis). A member of the pink family, moss campion or cushion pink is a dwarf plant with pink to violet flowers that forms mats at high altitudes in the East, from the Arctic south to New Hampshire's Mount Washington. It is also found in mountains in the West. The sunlight-seeking blossoms are usually grouped on the south side of the mat. The entire plant is edible when boiled.

BEARBERRY (Arctostaphylos uva-ursi). Found only in northern coniferous regions, this member of the heath family forms dense, spreading mats of evergreen leaves in colder, drier areas. The white to pale pink, urn-shaped, nodding flowers bloom briefly in early spring and are followed by clusters of red berries, which are said to be among the first fruit sought by bears when they emerge from hibernation.

MEXICAN HAT (Ratibida columnaris). Mexican hat, a member of the sunflower family, is distinguished by its long, blunt cone of tiny yellow disc flowers, surrounded by drooping, notched yellow ray flowers. The flowerheads, reminiscent of the traditional hats worn in Mexican fiestas, grow on long, leafless stalks. They are found along roads and on prairies on most of the Great Plains and south to Mexico.

HAREBELL (Campanula rotundifolia). This perennial member of the bluebell family, with its pendant violet-blue bells nodding on threadlike stalks, is found in open fields and roadsides and on rocky outcrops from northern Canada south through the northeastern and midwestern states. It is also native to Asia and Europe; its common name comes from Great Britain, where naming plants for animals was an old custom.

DESERT FIVE SPOT (Malvastrum rotundifolium). This handsome specimen is a member of the mallow family, which includes garden favorites like hibiscus and hollyhock. Each of its five rose-pink petals displays a large red-purple spot near its base. When light passes through the distinctive globe-like corollas, they resemble glowing lanterns. The sparsely leaved plants grow on desert flats in the Southwest.

SMOOTH SOLOMON'S SEAL (Polygonatum biflorum). Most authorities link this plant's name to the scars on the rootstock, which are somewhat signet shaped and resemble a royal seal. A member of the lily family, it displays pairs of greenish-white bell-like flowers that hang down from each leaf axil along the arching stem. It prefers shade and is found in woods of the East and Midwest.

RED MAIDS (Calandrinia ciliata). Red maids' flowers have three to seven bright reddish-pink, short-lived, round-tipped petals with white markings at the base and two sepals covered with coarse hairs. They bloom on short stalks growing from the axils of the upper leaves on spreading or erect stems. The plant is found in moist, open soil in the Pacific states, Arizona and New Mexico. It is edible raw or cooked.

YELLOW SKUNK CABBAGE (Lysichiton americanum). This large, leafy perennial is found in open swamps and wet woods from northern California to Alaska. Its yellow, unpleasant-smelling bract, surrounding a stout fleshy stem of numerous tiny, yellowish flowers, pushes through the ground ahead of the large green, oblong leaves. Carrion flies, attracted by the odor, perform the job of pollination.

RUE ANEMONE (Anemonella thalictroides). Rue anemone is named for Anemos, the Greek wind god. Its numerous fragile-looking white flowers on delicate stalks tremble in the slightest breeze, earning it another common name, windflower. The leaves have three rounded lobes. Rue anemone can be easily cultivated in wildflower gardens. It blooms in the early spring in open woods in the East, South and Midwest.

STANDING CYPRESS (Ipomopsis rubra). The red, tubular flowers of the standing cypress, also known as the scarlet gilia, have interior patterns of red spots against a yellow background. A member of the phlox family, it ranges across the South from Texas to North Carolina. Its name refers both to its leaf, which resembles the lacy cypress leaf, and the flowers, which are similar to those of the cypress vine.

WILD FLAX (Linum perenne). This perennial blooms all summer long on flatlands across the midsection of North America. A cousin of the common flax, the source of linen and linseed oil, it has slender, leafy stems bearing clusters of large blue flowers with a spot of yellow in the center. Funnel-shaped when they open in the morning, the flowers flatten during the day and are dropped the following day.

For some of these flowers, it was a repeat appearance on U.S. stamps. A variety of Indian paintbrush, the California poppy, the common sunflower, the sego lily and the pasqueflower are all state flowers (Wyoming, California, Kansas, Utah and South Dakota) and as such had been shown on the 1982 State Birds and Flowers pane. The sunflower and pasqueflower had also appeared prominently on the Kansas (1961) and South Dakota (1989) statehood centennial stamps, and a mountain meadow containing Indian paintbrush added color to the Wyoming statehood centennial stamp of 1990.

A field of California poppies decorated the Highway Beautification stamp of the 1969 Beautification of America block of four. The yellow lady's slipper was shown on one of the four Orchids stamps of 1984. Finally, Chuck Ripper used two of the flowers as backgrounds on stamps of the 1987 American Wildlife pane: the o'hia lehua, with the iiwi, a Hawaiian bird, and the trumpet honeysuckle, with the luna moth.

The 50-stamp Wildflower pane got top billing when, in August, 1990, USPS announced its 1991 stamp program. However, on December 17, 1990, came an announcement of a change of plan; the Wildflowers would be postponed until 1992.

"The design of the Wildflowers stamps could not be finalized until the new first-class rate is announced in January (1991)," the news release said. "In addition to this, with the large number of stamps needed to support the rate change, the stamps could not have been issued until late summer. Since that would not be the best time of year to issue the Wildflowers stamps, the decision was made to defer them."

Among the 50 wildflowers that made previous U.S. stamp appearances were the California poppy, on the Birds and Flowers pane; the trumpet honeysuckle (with the luna moth) and the o'hia lehua (with the iiwi) on the Wildlife pane; and the pasqueflower, on the South Dakota issue.

This postponement turned out to have a major impact on the choice of printer, and printing method, for the Wildflowers.

When the Wildflowers pane was approved, USPS officials expected that they would give the job to the Bureau of Engraving and Printing. They wanted the fine-screen detail and precision of printing that the offset method could give, in order to fully exploit the color of the subjects and the contrast between flowers and the black backgrounds Karen Mallary had given them. They assumed, however, that they would have to add an intaglio element — even if it was only the letters and numerals — to ensure security. BEP was the only printer that was already in the business of producing offset-intaglio combination stamps.

The decision to move the issue date back to 1992 gave the Stamps Division some time to re-examine its options. Officials had known all along that if they could justify the printing of stamps by 100 percent offset, they would not only save production costs but widen the field of potential competitors for the business. In 1988 USPS had introduced the first Official Mail stamps printed solely by offset, on the assumption that nobody would be tempted to counterfeit these items, which are used exclusively by federal agencies. The next step came in 1991, when all-litho production was ordered for three low-value definitive stamps, the non-denominated Makeup Rate stamp that sold for 4¢ and 1¢ and 3¢ denominated items.

Now USPS decided it was time for the last and biggest step. In mid-1990, Joe Brockert sent a memo to the Prevention and Countermeasures Branch of the USPS' Postal Inspection Service, asking clearance to print the Wildflowers stamps in offset without intaglio. Brockert, who at that time was serving as acting manager for the Stamp Product Development Branch, pointed out that the Wildflowers issue would have some inherent security features.

For one thing, there would be 50 different multicolor designs to a pane. For another, the paper used would be prephosphored — meaning that the phosphor taggant would be an integral part of the paper, and not applied in a post-printing step. Officials reasoned that counterfeiters would find it difficult to obtain paper that would emit a phosphor signal on the very discrete wavelength of stamp papers.

In August 1990 Brockert received approval from the Postal Inspection Service for offset-only production of the Wildflowers stamps on an experimental basis. The inspectors stressed, however, that the paper must be prephosphored — with the taggant a part of the paper itself — rather than phosphor-coated, which they considered less secure.

"This is one of the payoffs from prephosphored paper that we've known was coming," said Donald M. McDowell, director of the USPS Office of Stamp and Philatelic Marketing. "In the future, when we add intaglio to offset it will be because it can add value aesthetically to the stamp. It will be because it's the best production solution for interpreting the design, and not just an added security requirement."

In August 1990 USPS had no outside contractors qualified to do 100 percent offset work, and they still anticipated that their Wildflowers printer would be BEP. But near the end of 1990, when they knew that the Wildflowers stamps would be delayed until 1992, they began to explore the possibility of finding a private printer for the job. A request-for-proposal was publicized, but when the responses came back they were all from foreign firms.

One of the firms was Ashton-Potter Limited of Concord, Ontario, near Toronto. Ashton-Potter produces some 85 percent of Canada Post's stamps, and obviously had the expertise and experience to do the job for USPS. But, as it turned out, it would have been a political impossibility for the Postal Service to contract for the stamps to be printed in Canada.

That was because, in the spring of 1991, USPS was hit hard by criticism from members of Congress and segments of the philatelic press for allowing one of its prime stamp contractors, Stamp Venturers, to subcontract the printing of the 35¢ Dennis Chavez stamp in the Great Americans series to the Canadian Bank Note Company of Ottawa. The critics expressed shock and horror that a U.S. stamp should be printed outside the U.S. borders, and to mollify them Postmaster General Anthony M. Frank gave his assurances that it wouldn't happen again (with the exception of one additional Stamp Venturers subcontract, for the 29¢ Earl Warren definitive, that was already in the pipeline).

USPS contracting officials made it known that only if a foreign firm were to establish a U.S. branch for the actual production of the stamps could it hope to land the Wildflowers job, or any other stamp printing assignment. Coincidentally, Ashton-Potter's management was already considering setting up a subsidiary in the United States, to better compete in the U.S. commercial printing market and better serve the customers it already had south of the border.

The firm acquired the use of a building in Amherst, New York, a suburb of Buffalo. On December 12, 1991, the newly created U.S. firm, named Ashton-Potter America Inc., received a contract under which it would produce 550 million Wildflowers stamps.

Ashton-Potter America moved into its new quarters in February 1992 and began hiring a U.S. workforce. Prepress work — color separations and platemaking — began early in March. Color proofs were approved by USPS March 4. Printing followed immediately and was completed the first week in May.

In making the color separations, Ashton-Potter used two different size line screens to create the dot patterns that make up the printing surfaces: 250 and 300 lines to the inch. "Some of the flowers, such as the sunflower, had very 'busy' images, and on these we used the coarser screen," said Barry Switzer, vice president and general manager of Ashton-Potter. "On flowers with simpler contours, such as the stream violet, we used a higher line screen, to bring out the details."

As an added — and unpublicized — security measure, Ashton-Potter America used still another screen, to apply a patch of microscopic black dots over the white denomination numbers "29." This was a gradient

This tiny dot pattern, visible only through a magnifying glass, was added to the denomination figures as a safeguard against counterfeiting of the offset-printed stamps.

screen, which started at 390 lines at the top of the numbers and became finer as it descended until the dots disappeared at about the half-way point. The dots, which could only be seen through a strong magnifying glass, were too small to be reproduced by even the finest color copying machine that was presently available.

Ashton-Potter printed the Wildflowers stamps on pregummed, prephosphored paper supplied by the U.S. Paper Corp. of New York. The press was a sheetfed five-color offset press capable of handling a 40-inch-wide sheet. Four of the color stations applied the standard process colors of cyan, magenta, yellow and black, in that order. The black ink wasn't the normal process black, however, but was enhanced with the addition of a purple tone. The fifth color station — actually the first one — was used to condition and clean the sheets, removing paper dust and other minuscule contaminants, before the actual printing took place.

The company asked and received the Postal Service's permission to use two different size plates in order to cut down the time required for the job. Obviously, more stamps could be made in the same amount of time if part of the press run was printed on 300-unit plates rather than the standard 200-unit plates. The 200-unit (four-pane) sheets were printed first, followed by the 300-unit (six-pane) sheets. A total of 1.25 million sheets of each of the formats, "six-up" and "four-up," was printed, making 625 million stamps in all. This number included a normal allowance for spoilage and a reserve.

The plates were laid out in a way that was unusual for U.S. stamps. Normally, on a 400-subject or 600-subject plate made for sheet stamps, all the stamps line up in the same direction. With the Wildflowers, however, the upper panes — two on the 400-subject plates, three on the 600-subject plates — were upside down in relation to the lower panes.

This was done to accommodate Ashton-Potter's stroke comb perforator, which perforates two rows of stamps at a time and creates the bull's-eye perfs (perfs that intersect perfectly at the corners of each stamp) that USPS prefers. Arranging the upper panes on the plate head-to-head against the lower panes allowed the printer to leave a strip of blank paper between the panes that was exactly the width of a row of stamps. This strip became the selvage for the upper panes, wide enough to accommodate the inscriptions USPS wanted to print in the selvage but not so wide that an excessive amount of paper would have to be trimmed off and thrown away in order to cut the panes down to standard post-office size.

This wide selvage that contained plate numbers and other marginal markings was at the top of the panes on panes from the top half of the plates, and at the bottom on panes from the bottom half of the plates. The six-pane sheets were printed from even-numbered plates and the four-pane sheets from odd-numbered plates, which meant that an observer could tell, by looking at the plate number on a pane, which size plate it came from.

But USPS officials decided to add an extra method of identification. Adopting an idea credited to Assistant Postmaster General Gordon C. Morison, they created the small diagram by which the buyer of a pane of 50 stamps could tell not only which size plate his pane came from, but what was its position on the plate. The diagram — designed by Terrence McCaffrey of USPS on his Macintosh computer — was printed in the selvage immediately adjacent to the plate number. It consisted of four or six hollow rectangles with one rectangle, shaded in violet, that was marked: "This plate position during printing."

One requirement that USPS impressed on Ashton-Potter was that the selvage was to be left on all panes shipped from the plant. The company was accustomed to producing stamps for Canada Post, which requires selvage on philatelic stock only. For stamps that go to Canadian post offices, Ashton-Potter cuts off the selvage before shipping.

After the stamps were printed, they were perforated, a few sheets at a time, on the company's stroke comb perforator. Then, in larger stacks, the perforated sheets were guillotined into panes and the excess paper sliced off. Finally, each pane was individually inspected for printing and perforating quality by a team of 32 employees, and the panes were then packed for shipping.

USPS officially unveiled the design of the Wildflowers pane, along with the designs of many other 1992 stamps, on December 11, 1991. No issue date for the Wildflowers was given, but USPS said they would appear some time in June or July.

Later information came in installments. In March USPS told cachetmakers that the stamps would be issued July 15 in Columbus, Ohio, site of the six-month Ameriflora 92 International Floral and Garden Exposition. Early the following month, the Postal Service announced that the stamps would be printed by Ashton-Potter America Inc. At about the same time, Douglas Kelsey, executive director of the American First Day Cover Society, met with Assistant Postmaster

General Morison and Donald McDowell and suggested that they move the ceremony's date back nine days so it would coincide with the AFDCS national convention, also in Columbus. The postal officials agreed, and a May press release reported the change of date to July 24. Full details came in mid-June.

Concurrent with the stamps, USPS offered for sale a 64-page Wildflowers book, with color photographs, text by freelance writer Sara Day, and space for the stamps. The book, along with a pane of stamps (face value $14.50), sold for $21.95.

The Designs

From the beginning, USPS knew that it wanted the flower stamps to be commemorative size, vertically arranged. Beyond that, the Postal Service left it to Mallary to suggest the design treatment.

Mallary, who frequently places her flower paintings against black backgrounds, decided to do the same with these flowers. "I wanted these stamps to be really bright, and I wanted them totally different from anything I had seen before," she said. "I had gone through the Scott catalog, and used other stamp reference works at the library, and I dug out a stamp collection I had had as a child. Nobody, to my knowledge, had ever used black as a background for flowers; nobody had ever had them falling out of an imaginary frame. That makes sense to me, I thought, and it was my design format from the beginning."

Her supervisors at USPS liked the treatment. The black backgrounds gave the flowers "punch," said Derry Noyes. And Joe Brockert noted that the spillover design technique "tends to make the stamps, when they're removed from the pane, look bigger than they are."

For this assignment, Mallary decided, she would aim for something other than the sharp-definition realism she customarily achieves in her flower paintings. She wanted the paintings to be as "clean" as possible, without excess detail — leaves, stems, tiny floral parts — that might create visual clutter. She wanted to be able to emphasize the blossoms themselves, and de-emphasize the accessory elements.

Another influence was the fact that in painting the stamps she would have to refer, in many cases, to color photographs made by other people. "In my regular work," she said, "I prefer to paint only things that I can hold in my hand, and turn around, and look at from all sides. But that wasn't possible in this case. So most of the images I worked from were images that I had unearthed at the University of Alaska library or from my own library of reference books.

"I had to be extremely careful not to step on somebody else's copyright. That's why I chose to paint these flowers in a very stylized way."

As a further precaution against literal copying, Mallary would study all the pictures she had on a specific flower, then close the books and draw it from memory. She would also change the viewing angle of the plant, or alter it in other ways. Once she had made her sketch, however, she would return to the reference materials to make sure her memory hadn't betrayed her into erroneous representations.

One of the ingredients of her stylized treatment was the use of black lines, not only to outline the flowers but also for interior details. As Derry Noyes, the art director, pointed out, the interior linework looked somewhat heavy in the finished paintings, which were five times stamp size, but when reduced to stamp dimensions they lost their heaviness and gave the artwork a helpful clarity.

"I didn't set out to create a field guide," Mallary said. "The stamps aren't meant to be identifiers. They're not botanical drawings, and were never meant to be. They are — if I can wax poetic here — a celebration of nature's color and diversity and abundance, represented in a very stylized manner."

Mallary decided early on that it would be futile to try to paint all 50 flowers to the same scale. The stamps were meant to be used individually on letters, not viewed as a 50-part bouquet, and so it was important to show each one to its own best advantage. She said, "If the twinflowers had been shown at the same scale as the giant sunflower, they are so tiny and delicate that you would have seen nothing but black background. In fact, in some cases I was asked to repaint the flower because the postmaster general, looking at the original, felt there was too much black showing, and the flower itself should be enlarged."

Mallary created her paintings within an arbitrary rectangle 4¼ inches across by 6¼ inches deep; no portion of a flower protruding out of the black background could extend outside those dimensions. When the preliminary sketches, in batches of 10, would come back from Washington with CSAC's approval, the artist would make a pencil tracing and transfer that tracing lightly to illustration board. She would then paint the finished artwork, applying her watercolors with a sable brush. Because she dislikes pencil marks that show through watercolor, she created just enough of a pencil line to guide her, but not enough to be detectable in the finished product.

The amount of time required to complete a single painting varied. "Some of them took forever," she confessed. "I had fits over them. They just wouldn't come. But that's the nature of the creative process. Sometimes you feel like working, sometimes you don't. You've got to work whether you feel like it or not, and sometimes it comes easy and sometimes it doesn't.

"It's always a challenge. I always knew what my deadline was. I always knew I would get my work finished ahead of the deadline, because I pride myself on always meeting deadlines. I've never been late.

"Sometimes I'd do the black background first, sometimes I'd do the flower first, sometimes I'd do the leaves first. I had no set way of doing it. I'd do whatever appealed to me at the time. If the color was one that I really liked, or if it was going to pose a problem, I'd do that color first, because if I messed up I might as well know early on, and that would allow me time to re-do and still meet my deadline."

The typography, chosen by CSAC's Bradbury Thompson, was Galliard,

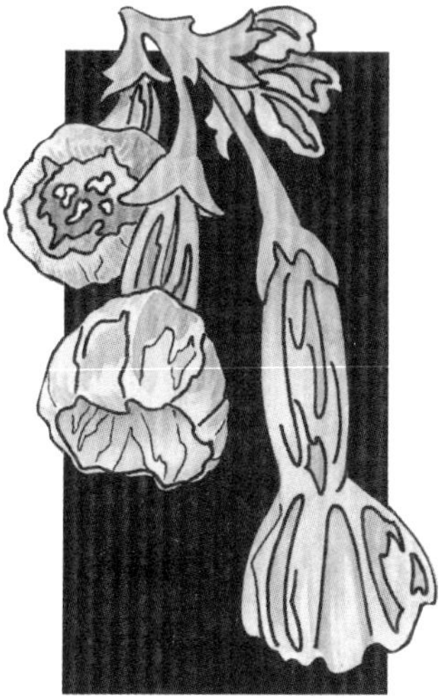

Karen Mallary's original version of the Virginia bluebells showed fewer blossoms and more black background than on the final design.

a 20th-century typeface designed by Matthew Carter and based on the 16th-century work of printer Robert Granjean. At Mallary's request, the "USA 29," which was dropped out of the black backgrounds, was placed at the bottom of each stamp. "As an artist I like to see work weighted on the bottom," she explained.

She found it a little more difficult, however, to convince Derry Noyes and CSAC that the location of the "USA 29" should vary between the lower right and lower left corners. Noyes pointed out that this approach had never been used on a 50-stamp pane; on the three previous panes, the typographical elements were in fixed locations. "I said, 'Well, then it's time to do something different,' " Mallary recalled, "because I wanted a balance without absolute conformity." Having this typographical element at the lower right on some stamps and the lower left on others would make the whole pane much more interesting, she told them: "The flower won't be coming out of the same corner on every stamp." Ultimately, Mallary won the argument.

The very bottom of each stamp was reserved for the name of the flower. The names were very small, black on white, and in uppercase and lowercase type. In most cases the names fit comfortably, but a few, such as the showy evening primrose, crowded the available space. Though some previous U.S. stamps depicting flowers had used the Latin names, the decision this time was to keep the use of wording to a minimum by using only the common names.

However, in the process of arriving at the final nomenclature for the stamps, the creative team almost always made the names more specific. Thus, what had been "poppy" in the early version became "California poppy"; "skunk cabbage" became "yellow skunk cabbage"; "lady's slipper" became "yellow lady's slipper"; "harlequin" became "harlequin lupine"; "sunflower" became "common sunflower"; "bluebells" became "Virginia bluebells"; "primrose" became "showy evening primrose";

Selvage Inscription: "This is the second in a series of World War II/50th anniversary stamp sheets being issued by/the U.S. Postal Service from 1991 through 1995./A series of five books focusing on each year's/stamps and war-related world events is being/offered for sale." "For ordering details, write:/WORLD WAR II BOOKS/USPS SALES DIVISION/PO BOX 449997/KANSAS CITY MO/64144-9997." Inscription appears twice on each pane of 2 miniature sheets.

Selvage Markings: "©/United States/Postal Service/1991" in selvage adjacent to each sheetlet of 10. Inscription appears twice on each pane of 2 sheetlets.

Designer: William H. Bond of Arlington, Virginia

Art Director and Typographer: Howard Paine (CSAC)

Project Manager: Jack Williams (USPS)

Engraver: John Smith Jr. (denomination and "USA", BEP)

Modeler: Peter Cocci (BEP)

Printing: printed by BEP on 6-color offset, 3-color intaglio D press (902)

Quantity Ordered: 120,000,000 stamps (12,000,000 sheetlets)

Quantity Distributed: 120,000,000 stamps (12,000,000 sheetlets)

Plate/Sleeve Number Detail: 1 group of 4 offset plate numbers and 1 single-digit intaglio sleeve number in corner of selvage adjacent to each sheetlet of 10; numbers appear twice on each pane of 2 souvenir sheets.

Plate/Sleeve Number Combinations: 1111-1, 1211-1, 1212-1, 1213-1, 2223-1, 3223-1, 3323-1, 3423-1, 4422-1, 4432-1, 4442- 1, 4532-1, 4542-1, 5354-1, 5632-1

Tagging: overall, large block covering stamps and part of selvage

The Sheetlet

The year 1992 saw the issuance of the second in a projected series of five annual sheetlets marking the 50th anniversary of U.S. participation in World War II. The sheet, labeled "1942: Into the Battle," was issued August 17 in Indianapolis, Indiana, at the national convention of the Veterans of Foreign Wars of the United States.

In 1985 the Postal Service had begun planning its extended commemoration of the war years. USPS wanted a program that would properly recognize the key events of the war and the principal aspects of national endeavor that contributed to Allied victory — but would do so without producing an extravagant number of stamps over the 50th anniversary period. This required a careful and credible process for selecting stamp subjects. In developing that process, a special subcommittee of the Citizens' Stamp Advisory Committee convened the historians for the Army, Navy, Air Force, Marines and State Department and solicited their recommendations.

The plan, as it evolved, called for five sheetlets to commemorate the events of 1941 through 1945. Each sheetlet would be issued in the 50th anniversary year and would contain 10 different stamps, in horizontal strips of five, above and below a panel displaying a Mercator map of the world. Allied and neutral nations would be colored yellow on the map; territory controlled by the Axis powers would be red. Map annotations would call attention to major military and political developments of the year, including events not featured on the individual stamps of the sheetlet.

For the sake of uniformity, one design team — artist William H. Bond and art director Howard Paine — was assigned to create the artwork for the entire project, 50 stamps in all. USPS contracted with the Bureau of Engraving and Printing to produce all five sheetlets and to print them by offset and intaglio. They would be distributed to post offices in panes containing two full sheetlets, or 20 stamps, so joined that they could be separated along a horizontal row of perforations.

Paine was one of the principal advocates of this procedure. "I think collectors like consistency," he said. "They like things that add up to a set. When I sold the idea of the map and the 10 stamps, I said, 'We want to do this for five years, so let's have no changing the rules in midstream.'

"When I went to the Bureau the last time to see the final proof I told them, 'What I want to do is match the previous sheetlet. I want to match the weight and the strength and the color and the detail and the feel and everything else of the first one.' It's like making Campbell's soup. The nine millionth can of tomato soup has got to taste like the first can."

Even so, there were some small differences — USPS considered them improvements — between the 1992 sheetlet and the prototype in 1991.

First, the caption on each individual stamp included the year being commemorated, 1942. Although the previous year's sheetlet had prominently displayed a "1941" on its central map, the stamps themselves had lacked this information. This meant they lost much of their educational effectiveness when detached and used on letters.

"We've done what people have asked us to do, and what we should have done with the 1941 sheet," said Jack Williams of USPS, the project manager. "We've added the year to the inscription in every case, so the stamps make more sense when they're separated."

The 1992 map also carried an explanatory line that hadn't been included on the first sheetlet: "Red areas controlled by enemy."

The Postal Service also added a marginal inscription to each pane of two sheetlets, in what had been blank space on the first year's panes, to describe the purpose of the issue and to promote another USPS marketing project: a series of hardcover books focusing on the subjects of each year's stamps. The 1992 book had an introduction by comedian Bob Hope, who traveled thousands of miles during the war to entertain U.S. troops. It sold for $15.95 and included two sheetlets (face value $5.80) for mounting inside, as a sheetlet and as individual stamps.

There was also a new die for the only intaglio element on the stamps, the "29 USA." BEP's Deborah Alexander had engraved a die for the 1991 sheetlets, and the Bureau had intended to use it to make the printing sleeves for the other four sheetlets in the series as well. However, during the press run of the 1991 sheetlet, the "29 USA" showed excessive war, and the decision was made to create another die with a different depth and line structure for the 1992 and subsequent sheetlets. John Smith Jr. engraved the new die, and the sleeves made from it proved satisfactory at holding ink during the run of the 1992 sheetlets.

USPS promoted the sheetlets and hardcover books in full-page ads in philatelic publications that plugged the message: "Time to re-up . . . and re-enlist in a remembrance of some of our nation's greatest heroes." To the Postal Service's obvious pleasure, the great majority of the sheetlets sold to the public were kept as collectibles. Like the stamps from the 1991 sheetlets, very few of the 1992 stamps turned up in the mailstream.

The events depicted on the 10 stamps of 1992, and their captions, were:

B-25S TAKE OFF TO RAID TOKYO APRIL 18, 1942. The Japanese belief that their island nation was divinely protected was shattered when 16 U.S. Army bombers, led by Lieutenant Colonel James H. Doolittle, swept in from the sea to bomb Tokyo and four other Japanese cities, then vanished westward. The raiders, whose objective was to shake Japanese confidence and boost American morale at a time when the enemy was advancing steadily across the Pacific, had made an unprecedented carrier takeoff from the *USS Hornet* some 700 miles from Tokyo. After dropping their bombs, they headed for sanctuaries in Russia and China. Of 80 crewmen, seven perished, including three who were executed by the Japanese.

FOOD AND OTHER COMMODITIES RATIONED, 1942. To keep inflation in check as national income expanded and the supply of consumer goods shrank, and to ensure a fair distribution of scarce products, the government launched an extended program of controlled consumption. Ceilings were placed on prices, wages and rents, production of cars for civilians was halted, and tires, gasoline, sugar, coffee, meats,

This U.S. stamp of 1944 showed an aerial view of the island of Corregidor and honored the American and Filipino troops who participated in its final defense.

shoes and other products were rationed. For a grocery shopping trip, the family ration-coupon books were as essential as money.

U.S. WINS BATTLE OF THE CORAL SEA MAY 1942. The world's first battle between aircraft carriers, and the first major battle between ships out of sight of each other, was fought May 4 and 5, when some 83 U.S. planes and 70 planes from a Japanese force that was threatening New Guinea attacked each other's home fleets. U.S. carrier *Lexington* was lost, and another carrier was hit. But the battle checked Japan's southward expansion, saved New Guinea and crippled two big Japanese carriers, making them unavailable to fight at Midway a month later.

CORREGIDOR FALLS TO JAPANESE MAY 6, 1942. Japanese troops pushing across Luzon drove combined U.S. and Philippine army forces from Manila and onto the 30-mile peninsula of Bataan. After weeks of fighting, Bataan's 76,000 defenders surrendered, leaving only the island of Corregidor at the mouth of the bay in Allied hands. For nearly a month, 13,000 troops were pounded day and night by more than 100 Japanese guns. On May 6, General Jonathan Wainwright was forced to surrender not only the island but the entire Philippines. (An aerial view of Corregidor is shown on the U.S. wartime stamp commemorating the defenders' final resistance, Scott 925).

JAPAN INVADES ALEUTIAN ISLANDS JUNE 1942. As the Pacific war raged, the 1,200-mile-long chain of islands just off Alaska became increasingly significant. On June 3, the Japanese invaded the Aleutians, in part to provoke Admiral Chester Nimitz into sending a portion of his fleet northward, away from the impending clash at Mid-

way. (Nimitz refused to take the bait.) The Aleutian fighting was difficult and frustrating, with more equipment lost and more casualties suffered because of foul weather than to enemy action. The major land battle, on Attu in May 1943, was the first of many island-hopping operations by which U.S. forces recaptured territory taken in Japan's powerful initial push.

ALLIES DECIPHER SECRET ENEMY CODES, 1942. Even before Pearl Harbor, U.S. cryptographers had broken "Purple," Japan's top diplomatic code. Unfortunately, they were unable to pinpoint the time and place of the Japanese strike that brought America the war. The results were better at Midway, where commanders knew the Imperial Fleet's attack plans, thanks to the work of a small team of Navy codebreakers in Hawaii. The team, known as Station Hypo, broke the Japanese operational code known as JN-25, a system based on five-digit numbers.

YORKTOWN LOST, U.S. WINS AT MIDWAY, 1942. The turning point in the Pacific came June 3-6, when Admiral Yamamoto's plan to seize the key U.S. island of Midway was smashed by seamen and flyers of the carriers *Yorktown*, *Enterprise* and *Hornet* and supporting vessels. American losses in men and planes were large; Midway was hammered; the *Yorktown* and a destroyer were sunk. But the Japanese, despite a 3-1 advantage in ships and aircraft, lost all four of their carriers, one cruiser, 322 planes and 3,500 men. Yamamoto was forced to turn away in defeat.

MILLIONS OF WOMEN JOIN WAR EFFORT, 1942. "Rosie the Riveter," celebrated in song, film and a Norman Rockwell illustration, personified the armies of American women who found themselves doing work they had never dreamed of as children. They toiled in war plants and shipyards, on farms and in warehouses, taking the place of men in uniform. Another 400,000 women were in uniform themselves, as members of the WACs, WAVES, SPARs and Marines, as military nurses and as ferry pilots. Old role stereotypes were broken, never to be put back together.

MARINES LAND ON GUADALCANAL AUG. 7, 1942. Japanese occupation of the jungle islands of Tulagi and Guadalcanal posed a threat

to Allied supply lines and to Australia. On August 7, 17,000 Marines came ashore, meeting light early resistance, and seized a partially built airstrip on "the Canal." But the enemy counterattacked by sea, air and land, the Marines were isolated without resupply, and bitter fighting raged into the winter. The Allies prevailed after suffering heavy losses to enemy fire and to disease. Japanese casualties topped 30,000.

ALLIES LAND IN NORTH AFRICA NOVEMBER 1942. Operation Torch, the war's first major Anglo-American campaign, began with the largest amphibious operation ever attempted. More than 107,000 troops landed November 7 at Casablanca in Morocco and Oran and Algiers in Algeria. Torch's major aims included squeezing the German Afrika Korps that was being pushed westward across Libya by the British. But strong German resistance gave green American GIs their baptism of fire and delayed the capture of the key ports of Tunis and Bizerte until the following spring.

The Designs

British-born artist William Bond of Arlington, Virginia, brought personal experience to the huge assignment of providing 50 different stamp paintings that would cover U.S. participation in World War II from start to finish. He himself had served as a signalman in the Royal Navy during the war.

Bond has created his acrylic paintings for the series in several different ways. Some of the stamp designs are near-literal representations of specific wartime photographs. Others are composites, based on several different photos plus his own imagination. Still others are still-life pictures that are intended to represent an ongoing theme of the war, such as civil defense, rationing and women in industry, rather than a specific event. "Those are the hardest," said art director Howard Paine.

Creating a stamp design for the series can be an involved process. Bond and Paine are the principal participants, but many people get into the act, including the Citizens' Stamp Advisory Committee; Jack Williams of USPS, project manager for the first two years' sheetlets; Susan Robb, a contract researcher who locates photographic reference material, much of it from the National Archives and Library of Congress, and tracks down answers to questions raised by Bond or Paine in the course of their work, and experts on various aspects of World War II, such as Colonel Charles A. Endress of the U.S. Army Reserve, who has been closely involved in the project from the beginning.

Several artistic problems fall under the general heading of "color." The Postal Service wants colorful stamps in colorful sheetlets, but, as Paine observed, "The war was camouflage and it was smoky and it was night and it was muddy and it was grim . . . We try to force some color where we can." The question of color accuracy also can be formidable. Most of the wartime photographs are black and white, and determining the actual colors of weapons, costumes and buildings half a century later isn't always easy. To add another complication, the stamps' dominant or background colors must vary from stamp to stamp on a given sheetlet, but they also must be distributed in a balanced way across the entire sheetlet.

Bond's painting illustrating the Doolittle raid on Tokyo showed a B-25 bomber a few feet above the waves, moments after it had cleared the flight deck of the carrier *Hornet*. He modeled the plane on drawings and photographs from various sources. One point of discussion with CSAC, USPS staff members and researchers was whether at that point early in the flight the flaps and wheels still would be down or would be retracted. The consensus was that they would be down, and Bond painted them in that position.

The second stamp on the sheetlet showed a close-up of a woman's hand (Bond's wife was the model) holding specimens of red, green and black food-rationing coupons over the tops of two cans. Paine provided coupons from his own collection for Bond to copy. Bond's first version showed the can lids imprinted with the price and the number of ration points they required, but "the stamps were getting overburdened with numbers," Paine said, so the artist deleted the markings.

For the Battle of the Coral Sea, Paine and Bond decided against using a naval battle scene like the one they planned for the Battle of Midway stamp elsewhere on the sheetlet. Instead, Bond painted a Douglas Dauntless dive bomber — a plane that played a key role in the Coral Sea engagement — taking off from a carrier deck as a signal officer drops his checkered flag. (Bond blurred the flag and the man's forearm to indicate motion.) Because the Navy photographs he used for reference were black and white, he asked Susan Robb to try to determine the signal officer's uniform color. She tracked down a veteran of World War II carrier duty who confirmed that the color was beige.

The Corregidor stamp was the darkest of the series so far, both in mood and in color. "Very depressing," Bill Bond called it; "a downer," were Paine's words. The first U.S. stamp ever to graphically depict an American surrender, it showed a Japanese Army's-eye view of a group of U.S. servicemen, their faces partly in shadow, with hands raised.

Bond used as reference several pictures taken by Japanese photogra-

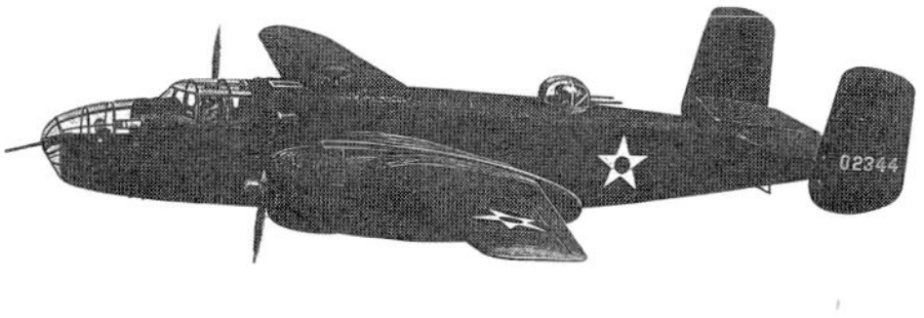

Published photographs and drawings of B-25s, such as this one, were used by William Bond in designing the stamp honoring the Doolittle raid on Tokyo.

phers, including one that was printed in *The Rising Sun*, part of the Time-Life Books series on World War II, and credited to Tsuguichi Koyanagi. "I tried to make it a bit abstract," Bond said of his painting. "I started out brightly on the left side, so the 29 USA would stand out, and I changed colors as I went through to the other side." The resulting stamp was darker than he intended, Bond said: "The black plate (in the printing operation) got a little heavy."

Survivors of the Philippine campaign have an organization called American Defenders of Bataan and Corregidor Inc. "We got a very angry letter from the organization after the unveiling of the designs in December," said Jack Williams. "What this sheet was all about was not fully understood, and newspapers just picked up and reported the subjects of the stamps. The subject of this particular stamp was Corregidor. We immediately got a protest, 'Why did you do Corregidor and not Bataan and not both?'

"I had to talk to the head of the organization, and I then wrote him a letter and pointed out that the stamp focused on Corregidor because that was the closing act in the Philippines for the U.S. forces — the final act of capitulation. Bataan had come earlier. And we had also covered it on the map by saying 'Philippines fall to Japanese: Bataan, April 9; Corregidor, May 6.' That seemed to satisfy them."

Bond's painting for the Aleutian invasion stamp showed a military

This published Navy photograph of a Douglas Dauntless dive bomber taking off from its carrier was part of William Bond's reference material in designing the Battle of the Coral Sea stamp.

installation identified as Fort Mears, in Dutch Harbor on Unalaska Island, with buildings ablaze from the Japanese bombing of June 3 and 4. His principal pictorial reference was a U.S. Navy photograph from the National Archives. "We enlarged the crop a little bit," Paine said — in other words, showed the picture from a greater distance — "to get the mountain and bay. If we had come in too close, it could have been Fort Dix or Fort Devon instead of Dutch Harbor."

To determine the color of the barracks roofs, Susan Robb sought the help of a National Park Service official in Anchorage, Alaska, named Sandra Faulkner. Faulkner unearthed plans for the buildings prepared in 1941 by the Department of the Navy's Bureau of Yards and Docks. These plans, plus the personal recollections of persons living near Fort Mears, disclosed that the roofing material was a bituminous sheeting with wood battens and had been left unpainted. Originally a light gray, the material in time weathered to a darker gray.

William Bond based his painting for the Corregidor stamp on several archival photographs such as this one. The picture shows American and Filipino troops giving up outside the Malinta Tunnel, where their garrison withstood 27 days of artillery bombardment.

That was the color Bond painted them. "I had hoped the roofs would be barn red, because it would have added color to the scene," Paine said. As it turned out, the only touches of bright color in the finished painting were the yellow and red of the flames.

The stamp honoring the cryptographers who broke the Japanese codes posed a real problem, Paine recalled. The solution turned out to be another of Bond's still-life paintings. It showed a sheet of paper with rows of letters, a radio headset, a pencil, and a portion of the green shade on a desk lamp that illuminated the scene. The caption read: "Allies decipher secret enemy codes, 1942."

The caption, and the juxtaposition of objects in the picture, suggested that the letters had been heard in a wartime radio intercept and transcribed in pencil by the operator. This entailed some creative license on Bond's part. The actual coded message on which he based his artwork was in the Purple Code and had been sent to Tokyo by Kichisaburo Nomura, the Japanese ambassador to the United States, April 17, 1941, more than seven months before Pearl Harbor. The letters were not hand-printed, but were printed on an electric typewriter connected to a coding machine.

Among the design ideas Paine and Bond considered for this stamp were a picture of a decoding machine (they couldn't find one that was

William Bond used this photograph as pictorial reference for his design for the Aleutian Islands invasion stamp. The picture shows burning buildings at Fort Mears, a U.S. military installation at Dutch Harbor, after a Japanese bombing attack. Additional research was needed to learn the color of the building roofs so the artist could depict them accurately.

both authentic and recognizable) and a room full of cryptographers ("It wouldn't work on a stamp," Paine said). At the Smithsonian Institution, they saw a cryptography exhibit that included a sailor with earphones taking down enemy radio transmissions, and from this they developed the idea of creating a symbolic design featuring some of the tools of radio message interception.

For the Battle of Midway, Bond based his design on a well-known Navy photograph from that engagement that showed a fiery explosion aboard the carrier *Yorktown*. Aside from converting a black and white picture to color, the only significant changes he made were in the shapes and locations of the black smoke puffs caused by bursting shells.

For the stamp saluting women in the war effort, Bond depicted a woman factory employee, wearing goggles, her sleeves rolled up, her hair in a scarf, working on the inside of some kind of unspecified military craft. The edge of an identification badge is visible on the bib of her overall. The undefined open space at the left of the action gave the artist a chance to introduce some spot color, in this case green.

Precisely what the worker was doing in the picture, and with what kind of tool, was left vague. Bond and Paine called the tool she was holding a rivet gun, but Jack Williams said it was a drill; and, in fact, in one of Bond's earlier versions of the design, the drill bit showed quite clearly.

Bond's Guadalcanal stamp featured Marines walking through the surf

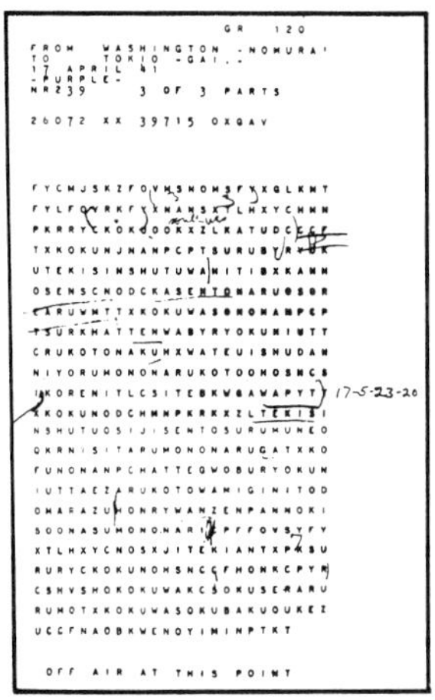

GR 120

FROM WASHINGTON -NOMURA'
TO TOKIO -GAI..-
17 APRIL 41
-PURPLE-
NR239 3 OF 3 PARTS

26072 XX 39715 OXQAV

FYCMJSKZFOVHSHOMSFYXQLKHT
FYLFOVRKFYXHANSXTLHXYCHHN
PKRRYCKOKOOOKXZLKATUDC
TXKOKUNJNANPCPTSURUBYR
UTEKISINSHUTUWAHITIBXKANN
OSENSCNODCKASENTONARUOSOR
CARUWNTTXKOKUWASONONANPEP
TSURKHATTENWABYRYOKUNIUTT
CRUKOTONAKUNXWATEUISNUDAN
NIYORUNONONARUKOTOONOSNCS
IKORENITLCSITEBKWGAWAPYT 17-5-23-20
XKOKUNODCHMNPKRKXZLTEKISI
NSHUTUOSIJISENTOSURUMUNEO
QKRNISITAPUMONONARUGATXKO
FUNONANPCHATTEQWOBURYOKUN
IUTTAEZARUKOTOWAMIGINITOD
OMARAZUHONRYWANZENPANNOKI
SOONASUMONONARI PFFOVSYFY
XTLHXYCNOSXJITEKIANTXPKSU
RURYCKOKUNOHSNCCFHONKCPYR
CSHVSHOKOKUWAKCSOKUSEAARU
RUMOTXKOKUWASOKUBAKUOUKEZ
UCCFNAOBKWENOYIMINPTKT

OFF AIR AT THIS POINT

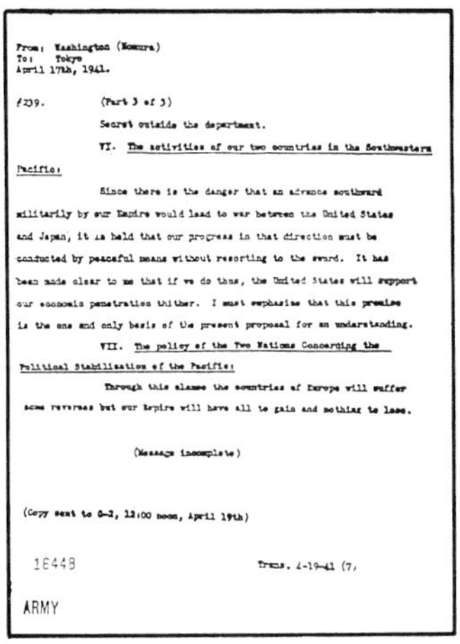

From: Washington (Nomura)
To: Tokyo
April 17th, 1941.

#239. (Part 3 of 3)

Secret outside the department.

VI. The activities of our two countries in the Southwestern Pacific:

Since there is the danger that an advance southward militarily by our Empire would lead to war between the United States and Japan, it is held that our progress in that direction must be conducted by peaceful means without resorting to the sword. It has been made clear to me that if we do thus, the United States will support our economic penetration thither. I must emphasize that this premise is the one and only basis of the present proposal for an understanding.

VII. The policy of the Two Nations Concerning the Political Stabilization of the Pacific:

Through this clause the countries of Europe will suffer some reverses but our Empire will have all to gain and nothing to lose.

(Message incomplete)

(Copy sent to G-2, 12:00 noon, April 19th)

16448 Trans. 4-19-41 (7)

ARMY

On the left is a reproduction of a prewar message in the Purple Code, sent to Tokyo by Japan's ambassador in Washington, which designer William Bond used as a reference in making his painting for the stamp commemorating U.S. code-breaking achievements. A decrypted version of the message is at right. It says in part: "Since there is the danger that an advance southward militarily by our Empire would lead to war between the United States and Japan, it is held that our progress in that direction must be conducted by peaceful means without resorting to the sword."

This well-known Navy photograph of a Japanese bomb scoring a direct hit on the carrier Yorktown *was an important pictorial reference for William Bond's painting for the Midway stamp.*

toward the beach, rifles at the ready. Elements of the picture were based on multiple photographs. The stamp, with white sky and white surf, was one of two on the sheetlet to have a colorless background (Coral Sea was the other). "We're trying each year to have a couple of stamps that have white backgrounds, just to bring some 'air' into the sheet, so they aren't all solid squares of color," Paine said.

The original Guadalcanal design that was shown to CSAC had its image area shifted somewhat to the left as compared to the finished stamp (see illustration). This shift put the helmet of the foreground Marine closer to the "29 USA," and revealed the trunk of a palm tree leaning diagonally into the picture at the right.

On CSAC's recommendation, the image was recropped. This opened up about 4 millimeters of white space between the helmet and the numeral "9," and revealed more of the left side of Bond's full painting. The trunk of the tree was lost in the process, and only some hanging fronds show on the stamp.

This is an earlier version of the stamp honoring women in war work. On the final version, the shape of the power tool was altered, and the caption was changed to read "Millions of Women Join War Effort 1942" in order to identify the year being commemorated.

The image on this earlier version of the Guadalcanal stamp is shifted more to the left than the image on the stamp as issued. The trunk of the palm tree on the right shows in this version, and the foreground Marine's helmet is closer to the "29 USA."

For his North Africa stamp design, Bond painted the sky yellow and gave the entire landscape a yellowish cast to evoke the heat and sand of the desert. He based his picture on a 35-millimeter color photograph of an American M3 light tank moving forward to probe German defenses at El Guettar in Tunisia. The picture was made by *Life* magazine photographer Eliot Elisofon.

A late addition to the design of the overall sheetlet was a series of dots

This photograph of an American M3 light tank in Tunisia, originally taken in color, was the basis for the design of the stamp commemorating the North Africa landing.

The dots representing Washington, D.C., Ottawa and other cities on the World War II sheetlet's centerpiece map are slightly off their proper locations. The dot representing Leningrad is on the east side of Lake Ladoga rather than the west side, where it belongs.

locating major cities on the map. The map had originally borne just the names of the cities, without dots. This added detail proved to be one detail too many. Critics pointed out that some of the dots were off target — too far off to be the result of color misregistration. The city that strayed the farthest was Leningrad, which the map placed on the east side of Lake Ladoga rather than on the west side, where it belonged.

However, one mistake that had been made with the previous sheetlet's map was corrected on this one. The 1991 sheetlet had shown the Danish island of Sjaelland, site of Denmark's capital city of Copenhagen, colored yellow, indicating that it was outside the area of Nazi occupation. The 1992 map correctly showed it in red.

The map captions were subject to extensive fine-tuning. One of the last to be changed was the one at the far right referring to the battle of Stalingrad. "At the last minute," said Jack Williams, "we still had it saying: 'Russian defenders destroy German forces at Stalingrad July 17, 1942-February 2, 1943.' The battle overlapped two years, but we didn't want to overlap sheets. So we changed it to read: 'Russian defenders battle German forces at Stalingrad, Summer 1942.'

"This gave us the option of including a map notation on the next sheet, for 1943, if we thought it was significant and if we had the room to do it."

First-Day Facts

The date of issue of the sheetlet was originally set for August 14, but in June it was changed to August 17 to coincide with the opening of the Veterans of Foreign Wars convention.

Deputy Postmaster General Michael S. Coughlin dedicated the stamps at a convention general session, substituting for Postmaster General

Marvin Runyon, whose name was on the program. The welcome and introduction of Coughlin were given by Howard Vander Clute, VFW national adjutant general.

USPS accommodated mail-order first-day cover customers by affixing individual stamps to addressed envelopes on request, but only stamps selected at random. The Philatelic Sales Division offered full sheetlets (10 stamps) or full panes of two sheetlets (20 stamps) preaffixed to envelopes and bearing first-day postmarks for face value plus $1.

29¢ DOROTHY PARKER
LITERARY ARTS SERIES

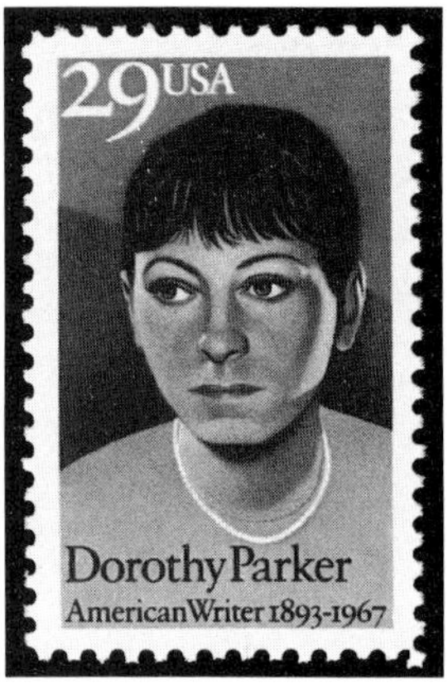

Date of Issue: August 22, 1992

Catalog Number: Scott 2698

Colors: magenta, yellow, cyan, purple, black

First-Day Cancel: West End, New Jersey

FDCs Canceled: 266,323

Format: Panes of 50, vertical, 10 across, 5 down. Gravure printing cylinders of 200 subjects (20 across, 10 around).

Perf: 10.9 (L perforator)

Selvage Inscription: "Dorothy Parker, U.S./writer noted for/sardonic satire in/poetry & short stories." "Drama and book/critic for literary/magazines, playwright/and screenwriter." "She joined in the/renowned gatherings/of a group of New/York's sharpest wits."

Selvage Markings: "Use Correct/ZIP Code/®/36 USC 380." "©/United States/Postal Service/1991." USPS Olympic logo.

Designer: Greg Rudd of Monroe, Connecticut

Art Director and Project Manager: Jack Williams (USPS)

Typographer: Bradbury Thompson (CSAC)

Modeler: Richard Sennett (Stamp Venturers)

Printing: Printed by Stamp Venturers on a Champlain gravure press in Richmond, Virginia. Stamps perforated, processed and shipped by Stamp Venturers in Milwaukee, Wisconsin.

Quantity Ordered: 105,000,000

Quantity Distributed: 105,000,000

Cylinder Number Detail:	1 group of 5 gravure cylinder numbers preceded by the letter S alongside corner stamp
Cylinder Number Combination:	S11111
Tagging:	phosphor-coated paper with block tagging included in printing sequence

The Stamp

A stamp depicting writer and humorist Dorothy Parker was dedicated in the seashore town of West End, New Jersey, on August 22, 1992, the 99th anniversary of her birth there. West End today is a section of Long Branch, New Jersey.

The stamp was the 10th in a rather arbitrary grouping of commemoratives that USPS calls the Literary Arts series. Parker was the third woman, after Edith Wharton and Marianne Moore, to be included, although previous stamps not listed in the series had honored poets Emily Dickinson and Edna St. Vincent Millay.

A biographer of Parker, Marion Meade, conceded that Parker was a literary lightweight compared to these predecessors. She "would be delighted to be in the company of them . . . whom she considered real writers," Meade told Bill McAllister of *The Washington Post.*

Meade, author of a book *Dorothy Parker: What Fresh Hell Is This?*, said she wasn't sure why USPS had picked Parker for postal honors, but that she suspected that the Postal Service was seeking women. "Secretly, she would have been terribly, terribly pleased, but publicly she would say that it was an honor she did not deserve," Meade told McAllister. "She had a very low opinion of herself."

Born Dorothy Rothschild, the writer married Edwin Pond Parker II in 1917, and although they later divorced and she remarried, she continued to use the name Parker professionally. After working for *Vogue* magazine, she became drama critic of the periodical *Vanity Fair* and later joined the staff of *The New Yorker*, where her sharply worded opinions on books and theater soon drew a following. *The New Yorker* also published many of her short stories. Her first book of verse, *Enough Rope* (1926), was a success, and she became a free-lance writer. She also collaborated on several plays and wrote for Hollywood. A painstaking craftsman, she once said: "I can't write five words but I change seven."

"In print and in person, Miss Parker sparkled with a word or a phrase, for she honed her humor to its most economical size," *The New York Times* wrote in her obituary. "Her rapier wit, most of it spontaneous, gained its early renown from her membership in the Algonquin Round Table, an informal luncheon club at the Algonquin Hotel in the 1920s, where some of (New York's) most sedulous framers of bon mots gathered." She was a co-founder, with Robert Benchley and Robert E. Sherwood. At one time or another, the group included Franklin P. Adams, George S. Kaufman, Harold Ross, Russel Crouse, Edna Ferber, Heywood

Broun, Ruth Gordon and Alexander Woollcott.

Among Parker's best-known comments are these:

- On actress Katharine Hepburn: "She ran the gamut of emotions from A to B."
- "The love affair between Margot Asquith and Margot Asquith will live as one of the prettiest love stories in all literature."
- "Brevity is the soul of lingerie — as the Petticoat said to the Chemise."
- "The reading of 'Dawn' (by Theodore Dreiser) is a strain upon many parts, but the worst wear and tear fall on the forearms."
- "Razors pain you;/Rivers are damp;/Acids stain you;/And drugs cause cramp./Guns aren't lawful;/Nooses give;/Gas smells awful;/ You might as well live."

The most famous Parker pronouncement of all was: "Men seldom make passes at girls who wear glasses," a couplet that appeared in *Enough Rope*. According to *The New York Times*, she took that advice seriously, and "although she was quite nearsighted, she refrained from wearing her horn-rimmed spectacles in public, or when men were present: She much preferred to blink her luminous hazel-green eyes."

In preparing the selvage inscription for the stamp, Jack Williams of USPS, the project manager, said: "I tried my best" to work in the "glasses" couplet. "But we're so limited in space that I couldn't do it," he said. Another omission from the selvage notes was the name of the Algonquin Hotel where the Round Table gathered. The inscription said simply that Parker "joined in the renowned gatherings of a group of New York's sharpest wits." The Citizens' Stamp Advisory Committee vetoed the use of the hotel's name on grounds that to use it would have publicized a commercial establishment, Williams said.

Parker was active in liberal causes and was national chairwoman of the Joint Anti-Fascist Refugee Committee during the Spanish Civil War. In 1951 she was cited by the House Un-American Activities Committee, with 300 other writers, professors, actors and artists, for affiliation with what the committee called "Communist front" organizations. One witness identified her as a member of the Communist Party, an accusation she persistently denied.

She was in frail health in later years and died in New York City June 7, 1967, at age 73. She left an estate estimated at only $10,000, the bulk of which she willed to Dr. Martin Luther King Jr. for his civil rights work.

The Design

Artist Gregory Rudd of Trumbull, Connecticut, prepared the painting that was used in making the stamp. Rudd, who does his portraits in oil on gesso board, had previously designed the Francis Ouimet stamp (1988) in the American Sports series and the Ernest Hemingway (1989) and Marianne Moore (1990) stamps in the Literary Arts series.

For the earlier assignments, the Postal Service had asked Rudd to do his own research and use his own ideas in developing the designs. This time CSAC had already chosen the image — a black and white photograph of a young, solemn-looking Dorothy Parker seated at a desk — as well as the arrangement of the visual elements, which had been worked out by USPS consultant John Boyd of Anagraphics, Incorporated.

The photograph that CSAC preferred was found in the *Encyclopedia Americana*, and USPS obtained the rights to use it from Culver Pictures Inc. On the way to this decision, CSAC considered and dismissed other portraits, including one showing Parker in a large flowered hat and another that depicted her holding her dachshund, Robinson. The latter was ruled out because of the design problem posed by the dog (should it be included or removed?). The committee felt that in the picture it selected "she had the nicest expression," said project manager Williams.

Rudd, however, said he was struck by the "pensive, unhappy" look in the large eyes and the unsmiling mouth of the photograph. "She seemed to exude a sadness, a disappointment, that I guess was a reflection of her life," he said. In his first painting based on the photo, he put "a little Mona Lisa smile" on her face, but the committee members sent word via Williams that they preferred the original expression, and Rudd repainted

This is the picture of a youthful Dorothy Parker on which Gregory Rudd based his painting for the stamp. Rudd shortened the bangs and added a backlighting effect.

the mouth accordingly.

Rudd did take some artistic license with Parker's hairline, which in the photograph all but concealed her eyebrows. He shortened the bangs slightly so he could "work with the brows and give a little more lift to the face," he said. The original portrait was flat, with no strong contrasts, so Rudd provided some backlighting in his painting to create a more three-dimensional effect.

The photograph showed Parker seated in a wing-back chair. Rather than reproduce the chair literally, Rudd decided to create abstract blocks of color in the same general form. He selected his prominent colors — green and blue graduating into purple — because they were muted, complemented each other and were pleasing to the eye, he said.

In translating Rudd's artwork, Stamp Venturers added a purple ink to the four standard process colors. The stamp as printed was a little lighter and brighter than the original painting, Rudd said.

In the typography of the stamp, the numerals in the denomination are exaggerated, with the horizontal stroke in the 2 extended and the tail of the 9 dropping well below the base of the 2. The numerals in the dates "1893-1967" show a similar variety of heights and depths.

First-Day Facts

Assistant Postmaster General Frank R. Power dedicated the stamp at an outdoor ceremony in West End Park at Brighton and Ocean Avenues. Parker's biographer, Marion Meade, spoke. Louise Poster portrayed Parker in a theatrical presentation, *The Darling of the Algonquin*, and three students read selections of Parker's poetry. Three grandnieces of the writer, residents of upstate New York, were introduced.

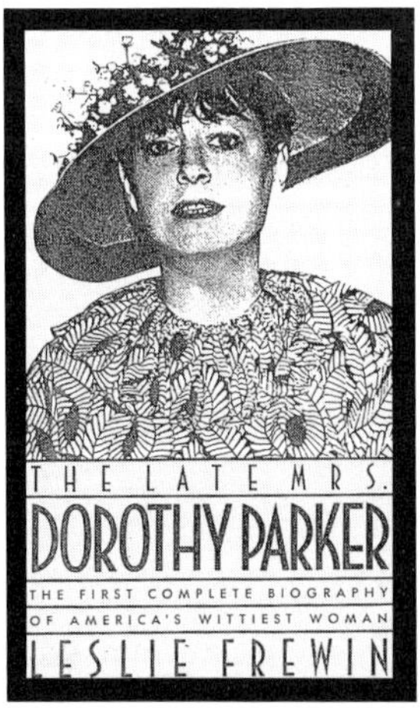

The Citizens' Stamp Advisory Committee also considered these photos of Dorothy Parker as models for the stamp design. One shows her in an enormous hat. In the other, she is holding her dachshund, Robinson.

29¢ THEODORE VON KARMAN

Date of Issue: August 31, 1992

Catalog Number: Scott 2699

Colors: magenta, yellow, cyan, black

First-Day Cancel: Washington, D.C.

FDCs Canceled: 256,986

Format: Panes of 50, vertical, 10 across, 5 down. Gravure printing cylinders of 200 subjects (20 across, 10 around) manufactured by Armotek Industries Inc., Palmyra, New Jersey.

Perf: 10.9 (L perforator)

Selvage Inscription: "Theodore von Karman/received the first/U.S. Medal of Science,/from President Kennedy." "A gifted aerodynamicist/and engineer, he was/called the 'architect/of the space age.' " "His discoveries enabled/supersonic flight and/the landing on the moon/by U.S. astronauts."

Selvage Markings: "©/United States/Postal Service/1991." "Use Correct/ZIP Code/®/36 USC 380." USPS Olympic logo.

Designer: Christopher Calle of Ridgefield, Connecticut

Art Director and Project Manager: Jack Williams, USPS

Typographer: John Boyd, Anagraphics Inc., New York, New York

Modeler: Richard Sennett, Stamp Venturers

Printing: Printed by Stamp Venturers on a Champlain gravure press in Richmond, Virginia. Stamps perforated, processed and shipped by Stamp Venturers in Milwaukee, Wisconsin.

Quantity Ordered: 144,000,000	
Quantity Distributed: 142,500,000	
Cylinder Number Detail:	1 group of 4 gravure cylinder numbers preceded by the letter S alongside corner stamp
Cylinder Number Combination: S1111	
Tagging: phosphor-coated paper	

The Stamp

Theodore von Karman, a pioneer in rocket research and one of the principal builders of the U.S. aerospace industry, was honored with a 29¢ commemorative stamp that was issued August 31 at the World Space Congress in Washington, D.C.

The Hungarian-born educator, scientist and engineer was a founder of what is now the Jet Propulsion Laboratory at the California Institute of Technology in Pasadena. This institution became America's first center for long-range missile development and space research.

Dedication of the stamp marked the successful conclusion of a 27-year campaign by Shirley Thomas, now a professor of writing at the University of Southern California, to obtain postal honors for von Karman. Her long-sustained effort was described in a report by Joan Zyda in the Jet Propulsion Laboratory's publication *Universe*.

"I decided not to give up,'' Thomas told Zyda. "It's a fitting tribute, a dedication to the man. We need to do something to preserve aerospace history. So many stamps mark what I would consider less worthy people and events.''

Thomas met von Karman in 1959 when she was working on his biography for inclusion in her book *Men of Space*, Volume I (published in 1960). She remained in touch with him until his death in 1963.

"We were not close friends,'' she said, "but I spent enough time with him to gather information to write about him.

"I was taken by the utter brilliance of the man and his ability to explain things, no matter what the concept, and his kindness and wit.''

Thomas began her campaign for a von Karman stamp in 1965 by writing letters to the postmaster general. In 1983 she organized the Committee for the Theodore von Karman Postage Stamp, with a membership that included Air Force test pilot Charles E. Yeager, astronauts Edwin "Buzz'' Aldrin and L. Gordon Cooper, and William J. Numeroff, the artist credited with leading the campaign for the 1964 U.S. airmail stamp honoring rocket pioneer Robert H. Goddard (Scott C69).

She also received support and endorsement from many other people in the fields of education, science, industry and government. She asked them to send their letters in support of the stamp to her. Periodically she would compile the letters in packets and mail them to the postmaster general. Usually, she said, she received a form letter in return, or nothing.

Her campaign was made difficult, Thomas said, by the fact that "outside of the scientific world, von Karman is not a magical name, unfortunately. But in the scientific world, he was a giant."

Belmont Faries, former chairman of the Citizens' Stamp Advisory Committee, wrote in *Stamp Collector* in 1991 that CSAC approved von Karman in 1985 (as Thomas would learn later) as a potential subject for a Great Americans series stamp.

"For several years Dr. Thomas had a promise of a stamp but not of a date of issue," Faries wrote. "This year there was to be a major event she considered ideal for a von Karman stamp announcement. The California Institute of Technology, with which Dr. von Karman was closely associated, is celebrating its 100th anniversary, and all of the activities are being dedicated to von Karman.

"Dr. Thomas saw an August 3 (1991) awards ceremony sponsored by the Aerospace Historical Committee of the California Museum of Science and Industry as an ideal time and place to make the announcement of the von Karman stamp. This time she reached the top with her request — Postmaster General Anthony M. Frank."

Frank came to the event, announced his approval of the stamp and accepted Thomas' suggestion that it be issued the following year on the opening day of the World Space Congress. According to Thomas, the postmaster general said jokingly that the von Karman stamp was approved because "I had to stop those letters from Shirley."

Frank added that the von Karman campaign file was "the thickest one ever received — except for the campaign for the Elvis (Presley) stamp," Thomas said. (See Year in Review).

Von Karman was born in Budapest, Hungary, May 11, 1881, and began his study of aerodynamics in 1906 at the University of Gottingen, where he obtained a grounding in mathematics and engineering. Here he produced an analysis of the periodic vortices that appear in the wake of an obstacle in a fluid stream. Now known as the "Karman vortex street," this effect can cause destructive vibrations in aerodynamic structures. His analysis was used to explain the 1940 collapse of the suspension bridge at Tacoma Narrows, Washington.

In 1929 von Karman became director of the Guggenheim Aeronautical Laboratory at Caltech, and he became a U.S. citizen in 1936. He was a founder of the Aerojet Engineering Company in addition to the Jet Propulsion Laboratory. Both were important elements in the advancement of the U.S. aerospace industry.

During World War II, von Karman pushed for establishment of a long-range missile program. Such a program, called ORDCIT (Ordnance Contract to Caltech) began in 1944 and carried into the postwar period. In an outgrowth of this project, at White Sands Proving Ground in New Mexico in February 1949, a high-altitude sounding rocket called the WAC Corporal, launched from the nose of a reconstructed German V-2 rocket, reached a height of 244 miles, thus becoming the first U.S. rocket to enter what von Karman called extraterrestrial space. Von Karman and his Caltech students also pioneered in designing supersonic jet aircraft.

The spacework laid by von Karman proved invaluable in later U.S. space achievements, climaxed by the Apollo moon landings beginning in 1969. In 1963 President John F. Kennedy presented him with the first National Medal of Science. Shortly afterward, on May 6, 1963, he died in Aachen, West Germany.

The Design

Christopher Calle of Ridgefield, Connecticut, had designed many previous Great Americans stamps for USPS, but the von Karman stamp was his first commemorative portrait assignment.

Calle's stamp, vertically arranged, showed a full-face portrait of von Karman in the left foreground. Up the right side of the stamp, in the background, a V-2 missile, with a WAC Corporal as its second stage, could be seen rising on its fiery exhaust. The phrase "Aerospace Scientist" appeared beneath von Karman's name.

To prepare for the project, Calle assembled a variety of photographs of his subject. He prepared several concept sketches in pencil — first in the Great Americans format, and later in commemorative size.

"When they decided to make a commemorative of it, I had to completely change not only the format, but the imagery," Calle said. "I went out and did a lot more research than I had done the first time. I must have done 10 sketches — some with the rocket, some just a straight portrait, some showing very determined looking von Karmans, some showing very thoughtful looking von Karmans. On one of them the background image bridged the time span in which he had worked, from an early

This photograph of von Karman provided the basis for the portrait Christopher Calle drew for the finished commemorative stamp.

These are two of the sketches Christopher Calle prepared for a Great Americans stamp depicting von Karman.

biplane to a jet plane of today.''

The portrait selected for the stamp was based on a photograph furnished by Aerojet General in La Jolla, California. To do the finished artwork, Calle employed what he called "mixed media,'' a combination of colored pencil, watercolors and dyes.

After the decision was made to make the von Karman stamp a commemorative, Christopher Calle made several sketches in commemorative format showing the scientist with and without background art.

From an artist's viewpoint, von Karman had a "great face,'' Calle said. "His face seemed to me to be characteristic of a scientist,'' the artist added. "It just has that 'look' of someone who is deeply committed to what he's doing and with a high regard for his work.

"It was a lot of fun to do his portrait, because each different sketch embodied a little different character. One sketch had a little more dramatic lighting, and he was holding some glasses and looking very, very thoughtful. In others he was just kind of looking 'ahead,' as if toward the coming technology. That's what I tried to convey.''

First-Day Facts

The stamp was unveiled during the inaugural ceremony of the World Space Congress August 31 at the Washington, D.C., Convention Center. The Congress, and the ceremony, were closed to the general public, although USPS had originally announced that they would be open. William Dowling, a USPS vice president, spoke to the estimated 4,000 persons attending.

The World Space Congress, one of the major events of the International Space Year, marked the first time that the Committee on Space Research (COSPAR) and the International Astronautical Federation (IAF) held a joint meeting. The themes of the Congress were "Discovery, Exploration and Cooperation.''

USPS supplied no first-day program. First-day cancellations were available to the public at Washington's main post office, at USPS headquarters and during the noon hour at the Smithsonian Institution's National Air and Space Museum. On the same day the stamp went on sale, the Smithsonian Institution Press released a 259-page biography, *The Universal Man: Theodore von Karman's Life in Aeronautics* by Michael H. Gorn.

A second-day ceremony was held in the von Karman Auditorium of the Jet Propulsion Laboratory in Pasadena September 1. Fred Bowen, NASA resident office director, presided, and Dr. Duane F. Dipprey and Caltech President Thomas E. Everhart spoke. The stamp was dedicated by Pasadena Postmaster Jose L. Castellanos.

29¢ MINERALS (BLOCK OF FOUR)

Date of Issue: September 17, 1992

Catalog Numbers: Scott 2700-2703 (single stamps); 2704 (block or strip of 4)

Colors: black, magenta, yellow, cyan, metallic silver (PMS 877) (offset); dark brown (PMS 412U), dark purple (PMS 276U) (intaglio)

First-Day Cancel: Washington, D.C.

FDCs Canceled: 681,416

Format: Panes of 40, vertical, 8 across, 5 down. Offset printing plates of 160 subjects (10 across,16 around); intaglio printing sleeve of 320 subjects (10 across, 32 around).

Perf: 10.9 by 11.2 (Eureka off-line perforator)

Selvage Markings: "Use Correct/ZIP Code/®." "©/United States/Postal Service/1991/36 USC 380." USPS Olympic logo.

Designer and Typographer: Leonard Buckley (BEP)

Modeler: Peter Cocci (BEP)

Engravers: Thomas Hipschen (BEP), azurite and wulfenite; Gary Chaconas (BEP), variscite; Kenneth Kipperman (BEP), copper; Dennis Brown (BEP), lettering.

Art Director and Project Manager: Joe Brockert, USPS

Printing: BEP's 6-color offset, 3-color intaglio D press (902)

Quantity Ordered: 150,000,000

Quantity Distributed: 147,324,000

Plate/Sleeve Number Detail: 1 intaglio sleeve number and 1 group of 5 offset plate numbers in selvage of adjacent corner stamps

Plate/Sleeve Number Combinations: 11111-1, 21111-1, 32111-1, 32121-1, 32221-1, 42232-1, 42233-1, 43233-1, 53233-1, 54233- 1, 55233-1

Tagging: phosphor-coated paper

The Stamps

Each year thousands of Americans try to persuade the U.S. Postal Service to issue stamps for their pet subjects, but only a handful succeed. One person who beat the odds twice within two decades — and with the same subject — was Lillian Turner of Bethesda, Maryland.

Turner's postal passion was American minerals. In 1974 she succeeded in getting USPS to issue a block of four stamps showing four polished gemstones from the collection of the Smithsonian Institution in Washington, D.C. That wasn't enough. She renewed her lobbying a few years later, and, on September 17, 1992, it paid off with another block of four, depicting yet another quartet of Smithsonian mineral specimens.

"Persuading the government to come up with a commemorative stamp issue is like shoving a tired elephant to make it join the parade,'' wrote *Smithsonian* magazine. "It takes huge effort, ingenuity, leverage, persistence, luck and, perhaps most of all, desire. The new (1992) stamps are here because of a backer with an abundance of all those requirements. Lillian Turner, winner of the 1981 Smithson Society Founder's medal and an enormously enthusiastic friend of the Institution, says that over the past 30 years she's donated so many possessions to our museums that 'the Smithsonian is like an extension of my living room.'

"Interested in minerals — and just about everything else — Lillian Turner began campaigning back in the mid-'60s for a stamp issue to celebrate the theme 'Our Mineral Heritage.' She tackled various government biggies, lined up all the clout she could and at last, in 1974, got the elephant to issue four stamps . . . (that pictured) purple amethyst, pink rhodochrosite, tourmaline of a tasteful mixture of pink and green called 'watermelon,' and petrified wood, which often has a rainbow effect . . .

"Some 18 years after that first issue, Lillian Turner renewed her vigorous espousal of minerals and again got the elephant to budge. Hence, (the new) issue . . . 'I'm a natural promoter,' she explained, 'and I want to publicize the new Hall of Geology, Gems and Minerals — so important for children to see.' ''

Bill McAllister, stamp columnist for *The Washington Post*, also spoke with Turner about her crusade. She told him her love of minerals dated to a 1961 gem and mineral show she attended at the Silver Spring, Maryland, armory. There, she said, she saw "nature in the rough" and "officially became a rock hound."

Even after the 1974 stamps appeared, she continued lobbying postmasters general, arguing: "There must be more than four minerals stamps . . . Think of all the bird and flower stamps." She became such a familiar figure at USPS headquarters that one member of the Citizens' Stamp Advisory Committee told her he was keeping a diary of her activities. It was a new postmaster general, Anthony M. Frank, in 1988 who finally made the critical decision for another quartet of minerals stamps, Turner told McAllister. "I showed him the first four stamps," she said, "and he said, 'Yeah, we've got to have more of them.' "

The designs of the 1992 Minerals stamps were first shown December 11, 1991, when the Postal Service announced its 1992 program. They were unveiled a second time on July 23, 1992, by Assistant Postmaster General Gordon C. Morison, in Brunswick, Ohio, in conjunction with the combined show and national convention of the American Federation of Mineralogical Societies and Mid West Federation.

To select the specific minerals for the block and create the designs, USPS turned to the same person who had done the job for the 1974

This is the 1974 Mineral Heritage block of four (Scott 1538-1541), also designed by BEP's Leonard Buckley and also showing specimens from the collection of the Smithsonian Institution.

Mineral Heritage stamps, Leonard Buckley, foreman of designers at the Bureau of Engraving and Printing.

Buckley went once again to the Smithsonian, where he consulted with Daniel E. Appleman, the Museum of Natural History's associate director for science. Because of the Postal Service's requirement that pending stamp projects be kept confidential, Buckley was able to tell Appleman only that he was looking for colorful minerals that could be engraved in small dimensions.

Appleman showed him the portions of the collection that were on public display. Then he led the way to the Smithsonian's vault where a much larger assortment of minerals reposed, and "began pulling out drawers," Buckley recalled.

Buckley made a preliminary choice of 30 to 50 promising specimens before narrowing the field to about 20. Chip Clark, a Smithsonian photographer who specializes in shooting the museum's material, was called in to make color transparencies of the 20 specimens, working to specifications provided by Buckley. With the help of Peter Cocci, a BEP stamp designer and modeler, Buckley developed a proposal for a booklet pane containing 10 stamps (two each of five different varieties).

One of the minerals he chose was bright blue azurite, a copper carbonate, from the Copper Queen Mine near Bisbee, Arizona. The Smithsonian had gotten that specimen in 1927 after the death of its owner, Washington Roebling, the builder of the Brooklyn Bridge. Another was blazing orange wulfenite, from the Red Cloud Mine, also in Arizona, which the museum obtained in 1969. There was green variscite, a mineral of gemstone quality from Fairfield, Utah; it arrived in 1972. There was also the gold nugget known as "the bird," from Telegraph Mine, California, and a specimen of microcline embedded in smoky quartz, from Crystal Peak, Colorado.

Among the minerals Buckley considered

Leonard Buckley prepared this mockup of a 10-stamp booklet pane containing two each of five mineral designs: gold, azurite, wulfenite, variscite and a smoky quartz and microcline combination.

but didn't use were apatite, a reddish-violet crystal from Maine; beryl, from North Carolina; two fluorite specimens, one from Illinois, the other from Westmoreland, New Hampshire; prenite, from New Jersey, and rutile, from North Carolina.

Color and geographical distribution were important considerations, Buckley said, but a distinctive shape was an equally important requirement. "When you see a stamp, you want to know what you're looking at," he said. "Minerals aren't readily recognizable per se, so I wanted to make sure that the specimens that I used had crystalline shapes or polished surfaces so that people could readily identify them — especially because I at first intended not to put the word 'minerals' on the stamps as I had done in 1974. In 1974 there had been a lot more wording on the stamps. I was trying to simplify that, to minimize the wording, and still get the message across."

Because Buckley wanted to use intaglio in combination with offset lithography, as he had done in 1974, he was looking for shapes and other features that would lend themselves to intaglio interpretation. The five finalists met all his requirements. The wulfenite, for example, consisted of crystals embedded in a rock matrix.

Buckley wanted to avoid repeating the format he had used in 1974. Each of those stamps was a square on which the design was arranged in a way that encouraged the mailer to see the stamp as diamond-shaped and place it on the envelope with one point down and another point up. (Habit proved too powerful, however, and the great majority of the stamps were affixed in the conventional way.) This time Buckley selected a vertical format in the semi-jumbo size, which is a kind of stamp BEP prints from 160-unit plates.

Use of this size would have required a booklet of larger-than-normal dimensions, and in the end USPS decided to issue the stamps in sheet form, as a se-tenant block of four varieties, rather than as a booklet of five. Two specimens, the smoky quartz-microcline and the gold, were dropped from the quintet Buckley had originally chosen, and one was added, a shiny chunk of copper crystals from

This is Buckley's concept sketch for a cover for the proposed minerals booklet, depicting variscite, wulfenite and smoky quartz/microcline.

Keweenaw Peninsula in upper Michigan. The Citizens' Stamp Advisory Committee also asked Buckley to incorporate the word "Minerals" into his final design for each stamp.

Buckley used the same sheet layout that had been used in 1974, a checkerboard from which the buyer of a pane could break out a multiple that contained all four varieties in either a block or a horizontal strip. The traditional layout of four-variety se-tenants (used earlier in the year on the First Voyage of Columbus commemoratives, for instance) yields only blocks. The difference is shown by the following diagrams:

Usual Format

A B A B A B A B
C D C D C D C D
A B A B A B A B
C D C D C D C D
A B A B A B A B

Minerals Format

A B C D A B C D
C D A B C D A B
A B C D A B C D
C D A B C D A B
A B C D A B C D

The 1974 Mineral Heritage block had been printed in two stages on sheetfed presses, but the new block was produced on BEP's D press, a webfed facility that hadn't been available in 1974.

The Minerals panes were the first printed by BEP that showed in the selvage a pattern of small squares that was associated with a new printing-press video system — albeit one that hadn't been installed yet. The video system, called CC1, was scheduled to be operational on the D press in late 1992 or early 1993.

CC1 was described as a "defect-free manufacturing system" that monitors color and register, displays printing errors and alerts printers when color or register are off. This allows for corrective action on a touch-interactive viewing screen.

The telltale marks appeared in the selvage of two of the four panes on each Minerals sheet, an upper pane and a lower pane. They consisted of eight 1-millimeter colored squares in two parallel rows of four each.

The marks had also been placed in the selvage of the World War II souvenir sheets, which were printed before the Minerals. However, because they were closer to the edge of the paper web than the marks on the Minerals sheets, the marks were trimmed off during the processing of the printed World War II web into post office panes.

The Designs

For the 1974 Mineral Heritage block, Leonard Buckley had made acrylic paintings of the four mineral specimens, which were then used to create the offset plates and guide the Bureau's engravers. Since then, however, BEP had acquired its electronic design center, where images can be scanned into a computer memory and then refined as needed.

Using the design center, Peter Cocci scanned Chip Clark's color photographs, then extracted from the images those elements that would be added by the engravers. What remained was used to make the color separations for the offset plates.

Clark had photographed the four mineral specimens against a neutral background that shaded from dark above to lighter below. He arranged his lighting so each specimen cast a shadow that would provide an artistic base for the design. Part of the shadow on each stamp was engraved, and this portion blended into the offset portion of the shadow in a calculated effort to visually marry the two printing methods.

BEP used the four standard process colors on the offset-printed portions. A fifth offset color, metallic silver, was used for the borders and the large typography. This ink had last been seen on the French Revolution Bicentennial airmail stamp of 1989. Two special intaglio inks were used for the engraved picture portions and the small type in which the minerals' names were set: dark purple for the azurite and dark brown for the other three stamps.

"As in 1974, I wanted to get the most brilliant and colorful part of each stamp in the mineral itself, so that it would stand out,'' Buckley said. "The lettering and backgrounds would be secondary.''

For his lettering and numbers, Buckley chose a typeface called Eras,

Buckley prepared this rough sketch to show CSAC what he had in mind for the size, shape and general design of a block of four mineral stamps.

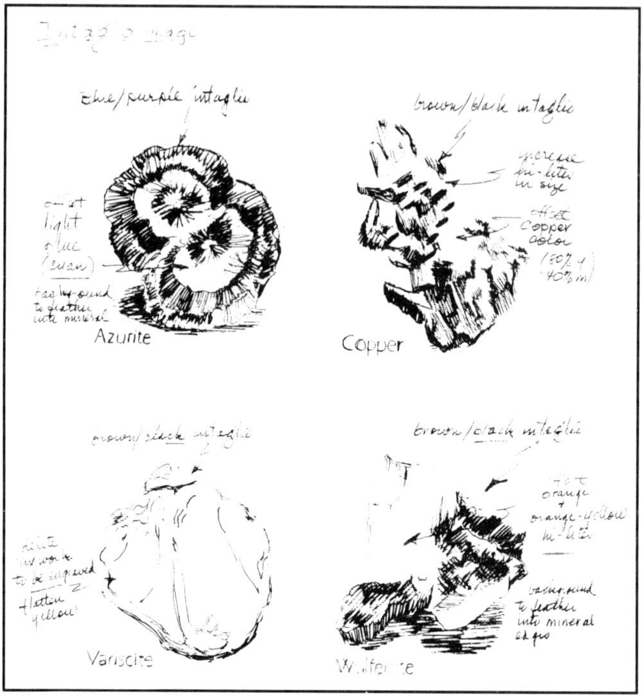

For the guidance of the engravers, Leonard Buckley prepared these pencil sketches of the design areas that were to be hand-engraved and printed in intaglio over the offset-lithographed backgrounds.

a sans-serif type with a slight, not-quite-italic slant to it. He had used Helvetica on the 1974 block, and this time he wanted something "a little different'' but still "as clean, noble and classic'' as Helvetica.

First-Day Facts

John N. Griesemer, vice chairman of the USPS Board of Governors, dedicated the stamps in a public ceremony in the Baird Auditorium of the Smithsonian Institution's National Museum of Natural History September 17. Frank H. Talbot, director of the museum, gave the welcome, and the speaker was Daniel E. Appleman, the associate director for science, who had helped Buckley find appropriate mineral specimens. Honored guests included Lillian Turner, whose advocacy led to the stamps' issuance; Jeffrey E. Post, chairman of the museum's Department of Mineral Sciences, and designer Buckley.

29¢ JUAN RODRIGUEZ CABRILLO

Date of Issue: September 28, 1992

Catalog Number: Scott 2704

Colors: cyan, magenta, yellow, red (PMS 187), black, buff (PMS 155) (offset); black (intaglio)

First-Day Cancel: San Diego, California

FDCs Canceled: 290,720

Format: Panes of 50, vertical, 10 across, 5 down. Offset printing plates of 200 subjects (20 across, 10 around); intaglio printing plate of 200 subjects (20 across, 10 around).

Perf: 11.1 (reciprocating stroke perforator)

Selvage Inscription: "On September 28, 1542,/explorers representing/Spain landed at San/Diego Bay, California." "Juan Rodriguez Cabrillo/led the expedition. He/named the area San/Miguel and claimed it/for Spain." "If he was Portuguese/as many believe, his/name would be spelled/Joao Rodrigues Cabrilho."

Selvage Markings: "©/United States/Postal Service/1991." "Use Correct/ZIP Code/®." USPS logo. Olympic rings with inscription: "OFFICIAL OLYMPIC SPONSOR/36 USC 380."

Designer: Ren Wicks of Beverly Hills, California

Art Director and Project Manager: Jack Williams (USPS)

Typographer: Bradbury Thompson (CSAC)

Modeler: Richard Sennett, Stamp Venturers

Engraver: Yves Baril, Canadian Bank Note Company, Ottawa, Canada

Printing: Printed by Stamp Venturers. Offset printing on a six-color Heidelberg sheetfed press at The Press, Inc., Chanhassen, Minnesota. Intaglio printing by Stamp Venturers on a T.A. sheetfed press at Ogdensburg, New York.

Quantity Ordered: 85,000,000

Quantity Distributed: 85,000,000

Plate/Sleeve Number Detail: 1 black intaglio plate number preceded by letter S and 1 group of 6 offset plate numbers preceded by letter S in selvage of adjacent corner stamps.

Plate/Sleeve Number Combinations: S111111-S1, S222222-S1, S333333-S1, S444444-S1

Tagging: phosphor-coated paper

The Stamp

Juan Rodriguez Cabrillo, the first European to visit what is now California, landed on the shores of San Diego Bay September 28, 1542. Four hundred fifty years to the day afterward, a stamp depicting the explorer was issued in San Diego.

The stamp's principal advocates, members of the Portuguese-American Cabrillo Civic Clubs of California, received an unusual amount of advance notice that their hopes would be realized — more than 3½ years' worth. The news that the stamp would be issued in 1992 was announced by Postmaster General Anthony M. Frank in a speech to the organization's state convention January 28, 1989.

According to *The San Diego Union-Tribune*, the individual who worked longest and hardest for the stamp was Marge Perry, a member of a Cabrillo club in Concord, California, and the wife of a Portuguese immigrant. She had written letters and otherwise promoted the idea for 33 years. She lived long enough to learn that her campaign was successful, but died at the age of 84 in March 1992, a few months before the stamp was actually issued.

One of the people Perry had enlisted in her campaign was then-U.S. Representative Tony Coelho of California, the House Democratic whip. Gary Griffith, writing in *Linn's Stamp News*, reported that Coelho, a Portuguese-American himself, personally lobbied Postmaster General Frank for the stamp.

"I'd known Tony for years," Coelho told Griffith. "So I made a plea and a presentation to him, and we got it through."

The 3,000-odd members of the Cabrillo Civic Clubs claim Cabrillo as a fellow Portuguese, and the Postal Service's first written announcement of the stamp, in February 1989, described him as a "Portuguese explorer." Several encyclopedias, including the *Encyclopedia Britannica*, agree with that historical statement.

However, when the time came to plan the design, USPS was much less certain than before. After the design was completed and released, some Portuguese-Americans objected because the Spanish spelling of the explorer's name, not the Portuguese spelling ("Joao Rodrigues Cabrilho") was to be used on the stamp. In letters of response, the Postal Service explained its position this way:

"Quite frankly, these suggestions (to use the Portuguese spelling) resulted in one of the most exhaustive stamp subject research efforts we have ever undertaken. We learned, for example, that there is widespread scholarly dispute over his birthplace, and many scholars argue that he may not have been Portuguese.

"The Postal Service does not intend to enter that dispute, nor can we resolve it. Whether he was Portuguese or Spanish, virtually all scholars — especially those in the United States — seem comfortable with the familiar Spanish spelling of his name. We chose not to oppose the overwhelming odds, the scholars and the familiarity of countless Americans — especially Californians — by using anything but the traditional Spanish spelling on the stamp design itself."

In its news release announcing details on the stamp's issue, USPS hedged by saying that "though he sailed under the Spanish flag, some historians believe Cabrillo was born in Portugal." And postal officials attempted to satisfy Portuguese-American sensitivities by including this wording in the marginal inscription of each Cabrillo stamp pane:

"If he was Portuguese as many believe, his name would be spelled Joao Rodrigues Cabrilho."

Eighty years earlier, the Post Office Department had planned to use a portrait of Cabrillo on the 10¢ value of the Panama Pacific commemorative set of 1912. "All efforts to find a picture of him proved futile," according to U.S. stamp historian Max G. Johl. After considering an essay that showed two galleons at anchor above the inscription "Cabrillo 1542," the Post Office used a picture labeled "Discovery of San Francisco Bay" instead.

No authentic portrait of Cabrillo turned up in the intervening decades, but officials of the modern-day Postal Service turned out to be less concerned about verifiable accuracy than their long-ago predecessors. They told the artist to invent a likely looking face and call it Cabrillo. Earlier, a similar dispensation had been granted the sculptor of a heroic statue of the explorer that stands in Cabrillo National Monument, at the tip of San Diego's Point Loma.

Stamp Venturers printed the stamp by a combination of six-color offset and single-color intaglio, the intaglio portion being the black typography at the top of the design. It was the company's first stamp to be made by the combination process. The offset work was done at The Press, a company in Chanhassen, Minnesota, and the printed sheets were then sent to Stamp Venturers' new installation in Ogdensburg, New York, for the application of the intaglio portion.

Only 85 million Cabrillo stamps were ordered and distributed, an unusually small number for a single commemorative. Most such issues in recent years have had press runs of 150 million or more.

Cabrillo, whose date of birth is unknown, was a navigator in the Spanish service when he arrived in what is now Mexico in 1520. He participated in the Spanish conquest of Mexico in 1521 and of present-day Guatemala and Honduras in 1523 and 1524.

Leaving Navidad in northwest Mexico on June 27, 1542, with two ships, the *San Salvador* and the *Victoria*, Cabrillo explored the Pacific coast of Lower California and then sailed northward, hoping to find rich cities and a water passage between the Pacific and Atlantic Oceans. He discovered San Diego Bay, San Pedro and Santa Monica Bays, Santa Catalina Island and the islands of the Santa Barbara Channel. He went as far north as Point Reyes, but missed the Golden Gate. Returning south to winter on San Miguel Island, Cabrillo died January 3, 1543, of injuries sustained in a fall. His pilot, Bartolome Ferrelo, continued his explorations later that year and probably reached the Oregon coast.

The Design

For the challenging assignment of painting a portrait of an explorer whose likeness had been lost to history, USPS picked a veteran artist, Ren Wicks of Beverly Hills, California.

Wicks, who was 78 when he began the project in 1990, had previously designed the 10¢ Crossed Flags definitive stamp of 1973, the 29¢ William Saroyan commemorative of 1991 and the 36¢ Sikorsky and 40¢ William Piper airmail stamps. His large output of non-stamp artwork included paintings for the aerospace industry — and the famous poster of actress Jane Russell for Howard Hughes' 1943 movie *The Outlaw*.

The portrait Wicks produced for the Cabrillo commemorative showed a head-and-shoulders view of a handsome, bearded man in casque and cuirass (helmet and breastplate), gazing into the distance. He modeled his imaginary Cabrillo, in part, on two of his acquaintances.

One was Rosario Ullio, the manager of the Sumitomo Bank branch in the Wilshire Boulevard building where Wicks had an office. "He's a handsome Latino, and he had the look I wanted," Wicks said. The artist asked Ullio to let him photograph his face and work from the pictures, but the banker declined. However, Wicks did bestow at least a bit of philatelic immortality on his reluctant model by developing a Cabrillo face whose features, particularly the eyes, mouth and cheekbones, were similar to Ullio's. There were significant differences, as well: The banker was younger than the Cabrillo on the stamp, and was clean-shaven. "But he could see the likeness, and he was actually quite pleased," Wicks said.

Some members of the Citizens' Stamp Advisory Committee said this Cabrillo reminded them of Franco Harris, the former running back of the Pittsburgh Steelers, whose beard and mustache were similar to the ones with which Wicks endowed his explorer. Wicks himself told a newspaper reporter that he saw a similarity in the face to actor Tom Selleck.

At the Western Costume Company of Los Angeles, Wicks rented for $250 a period costume, relying on the advice of a staff member who specialized in the 15th- and 16th-century age of exploration. "Western Costume is a six-story museum of every conceivable prop, outfit, dress and costume — over 2 million of them — and has served the motion picture industry for 66 years," the artist wrote in a letter to Jack Williams. "I have every confidence that their coaching is absolutely accurate and this is the correct uniform for Senor Juan."

Norman Merritt, a designer-illustrator and a former business associate of Wicks, agreed to put on the costume, and Wicks made about 25 photographs of his friend in various heroic poses appropriate to a discoverer. The artist then sketched a series of possible stamp design treatments. CSAC chose a vertical design showing Cabrillo against a background of a sailing ship and a map, and Wicks developed this concept into finished art.

While painting, Wicks added a few refinements. His rented costume helmet was smooth, with no decorations, but he had seen a series of paintings of Cabrillo at the National Monument in which the explorer's casque was covered with raised designs. So Wicks added similar embellishments to his own artwork, including an eagle and other devices borrowed from flags of the period. "It gave the casque a little richer look," he said.

The ship on the stamp, a caravel, was based on a picture in a publication produced by the U.S. Department of the Interior for the National Monument. Wicks' reference for the outline map of San Diego Bay came from an atlas published by the National Geographic Society. Shown prominently on the map is Point Loma, the peninsula that thrusts down from the city of San Diego and forms the western shore of the bay. An aerial view of this peninsula can be seen in the background of the 1935

These are two of some 25 photos artist Ren Wicks made of his friend Norman Merritt in Cabrillo costume for Wicks' use in preparing the stamp design.

Ren Wicks made this group of pencil sketches for CSAC's review as part of the process of finding the most effective combination of Cabrillo image and map background for the stamp design.

stamp that commemorated the California Pacific International Exposition, which was held in San Diego's Balboa Park (Scott 773).

An early plan had been to show a map with a red line that traced Cabrillo's sea route along the California coast, from bay to bay, as far north as Monterey. But it soon became obvious that this was too extensive an area to reduce to tiny dimensions and tuck into a corner of a stamp design, so the decision was made to use a map of San Diego Bay instead.

Wicks' preliminary sketches incorporated the inscription "Discoverer of San Diego Bay." "As we got further into it, we realized he was more than that," Jack Williams said. "He went on to explore the rest of the coast, up the line. So the inscription was changed." The final choice of wording was "Explorer of California 1542."

Cabrillo wasn't the first historical personage to be pictured on a U.S. stamp despite the lack of a known portrait for reference. A previous stamp to bear an artist's conception of a face was the Black Heritage commemorative of 1987 that honored Jean Baptiste Pointe Du Sable, first settler of what is now the city of Chicago.

First-Day Facts

The stamp was dedicated September 28, 1992, at the Cabrillo National Monument by Joseph R. Caraveo, chief operating officer of USPS. Participants in the ceremony included Terry DiMattio, superintendent of the National Monument; Gene Santos, president of Cabrillo Civic Club No. 16; and Mary Giglitto, president of the Cabrillo Festival Inc. Everett Ellis Briggs, U.S. ambassador to Portugal, was an honored guest.

Also on hand was Geraldine Weiss, daughter of the late Marge Perry, the Cabrillo stamp's long-time advocate. Weiss accepted a plaque on behalf of her mother, saying she was sure she was present in spirit.

$5.80 WILD ANIMALS BOOKLET

Date of Issue: October 1, 1992

Catalog Numbers: Scott 2705-2709 (single stamps); 2709a (booklet pane of 5)

Colors: magenta, yellow, cyan, black

First-Day Cancel: New Orleans, Louisiana

FDCs Canceled: 604,205

Format: 4 panes of 5 different horizontal stamps, arranged vertically. Gravure printing cylinders of 200 subjects (10 across, 20 around).

Perf: 10.9 by imperforate (L perforator)

Selvage Markings: Cylinder numbers printed on each pane binding stub. Vertical guidelines sometimes appear on left or right selvage of Flamingo stamp

Cover Markings: "© United States Postal Service 1991 K" and promotional paragraph for National Stamp Collecting Month on inside of front cover. Universal Product Code (UPC) and promotion for Wild Animals activity book for children on outside of back cover. Coupon for children's activity book on inside of back cover.

Designer: Robert Giusti of New Milford, Connecticut

Art Director: Derry Noyes

Project Manager: Joe Brockert (USPS)

Typographer: John Boyd

Printing: Printed for KCS Industries Inc. by Sennett Enterprises in Richmond, Virginia, on a Champlain gravure press. Booklet covers printed on a 6-color Heidelberg sheetfed offset press by The Press, Chanhassen, Minnesota. Perforated and formed into booklets at KCS.

Quantity Ordered: 400,000,000 stamps

Quantity Distributed: 329,244,000 stamps

Cylinder Number Detail: 1 group of 4 gravure cylinder numbers preceded by the letter K on each pane binding stub

Cylinder Number Combination: K1111

Tagging: phosphor-coated paper

The Stamps

As it does each year, USPS in 1992 issued a set of richly colored topical stamps in conjunction with its October celebration of National Stamp Collecting Month.

The 1992 stamps, placed on sale October 1, consisted of a 20-stamp booklet of five varieties featuring wild animals: a giraffe, a giant panda, a flamingo, two king penguins and a white Bengal tiger. Of the five species, only the flamingo is found wild in North America.

This seemed to run counter to the Citizens' Stamp Advisory Committee's first criterion for subject selection, which reads: "It is a general policy that U.S. postage stamps and stationery primarily will feature American or American-related subjects." When a reporter pointed this out at the unveiling of the 1992 stamp program December 11, 1991, Postmaster General Anthony M. Frank defended the Wild Animals stamps by noting that the creatures "are in our zoos." Besides, he said, they would "help educate kids and get kids interested in collecting."

The issue, in fact, was originally called "Zoo Animals." Later CSAC decided to change the name to "Wild Animals" out of its continuing concern that stamps be "politically correct." In this case, CSAC members were afraid that the designation would offend animal-rights activists who believe money spent on zoos would be put to better use protecting animals in their natural habitat.

CSAC left the selection of animals for the booklet to the artist, Robert Giusti of New Milford, Connecticut. When Giusti was asked in 1989 to submit concept sketches for the project, Derry Noyes, the art director, relayed to him only two requirements. First, each stamp had to have a distinctive appearance in terms of the animal's color and the color of the background. Second, the choices had to reflect geographical diversity, with widespread areas of the globe represented.

"I tried to pick animals that were interesting in themselves, animals that were a little unusual," Giusti said. "I wanted to stay away from the totally mundane, and I also wanted to stay with the popular. Pandas, for instance; there was so much publicity about the Washington Zoo pandas and the attempts to breed them. White tigers have always had a fascination for people, including myself.

"I also had to keep color in mind. I didn't want to pick animals that were too bland. Each one I chose has distinctive color or distinctive markings."

Giusti selected and painted stamp art for more than five species, but USPS wouldn't identify the leftovers because of the possibility it will use them for stamps later on.

After the designs of the Wild Animals stamps were made public, USPS learned to its surprise that it had mislabeled one of the species. The design of the stamp showing the heads of two penguins bore the inscription: "Emperor Penguins." However, Ron Knight of San Diego, who saw a full-color illustration of the design in *Linn's Stamp News* for December 30, 1991, was convinced by the shape and size of the orange markings on the birds' heads that they weren't emperors, but were the similar but smaller king penguins.

Knight's letter to *Linn's*, published January 20, 1992, asserted that either the illustration or caption was wrong, and added: "Perhaps you'd better inform the United States Postal Service. Tell them to double-check the design in order to avoid a possible boo-boo."

At *Linn's* request, ornithologists at the Smithsonian Institution's National Museum of Natural History looked at the color transparency of

This is the design of the penguins stamp as USPS first made it public, wrongly identifying the birds as emperor penguins.

the stamp artwork USPS had released. "There's no question that the markings say this is a king penguin, not an emperor," Storrs L. Olson, curator of the Division of Birds, said after comparing the art to published illustrations and stuffed specimens.

Linn's notified USPS of these findings January 14. On January 18, Donald M. McDowell, director of the Office of Stamp and Philatelic Marketing, told the publication that USPS was doing its own double-checking. If an error had been made, he said, there would be time to correct it before the stamps were printed.

Finally, on January 28, McDowell said his office was satisfied, after talking with Storrs Olson and also with Joan Smith, a curator at the National Zoo, that the birds were, in fact, king penguins. Correcting the mistake, he told *Linn's*, would be a simple matter of revising the caption.

The decision was praised by Michael Laurence, editor-publisher of *Linn's*. The fact that the error could be fixed without any great expense or delay, Laurence wrote in his column, was a collateral benefit of the Postal Service's decision to unveil the entire year's stamp designs before the year began. "The mislabeled penguins might not have been detected had USPS followed its traditional practice of withholding stamp images until fairly late in the production process," he explained.

How did the mistake happen? The artist got his birds mixed, according to Joe Brockert, USPS project manager for the booklet.

"Originally, they were labeled just 'penguins,' " Brockert said. "We had 'tiger,' we had 'penguins,' we had 'flamingo,' we had 'panda.' We thought the captions should be more specific, so we went back and called them 'white Bengal tiger' and 'giant panda' . . .

"We asked the artist to please identify the penguins. He identified them as emperor penguins. But he had painted king penguins . . . (Afterward), he said, yes, I was researching both and I simply mixed up my research when I came back and told you I had done one rather than the other.' "

The Postal Service never considered the option of having Giusti change his painting to convert the king penguins into emperors, Brockert said. "The committee hadn't specified that it wanted emperor penguins," he said. "They didn't care if they were emperors or kings. We knew that the painting was good, and we knew that if we went back and thought to do emperor penguins, the emperors would have been a poorer choice. They are fatter, less attractive birds with less coloration. It would have been a less attractive stamp.

"No plates had been made at that point. So it was just a matter of changing the black color separation before the printer (KCS Industries) made the plates."

GIRAFFE. The giraffe (Giraffa camelopardis) of eastern Africa is the tallest of all living land animals. Adult males stand as high as 20 feet. The height comes mostly from the legs and neck; the body is smaller than that of the average horse. The giraffe's neck has only seven vertebrae — the same as in man — but each vertebra is very long, which makes the animal's neck so stiff that it must spread its legs far apart to reach down to drink. Its mottled brown and yellow coat blends with the play of light and shadow among the mimosas and other trees on whose leaves it feeds.

GIANT PANDA. Giant pandas (Ailuropoda melanoleuca), related to bears, live in the mountainous forests of southwestern China, where they feed on bamboo (as the panda shown on the stamp is doing). They are 4 to 5 feet long and can weigh 300 pounds or more. Only about 1,000 specimens are believed to survive. Because the giant panda is a unique mammal and of great appeal to the public, it has become a status symbol for zoos. One of the world's most famous pandas, Ling-Ling, died at Washington's National Zoo December 30, 1992, at the age of 23. She and her mate, Hsing-Hsing, were gifts to the United States from the People's Republic of China.

FLAMINGO. Flamingos stand up to 6 feet tall and have long, sinuous necks, long legs, webbed feet and large, downcurved beaks. Adults are a rich vermilion, shading underneath to rose and pale pink. They breed in colonies, sometimes in enormous numbers, and favor warm brackish or saltwater lakes or lagoons. Here they dine on bottom-dwelling mollusks, using ridges along the sides of their beaks to filter out mud and sand. The American flamingo (Phoenicopterus ruber) is found on Caribbean islands and the coasts of tropical America. Large flocks of captive birds live at Florida's Hialeah Park racetrack and Parrot Jungle.

KING PENGUIN. Penguins are flightless sea birds of the Southern Hemisphere. Their wings are strong narrow flippers with which they propel themselves through the water. The king and emperor are the largest and most colorful species. Emperors, standing 3 feet high and weighing up to 100 pounds, are the world's largest and heaviest sea birds. Kings, at 30 to 40 pounds, are still more than twice as heavy as any of the smaller penguin species. The emperor breeds only on the Antarctic continent, while the king (Aptenodytes patagonica) breeds on South Georgia and other islands in the Antarctic seas. A stamp of South Georgia (Scott 54) depicts the king penguin.

WHITE BENGAL TIGER. Tigers are the largest of all the big cats and are native to Asia. The normal coloration is yellow to brown on the upper side, striped with black. White Bengal tigers (Panthera tigris tigris) are mutants, colored a light ivory to white. Their eyes are blue, but often turn yellowish when the animal is excited and the pupils are opened wide. All zoo-kept whites are descendants of a male that was captured in Rewa, India, and bred with a normally pigmented female. His mate bore young of normal color, but when the father was then mated with one of his daughters the resulting young were likewise white.

The Designs

Robert Giusti's acrylic-on-canvas paintings are posterlike, with hard edges and bright colors. CSAC liked his work on the Wild Animals booklet so much that he was assigned another stamp project as well: to prepare paintings of American wildlife to use on definitive stamps as they became necessary. As it turned out, two of those definitives — the Wood

Duck booklet and Cardinal sheet stamp — were issued in 1991, before the Wild Animals booklet, even though they were designed afterward.

Joe Brockert, the Wild Animals project manager, expressed the general enthusiasm at USPS for Giusti's work. "His originals are just so incredibly lifelike," he said. "They have a rather stylized look to them; I mean, they aren't absolutely 100 percent scientifically accurate, perhaps, but they are so real and lifelike and three-dimensional . . . that that is the overriding factor. And they reproduce very well down in stamp size.

"With the Wild Animals, the artwork remained virtually unchanged from start to finish. I can't think of a single change we had him make in any of the original paintings. They basically came in finished."

For reference, Giusti used photographs from his own files and other sources, but he adapted the creatures' poses as necessary to fit the animals within the narrow horizontal framework prescribed for each stamp.

"To zoom in on the images and show each one from about the neck up was my idea, because I wanted to make them as graphic as possible," Giusti said. By zooming in, he said, he could make "the yin and yang" — the negative and positive shapes — work. "In other words," he said, "the outer shape, the background shape, the part that's not the animal, becomes part of the design, really, and you can do that when you close in on something. It's awfully hard to do it when you add other elements to the picture."

For example, Giusti said, he had to stretch and loop the flamingo's neck merely to fit it into the space. "It would have looked awkward, and peculiar, to have had just the head and a small piece of neck and then have a lot of space on the left and right," he said. "I used the neck as space filler. The same with the giraffe. The penguins — by adding a second one, I also helped fill space. So I used different devices to utilize that space, leaving room for the denominations and the captions."

If the layouts had been vertical, the task

This is how the Wild Animals booklet was intended to look until Postal Service officials decided that the stamps needed to be narrower so as not to encroach on the FIMs (facing identification marks) printed on business reply envelopes. To change the aspect ratio, a white line bearing the creature's name was added to the bottom of each stamp.

would have been easier in the case of the giraffe and flamingo, and a single penguin would have filled the allotted space, Giusti said. But the tiger, in a vertical format, probably would have required a frontal view.

"As it turned out," he said, "I'm happy I was able to do it the way I did. I particularly liked the flamingo because I liked the way it curved into that space. And it was true to life; flamingos can twist around, and can actually loop their necks."

For his backgrounds, Giusti was told to stick with solid, basically primary colors that would be light enough to show an overprinted black "USA 29" to good advantage. He made the background blue for the giraffe, yellow for the panda, bluish-green for the flamingo, violet for the penguins and a yellowish-green for the tiger, and he graded each one from light to dark tones for added artistic interest.

As originally designed, the booklet stamps had an elongated aspect

Postal Service officials considered using this poster, created for National Stamp Collecting Month, as the basis for the Wild Animals booklet cover, but decided it contained too much detail.

These were two of Robert Giusti's preliminary sketches for the Wild Animals booklet cover. The final version combined giraffe, panda and leafy branch.

ratio, 1.75 inches wide by .88 inches deep, like the Classic Cars of 1988, the Steamboats of 1989 and other topical booklets prior to 1990. But it turned out that stamps of these dimensions, when arranged horizontally, were causing trouble in mail processing. They sometimes intruded on the facing identification marks (FIMs) imprinted at the top of business reply envelopes, which interfered with the FIMs' purpose: to identify pre-barcoded mail to automated postal equipment.

As a result, USPS decided to make future booklet stamps in the standard commemorative dimensions, 1.56 inches wide by .99 inches deep. But rather than ask Giusti to repaint his animals, or crop his artwork so tightly at the sides that it was spoiled, USPS merely changed the aspect ratio of the Wild Animals stamps by adding a white strip beneath each picture on which the name of the creature could be printed in black type. This also helped avert another potential problem by providing enough white space on the stamp to allow a good read of the tagging by automatic facer-canceler machines.

Giusti also designed the booklet cover. USPS officials at first considered adapting the Stamp Collecting Month poster ("Do Something Wild! Collect Stamps") for use on the booklet. However, they concluded that the poster, showing all five of the featured species in a junglelike setting, was too detailed to be reduced effectively to booklet size.

The booklet cover assignment called for vertically arranged artwork, and Giusti depicted a stylized, almost whimsical giraffe, its neck extended, munching on leaves, alongside a panda bear. His original sketch for the cover had included a penguin, but it crowded the design too much, so the bird was removed and replaced with a piece of the branch on which the giraffe was feeding.

First-Day Facts

William T. Johnstone, one of USPS' newly named vice presidents, dedicated the booklet October 1 in a public ceremony at the Odenheimer Sea Lion Pool at the Audubon Zoological Garden in New Orleans, Louisiana. Craig Dinsmore, general curator of the Audubon Zoo, was the principal speaker.

Although it was announced that New Orleans would be the only place where the booklets would be sold October 1, they were actually released in locations across the country on that date as a result of a USPS communications lapse.

Instructions in the *Postal Bulletin*, an internal USPS publication distributed to all post offices, had stated: "Do Not Place (the Wild Animals stamps) on Sale Before October 1, 1992." This in itself wasn't unique; several other stamp issues of recent years have had similar misinformation published in the *Postal Bulletin*. Each time, however, the misinformation was later corrected in communications to post offices.

In this case, however, other USPS messages to postmasters regarding the Wild Animals stamps also indicated that the stamps could be sold as of October 1. One such communication was an Advice of Shipment form (3309), which serves as a stamp invoice to post offices but also gives the date when the stamps may be sold to the public. The form for the Wild Animals stamps listed October 1 as the public sale date. *Linn's Stamp News*, in its first report on the subject, said the stamps had been sold in Pittsburgh, Pennsylvania, on that day, as well as in *Linn's* hometown of Sidney, Ohio.

What this meant was that the Wild Animals stamps were — uninten-

USPS authorized these special pictorial cancellations for the Wild Animals booklet, one for first-day covers and the other for canceling machines in post offices throughout the country.

The pandas on this pictorial postmark for Stamp Collecting Month visually overwhelm the panda on the stamp beneath.

tionally — a part of a select group of modern U.S. stamp issues that were released across the country on a single date, a group that includes the 4¢ Project Mercury (Scott 1193), 5¢ John F. Kennedy (Scott 1246) and 8¢ U.S. Postal Service (Scott 1396).

Like most other U.S. stamps of 1992, the Wild Animals also turned up on mail with postmarks much earlier than the scheduled release date. The earliest known use of a Wild Animals stamp, in the *Linn's Stamp News* year-end tally of such usages, was September 2.

For first-day covers from New Orleans, USPS created a square pictorial handstamp cancellation. It depicted outline drawings of a panda, giraffe and flamingo in a tropical setting.

USPS also authorized a special machine cancellation die to promote stamp collecting. It was used beginning September 1 at 155 participating postal facilities in all 50 states. The die, showing the faces of two pandas in outline, carried the Stamp Collecting Month slogan: "Do Something Wild: Collect Stamps!" Unfortunately, the choice of image for the die-hub cancellation wasn't an aesthetic success: The panda faces, with their solid black ears, noses and eye patches, tended to visually overwhelm the stamps they canceled.

SPECIAL STAMPS

Special stamps are issued for specific mailing purposes, are customarily printed in greater quantities than commemoratives and are on sale for longer periods. The year 1992 saw 12 such issues.

One was the Love stamp, which this year was issued only in sheet form, at the first-class rate. The other 11 specials were Christmas stamps in various designs and formats.

The traditional Christmas stamp was made in both sheet and booklet form, as usual. The contemporary Christmas issue, however, was available in an unprecedented three different formats: sheet, booklet and self-adhesive. The last-named was made in dollar-bill-sized sheetlets for dispensing from automatic teller machines (ATMs).

Both the sheet and booklet versions of the contemporary Christmas stamp included four different designs, arranged in se-tenant blocks of four. For the ATM version, only one of the four designs was used.

29¢ LOVE

Date of Issue: February 6, 1992

Catalog Number: Scott 2618

Colors: green, blue, red, black, purple

First-Day Cancel: Loveland, Colorado

FDCs Canceled: 218,043

Format: Panes of 50, vertical, 10 across, 5 down. Gravure printing cylinders of 300 subjects (20 across, 15 around).

Perf: 10.9 (L perforator)

Selvage Markings: "© USPS 1991." "USE CORRECT ZIP CODE ®."

Designer: Uldis Purins of Boston, Massachusetts

Art Director and Typographer: Richard Sheaff

Project Manager: Joe Brockert (USPS)

Printing: printed by American Bank Note Company, Los Angeles, California, on 8-color combination gravure-intaglio webfed press. Color separations by Intaglio Corporation, Chicago, Illinois. Cylinders by Intaglio Corporation.

Quantity Ordered: 900,000,000

Quantity Distributed: 835,000,000

Cylinder Number Detail: 1 group of 5 gravure cylinder numbers preceded by the letter U alongside corner stamp

Cylinder Number Combinations: U11111, U21111, U21112, U21212, U21222, U22222, U22223, U32223, U33223, U43234, U43334

Tagging: phosphor-coated paper

The Stamp

A new 29¢ Love stamp in sheet form made its debut in Loveland, Colorado, February 6, in time for at least some postal customers to use on Valentine's Day cards and letters. Depicting a large red heart emerging from an open envelope, it replaced another 29¢ Love stamp, featuring a heart-shaped Earth, that had been in service for less than nine months.

The stamp covered the basic rate for first-class letters and was the only Love item to make its appearance in 1992. There was no new Love booklet, no new 52¢ Love stamp and no new Love stamped envelope. Quantities on hand of the 1991 versions of those items were sufficient to meet customer demand, USPS said.

The heart-in-envelope design was the 12th in the long-running Love series, which began in 1973. The stamp was printed by Jeffries Bank Note of Los Angeles, California, a division of the American Bank Note Company. Jeffries had also produced the 25¢ sheet and booklet Love stamps of 1990, the 29¢ sheet and booklet Love stamps of 1991 and the 52¢ Love sheet stamp of 1991.

However, contrary to preliminary reports, the 1992 stamp, unlike its 1991 counterpart, came in only one perforation-gauge variety.

Several months after the 1991 Love stamps first appeared, *Linn's Stamp News* disclosed that the sheet version existed in two forms: with bull's-eye perforations that met in a perfect matchup at the points where horizontal and vertical perforations crossed (perf 13), and L perforations that produced imperfect holes at the intersections (perf 10.9).

This happened, ABNC said, because of equipment failure. The stamps were originally processed on an Ormag rotary perforator, which is an on-press harrow perforator. But the Ormag broke down, and processing was switched to an off-line L perforator.

Because a long delay in repairing the Ormag was anticipated, ABNC originally planned to begin production of the 1992 Love stamps on the L perforator and move it to the repaired Ormag in mid-run. Thomas Harris, vice president in charge of government sales for ABNC, told *Linn's* that collectors should expect the same two perf varieties on the 1992 stamp that they had seen on the 1991.

Later, however, postal officials decided to keep production of the stamp consistent and avoid unnecessary varieties by processing the entire run of the 1992 Love stamp on the L perforator.

The Design

The 1992 Love stamp design was the work of Uldis Purins of Boston, Massachusetts. Purins was a staff designer at Sheaff Design Inc. of Needham, Massachusetts, a company with which USPS had contracted to provide design support services. The firm was founded by Richard Sheaff, a design coordinator for USPS who has personally designed many stamps and served as art director for others. Sheaff later sold his interest in the company, although it continued to bear his name.

Purins' original heart-in-the-envelope design was one of a number of

In developing Uldis Purins' heart-in-the-envelope concept sketch into a finished design, art director Richard Sheaff proposed this variation in which the word "Love" would have been given a definition, "Giving is Love." CSAC preferred to stay with the practice of using the word "Love" by itself.

concept sketches for Love stamps and other recurring types prepared by Sheaff Design staffers and shown to CSAC. After the committee gave its approval, Richard Sheaff reworked the concept into the finished stamp design, using his Macintosh computer to generate the image and typography. The word "LOVE" was in a typeface known as Berkeley Medium.

Like all previous Love stamps, this one was printed by gravure, but instead of the customary process colors, which blend to form the full range of tones, the printer used individual or self colors. Purins' original sketch had placed the red heart inside an orange envelope with a rose pink background shading from dark at the top to light at the bottom. Sheaff changed the colors to a cooler combination. He retained the red heart, but prescribed blue for the envelope paper, black for the envelope outline, green for the background and purple for the word "LOVE."

First-Day Facts

Regional Postmaster General John G. Mulligan dedicated the Love stamp in a public ceremony at the Hatfield Chilson Center in Loveland, a Denver suburb.

Loveland has been a favorite postmark of Valentine's Day correspondents since 1947. In that year Elmer Ivers, the local postmaster, and Ted Thompson, president of the Loveland Chamber of Commerce, began an organized remailing operation for the holiday. The program included a valentine cachet with imprinted verse written by Thompson and his wife, Mabel. Some 300 valentines were remailed that first year. In the years that followed, as the number of cards sent for the postmark grew, the Thompsons continued to write the poetry imprinted on the cachet. An estimated 300,000 cards passed through the Loveland post office during the 1991 Valentine's Day mailing season, USPS said.

Mabel Thompson spoke at the first-day ceremony for the 1992 Love stamp. Her husband Ted was scheduled to attend, but illness prevented him from being there. He died a month later.

29¢ CHRISTMAS MADONNA AND CHILD SHEET STAMP

Date of Issue: October 22, 1992

Catalog Number: Scott 2710

Colors: red, yellow, pink, blue (offset); red, brown (intaglio)

First-Day Cancel: Washington, D.C.

FDCs Canceled: 201,576 (includes booklet stamps)

Format: Panes of 50, vertical, 10 across, 5 down. Offset printing plates of 300 subjects (15 across, 20 around) and intaglio printing sleeves of 600 subjects (15 across, 40 around).

Perf: 11.2 (Eureka off-line perforator)

Selvage Markings: "© UNITED STATES/POSTAL SERVICE 1991." "USE CORRECT ZIP CODE ®."

Designer and Typographer: Bradbury Thompson (CSAC)

Project Manager and Art Director: Jack Williams (USPS)

Engravers: Thomas Hipschen (vignette, BEP); Gary Slaght (lettering and numerals, BEP)

Modeler: Clarence Holbert (BEP)

Printing: printed by BEP on 6-color offset, 3-color intaglio D press (902)

Quantity Ordered: 300,000,000

Quantity Distributed: 300,000,000

Plate/Sleeve Number Detail: 1 group of 4 offset plate numbers and 1 single-digit intaglio sleeve number in selvage of adjacent stamps above or below left or right corner (outer panes), or 1 group of 4 offset plate numbers and 1 single-digit intaglio sleeve number in selvage of adjacent stamps alongside upper-left or upper-right corner (middle panes).

Plate/Sleeve Number Combinations: 1111-1, 1112-1, 2223-1, 3334-1, 4445-1

Tagging: overall

The Stamp

In 1991 both the traditional and contemporary Christmas stamps were non-denominated. That's because at the time they were produced USPS wasn't certain whether the first-class letter rate during the holiday season would be 29¢ or 30¢. Once it was certain that the rate would remain at 29¢, the Postal Service formally assigned that value to the stamps. So the Christmas stamps of 1992 were the first in the annual series to actually include the 29¢ denomination in their designs.

Each year, the traditional Christmas stamp reproduces a centuries-old image of Mary and the Infant Jesus. The source of most of those images, in recent years, has been the collection of paintings in the National Gallery of Art in Washington, D.C. In 1991 the Postal Service broke from that pattern and reproduced a detail from a 15th-century work in the Museum of Fine Arts in Houston, Texas. But in 1992 the Postal Service returned to the National Gallery for its artwork.

The painting chosen was *Madonna and Child With Saints* by Giovanni Bellini, an artist of the Italian Renaissance. Bellini (circa 1430-1516) made his native city, Venice, a center of Renaissance art comparable to Florence and Rome. Most of the major Venetian painters of the early 16th century were his pupils. A painter of natural light, he worked in tempera in his early years, and later became a master of oil painting.

The National Gallery owns a large collection of Bellini works, which occupy three main floor galleries in the west building. One of those rooms is devoted to a single painting, *The Feast of the Gods,* which the Citizens' Stamp Advisory Committee's vice chairman, C. Douglas Lewis, curator of sculpture at the National Gallery, calls "arguably the most important Renaissance painting in America."

The madonna painting from which the stamp design was adapted is on wood, approximately 29¾ inches deep by 20 inches wide, and was painted circa 1490. It depicts a standing nude Christ child in the embrace of Mary. At the left is St. Peter, identifiable by the key he holds, and at the right is a female saint — a curiously sly look in her eyes — whose identity is unknown. David Brown, a curator of Renaissance painting at the National Gallery, said at the first-day ceremony that because she holds a cross she may be St. Helena, to whom is attributed the discovery of the cross on which Christ died. She may also be St. Margaret, he said.

The painting was purchased by the Samuel H. Kress Foundation in New York in 1940 and given to the National Gallery in 1943, only two years after the museum was founded.

Each year since 1988, USPS has marketed silverplated Christmas ornaments containing specimens of the current year's Christmas stamps sealed inside transparent epoxy. These have been available in pairs, one containing a traditional Christmas stamp, the other containing a contemporary stamp. Similar ornaments were made for 1992, but in only limited quantities, according to the manufacturer, The Heritage Collections, Ltd., of Falls Church, Virginia.

"Production of the ornaments has been sharply reduced — from an average of about 75,000 a year — to a 1992 edition of only 1,000," the company said in a news release. "Moreover, none are available at post offices. The cutback is a direct result of actions taken this year by the U.S. Postal Service. The reason can be attributed to the Postal Service's reorganization and its across-the-board curtailment of all collectible products."

The company said it would take orders for the ornaments at $14.95 each, or $25 per pair, until January 18, 1993.

The Design

For the past two decades, the great majority of designs for the traditional Christmas stamps have been the work of Bradbury Thompson, design coordinator for CSAC. Thompson performed that task again with the 1992 stamp.

The design conformed to the formula Thompson had fol-

These are the 1992 Christmas stamp ornaments. The manufacturer reported that only 1,000 were produced this year, compared to an average of 75,000 sold annually by USPS in previous years, because of the Postal Service's curtailment of product sales.

lowed since 1986. He cropped the Bellini painting so as to show only the head, shoulders and chest of the nude Christ child, and to eliminate the figures on either side of Mary. He placed this image inside a rectangular frame, with the denomination and "USA" in an upper corner of the frame in dropout white lettering. Across the top of the stamp, in red capitals, was the word "Christmas." Across the bottom, in small black type, was the line identifying the painting: "Bellini c. 1490 National Gallery."

This design formula has varied only slightly from year to year. The date of the painting was included for the first time in 1991. And in that year, because the Christmas stamps were non-denominated, the word "Christmas" at the top of the design was augmented by "1991 USA," so that postal clerks, seeing the stamp on mail in the future, could confirm that it had a value of 29¢.

This is the painting **Madonna and Child with Saints** *by Giovanni Bellini on which the 1992 traditional Christmas stamp design was based. The male saint is Peter; the female is unidentified, but may be Margaret or Helena.*

All traditional Christmas stamps since 1988 have been printed by the Bureau of Engraving and Printing in a combination of offset and intaglio. Certain combination-press stamps are classified by USPS as basically offset with intaglio support — meaning that only the typography is engraved, or that engraving is added to the design in limited amounts to strengthen some of the details. The Christmas stamps are in the opposite category: They are intaglio stamps with offset support.

Each year, Thomas Hipschen, BEP's premier engraver, has recreated the madonna, child and background within complex patterns of finely engraved lines, curves and dots that could stand alone as a complete design. The effect of the offset printing beneath the intaglio has been to contribute a multicolored glow to the work. For the 1992 stamp, the Bureau used an unusual combination of offset colors: red, yellow, pink, and blue. The intaglio portion of the vignette's design was in brown, and the intaglio lettering at the top was red.

First-Day Facts

Both the sheet and booklet versions of the 1992 traditional Christmas stamp were dedicated October 22 at a ceremony at the Main Auditorium of the East Building, National Gallery of Art.

Joseph J. Mahon Jr., USPS vice president for labor relations, officiated. David Brown, the Gallery's curator of Southern Renaissance painting, was the principal speaker.

First-day cover collectors were given 60 days to submit addressed envelopes for first-day cancellations. Collectors were encouraged to buy the stamps and affix them to the envelopes themselves. However, as usual, USPS offered to affix Christmas stamps to customer-supplied, addressed envelopes in return for payment of the face value of the stamps. The Postal Service declined to affix combinations of traditional and contemporary stamps, but would postmark customer-prepared covers bearing combinations. Those submitting such covers were instructed to specify which cancellation they wanted: Washington, D.C., or Kansas City, Missouri, the first-day city for the contemporary Christmas stamps.

$5.80 CHRISTMAS MADONNA AND CHILD BOOKLET

Date of Issue: October 22, 1992

Catalog Number: Scott 2710 (single stamp); 2710a (booklet pane of 10)

Colors: blue, yellow, pink, red (offset); red, brown (intaglio)

First-Day Cancel: Washington, D.C.

FDCs Canceled: 201,576 (includes sheet stamps)

Format: 2 panes of 10 stamps each, arranged vertically, 2 across by 5 down. Offset printing plates of 300 subjects (15 across, 20 around) and intaglio printing sleeves of 600 subjects (15 across, 40 around).

Perf: 11.2 by 11.2 by imperforate (Eureka off-line perforator)

Selvage Markings: Sleeve number on binding stub of each pane. Pattern of 6 1-millimeter-square colored marks arranged in 2 parallel rows of 3 marks each to left of sleeve number on 7 percent of booklet panes.

Cover Markings: "© United States Postal Service 1991" and promotion for printed stamped envelopes on inside of front cover. Universal Product Code (UPC) and promotion for 1992 Commemorative Stamp Collection on outside of back cover. Coupon for Commemorative Stamp Collection on inside of back cover.

Designer and Typographer: Bradbury Thompson (CSAC)

Project Manager and Art Director: Jack Williams (USPS)

Engravers: Thomas Hipschen (vignette, BEP); Gary Slaght (lettering and numerals, BEP)

Modeler: Clarence Holbert (BEP)

Printing: Printed by BEP on 9-color intaglio-offset D press (902). Booklet covers printed on a 6-color Goebel Optiforma offset press (043). Booklets formed on standard bookbinding equipment.

Quantity Ordered: 342,234,000 in booklets; 7,020,000 in unfolded panes

Quantity Distributed: 342,234,000 in booklets; 7,020,000 in unfolded panes

Plate/Sleeve Number Detail: 1 intaglio sleeve number on each pane binding stub

Sleeve Number: 1

Tagging: overall

The Stamp

As in previous years, the booklet version of the traditional Christmas stamp was identical to the sheet version except that each booklet stamp had at least one straight edge. This difference was accurately reflected in the full-color reproduction of the stamp that appeared on the booklet cover; the stamp had a straight edge along the left side.

Even though this reproduction was considerably larger than the actual stamp, USPS took the precaution of canceling it with a diagonal black line across the upper-left corner. The same kind of defacing line was used on the enlarged images of the Toy Locomotive stamp that decorated the covers of the Christmas Toys booklet and the sheetlet of Christmas stamps made for sale in automatic teller machines (ATMs).

Information on the Washington, D.C., first-day ceremony can be found in the preceding chapter. For first-day covers of the booklet stamp that were fully serviced by USPS, only full panes of 10 stamps were affixed at a cost of $2.90.

29¢ CHRISTMAS TOYS SHEET STAMP (BLOCK OF FOUR)

Date of Issue: October 22, 1992

Catalog Numbers: Scott 2711-2714 (single stamps); 2714a (block of 4)

Colors: black, yellow, magenta, cyan, green

First-Day Cancel: Kansas City, Missouri

FDCs Canceled: 461,937 (includes booklet stamps)

Format: Panes of 50, horizontal, 5 across, 10 down. Offset printing plates of 300 subjects (15 across, 20 around).

Perf: 11.2 (reciprocating stroke perforator)

Selvage Markings: "Use Correct/ZIP Code ®." "© United States/Postal Service 1991." Plate position diagram with one block shaded and inscription "This plate position/during printing."

Designer and typographer: Lou Nolan of McLean, Virginia

Art Director and Project Manager: Elizabeth A. Altobell (USPS)

Printing: Printed by Ashton-Potter America Inc., Amherst, New York, on 5-color sheetfed offset press. Stamps perforated, processed and shipped by Ashton-Potter America.

Quantity Ordered: 500,000,000

Quantity Distributed: 500,000,000

Plate Number Detail:	1 group of 5 offset plate numbers preceded by the letter P on selvage above the corner stamp on top pane, below the corner stamp on bottom pane
Plate Number Combinations:	P11111, P22222, P33333, P44444
Tagging:	phosphor-coated paper

The Stamps

The 1992 contemporary Christmas stamp issue consisted of a se-tenant block of four depicting antique Christmas toys. It was the fourth se-tenant block in the 30-year history of Christmas stamps; the others appeared in 1964, 1970 and 1982.

The toys, all on wheels, were a race horse with jockey, a locomotive with coal car, a horse-drawn fire pumper (which the Postal Service announcement erroneously described as "a steam engine") and a steamship. The block was similar in appearance to another se-tenant block of Christmas stamps, issued in 1970 (Scott 1415-1418). That block, like this one, displayed antique toys against a plain white background.

The 1992 stamps were printed by Ashton-Potter America Inc. of Amherst, New York. Like the 50-stamp American Wildflowers pane, which Ashton-Potter had produced earlier in the year, the Christmas toys were printed by offset lithography, without an intaglio element. USPS had previously considered the intaglio printing an essential addition to offset stamps to deter counterfeiting. Instead, Ashton-Potter took other steps for security.

First, a special green ink containing metallic elements was used to print the "29 USA" inscription. In its announcement, USPS said this ink "blackens when photocopied or scanned during the color separation

This earlier se-tenant block depicting antique Christmas toys, designed by Stevan Dohanos, was issued in 1970.

This photograph shows the location of the hidden dates on the contemporary Christmas stamps printed by Ashton-Potter America Inc.

process." Actually, according to Barry Switzer, vice president and general manager of Ashton-Potter America, if the stamps were copied on a color copier the letters and numbers printed in this ink would tend to break up rather than blacken.

Second, each of the four designs included a "© 1992" inscription, in microscopic black characters. These inscriptions were reminiscent of the hidden dates that Canada included in its stamp designs for several decades, beginning in the 1920s, to show off the skill of its steel engravers. The dates on the Christmas Toys stamps, which require a strong magnifying glass to see, were located on the vertical support beneath the pony; along the lower edge of the locomotive boiler just in front of the large wheel; on the left side of the front crossbar of the fire pumper, and on the red trim on the top deck of the steamship, at the very front. The printers incorporated them into the designs from type when they made the black color separation.

Third, an extra-fine screen, 300 lines to the inch, was used to make the four color separations that together form the colors on the finished stamps, and a small patch of magenta dots, made with a super-fine 390-line screen, was added to each stamp image. These patches, which also require a strong glass to detect, were located between two wheel spokes on the racehorse, locomotive and fire pumper stamps, and on the covered open deck at the stern of the steamship between two of the roof supports. Ashton-Potter America had previously incorporated similar patches of microscopic dots into its Wildflowers stamps.

An additional security measure was the use of prephosphored paper, a step the company had also taken with the Wildflowers issue. The paper had the phosphorescent compound zinc orthosilicate embedded in it, rather than suspended in a lacquer and applied as a coating.

The stamps were printed in sheets of 300, which were then divided into panes of 50 for distribution to post offices. As it had done with the Wildflowers stamps, Ashton-Potter America included a diagram in the selvage of each pane, next to the plate numbers, indicating which position that pane had occupied on the sheet.

The contemporary Christmas stamps were also issued in booklet form, using the same four designs, but the booklet stamps were produced by Multi-Color Corporation for the American Bank Note Company. Because these stamps were printed by the gravure process, there was no

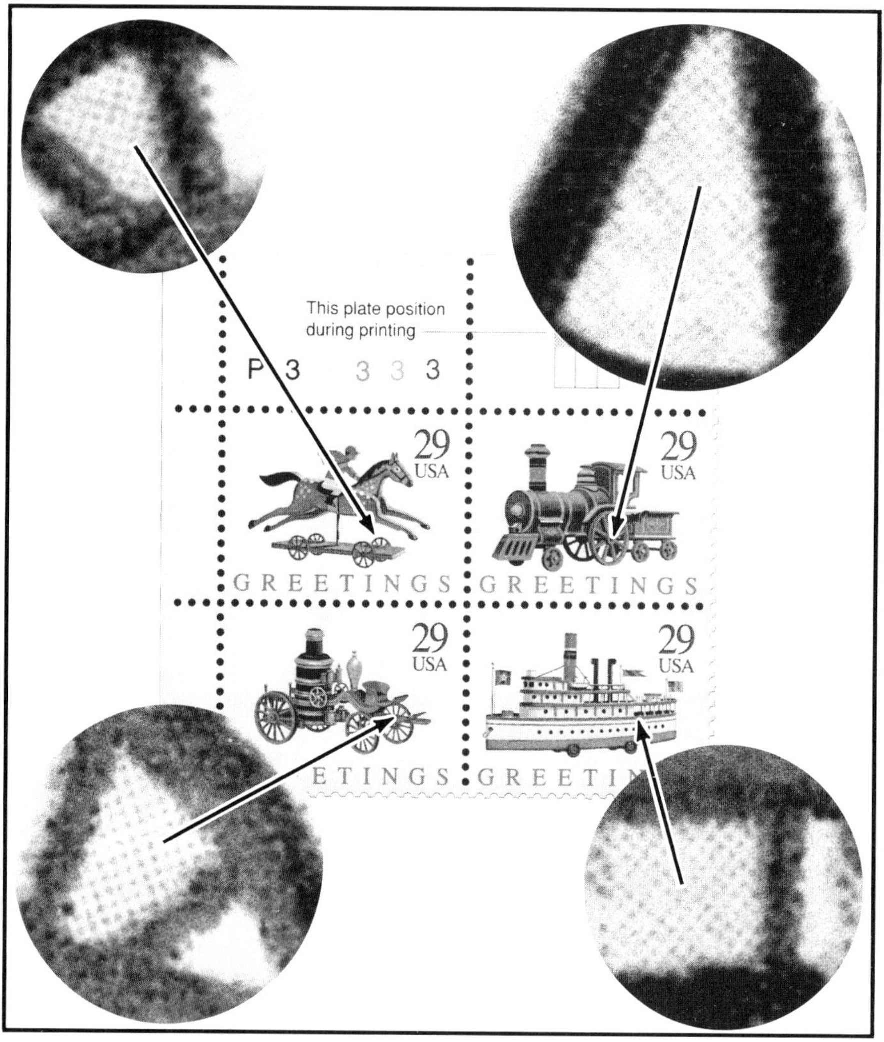

These blowups show the location of the patches of extra-fine screen dots placed in the designs of the contemporary Christmas stamps as a security measure.

need to add dates and dot patches to the designs for security. In addition, the toy locomotive stamp was issued in self-adhesive form for vending through automatic teller machines. (See the next two chapters.)

The Designs

Lou Nolan of McLean, Virginia, designed the stamps, painting his pictures in water-soluble designer colors on illustration board. Nolan had previously designed several stamps in the Transportation series, as well as the 22¢ Certified Public Accountants commemorative and 14¢ Take Pride in America postal card of 1987.

The artist submitted three different design ideas for Christmas stamps in the form of layouts to the Postal Service. The Postal Service chose one of them, an antique toy, and asked him to develop three other designs with similar subject matter.

While searching for pictorial reference material, Nolan visited a friend, William Sharon Farr Jr., at his home in Washington, D.C. Farr was a former graphic artist in the advertising business who had taken up the trade of making and selling items of folk art, including toys, out of wood and other materials. Two of the toys in the block of stamps — the horse with jockey and the steamboat — were based on photographs Nolan took of toys made by Farr.

The horse on the stamp was actually a composite of two wooden horses

Lou Nolan based two of his paintings for the Antique Toys block of four on these wooden toys made by his friend, William Sharon Farr Jr. of Washington, D.C. Nolan also incorporated elements of another of Farr's carved horses in his design. On the stamps, the colors are somewhat different from those on the original toys: The jockey on the stamp has a red rather than a blue coat, and the steamboat is cream-colored and blue rather than white and blue.

This Transportation coil stamp issued in 1981 (Scott 1908) depicted an Amoskeag fire pumper of the 1860s. One of the toys on the 1992 Christmas se-tenant block is a replica of this vehicle.

Farr had made as part of a large set that included several racing thoroughbreds and a portion of the grandstand at Churchill Downs in Louisville, Kentucky, site of the Kentucky Derby. Nolan, in his painting, added the wheeled platform beneath the horse.

Nolan found the model for his fire pumper in the collection of the Smithsonian Institution. The toy, located in the National Museum of American History's Division of Domestic Life, was of painted cast iron, and came with three horses and a driver. In his painting, Nolan changed the pewter-colored trim to gold, and depicted only the vehicle. The toy measured 8½ inches high, 6½ inches wide and 21½ inches long (with horses included). Made around 1910 or 1915 by the Wilkins Toy Works of Keene, New Hampshire, it was one of a number of objects given to the Smithsonian in 1968 by a Mrs. Margaret White Fink.

A reader of the *American Philatelist*, Peter Arth, wrote to the magazine to say that the toy pumper was a replica of a 19th-century New England fire engine, equipped with a steam-driven water pump, called the "Amoskeag Steamer." Coincidentally, the Postal Service had reproduced the image of a real Amoskeag fire pumper on its 20¢ red Transportation coil stamp of 1981 (Scott 1908).

Nolan based his painting of the toy locomotive on an illustration in a book. He could no longer remember the book's name or where he had obtained it, he said.

The artist also offered the Postal Service a layout for a fifth stamp, depicting a toy circus wagon with a lion inside. But the concept of a caged animal didn't appeal to some members of the Citizens' Stamp Advisory Committee, and the design wasn't used.

One of Lou Nolan's proposed Christmas toy designs, showing a circus wagon with a lion, wasn't used for the block of four.

First-Day Facts

The contemporary Christmas stamps, both panes and booklets, were dedicated in a ceremony at Hallmark Cards Corporate Headquarters in Kansas City, Missouri.

William Brown, St. Louis, Missouri, area manager for USPS, dedicated the stamps, substituting for Deputy Postmaster General Michael S. Coughlin. The principal speakers were Mary Harris Francis, co-founder of the Toy and Miniature Museum of Kansas City, and Kansas City Mayor Emmanuel Cleaver. Other speakers included two Hallmark executives, Laurie Beeson, vice president for marketing, and Charles Hucker, division vice president for public affairs and communications.

For mail-order first-day cover customers, USPS affixed stamps to envelopes on request, but only in specified ways: a random single pane stamp, a block of four pane stamps, a random single booklet stamp or a booklet pane of four stamps. On request, USPS also applied either a Washington, D.C., or Kansas City first-day cancellation to any combination of the 1992 contemporary and traditional Christmas stamps, but only if the stamps were already affixed.

$5.80 CHRISTMAS TOYS PANE OF FOUR BOOKLET

Date of Issue: October 22, 1992

Catalog Numbers: Scott 2715-2718 (single stamps); 2718a (booklet pane of 4)

Colors: yellow, magenta, cyan, black, red, green

First-Day Cancel: Kansas City, Missouri

FDCs Canceled: 461,937 (includes sheet stamps)

Format: 5 panes of 4 stamps each, one of each of 4 designs. Gravure printing cylinders of 320 subjects (20 across, 16 around).

Perf: 10.9 (L perforator)

Selvage Markings: cylinder numbers printed on each pane binding stub

Cover Markings: "© United States Postal Service 1992" and mailing information on inside of front cover. Universal Product Code (UPC) and advertisement for 1992 Commemorative Collection on outside of back cover. Coupon for Commemorative collection on inside of back cover.

Designer and Typographer: Lou Nolan of McLean, Virginia

Art Director and Project Manager: Elizabeth A. Altobell (USPS)

Printing: Printed for American Bank Note Company by Multi-Color Corporation, Scottsburg, Indiana, on a Schiavi 10-color webfed gravure press. Perforated and formed into booklets at ABNC, Bedford Park, Illinois.

Quantity Ordered: 400,000,000 stamps (19,851,500 booklets; 2,970,000 unfolded panes) plus additional order for 8,550,000 stamps (427,500 booklets)

Quantity Distributed: 408,550,000 stamps (20,279,000 booklets; 2,970,000 unfolded panes)

Cylinder Number Detail: 1 group of 6 gravure cylinder numbers preceded by the letter A on each pane binding stub

Cylinder Number Combinations: A111111, A112211, A222222

Tagging: phosphor-coated paper

The Stamps

The story of the Christmas Toys booklet of 1992 was the story of an extra variety that wasn't.

When USPS announced details of the Christmas stamps, it included this information in its news release:

"The manufacturing of the contemporary Christmas booklet stamps was contracted to American Bank Note (Company) and the stamps were printed by the Multi-Color Corporation at its Scottsburg, Indiana, facility. Because of a flood at Multi-Color, printing was transferred to the Jeffries Bank Note Company in Los Angeles. However, an estimated 10-12 million booklets were printed by Multi-Color and bear plate numbers 1 and 2. Jeffries printed the remaining booklets starting with plate number 3.

"Because Multi-Color printed the stamps by gravure and Jeffries by a combination gravure/offset (the green 'USA 29' prints offset), the two stamps will appear different when placed side by side. The Philatelic Sales Division will have both versions and each will have its own item number in the *Stamps etc.* catalog. The Sales Division also will sell loose booklet panes of both the contemporary and the traditional stamps."

The news release gave ordering instructions for first-day covers of the two different varieties of Christmas contemporary booklet stamp, including separate item numbers, with a "J" suffix, for singles and panes of four of the Jeffries-produced items.

All of which was impressively detailed and appeared to be definite. But it also turned out to be inaccurate. All the booklet stamps were, in fact, produced by Multi-Color. Collectors were spared an additional four varieties of Christmas stamp — although the Jeffries varieties, had they been produced, would have been a novelty: No U.S. stamp had ever been printed by a combination of the gravure and offset methods.

Wayne L. Youngblood told the full story in *Linn's Stamp News* after interviewing Thomas C. Harris, vice president of government sales for the American Bank Note Company.

The August 8 flood at Multi-Color did leave some three feet of water on the plant floor, halting production of the booklets, Harris said. An estimated 10 million to 12 million booklets (about 200 million to 240 million stamps) had been printed, which represented about half the initial print order of 400 million stamps. Cleanup was estimated at three months, so plans were made to transfer printing to Jeffries (which the parent company officially refers to as ABNC, Los Angeles).

But the press and the cylinders weren't permanently damaged, Harris said, and the insurance company involved in the cleanup hired the Multi-Color employees whose jobs were affected to help with the task. As a result, it went much more quickly than had been originally estimated, and the stamps went back to press September 29. The plan to shift the remainder of the printing to Jeffries was scrapped.

The Postal Service duly issued another press release. "All 1992 contemporary Christmas booklet stamps have been produced by the Multi-Color Corporation," the release said. "There will be no varieties of the booklet stamp and all references to the Jeffries stamp, including item number and first day of issue ordering instructions, are no longer valid."

The Christmas Toys booklets were issued in the same format — five panes of four stamps each — as the 1991 Santa Claus stamp booklets, which were also printed by Multi-Color for ABNC. But whereas each pane in the five-variety Santa booklets contained stamps of only one design, each pane in the four-variety Toys booklet was a se-tenant block containing all four designs.

Actually, that 1991 booklet included six collectible varieties rather than five, because collectors discovered an unintended — and unprecedented — difference between identical Santa stamps on the top pane. The computer that cropped the original design, or cut it down to finished-stamp size, left a small amount of additional chimney brickwork showing on the two stamps on the left side of the pane. The stamps on the left and right sides were given separate listings in the Scott *Specialized Catalogue of United States Stamps*.

That didn't happen with the 1992 booklet, and in fact couldn't have happened, because the panes consisted of four se-tenant designs rather than four copies of a single design.

Like the 1991 booklet panes, the 1992 versions had larger-than-usual tabs. Even so, the overall booklets were smaller than normal stamp booklets — 3.15 inches long by 1.74 inches wide — because they contained only four stamps per pane.

The Designs

The same four Lou Nolan paintings of Christmas toys that were used to create the sheet stamps were used for the booklet versions. Both versions also displayed the same color typography: green for the "29 USA," red for the "Greetings."

The easiest way for a collector to distinguish a sheet stamp from a booklet stamp was to look at the edges. If the stamp was perforated all the way around, it came from a pane of 50; if it had one straight edge (horse and jockey, fire pumper) or two straight edges (locomotive, steamboat) it came from a booklet pane of four.

But because the sheet and booklet stamps were printed by different methods — offset and gravure, respectively — collectors could readily see other differences between them. The most basic was the absence from the booklet stamps of the design security elements that could be found in the sheet stamps. USPS considers gravure an inherently more secure printing process than offset; consequently, there was no need for ABNC to utilize the tiny dates, patterns of microdots or copier-resistant green ink that Ashton-Potter America Inc., printers of the sheet stamps, had relied on to frustrate counterfeiters.

There were also minor size differences. Overall, the sheet stamps were larger than the booklet stamps. However, the images of the horse and jockey and the fire pumper were slightly larger in the booklets. The other two toys were virtually the same size on both versions.

First-Day Facts

Both sheet and booklet varieties of the Christmas Toys stamps were dedicated October 22 at Hallmark Cards Corporate Headquarters in Kansas City, Missouri. Details on the first-day ceremony can be found in the preceding chapter.

For first-day cover collectors who didn't wish to affix their own stamps, USPS offered to affix a random single or a booklet pane of four to addressed envelopes submitted with the appropriate payment.

$5.22 CHRISTMAS LOCOMOTIVE SHEETLET (ATM-VENDED)

Date of Issue: October 28, 1992

Catalog Number: Scott 2719 (single stamp); 2719a (pane of 18)

Colors: yellow, red, cyan, black, green

First-Day Cancel: New York, New York

FDCs Canceled: 48,873

Format: Self-adhesive. Pane of 18 horizontal stamps arranged horizontally, 6 across, 3 down. Stamps printed from gravure printing cylinders of 540 subjects (30 panes), 5 panes across, 6 around. Backing paper printed from gravure printing cylinders of 30, 5 across, 6 around.

Perf: die cut, no perforations

Markings: Removable strip vertically across center of pane contains gravure cylinder numbers and messages: "Peel here to fold * Self-adhesive stamps * DO NOT WET *." On backing paper, "ExtraValue/Stamps ™," "Patent Pending © USPS 1992," "Happy/Holidays/from your/ Postal/Service" and Universal Product Code (UPC).

Designer: Lou Nolan of McLean, Virginia

Project Manager and Art Director: Elizabeth A. Altobell (USPS)

Modeler and Typographer: John Boyd of New York, New York

Printing: Stamps and backing paper printed by Avery Dennison, Clinton, South Carolina, in single pass on custom-designed 8-color webfed gravure press. Laminated paper furnished by Fasson. Stamps lacquer-coated, die cut and separated into panes by Avery Dennison, Pasadena, California, on Chesnut press.

Quantity Ordered: 21,600,000 stamps (1,200,000 panes)

Quantity Distributed: 21,600,000 stamps (1,200,000 panes)

Cylinder Number Detail: 1 group of 5 gravure cylinder numbers preceded by the letter V on removable center strip

Cylinder Number Combination: V11111

Tagging: phosphor taggant contained in a lacquer coating

The Stamp

In 1962 the U.S. Post Office Department began issuing Christmas stamps on an annual basis. In 1988 its successor, the U.S. Postal Service, issued Christmas stamps in booklets for the first time, and also created a Christmas stamped envelope (an innovation that hasn't been repeated). And in 1992 USPS created its first self-adhesive Christmas stamp.

The new 29¢ item was printed in dollar-bill-sized sheetlets of 18 for vending through automatic teller machines (ATMs). Its design was an adaptation of one of the four Christmas Toys designs that had been created for the 1992 Contemporary Christmas sheets and booklets. The stamp was the fourth face-different ATM stamp since USPS began experimenting with that format and dispensing method in 1989.

USPS issued the stamp October 28, on only a few days' notice. First-day sale was at the American Stamp Dealers Association's Postage Stamp Mega-Event in New York City. The issuance brought the number of Christmas stamp varieties to 11, an all-time high for a single year: sheet and booklet versions of the Madonna and Child stamp, sheet and booklet versions of four different Christmas Toys stamps, and the ATM stamp.

Valerie Welsch, a spokeswoman for USPS, told *Linn's Stamp News* the idea for a Christmas ATM stamp came from one of the banks participating in the ATM stamp program. "They suggested that they wanted something unique," she said, "and, in fact, one of them suggested a Christmas stamp."

The stamps were dispensed by some 400 ATMs belonging to the participating banks, which included Seafirst Bank, Seattle, Washington, the Postal Service's original partner in the experiment; BayBank Systems, Boston, Massachusetts; Equibank, Pittsburgh, Pennsylvania; First State Bank, Key West, Florida; Huntington Bank, Columbus, Ohio; and First National Bank of Southwestern Ohio, Cincinnati, Ohio.

Shortly before the stamps were issued, USPS invited other banks having Interbold, NCR or Fujitsu machines to join the ATM stamp program. Testing had shown there was "a viable market" for stamps dispensed in this manner, said Edward E. Horgan Jr., vice president of marketing and sales for the Postal Service. Banks could obtain the stamps on either a consignment or pay-on-delivery basis, USPS said.

The Christmas panes, like the Liberty Torch panes with which ATMs were normally stocked, were sold at their $5.22 face value. Bank customers could select the stamps from a menu of banking options. The cost of the items was deducted automatically from their accounts. Collectors could also obtain the panes from the Philatelic Sales Division.

Like all previous ATM stamps, these were printed by Avery Dennison, a leading manufacturer of pressure-sensitive labels. The company delivered a total of 1.2 million panes, which was only half the number of Liberty Torch panes that it made in 1991.

Avery Dennison printed the stamps on an eight-color webfed gravure press at its Clinton, South Carolina, plant. All eight ink fountains were used: five for the stamps (yellow, red, cyan, black and a special green for the "29 USA") and three for the backing paper (red, green and black).

The stamps were then sent to Avery Dennison's headquarters plant in Pasadena, California, to be die cut and given a lacquer coating on both back and front. The lacquer on the front was applied to keep the ink from flaking. The back coating was applied to counter the tendency of the front coating to cause the panes to curl. The front lacquer also contained a phosphorescent taggant. (For a fuller description of how this procedure evolved, see the section on the Liberty Torch ATM stamps in the chapter "Revised Definitives.")

The Design

The dimensions of the ATM stamp were smaller than those of the Christmas Toys sheet and booklet stamps: 25 millimeters by 22mm, compared to 28.96mm by 22.1mm for the booklet stamp and 30.2mm by

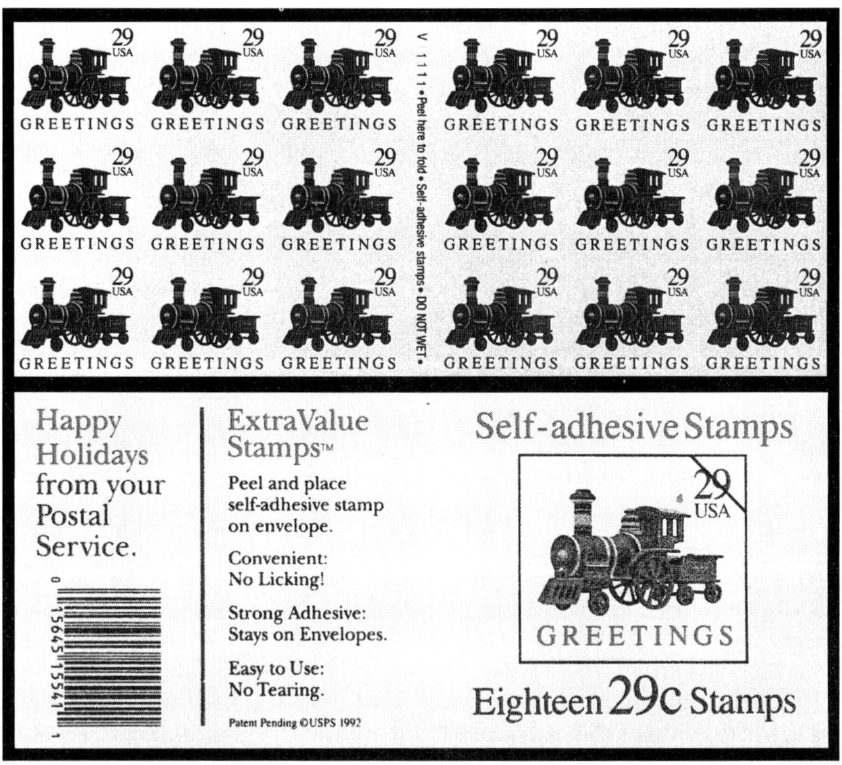

Shown here are the stamps and backing paper of a Christmas 1992 ATM sheetlet. The two sides were printed in a single pass of the paper through Avery Dennison's gravure press.

23.1mm for the sheet stamp. Although the aspect ratios were only slightly different, they were different enough that whichever design was chosen for the ATM variety would have to be reformatted.

Before deciding which of Lou Nolan's four Christmas Toys designs — horse and jockey, steamboat, fire pumper and locomotive — to adapt, USPS considered all the logical possibilities.

Using all four designs wouldn't have worked, officials said, because four doesn't divide evenly into 18, the number of stamps on the pane. They might have used two of the four designs in a checkerboard pattern, but, as one official said, "We would have had to decide which two, and, since the design had to be resized and reformatted, that would have been twice the trouble, so we decided that picking one was our best bet."

The final choice was the locomotive. "This was the strongest design of the four, and it worked the best," said Elizabeth A. Altobell, the project manager. "It didn't fall apart when we started resizing the design elements.

"What we did was make the train bigger in relation to the type. That way we got maximum design." On the ATM stamp, the tip of the cowcatcher of the locomotive was flush with the letter G in "GREETINGS," whereas on the sheet and booklet stamps it stopped short of the letter. The "29 USA" also sat higher in relation to the vignette than it does on either of the perforated varieties.

John Boyd of Anagraphics Inc., New York City, did the detail work involved in the reformatting. Boyd also designed the backing paper of the ATM pane, which reproduced the stamp in three colors (the locomotive was shown in black). The backing paper also bore a cheery "Happy Holidays from your Postal Service" in red and green.

First-Day Facts

The stamp was issued October 28, a few minutes after the opening ceremony for the ASDA Mega-Event at the Jacob K. Javits Convention Center in New York City.

The stamp was dedicated by William T. Johnstone, a USPS vice president. Speakers included Keith A. Wagner, executive director of the American Philatelic Society; Joseph B. Savarese, executive director of ASDA; and Arthur Morowitz, ASDA president. Santa Claus — in reality Andy Sozzi of USPS — made a special appearance.

First-day cover collectors were given 60 days to submit addressed envelopes for the first-day postmark.

29¢ HAPPY NEW YEAR

Date of Issue: December 30, 1992

Catalog Number: Scott 2720

Colors: red (PMS 485), yellow, magenta, cyan (offset); red (PMS 1795) and red (PMS 485) (intaglio)

First-Day Cancel: San Francisco, California

FDCs Canceled: final total not available

Format: Panes of 20, horizontal, 4 across, 5 down. Offset printing plates of 180 subjects (12 across, 15 around); intaglio printing plates of 180 subjects (12 across, 15 around).

Perf: 11 by 11.1 (Bickel reciprocating stroke perforator)

Selvage Inscription: "Many countries/celebrate/the New Year/on the first/of the year." "Ancient/cultures often/celebrated the/lunar calendar." "The lunar/calendar/in 1993 is/symbolized by/ the rooster." "The rooster/is the 10th/animal in a/12 animal/cycle."

Selvage Markings: "©/United States/Postal Service/1992." "Use Correct/ZIP Code/®."

Designer: Clarence Lee of Honolulu, Hawaii

Art Director and Typographer: Richard Sheaff

Project Manager: Elizabeth A. Altobell (USPS)

Engraver: Dick Jones, American Bank Note Company, Los Angeles, California

Modeler: Jack Barnett, American Bank Note Company, Los Angeles, California

Printing: Printed by ABNC-LA on a 6-color Miller sheetfed offset press and 3-color Giori Simplex sheetfed intaglio press.

Quantity Ordered: 105,000,000

Quantity Distributed: 105,000,000

Plate/Sleeve Number Detail: 1 intaglio plate number preceded by letter A, and 1 group of 4 offset plate numbers, in selvage above or below each of 4 corner stamps on a 20-stamp pane.

Sleeve/Plate Number Combinations: A1-1111, A2-2222, A2-3333, A2-6622, A3-3333, A4-1111, A4-4444, A4-6226, A4-6266, A4-7266, A5-3333, A5-4444, A5-7333, A5-8333

Tagging: phosphor-coated paper with block tagging over printing or phosphor-coated paper with block tagging under intaglio printing

The Stamp

The final stamp of 1992 carried the message "Happy New Year!" and was issued December 30. Not since the Blanche Stuart Scott and Glenn Curtiss airmails of 1980 (Scott C99-100) had a U.S. stamp been released so late in the year, and only one stamp of the modern era had ever been issued later: the 2¢ George Washington endwise coil (Scott 606) of December 31, 1923.

But, then, no previous stamp had incorporated a New Year's theme. This one had two primary purposes. One was to give all mailers a chance to express New Year's greetings in the early weeks of 1993 with a postage stamp. The other was to appeal specifically to Asian-Americans by calling attention to the Year of the Rooster — 4691 on the lunar calendar — that would begin the following January 23.

Besides its message in English, the stamp also bore two ideographs in Kanji, a written language developed by the Japanese from Chinese characters. A stylized image of a rooster completed the unusual design.

The stamp came about as a result of several unconnected events, according to Donald M. McDowell, who headed the Office of Stamp and Philatelic Marketing when the project was conceived and planned.

One was a continuing series of requests to the Citizens' Stamp Advisory Committee for stamps for various holidays, such as New Year's, Easter, the Fourth of July and Thanksgiving. Periodic requests had also come in for stamps for the signs of the Zodiac, and even for stamps for the 12 animal characters of the lunar calendar cycle.

Another was a growing realization among USPS staffers, CSAC members and others that Asian-Americans were "ideally situated" to become interested in philately — but that it wasn't happening.

"They are very studious people, very industrious people, people who are taking full advantage of the opportunities that our society offers and who tend to move rapidly up the economic ladder," McDowell said. "They have bright and industrious kids. But you go to a stamp show, and you don't see them." This was a topic of conversation one day at World Stamp Expo in Washington, D.C., in 1989, he said, when "10 or 12 of us, postal folks from two or three different postal administrations and folks from the hobby, were sitting around a couple of tables drinking coffee and just jawing."

Out of this and other conversations began to form the idea of a stamp for Chinese New Year. "It promised to be fun to do," McDowell said. "It would be a different-looking U.S. stamp, with different graphic possibilities. We have some 'arty' folks on CSAC who share the belief that calligraphy is gorgeous, whether or not you can read it."

As 1992 approached, USPS noticed what McDowell called "the four-year phenomenon" — an increase in requests by members of Congress, coinciding with the arrival of a congressional and presidential election year, for stamps that would appeal to specific voter groups. The California and New York congressional delegations, among others, let USPS know that they would favor a stamp that would recognize the contributions of Asian-Americans to the nation's development.

Finally, there came to CSAC's agenda a proposal by the Organization of Chinese Americans for a stamp to honor the Chinese who were instrumental in building the U.S. transcontinental railroads. The committee wasn't enthusiastic about that proposal, McDowell said, but did bring up — and endorse — the idea of a stamp for the Chinese New Year.

When the Chinese Americans' group inquired about its request, "we said the committee had been scratching its head, and thought something along the lines of the Lunar New Year might be a better way to cause some interest and excitement in the Asian community," McDowell said. "We hardly had the words out of our mouth when they embraced the idea."

USPS announced the stamp in mid-July, saying merely that "a Happy New Year stamp will be issued in December." Its design, and the fact that it would celebrate the Lunar New Year, were disclosed August 1 at the gala banquet of the 14th annual national convention of the Organization of Chinese Americans in San Jose, California. Joseph Peng, general manager of the USPS Stamp Manufacturing Division and a Chinese-American, unveiled the design.

The Happy New Year item was the first non-high-value stamp to be issued in panes of 20, four across by five down, rather than the 50 that is standard for commemorative-size stamps. The American Bank Note Company produced it in sheets of 180 and cut them into nine small panes for distribution. Each pane bore offset plate numbers and an intaglio plate number in each of its four corners, making it possible to extract plate number blocks of four from all available positions from one pane, leaving only four loose stamps.

There were two different pane varieties, however. Because of the way ABNC's Bickel sheetfed reciprocating stroke perforators work, the bottom six panes on each printed sheet had vertical perforations that ran from selvage edge to selvage edge. On the top three panes, however, the vertical perfs stopped at the top row of horizontal perfs. Therefore, persons who collected full panes would need an example of each type for the sake of completeness.

The Bickel perforator was capable of perforating five or six printed press sheets at a time. The perforating action began just above the top row of stamps on each press sheet of 180 subjects.

The perforator punched holes two stamp rows at a time, with the second stamp row lacking the bottom row of horizontal holes. When the perforating action was repeated, the second row of stamps received its bottom horizontal row of perforations that also served as the top row of horizontal perforations for the third row of stamps.

The sheet layout was experimental, said Joe Brockert of the Postal Service's Design Section.

This press sheet shows how the vertical perforations on the upper row of panes differ from those on the lower two rows.

The top pane of Happy New Year stamps, only a portion of which is shown, is from the top row of the press sheet of nine panes, with vertical perforations not extending through the top selvage. The bottom pane of 20 is from the middle or bottom row of the press sheet. Its vertical perfs extend through the top selvage.

"Based on vending machine sales and other information, we've found that people's preferred stamp purchasing unit is 20," Brockert said. "We want to see if that will hold true here — if people are more likely to buy a pane of these than to buy half of a pane of 50 stamps.

"This may ultimately save a lot of clerk's sales transaction time. Instead of having to tear off parts of panes to sell to people, they can sell complete panes. We'll be doing the same thing with a number of stamps in 1993 just to see what the reaction is.

"And, of course, there's the plate block factor. With four plate blocks per 20 stamps, this will probably reduce waste and excess stamps as clerks tear off plate blocks for customers."

USPS had introduced the mini-sheets of 20 a few years earlier with $1, $2 and $5 stamps. This was primarily to address a problem of stamp-clerk accountability, Brockert said.

"A pane of 100 $5 stamps puts $500 worth of accountability in one pane of stamps in a clerk's drawer," he said. "They have a limit as to how much cash value they can keep in a drawer at any one time. So having just one pane of $5 stamps made it much more difficult for a clerk to stock a whole lot of different commemoratives at one time."

Did the new stamp signal the start of an annual Lunar New Year series? As of this writing, there has been no announcement of another one. "We had preliminary discussions about making it an annual event," said McDowell. "But there's always a hesitancy to make a commitment to a series until you see what kind of response you get to the first one. We thought that if this turned out to be popular we might consider running through the whole 12-year cycle."

In fact, the stamp was quite popular in communities with a large Chinese-American population. Betty Liu Ebron, writing in *The New York Daily News*, said the Doyer Street post office, serving New York City's Chinatown, sold 80,000 Happy New Year stamps in the first three weeks. The station's normal order for a commemorative was 5,000 stamps. "The Flushing station (also in New York City) is also under siege: 218,000 rooster stamps flew out the door in two weeks, and 140,000 more have been ordered," Ebron added. *Linn's Stamp News* reported that the post office serving the Chinatown section of San Francisco, California, sold some 2 million Happy New Year stamps through the first week of February 1993.

The stamp was also reportedly popular in Asia, where some countries, such as Taiwan and Hong Kong, also marked the Year of the Rooster postally. Postal administrations in several countries ordered "significant numbers" of stamps for use on combination covers with their own stamps, according to McDowell.

And a collector named Zhu Nie of Nanjing, China, wrote to *Linn's* that "news of the stamp has been published widely, and most collectors are looking for a way to acquire one."

"The People's Republic of China has more than 10 million philatelists, and the hobby is growing," Zhu Nie wrote. "If these collectors each owned only one of the stamps, that would account for more than 10 million copies. However, in China about 100 million people actually were born in each of the 12 lunar years, including the Year of the Fowl. They are interested in anything having to do with their natal animals, including the one on this U.S. stamp. Mothers and fathers, for example, always buy something with fowl for children who will be born in 1993.

A Linn's Stamp News reader from Dearborn Heights, Michigan, bought these Happy New Year stamps with the stairstep perforations between the bottom two rows of the pane. The Bickel reciprocating stroke perforator perforates two horizontal rows at a time. In this case, a slight shift of the sheets being perforated created the misaligned vertical perforations.

This early vertical version of the stamp showed a rooster with feathers that were more detailed than on the final design. The ideographs can be translated: "Americans of Chinese Ancestry."

"If the Happy New Year stamp was made available to these people, there would be few of the stamps left in the United States."

The vote of approval wasn't unanimous. Betty Liu Ebron, the *Daily News* writer, said: "The stamp helps and hurts. It's better than nothing. But it belies the sweat, blood and lives that Chinese immigrants sacrificed for this country." She told *Linn's Stamp News* that a better design would have included "the face of a sweating laborer."

USPS also offered three collectible products related to the stamp: a pane of 20 in a red and gold folder ($7), a first-day ceremony program bearing a single stamp with first-day postmark ($5.95), and an 8- by 10-inch collector folder that included a block of four stamps with the first-day postmark and descriptive text, in English and Chinese ($7.95).

The lunar calendar used in China, Japan and neighboring countries consists of 12 months alternating between 29 and 30 days each. A year is equal to 354 days, or approximately 12 full lunar cycles. Intercalary months have been inserted to keep the calendar year in step with the solar year of 365¼ days. The months of the year and the hours of the day share the same 12 animal designations that are appended to the years: rat, ox, tiger, hare, dragon, snake, horse, sheep, monkey, rooster, dog and pig.

The Chinese New Year falls on the first day after the first full moon after the sun enters Aquarius, which can occur between January 21 and February 19. Its arrival is celebrated with fireworks, food and family reunions. Before a New Year, many housekeepers clean house thoroughly to sweep away any lingering bad spirits from the previous year, and some people cut out artistic floral patterns from red paper to decorate the walls at home or work. Traditionally, during the first week of the New Year, elders don't punish children.

According to *The New York Times*, Chinese debated whether the Year of the Rooster would be auspicious. Some said roosters are unstable,

The English inscription on this late version of the design reads, "The Year of Rooster." It was changed to "Happy New Year!" to make the stamp more understandable, and appealing, to English-speaking postal customers.

running this way and that, which boded ill for the year. Young couples hurried to be married before January 23 so their weddings wouldn't be linked to instability. Optimists, however, noted that "ji," the word for chicken, is similar to the word for "luck." Both words are pronounced "gee," like the American expression, but the chicken "ji" is in a steady tone, while luck is in a rising tone, like a question. The optimists also pointed out that roosters traditionally are well regarded and have good associations in Chinese folklore.

The Design

The stamp depicted a rooster in yellow with tones of orange, green and blue, silhouetted against a red background. The Kanji characters for "Year of Rooster" and "Happy New Year" were at the left in dropout white. At the right, also dropped out, in a serif typeface called Trump Medieval Bold, were the words HAPPY NEW YEAR! and the USA initials. The denomination, 29, was in Sabon Bold.

The artwork was done in airbrush by first-time stamp designer Clarence Lee, a Chinese-American artist. Lee, a top graduate of Yale's School of Art and Architecture, had headed a design firm in his hometown of Honolulu, Hawaii, since 1966, creating designs ranging from annual reports to signs and exhibits for some of Hawaii's largest companies.

"We knew that we wanted a modern Chinese, cut-paperish-looking sort of rooster, and that was the instruction given to the artist, and that's what he gave us," said Richard Sheaff, the art director. Lee painted the bird, photographed the painting and made a negative, which he overlaid on a solid background so the background color would show through the transparent parts of the rooster.

Lee subcontracted the Kanji characters to a professional calligrapher in Honolulu. Kanji, which is readable by most Oriental groups, is a Japanese adaptation of Chinese characters in which the original squarish and complicated symbols have been made more cursive and simplified.

"It was all made more difficult by the fact that in Kanji there are probably 10 ways to say the same thing," Sheaff said. "If you go to 10 calligraphers, you'll get 10 pieces of art that look radically different." But Elizabeth Altobell, the project manager, checked with experts through the Postal Service's International Business Department, which in turn consulted Chinese officials via the Universal Postal Union in Switzerland. The assurances came back that USPS was saying on the stamp what it had wanted to say.

The much-derided "chicken stamp" of 1948 (Scott 968) was the first U.S. postal item to depict poultry.

In one version of the design, the English inscription read: "Year of Rooster." "Then, the committee got to thinking about making it more general," said Sheaff, "not only by using Kanji, so all Oriental groups could read it, but by using the words 'Happy New Year!' in English so Americans would know why we were issuing the stamp, and so it could be used as a New Year's greetings stamp by English-speaking people." The exclamation point, Sheaff admitted, was his own contribution.

The American Bank Note Company produced the stamp by a combination of offset and intaglio, with the stylized details on the rooster's body being engraved. Four red inks were used, two intaglio reds and an offset red and magenta.

The stamp wasn't the first U.S. postal issue to depict poultry. That honor went to the often-derided 1948 chicken stamp, issued on orders of Congress to mark the "centennial of the American poultry industry" (Scott 968). It depicted a Light Brahma rooster, along with an egg — a juxtaposition that amused collectors. And a Rhode Island Red rooster was shown on the Rhode Island stamp of the 1982 State Birds and Flowers pane (Scott 1991).

Nor was the stamp the first to depict written Oriental characters. A 5¢ stamp of 1942 (Scott 906), issued to mark the fifth anniversary of the resistance of China to Japanese invaders, displayed Chinese ideographs representing Generalissimo Chiang Kai-shek's war motto, translated as "Fight the War and Build the Country," and the Chinese equivalent of Abraham Lincoln's phrase, "Of the people, by the people, for the people." Chinese characters also appeared on a 1961 stamp (Scott 1188) that depicted Sun Yat-sen and commemorated the 50th anniversary of the Republic of China.

First-Day Facts

The Happy New Year stamp was dedicated in a public ceremony December 30 at the St. Francis Hotel in San Francisco by Joseph R.

This 1942 commemorative honoring Chinese resistance to Japanese invaders (Scott 906) was the first U.S. stamp to bear Chinese ideographs.

Caraveo, USPS chief operating officer and executive vice president.

Speakers included San Francisco Mayor Frank Jordan; Sydney Chan, president of the Chinese Chamber of Commerce; Timothy Lau, presiding president of the Chinese Consolidated Benevolent Association; and Claudine Cheng, national president of the Organization of Chinese Americans. The Oriental Horizons Lion Dance Group performed the traditional lion dance during the program.

A first-day postmark and pictorial postmark were available during the day at the hotel and also at San Francisco's Chinatown Station.

The year 1992 saw no change in the basic postal-rate structure, which made it possible for the number of new definitives issued during the year to be held to a relatively modest 13. There were also five tagging or printing variations of previously issued definitive stamps.

The Postal Service's *Stamps etc. Catalog* for January-March 1993 listed two previously unknown tagging varieties as having been printed in 1992. These were the 50¢ Nimitz and 75¢ Willkie Great Americans stamps on prephosphored paper. Lacking information on these varieties, the *Yearbook* hasn't counted them in the 1992 total for definitives, or the overall stamp total.

The most novel of the new issues was a variable-rate coil, created to be dispensed by an experimental machine called a Postage and Mailing Center (PMC). It's counted here as one variety, although it theoretically could be counted as 9,999 varieties — which is the number of different denominations, from 1¢ to $99.99, a PMC customer could select.

For the first time, USPS distributed nationwide a pressure-sensitive stamp. This one is counted as three varieties. Although the Postal Service used only one design, it contracted with three different private printers to make the stamp. Each used a different color of typography to make its product readily identifiable.

The unannounced, but de facto, Wildlife series continued, with a 45¢ stamp picturing a pumpkinseed sunfish. Meanwhile, two long-running series also had modest extensions. The Great Americans series of sheet stamps grew to 52 face-different varieties by adding Wendell Willkie and Earl Warren to its gallery. And the Transportation coil series added a 53rd face-different variety with a gravure version of the Circus Wagon stamp that was previously issued in intaglio.

Two new U.S. Flag stamps made their debut, and although they were definitives, both did double duty by commemorating significant anniversaries. A coil stamp that pictured the flag over the White House marked the 200th anniversary of the Executive Mansion. And a booklet stamp, depicting Old Glory fluttering in the breeze, was issued on the 100th anniversary of the publication of the Pledge of Allegiance.

75¢ WENDELL WILLKIE
GREAT AMERICANS SERIES

Date of Issue: February 16, 1992

Catalog Number: Scott 2193

Color: maroon

First-Day Cancel: Bloomington, Indiana

FDCs Canceled: 47,086

Format: Panes of 100, vertical, 10 across, 10 down. Intaglio printing sleeve of 800 subjects (20 across, 40 around).

Perf: 11.2 (Eureka off-line perforator)

Selvage Inscription: "Wendell Willkie,/lawyer, businessman/and politician." "Candidate for the/U.S. presidency in/the 1940 election." "In One World, 1943,/he pleaded for/global cooperation."

Selvage Markings: "© United States/Postal Service 1991." "Use Correct/ZIP Code ®."

Designer: Christopher Calle of Ridgefield, Connecticut

Art Director and Project Manager: Jack Williams (USPS)

Typographer: Bradbury Thompson (CSAC)

Engraver: vignette, Tom Hipschen (BEP); lettering, Richard Everett (BEP)

Printing: printed by BEP on 3-color intaglio unit of 9-color offset-intaglio D press (902)

Quantity Ordered: 215,000,000 (continuing item)

Quantity Distributed: 161,080,000

Sleeve Number Detail: 1 intaglio sleeve number alongside corner stamps

Sleeve Number: 1

Tagging: phosphor-coated paper

The Stamp

Wendell Willkie was a politician who never held public office. He was a well-known public figure for fewer than five years. He lost the only election campaign he ever entered — for president of the United States.

Nevertheless, on February 16, 1992, two days before the 100th anniversary of his birth, he was honored with a stamp in the Great Americans series.

Although he was defeated in that 1940 presidential contest by President Franklin D. Roosevelt, Willkie won enormous respect from his fellow Americans. With World War II raging overseas, he threw his support behind Roosevelt's program of aiding the Allies and rearming the United States.

A dedicated internationalist, he wrote a book, *One World*, during the war. In it he stressed the need for global cooperation in the postwar world. The book became a best seller, with all proceeds going to war charities and public service organizations.

The nation was stunned at his death from heart failure October 8, 1944, at the age of 52. *The New York Times* commented that Willkie "had before him the prospect of long years of service to the fine causes on which his faith was founded . . . A man has gone who cannot be replaced."

The first recorded public mention of a stamp for Willkie took place in September 1945, less than a year after he died. It happened this way:

That month, President Harry Truman's postmaster general, Robert E. Hannegan, announced that a commemorative stamp would be issued honoring Alfred E. Smith, former Democratic governor of New York and his party's unsuccessful candidate for president in 1928. Smith — like Willkie — had passed away the previous October.

The surprise announcement drew considerable criticism, according to stamp historian Max Johl. "A defeated candidate for the presidency dead only a year hardly seemed an appropriate reason for issuing a commemorative stamp," Johl wrote. And James Waldo Fawcett of *The Washington Star* reported the news this way:

"The political significance of the stamp allegedly will be that it may help to heal the existing breach between the conservative wing and the Roosevelt wing of the Democratic Party.

"When Post Office Department officers were asked if consideration had been given to a stamp in memory of Wendell Willkie, Republican presidential candidate in 1940, they answered: 'No.' "

More than 46 years later, Willkie finally got his stamp. This time there was no hidden political motivation. The non-partisan U.S. Postal Service had replaced the very partisan Post Office Department, and the Postal Service's purpose was to honor a man remembered in history less as a political figure than as a "statesman" — the word that appeared beside his portrait on the stamp.

The stamp was issued in Bloomington, Indiana, as part of a three-day celebration by Willkie's alma mater, Indiana University, of the centennial of his birth on February 18. It bore a 75¢ denomination, which covered the three-ounce rate for first-class mail, and was the first U.S. stamp of that value since the 75¢ parcel post stamp of 1913 (Scott Q11).

The Willkie stamp was the 51st face-different variety in the Great Americans series, and the second in a row to depict a defeated presidential candidate. Hubert Humphrey, who lost the 1968 election to Richard Nixon, was shown on a 52¢ Great Americans stamp issued in 1991. Two other unsuccessful candidates for president, Henry Clay and William Jennings Bryan, had previously appeared on stamps in the same set.

Willkie was born in Elwood, Indiana, in 1892. He earned his law degree from Indiana University in 1916 and, after Army service in World War I, became a corporate lawyer. In 1933 he was named president of the Commonwealth and Southern Corporation, a public utilities firm selling electricity. He left the Democratic Party in the 1930s because he believed the party no longer held to Woodrow Wilson's ideals of international cooperation and limited government.

His capture of the 1940 Republican presidential nomination was one of the most dramatic events in U.S. political history. He came to the GOP convention in Philadelphia the darkest of dark horses, but his strong call for aid to the European democracies facing the Nazis had gained him the active support of powerful publishers. When in the spring of 1940 Hitler's armies rolled over France, Norway and the Low Countries and threatened Great Britain, the American public took serious notice of Willkie and his message.

At Philadelphia, the galleries packed with his supporters took up the chant "We want Willkie," and the candidacies of the favorites, Robert A. Taft, Thomas E. Dewey and Arthur Vandenberg, began to falter. On the sixth ballot this unlikeliest of candidates won the nomination.

"Almost overnight, Willkie moved the Republican Party out of its hidebound isolationism and sent a message to the world that Americans stood together against Axis aggression," wrote his biographer, Steve Neal. "As the Republican standard-bearer, he waged the most energetic campaign of any presidential candidate since Teddy Roosevelt. By the end, his voice was reduced to a hoarse whisper. The same factors that had compelled his nomination worked against his election, for FDR was the political beneficiary of the worsening international situation."

The contest proved to be the closest presidential race in a generation. In losing, Willkie received more votes than any previous Republican candidate. After his defeat, he grew in public esteem, and in time, Roosevelt would say of him: "We might not have had lend-lease or Selective Service or a lot of other things if it hadn't been for Wendell Willkie. He was a godsend to this country when we needed him most." His wartime service at FDR's behest included special missions to London during the blitzkrieg and later to the Middle East, Russia and China. On the home front, he spoke out against isolationism, imperialism and racial and religious discrimination.

In the process, he alienated the power elite of the Republican Party, which blocked his attempted comeback in 1944. Before the end of the year, he was dead.

The Design

Christopher Calle of Ridgefield, Connecticut, designer of several previous Great Americans stamps, executed the artwork for the Willkie stamp. He based his pencil drawing of the handsome, tousle-haired lawyer-executive on a 1940 campaign photo by the Fabian Bachrach studio in New York City, although he used some additional pictures from his own research for reference.

"Willkie had a really strong face with interesting features," Calle said. "Doing his portrait was a pretty straightforward job. There wasn't a real exploratory sketch phase, where I was working on a number of different 'looks' and a number of different expressions. The family had a clear preference for the one image, and when that happens you have to honor that wish.

"As usual, I did the best I could for the engravers, giving them pencil lines to use as a guide. And they did a great job. I think Willkie is one of the best portraits that I've done, and I think it was one of the best engravings that's been done, too." Thomas Hipschen, who is widely acknowledged as the top picture engraver at the Bureau of Engraving and Printing, was responsible for the intaglio work on the portrait.

For this picture, Calle provided only a touch of background shading. "On many of my other Great Americans, I've put a dark background because it's a real strong way to bring out the face," he said. "But Willkie had that dark, dark hair, and the design concept wouldn't work with a dark background. So I put in just a little feathering to kind of blend in the background and to 'hold' his ear a little bit so the engraver wouldn't have

This is the Bachrach portrait of Willkie on which designer Christopher Calle based his pencil portrait for the stamp.

to outline the ear to keep it from fading away. That's all it really needed. The features were strong enough, and the contrast between the dark and the light gave a nice visual impact.''

In choosing a color for the stamp, USPS honored Indiana University and its official color, crimson. The shade used in the printing was actually more of a maroon, however; it was similar to a hue featured on an earlier Great Americans stamp, the 15¢ Buffalo Bill Cody stamp of 1988.

First-Day Facts

John G. Mulligan, Central Region postmaster general, dedicated the stamp at an academic convocation at 2 p.m. Sunday, February 16, in the Indiana Memorial Union. Speakers at a symposium that day included Willkie's grandson, Wendell L. Willkie II, general counsel of the U.S. Department of Commerce. Four other grandsons were also on hand: Frank, Philip, Benjamin and David, the latter a member of the Indiana University Class of 1992. Also present was Rosalie Hall, first wife of Willkie's son Philip and mother of Wendell II, Frank and Philip Willkie, and Virginia Z. Willkie, mother of Benjamin and David.

There were two unveilings of an enlarged replica of the Willkie stamp, one at a luncheon meeting and the other at the afternoon dedication ceremony. Frank Willkie did the honors both times.

The Indiana delegation to Congress was well represented at the academic convocation, with the presence of U.S. Senator Richard Lugar, Republican, and Representative Frank McCloskey, Bloomington's congressman, chairman of the Subcommittee on Postal Operations and Services, and Representative Lee Hamilton, both Democrats.

USPS distributed folders containing copies of the Willkie stamp with the Bloomington first-day cancellation. The folders looked like first-day ceremony programs, with the Bachrach photograph of Willkie on the cover and a brief biography of the honoree inside. The folder contained no listing of speakers and wasn't considered a USPS program, USPS spokesman Frank Thomas told Scott Pelcyger, president of the American Ceremony Program Society. It wasn't included in USPS' ceremony subscription program or made available optionally to collectors.

Bloomington had previously been the site of the first-day sale of the 20¢ Horace Moses commemorative stamp in 1984.

29¢ FLOWER COIL STAMP (PERFORATED)

Date of Issue: March 3, 1992

Catalog Number: Scott 2526

Colors: yellow, magenta, cyan, black

First-Day Cancel: Rochester, New York

FDCs Canceled: 35,877

Format: Coils of 3,000. Gravure printing cylinders of 429 subjects (13 across, 33 around) manufactured by Armotek Industries Inc., Palmyra, New Jersey.

Perf: 10.9

Designer: Wallace Marosek of Boston, Massachusetts

Art Director and Typographer: Bradbury Thompson (CSAC)

Project Manager: Jack Williams (USPS)

Modeler: Richard Sennett of Stamp Venturers

Printing: Printed on a Champlain gravure press and perforated by Stamp Venturers in Richmond, Virginia. Coiled and finished at Stamp Venturers in Milwaukee, Wisconsin.

Quantity Ordered: 150,000,000

Quantity Distributed: 150,000,000

Cylinder Number Detail: 4 cylinder numbers preceded by the letter S on every 33rd stamp

Cylinder Number Combination: S2222

Tagging: phosphor-coated paper

The Stamp

In 1991 USPS issued no fewer than eight different varieties of stamps bearing the same design — a red tulip with green leaf and stem against a yellow background. On April 3, 1992, the appearance of a perforated coil version bearing a 29¢ denomination brought that count to nine.

The previous stamps that carried this hard-working design were:

(1) F sheet stamp, issued January 22, 1991, to meet the first-class rate of 29¢ that would take effect February 3.
(2) F coil stamp, same date.
(3) F booklet stamp, same date, printed by the Bureau of Engraving and Printing.
(4) F booklet stamp, same date, printed by KCS Industries.
(5) and (6) 29¢ sheet stamp, issued April 5, with two different types of perforations.
(7) 29¢ booklet stamp, same date.
(8) 29¢ coil stamp, rouletted, August 16.

This rouletted coil, the first of its type, was made by Stamp Venturers in rolls of 100. USPS, which called the roulette cuts "slit perforations," said it wanted to find out how the public would react to this less-expensive production technique.

One practical problem with slit perforations, as USPS knew, was that they couldn't be used with post office stamp vending machines or with business machinery that dispenses and applies coil stamps directly onto cards and envelopes. Those machines use the round-hole perforations to advance the coil through their mechanisms. Late in 1991, it was disclosed that Stamp Venturers had printed 150 million of the 29¢ Flower coil stamps with conventional round-hole perfs especially for business use. These stamps were in rolls of 3,000, which is one of the sizes used in stamp-affixing machines.

The perforated stamps — the ninth variety to bear the tulip design — would be distributed as soon as USPS gave the word, according to Richard Sennett, Stamp Venturers manufacturing director. The shipments were made early in January 1992, and shortly afterward USPS announced that the stamps would be issued March 3 in Rochester, New York, the same city where the sheet, booklet and rouletted coil versions of the denominated Flower stamp had first gone on sale. However, as early as January 9 some of the stamps were sold to the public.

The Design

The design, which was first used on the F stamps of early 1991, was the work of Wallace Marosek of Boston, Massachusetts. He had done the design as a student project while studying at the Yale University School of Art and Architecture under Bradbury Thompson, long-time design coordinator and stamp typographer for USPS. Marosek based his painting on tulips at his late grandmother's home on Lake Otsego in Cooperstown, New York.

First-Day Facts

Rochester was chosen as the first-day site for all the denominated Flower stamps because of its nickname, the "Flower City." However, no ceremony was held for any of the items. First-day postmarks for the perforated Flower coil were available at the Rochester main post office March 3, and by mail.

29¢ EARL WARREN
GREAT AMERICANS SERIES

Date of Issue: March 9, 1992

Catalog Number: Scott 2184A

Color: blue (between PMS 540 and 541)

First-Day Cancel: Washington, D.C.

FDCs Canceled: 175,517

Format: Panes of 100, vertical, 10 across, 10 down. Intaglio printing plates of 600 subjects (30 across, 20 down).

Perf: 11.2 (reciprocating stroke perforator)

Selvage Inscription: "Earl Warren/(1891-1974),/prominent jurist." "Elected governor/of California/for three terms." "14th chief justice/of the U.S.,/from 1953 to 1969."

Selvage Markings: "© United States/Postal Service 1991." "Use Correct/ZIP Code ®."

Designer: Christopher Calle of Ridgefield, Connecticut

Art Director and Project Manager: Jack Williams (USPS)

Typographer: Bradbury Thompson (CSAC)

Engraver: Czeslaw Slania

Modeler: Richard Sennett, Stamp Venturers

Printing: printed by Canadian Bank Note Company, Ottawa, Ontario, on a TA-2 intaglio press for Stamp Venturers of Fairfax, Virginia

Quantity Ordered: 250,000,000

Quantity Distributed: 250,000,000

Sleeve Number Detail: 1 number preceded by letter S in selvage at left or right of corner stamp (outer panes) or above or below right corner stamp (middle panes)

Sleeve Numbers: S1, S2

Tagging: prephosphored paper

The Stamp

Earl Warren, who was chief justice of the United States when the Supreme Court ended school segregation and issued other tradition-shattering rulings, was honored with a 29¢ Great Americans stamp issued in Washington, D.C., on March 9.

The Postal Service originally announced that the stamp would carry a 75¢ denomination, covering the three-ounce first-class rate, and would be issued in 1991, the 100th anniversary year of Warren's birth.

Later events caused a change of plans. USPS appealed the Postal Rate Commission's decision setting the first-class rates that took effect February 3, 1991. On August 8, the Postal Service announced that uncertainty over these rates would require that the Warren stamp be postponed until 1992.

The appeal failed, the one-ounce rate remained at 29¢, and the Warren stamp was rescheduled for March 9, 1992. Meanwhile, the 75¢ denomination was reassigned to another Great Americans stamp, depicting Wendell Willkie, and the Warren stamp was denominated at 29¢. When the Warren stamp finally appeared, more than 13 months had elapsed since the rate change.

The Warren stamp was an international production. Its engraver was Polish-born Czeslaw Slania, who is widely considered to be the world's premier stamp engraver, with hundreds of stamps from several countries to his credit. Its printer was the Canadian Bank Note Company in Ottawa, under a subcontract with Stamp Venturers.

These developments were received quietly by Congress and the philatelic press. A year earlier, things had been different. Then, the announcement that Canadian Bank Note would print two Great Americans stamps for Stamp Venturers — the 35¢ Dennis Chavez of 1991 and the Earl Warren — had stirred a storm of "buy American" protest and helped generate a congressional investigation of the Postal Service's stamp procurement policies. To quiet the controversy, Postmaster General Anthony M. Frank had promised that, after the Warren, no more U.S. stamps would be printed outside the country.

The selvage inscriptions on the Warren stamp were checked for accuracy by Sara Day, a contract researcher for USPS. The Postal Service began taking extra care with this phase of its stamp development after some of its early, hastily drafted selvage inscriptions turned out to contain factual errors. The most embarrassing of these occurred with the Hubert Humphrey Great Americans stamp, which was printed with incorrect dates for Humphrey's vice presidential term in the pane margins.

A September 18, 1991, memo to Project Manager Jack Williams from Day illustrates how careful USPS had become.

"This is OK," she wrote of the proposed Earl Warren selvage information, "except that governor and chief justice used in the general sense should not begin with uppercase letters.

"I did question the starting date — 1953 — for his term as 14th chief justice because I saw in one of your sources that he was not confirmed by the Senate until March 1954. I checked this out in the Library of Congress Law Library today in two sources ('Judges of the United States, 1983,' and 'A Reference Guide to the United States Supreme Court'). You will see from the copy of p. 349 in the latter that Warren was 'confirmed by a voice vote of the Senate on March 1, 1954.'

"A reference librarian in the Law Library called the Supreme Court Library for an explanation. Apparently, since President Eisenhower appointed Warren following Chief Justice Fred Vinson's sudden death when Congress was in recess it was considered to be a presidential interim appointment and, therefore, Warren's term began when he took the oath of office on October 5, 1953."

Earl Warren was born March 19, 1891, in Los Angeles, California. He was elected district attorney of Alameda County in 1925, California attorney general in 1938 and governor in 1942. In three terms as governor he reorganized the state government and secured major reform legislation, modernizing the hospital system, prisons and highways and expanding old-age and unemployment benefits.

In 1948 he sought the Republican nomination for president. Instead, the GOP named him to run for vice president on a ticket with presidential candidate Thomas E. Dewey. Although poll results indicated the ticket was a sure winner, it was upset by the Democratic team of President Harry Truman and Senator Alben Barkley.

Although several losing candidates for president have been depicted on U.S. stamps, only one other defeated candidate for vice president besides Warren has appeared on a stamp. He was Franklin D. Roosevelt, who ran unsuccessfully for vice president in 1920 only to win the presidency four times beginning in 1932.

In 1953 President Dwight D. Eisenhower appointed Warren the 14th chief justice of the United States. Eisenhower was later surprised — and somewhat chagrined — at the activist role his appointee staked out at the Supreme Court. Warren's biographer, Bernard Schwartz, wrote that the Warren era was one of "two great creative periods in American public law." The other was the early years of the 19th century, when the Supreme Court under John Marshall laid down the foundations of the American system.

As chief justice, Warren was a forceful leader who exercised great influence over the outcomes of the cases before the court. In the most important of all these cases, Brown vs. Board of Education of Topeka (1954), he fashioned a unanimous decision that school segregation was unconstitutional — even though, when the justices had first discussed that case under Warren's predecessor, they were sharply divided. The Brown case, and other Warren Court decisions furthering racial equality, helped inspire the civil rights movement of the 1950s and 1960s and the civil rights laws passed by Congress, which in turn were upheld by the high court.

In other major — and controversial — decisions under Chief Justice Warren, the court held that the "one man, one vote" principle must apply in legislative apportionment; that indigent criminal defendants must be provided counsel; that arrested persons must be advised of their right to a lawyer, whether or not they could afford to hire one; that the media have a far-reaching right to criticize public figures, absent a showing of actual malice; and that public schools could not sponsor periods of prayer.

In 1963 President Lyndon B. Johnson named Warren to head a commission to investigate the assassination of President John F. Kennedy. The panel, popularly known as the Warren Commission, reported that in its judgment Kennedy was slain by Lee Harvey Oswald and that Oswald acted alone.

Warren retired from the court in 1969. He died in Washington, D.C., July 9, 1974.

The Design

The designer of the Earl Warren stamp, Christopher Calle of Ridgefield, Connecticut, had also designed the Wendell Willkie stamp, also in the Great Americans series, that had been issued a few days earlier. USPS gave Calle some photographs to work with, but, as usual, the artist supplemented the material with other pictures that he found himself.

Calle based his pencil drawing of the former chief justice on three or four very similar images. The principal one was a photograph made in 1967 by Robert Oakes of the National Geographic Society. It showed Warren in his judicial robes, and was one of the favorite photographs of the jurist's wife, according to Warren's daughter, Virginia Warren Daly, whom USPS consulted.

"This was a little more difficult than the Willkie portrait," Calle said. "Willkie had a strong looking face, with great, interesting features, and that little half smile. The face was so recognizable. Warren had a more 'normal,' grandfatherly type of face.

"I came across many different images of Warren. Smiling just didn't seem to work with him. Smiling made him look too jovial and not serious enough. It didn't express his personality the way I thought it should."

Warren's eyeglasses gave Calle no problem. "Glasses are fine," he said. "They're just another interesting element, like a mustache — just another thing that defines that person's personality.

"I must admit that I would love to work on somebody who has a nice grizzly gray beard or a thick handlebar mustache. The one person I would have loved to do was Bret Harte. He had really interesting sideburns." (The Great Americans stamp showing Harte, issued in 1986, was designed by Arthur Lidov.)

Calle gave the Warren portrait a solid dark background. "The darkness was sort of an extension of his robe, and the robes are synonymous with Supreme Court justices," Calle said. "Also, because Warren's features weren't as strong and as delineated as Willkie's, the dark background kind of held the whole shape of his face."

Calle noted that the engraving that Czeslaw Slania had made from his pencil sketch was different in style from the engravings done from his work in the past by BEP craftsmen. The BEP's intaglio specialists faithfully translate Calle's multiple pencil strokes into engraved lines, but Slania — perhaps because he was more accustomed to engraving from photographs — produced a softer, more modulated rendition of the original artwork, Calle said.

The color of the stamp was dark blue. Blue has been the most frequently used basic color in the Great Americans series; the Scott catalog describes 13 of the 52 face-different stamps in the series as having some variation of the shade.

First-Day Facts

Chief Justice William H. Rehnquist, a self-described "amateur stamp collector" who takes a personal interest in stamps pertaining to the U.S. Supreme Court, was the principal speaker at the public first-day ceremony, held in the Lower Great Hall of the Supreme Court Building. The

This is Robert Oakes' photograph of Earl Warren on which Christopher Calle based his pencil portrait for the stamp.

chief justice had previously been the speaker at the dedication of the Supreme Court Bicentennial commemorative of 1990, and at that time he had complained about the small number of Supreme Court justices who had appeared on stamps. In this speech he noted with satisfaction that the Warren definitive bore the current first-class rate and would therefore be widely used, unlike the John Marshall definitive of earlier in the century, which carried a $5 denomination.

The stamp was dedicated by Postmaster General Anthony M. Frank. Honored guests included Chief Justice Warren's daughters, Virginia Warren Daly and Nina "Honeybear" Elisabeth Brien, and sons, Earl Warren Jr. and Robert Warren. The chief justice's widow was listed on the program but was unable to attend.

29¢ FLAG OVER WHITE HOUSE

Date of Issue: April 23, 1992

Catalog Number: Scott 2609

Colors: red (PMS 185), blue (PMS 295)

First-Day Cancel: Washington, D.C.

FDCs Canceled: 56,505

Format: Coils of 100, 500 and 3,000. 100-stamp coils printed from intaglio sleeves of 960 subjects (20 across, 48 around). 500-stamp and 3,000-stamp coils printed from intaglio sleeves of 864 subjects (18 across, 48 around).

Perf: 9.8 (Goebel stroke perforator for coils of 100; Huck rotary peforator for longer coils)

Designer and Typographer: V. Jack Ruther (BEP)

Art Director: Leonard Buckley (BEP)

Project Manager: Joe Brockert (USPS)

Modeler: Peter Cocci (BEP)

Engravers: Thomas Hipschen (BEP, vignette); Deborah Alexander (BEP, lettering and numerals)

Printing: printed on BEP's 3-color intaglio C press (901) and the 3-color intaglio station of BEP's offset-intaglio D press (902)

Quantity Ordered: 7,035,928,000 (6,020,800,000 in coils of 100; 675,000,000 in coils of 500; and 340,128,000 in coils of 3,000)

Quantity Distributed: 5,561,196,000 (4,756,020,000 in coils of 100; 612,600,000 in coils of 500; and 192,576,000 in coils of 3,000)

Sleeve Number Detail: 1 sleeve number on every 48th stamp

Sleeve Numbers: 1, 2, 3, 4, 5, 6, 7, 8

Tagging: prephosphored paper

The Stamp

The 29¢ coil stamp issued April 23, 1992, depicting the American flag over the White House, was a definitive stamp with a commemorative purpose. Unlike any of its predecessors in the long-running series of flag definitives, the new item was issued to mark the anniversary of a specific historic event. The event was the laying of the White House cornerstone October 13, 1792, and the stamp, in the fashion of a commemorative, bore the wording: "The White House/1792/1992."

Its design was the third in the flag series to picture the executive mansion at 1600 Pennsylvania Avenue, Washington, D.C. The very first flag definitive, in 1963, was a 5¢ sheet stamp displaying Old Glory over the White House (Scott 1208). That stamp, unlike any other U.S. stamp, bore only the denomination, with no wording. A second Flag Over White House design was used on five different sheet and coil stamps between 1968 and 1971 (6¢ and 8¢, Scott 1338 and 1338A-D-F-G).

The 1992 Flag Over White House coil replaced a previous 29¢ coil in the Flag series, issued a little more than a year earlier, on which the Stars and Stripes flew over Mount Rushmore. Although that stamp, too, had appeared in an anniversary year — the year when the Mount Rushmore National Memorial turned 50 — there was no indication, in the design or in USPS publicity, that its purpose was commemorative.

The White House stamp was originally scheduled for release in March 1992, but it was held up because of the difficulty in scheduling a first-day ceremony that fit the schedule of the building's chief resident, President George Bush. Eventually it was issued April 23, with the president participating in the dedication.

Postal Service officials asked the Bureau of Engraving and Printing in August 1991 whether the Bureau could prepare a new engraved flag stamp featuring the White House for release early in 1992. BEP said it could do the job.

At that time, USPS management was still hoping to get approval from the Postal Rate Commission for a 30¢ first-class rate or, failing that, to get the unanimous vote of the USPS Board of Governors that would be needed to override a Rate Commission turndown. Consequently, BEP had to proceed with the preparation of the new stamp without knowing what the denomination would be. When engraver Thomas Hipschen prepared the die, he left the denomination corner blank. Later, after it was determined that the 29¢ rate would remain in effect, the other engraver on the project, Deborah Alexander, added the "USA 29."

The White House previously had been depicted on 10 face-different U.S. stamps. These included the 5¢, 6¢ and 8¢ Flag designs mentioned earlier, as well as the Christmas stamp of 1963. The building's first postal appearance was on the 4½¢ value in the Presidential definitive series of 1938. In addition, the White House was displayed on both sides of the Postal Service's first picture postal card, issued in 1989.

The 200th anniversary of the White House was commemorated not only postally, but also numismatically, with a $1 silver coin produced by the U.S. Mint. The coin initially sold for $28 (proof) and $23 (uncirculated). Ten dollars of the surcharge benefited the White House Endowment Fund, which purchases art and antiques for the public rooms of the president's mansion. Only 500,000 of the coins were authorized, the lowest mintage for a commemorative silver dollar in nearly a century.

The coin's obverse, designed by Edgar Z. Steever IV, a sculptor-engraver for the Mint, showed a view of the north front of the White House. The reverse, designed by Chester Y. Martin of Philadelphia, depicted a bust of James Hoban, the Irish-American architect of the White House. It was similar to the portrait that had been shown on two stamps issued in 1981 to honor Hoban (Scott 1935-1936).

Hoban's design for the president's home was selected in a 1792 competition sponsored by the three commissioners for the planned new capital city. Conscious of cost, the commissioners specified a building that could be completed in stages after its initial occupation. It would be placed at the opposite end of a grand avenue from the planned capitol, on a site where Pierre Charles l'Enfant, the French city planner, had already begun an excavation.

Hoban's winning design netted its creator $500. Among the entries it defeated was a drawing of a domed structure submitted anonymously by Thomas Jefferson, who later would occupy the White House as president. Hoban envisioned a building in the Neoclassical style, quite unlike any house in the colonies or early republic, and bigger than any of them. The most striking feature of his floor plan was the oval drawing room on the south side, extending out into the garden area. This "elliptic saloon" would become the Blue Room, the central reception chamber.

Because of the uncertainty of funding, construction dragged on for years, and the building was still unfinished when John Adams, the second president, moved in during November 1800 near the end of his term. Jefferson, who followed Adams, declared the house "big enough for two

This is the commemorative silver dollar issued by the U.S. Mint to mark the 200th anniversary of the White House. The obverse shows the building's north front, while the reverse bears a bust of architect James Hoban and the main entrance of the White House he designed.

emperors, one pope and the grand lama," and set about to complete the basic work — and add touches of his own, such as east and west wings.

In 1814, during the War of 1812, British troops captured the city and set a fire that gutted the president's house. Hoban was hired to supervise the rebuilding, but had to replace much of the weakened shell. While he was at it, he added the lovely semicircular south portico, a modified version of one he had shown in his original design. Later, he added the colonnaded north portico that is prominently seen on the 1992 stamp.

During the administration of President Harry Truman, the building was completely renovated and its interior reconstructed. Truman also added the second-floor balcony inside the south portico. In 1991 the building was stripped of an accumulated 42 coats of paint and repainted with a single coat that approximated the whitewash sealer first applied by Scottish stonecutters in the 1790s.

The Design

Because the White House had appeared so often on U.S. stamps, finding a view and a treatment that hadn't been used before posed a challenge to BEP artist V. Jack Ruther.

For reference material, Ruther was given color photographs made by Sid Burch and Randy Eshpeter in August 1991, during the renovation of the building's exterior and grounds. He made at least one preliminary sketch of the building's south side, but his final design was based on a photograph made from the northeast corner of the building, showing the morning sun shining on the east side and the north portico.

This is the 1991 photograph of the White House, showing its east and north sides and the familiar colonnaded north portico, that V. Jack Ruther used for reference in creating his design for the 1992 Flag stamp. The lawn in the foreground was torn up because of extensive exterior renovation work that was then in progress.

Working from this photo, the artist made a black-and-white acrylic rendering of the building. In the process he artistically removed some of the trees and foliage that concealed the east wall and its distinctive windows. He also eliminated evidence of the restoration project, including scaffolding and dug-up portions of the lawn and driveway.

Although most previous flag coil stamps had utilized three colors, Ruther and Leonard Buckley, the BEP foreman of designers who served as art director for the stamp, decided to use only the colors needed for the flag — red and blue — on this one.

"Rather than print the White House portion in black, we wanted to get the feel of morning light and shadow in this picture," said Buckley. "We chose to carry the blue of the flag down into the vignette because it has a coolness that we liked and because it conveys shadows well."

In Ruther's original design, a flag flew on the flagpole on the roof of the White House, where the U.S. flag has traditionally flown. But because some members of the Citizens' Stamp Advisory Committee, as well as some Bureau officials, were afraid the small flag would appear as only a dot when it was reduced to stamp size, a second version of the design was made without it.

The design the Postal Service disclosed during its mass unveiling of 1992 stamp designs December 11, 1991, was the version without the flag and flagpole. But on the stamp as issued, the flag and pole were there.

According to Charles Yeager, writing in *The United States Specialist*, when the design was sent to the White House for approval in November or early December 1991, John Sununu, the president's chief of staff (and a well-known stamp collector), pointed out the absence of the flag, and

This is V. Jack Ruther's black-and-white acrylic rendering of the White House that was combined with his flag painting and typography to produce the finished stamp design.

V. Jack Ruther made these two pencil sketches while developing his design for the Flag Over the White House stamp. One showed the north portico, which was the view that was used on the finished stamp. In this sketch, Ruther placed a large tree at the left, which he pruned extensively in his finished art, and drew people and a horse and buggy in the driveway, figures that he eventually removed. The other sketch showed the beautiful south portico. This is the side that appears on the current $10 bill. Note that in this drawing Ruther included the flag that flies over the White House roof. In fact, it was superimposed over the two lower stripes of the large flag in the design.

it was subsequently put in.

"I just said it would be more accurate with it there," Sununu told Bill McAllister of *The Washington Post*. He said he cautioned that millions of tourists visit the White House every year, and some would be certain to complain to the Postal Service about the missing flag. "I'm not trying to design the stamp," Sununu told the officials, according to McAllister. "You have to make that decision . . . I am merely commenting as a private citizen who cares about stamps."

However, Donald M. McDowell, director of the Office of Stamp and Philatelic Marketing for USPS, gave a somewhat different version to *Linn's Stamp News*. McDowell said the Postal Service's "original plan was to let the engraver put the flag in and determine which way the wind

The original design of the Flag Over the White House stamp that was released to the press and public had a large free-floating flag, but lacked the smaller image of the flag that flies over the presidential residence. On the issued stamp, this flag was in its rightful place.

should blow." Production considerations and the direction of the press in printing the tiny flag were also to be considered, with an eye to preventing its blue ink and the red ink of the big flag's bottom stripe from contaminating each other, McDowell said.

"We were the ones who told John Sununu that it wasn't on there," he said. "And he agreed with us that the flag ought to be there." The story "got a little out of proportion," McDowell opined.

The typeface Ruther chose for the lettering and numerals was Galliard, a favorite of veteran CSAC typographer Bradbury Thompson. The commemorative inscription was placed in the upper-right corner in small type, and the "29 USA" was dropped out of the vignette in the lower-left corner and given a double outline of dark and white.

USPS officials originally wanted the small lettering to be red, but their BEP counterparts persuaded them that the red color should be reserved exclusively for the stripes on the flag.

"That way, the shape of the flag would stand out," said Buckley. "To make the lettering red would have compromised the stripes."

Although just two colors were used, the first printings of the stamp used the full three-color potential of BEP's intaglio C press and the virtually identical intaglio portion of the offset-intaglio D press.

As reported by Ken Lawrence in *Linn's Stamp News*, blue ink was applied to the printing sleeve by two different inking-in rollers while red was applied by the third. The purpose, again, was to prevent ink contamination — in this case, to ensure that the blue inscription above the flag wouldn't bleed into the flag's stripes during wiping. The blue ink for this inscription, and the blue for the White House vignette, were applied by separate inking-in rollers.

Later, with plentiful supplies of the stamp in the vault, BEP printers experimented with a single blue inking-in roller and found that they could

Early printings of the White House stamp used this configuration of inking-in rollers on the intaglio C press. Blue ink was applied by both bottom rollers, and red by the next one up. Later printings of the stamp used a single blue inking-in roller.

adequately control the contamination problem without the necessity of a second application of blue. All subsequent printings used just two inking-in rollers, one red and one blue.

Varieties

The Plate Number reported the finding of full rolls of imperforate White House stamps, from plates 3 and 6. In November an imperforate pair was auctioned by Lowell S. Newman and Company for $50.

First-Day Facts

With little advance notice, President George Bush and his wife Barbara took part in a brief first-day ceremony for the stamp in the White House Rose Garden at 3:30 p.m. April 23. Difficulties in scheduling a date with the White House prevented the Postal Service from announcing a first-day ceremony or holding a public event.

Deputy Postmaster General Michael Coughlin, who was serving as acting postmaster general until a successor to Anthony M. Frank was named, appeared with the president and first lady at the ceremony. Also attending were Edward E. Horgan Jr. and Kenneth Hunter, associate postmasters general; George Haley, chairman of the Postal Rate Commission; and stamp designer V. Jack Ruther.

In his remarks, President Bush briefly traced the history of the executive mansion, noting along the way that James Hoban's plan had "won out over grander designs, some of which included vast central courts, rotunda — and here's an intriguing idea, a draped throne for the

V. Jack Ruther, left, BEP designer of the White House stamp, poses for an Associated Press photograph with President George Bush at the stamp's April 23 first-day ceremony at the White House.

president." After Hoban won the contest, the president continued, he "began another capital tradition. He promptly leaked the news to his hometown papers in Charleston."

"I hope the stamp serves as a reminder to every American that this place is truly the people's house," he concluded. "One of the great blessings of the presidency, obviously, is to live within the walls of this house, to roam its hallways, to absorb its history and to be reminded at every turn of the noble men who have lived here and of their families. But a president can never obviously be more than a caretaker or a tenant in this house, for the White House belongs, as it has for 200 years, to every American."

23¢ USA FIRST-CLASS PRESORT RATE COIL (ABNC)

Date of Issue: July 21, 1992

Catalog Number: Scott 2608

Colors: yellow, magenta, cyan, black

First-Day Cancel: Kansas City, Missouri

FDCs Canceled: 35,673

Format: Coils of 10,000. Gravure printing cylinders of 456 subjects (19 across, 24 around).

Perf: 9.8 (stroke perforator, designed and built by Guilford Gravure Division of George Schmitt and Company)

Designer: Lon Busch of St. Louis, Missouri

Typographer and Art Director: Richard Sheaff

Project Manager: Joe Brockert (USPS)

Modeler: Acitronics Division of George Schmitt and Company

Printing: Printed by Guilford Gravure for American Bank Note Company on an Andreotti 5-color webfed gravure press. Perforated and coiled at Guilford Gravure. Color separations by Image Processing, a division of George Schmitt and Company. Cylinders by Acitronics.

Quantity Ordered: 150,000,000

Quantity Distributed: 150,000,000

Cylinder Number Detail: 1 group of 4 gravure cylinder numbers preceded by the letter A on every 24th stamp

Cylinder Number Combinations: A1111, A2222

Tagging: untagged

The Stamp

On July 21, the Postal Service issued a new 23¢ coil stamp for use by first-class bulk mailers who presorted their mail by ZIP code in minimum quantities of 500 pieces. Prominently bearing the words "Presorted First-Class," the stamp was considered a precancel by USPS, was made without tagging, and required a precancel permit for use.

The stamp, gravure-printed by the American Bank Note Company, was issued in coils of 10,000. Later in the year, coils of 3,000 and 500 were issued. These bore the same design, but were printed by the Bureau of Engraving and Printing and were perceptibly different in appearance (see next chapter).

The ABNC-printed item was the second coil stamp in less than a year to bear the 23¢ rate and to be intended specifically for users of first-class presorted mail. The first, issued September 27, 1991, in coils of 500 and 3,000, was hastily designed, depicting only the American flag waving over the words "Presorted First-Class." The new design was more imaginative and colorful, which are attributes that USPS is convinced customers want in their stamps.

The purpose of these stamps was to satisfy mailers who were paying 23¢ per piece and wanted a stamp that said so. Previously, USPS had expected them to use stamps bearing the 10¢ denomination and to pay the extra 13¢ per letter at the time of mailing. The mailers were afraid that the use of 10¢ stamps gave the public the mistaken idea that the mailings were excessively subsidized.

The new stamp was announced in June.

After ABNC had printed the 10,000-stamp rolls of the new design, USPS requested an additional quantity of 3,000-stamp rolls of the 1991 Flag design. According to Dr. Robert Rabinowitz, writing in *Stamp Collector*, a shortage had occurred because of heavy election campaign mailings. The new batch of rolls, bearing a new cylinder number, A333, began appearing in post offices in mid-August, Rabinowitz wrote.

The Plate Number reported that ABNC used the same wrapper labels for the newly designed stamp that it had used for the old Flag stamp. As a result, the labels for the USA stamps had the wrong copyright date.

The Design

The design of the new presort stamps was a variation on the traditional American flag subject. Instead of waving freely, the flag is partially reflected in the chromelike surface of the block letters "USA." The background is a deep blue, with the service inscription "Presorted First-Class 23" in dropout white.

"Because the 'USA' was a big design element, we didn't have to put in 'USA 23,' " said Joe Brockert, the project manager. "We were hoping that people wouldn't miss the forest for the trees and tell us we had left the 'USA' off."

The concept for the design came from Bob Brunsdon, who at the time was an employee of Sheaff Design in Needham Heights, Massachusetts.

Bob Brunsdon, an artist with Sheaff Design, used color markers to make this concept sketch on which Lon Busch based his finished airbrush painting for the 23¢ presort-rate coil stamp.

Sheaff Design, which was founded by Richard Sheaff, a design coordinator for USPS, has a contract with USPS for design support services. Sheaff himself no longer is connected with the firm.

"We (the USPS staff and its art directors) are always either hiring artists to come up with concepts for icons, or coming up with them ourselves," Sheaff said. "We ask, what else can we do besides eagles and flags? And there's sort of a constant stream of these going through.

"At a time when we were asking every artist we could think of, because the committee said it wanted more icons, we asked Sheaff Design to have their staff people submit some sketches. They sent in a pile of them. One of them was the USA, which Brunsdon had done with color markers.

"It caught my eye, and I took it to Washington, and Joe Brockert (of the USPS design staff) liked it. He knew there was going to be a need for a first-class presort stamp. So we took that rough concept and sent it to Lon Busch, to do a nice airbrush treatment of it. That's what he did."

Busch, of St. Louis, Missouri, was an airbrush specialist who had previously designed the Pan American Games commemorative stamp of 1987 and the Basketball Centennial stamp of 1991.

ABNC used the standard four process colors, yellow, magenta, cyan and black, to print the stamp. BEP, for the version issued later, used red, cyan, blue and black. The differences between the two versions were quite apparent to the eye and will be described in the next chapter.

First-Day Facts

The stamp was issued without ceremony in Kansas City, Missouri, home of the Philatelic Sales Division. However, first-day cancellations were available at the Kansas City main post office July 21, and by mail order through September 19. For first-day covers completely serviced by USPS, one 23¢ "USA" stamp and two 3¢ Conestoga Wagon stamps were used to make up the 29¢ regular first-class rate.

23¢ USA FIRST-CLASS PRESORT RATE COIL (BEP)

Date of Issue: October 9, 1992

Catalog Number: Scott 2608A

Colors: red, cyan, blue, black

First-Day Cancel: Kansas City, Missouri

FDCs Canceled: figure unavailable

Format: Coils of 500 and 3,000. Gravure printing cylinders of 432 subjects (18 across, 24 around).

Perf: 9.8 (Huck rotary perforator)

Designer: Lon Busch of St. Louis, Missouri

Typographer and Art Director: Richard Sheaff

Project Manager: Joe Brockert (USPS)

Printing: printed by BEP on 7-color Andreotti gravure press (601). Coils processed on Huck coiling equipment.

Quantity Ordered: 1,320,000,000 (150,000,000 in coils of 500; 1,170,000,000 in coils of 3,000)

Quantity Distributed in 1992: 280,000,000 (40,000,000 in coils of 500; 240,000,000 in coils of 3,000)

Cylinder Number Detail: 1 group of 4 gravure cylinder numbers on every 24th stamp

Cylinder Number Combination: 1111

Tagging: untagged

The Stamp

On October 9, USPS issued the Bureau of Engraving and Printing's version of the 23¢ first-class presort rate coil that depicted the chromelike letters "USA" with a waving American flag reflected.

Earlier, a stamp with the same design, but printed by the American Bank Note Company, had been issued in coils of 10,000. (Under an agreement between USPS and BEP, the Bureau would print no coil rolls larger than 3,000.) The BEP stamp, in coils of 500 and 3,000, was scheduled for issue October 30, "but increased demand by mailers prompted the earlier release date," USPS said.

When plans for a second version of the stamp were first announced, USPS said it would be printed by intaglio. Shortly afterward the Postal Service corrected itself. The new stamp, like the one produced by ABNC, was a gravure product.

The split printing was the third for coil stamps in two years. In 1991 BEP printed the intaglio versions of the Flag Over Mount Rushmore and Canoe coils, while gravure versions, in larger rolls, were printed by ABNC and Stamp Venturers, respectively.

The Design

Both BEP and ABNC used four gravure colors to produce their versions of the stamp. ABNC used the standard process colors: yellow, magenta, cyan and black. BEP used red, cyan, blue and black. The two versions are easily distinguished when placed side by side.

On designer Busch's original airbrush painting, the background blue graduated from dark blue to a lighter blue going downward. ABNC reproduced that effect by using a blend of cyan and black for the background color. This meant that the white typography had to drop out of two colors rather than one, and a close examination of some of the ABNC stamps will show a slight misregistration along the edges of the denomination numbers. BEP avoided this problem by making the background a single tone, using blue for this purpose; but its stamp was somewhat less faithful to the original art. The ABNC stamp also gave a somewhat crisper, clearer reflection in the chrome letters.

First-Day Facts

The stamp was issued without ceremony in Kansas City, Missouri, home of the Philatelic Sales Division. However, first-day cancellations were available at the Kansas City main post office October 9, and by mail order through December 8. For first-day covers completely serviced by USPS, one 23¢ "USA" stamp and two 3¢ Conestoga Wagon stamps were used to make up the 29¢ regular first-class rate.

VARIABLE-RATE COIL (BEP)

Date of Issue: August 20, 1992

Catalog Number: Scott 31 (under heading Computer Vended Postage) for 29¢ single. No numbers assigned to other values.

Colors: blue, red

First-Day Cancel: Oklahoma City, Oklahoma

FDCs Canceled: figure unavailable

Format: Coils of 3,000. Intaglio printing sleeve of 864 subjects (18 across, 48 around).

Perf: 9.8 (Huck rotary perforator)

Designer: Richard Sheaff of Needham Heights, Massachusetts

Art Director and Project Manager: Joe Brockert (USPS)

Engraver: Gary Chaconas (BEP, vignette); Dennis Brown (BEP, lettering)

Modeler: V. Jack Ruther (BEP)

Printing: printed by BEP on 3-color intaglio C press (901). Denominations applied by printer and ribbon in ECA GARD Postage and Mailing Center machine.

Quantity Ordered: 3,840,000

Quantity Distributed: 3,840,000

Sleeve Number Detail: 1 intaglio sleeve number on every 48th stamp

Sleeve Number: 1

Tagging: phosphor-coated paper

The Stamp

On August 20, 1992, USPS began a test program using a new kind of postage stamp and stamp-dispensing system. The stamp, called a variable-rate coil, or VRC for short, was vended from a computerized machine that USPS called a Postage and Mailing Center (PMC).

The basic stamps bore no denomination. Customers could program the PMCs to print any denomination from 1¢ to $99.99 on a stamp before it was dispensed. A built-in scale allowed the customer to determine the amount of postage needed for the desired level of service. The machines gave receipts on request.

The stamps were made by the Bureau of Engraving and Printing, by intaglio, in coils of 3,000 in which the perforations ran horizontally, above and below the design on each stamp. They were dispensed by PMCs manufactured by the ECA GARD company of Chicago, Illinois.

VRC test coils, such as this pair, show a " 0.00" denomination. The machine technicians cannot print any other type of stamp. Only when money is deposited in the machine are denominated stamps dispensed.*

A second type of PMC, dispensing a different variety of the variable-rate coil stamp, was scheduled to go into service "in mid to late summer," USPS said. But this debut didn't take place in 1992 at all. The stamps were gravure-printed by the American Bank Note Company in 3,000-stamp coils, with the perforations running vertically, for use in machines manufactured by Unisys. As of this writing, they were expected to be available in the spring of 1993.

From the beginning, the PMC-VRC program was plagued with problems and complications — including some relatively obvious ones that USPS apparently failed to foresee. These will be described later in the chapter. Several leading philatelic writers were outspoken in their criticism of the entire experiment.

The Postal Service's original announcement said the ECA GARD PMCs would be set up in five sites: the Oklahoma City, Detroit, Miami, Santa Ana and Southern Maryland divisions. USPS subsequently listed 14 specific post offices that would have the machines. These were in Oklahoma City and Norman, Oklahoma; Detroit and Ann Arbor, Michigan; Miami, Florida (four offices); Irvine and Monterey Park, California, and Washington, D.C. (four offices). It later turned out that two Detroit post offices had PMC machines, making a total of 15.

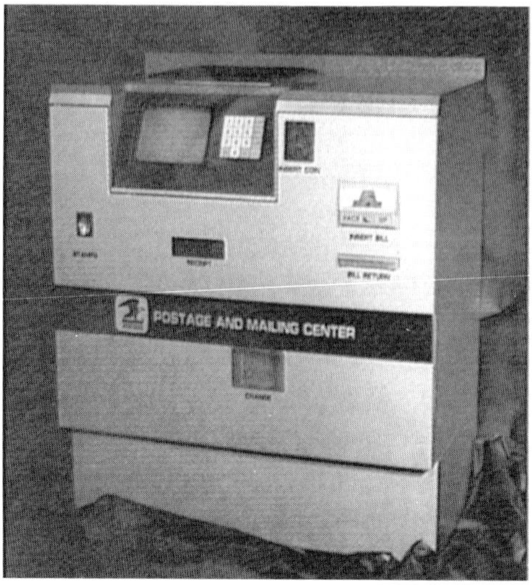

This is an ECA GARD Postage and Mailing Center that dispenses variable-rate coil stamps.

The first ECA GARD PMC began service August 20 in the lobby of Oklahoma City's main post office. The next day the machines were scheduled to begin operations in 12 of the 13 remaining sites. The site in Irvine, California, wasn't scheduled to go on line until September 18.

Several of these machines didn't start up on schedule, however, and others were out of order most of the time they were available to the public. Ken Lawrence, writing in *The Plate Number*, asserted that "within two weeks of installation, the majority of ECA GARD machines were not in working order most of the time, and any time one is found to be working, it is quickly emptied of coils by stamp collectors and dealers."

USPS announced in advance how the machines would work. "The ECA GARD PMC will allow a customer to print a maximum of 20 stamps, in up to three different denominations, per transaction," its news release said. "For example, a customer could order 10 29¢ stamps, five 52¢ stamps and five 75¢ stamps in one transaction.

"After the transaction is complete, the machine is ready for the next customer. The complete cycle, including selecting the type of transaction, making payment, and printing up to 20 stamps, takes approximately four minutes."

For collectors, the new product posed many questions and created some unique problems.

The first question was: Were these really stamps, suitable for collecting by mainstream collectors, or were they a form of postage meter label? The consensus answer quickly turned out to be that they were stamps.

Unlike meters, they required no permit to use, they bore no date or place of issue, and they were usable by anyone, any time, on any kind of mail, exactly like conventional stamps. They were similar in this respect to the experimental Autopost stamps of 1989-90, which are listed in a special section ("Computer Vended Postage") in the Scott *Specialized Catalogue of United States Stamps.*

Autopost stamps, however, looked like meter labels. Variable-rate coils, on the other hand, had all the physical attributes of regular machine-vended coil stamps. They were the same size, they were produced by high-quality security printing methods, and they had perforations, sleeve numbers and tagging.

Once that question was disposed of, the next one was: What would constitute an acceptable degree of completeness for this issue?

Would any stamp, of any denomination — say, 1¢ — fill the bill? Or should a specimen be acquired of each denomination matching a current major postal rate: 19¢ for postal cards, 29¢ for first-class (first ounce), 23¢ for first-class (second ounce), 52¢ for first-class (two ounces), $2.90 for Priority Mail, $9.95 for Express Mail?

Or should the collector strive for as many different denominations as possible, knowing that obtaining a single of every available denomination was a practical impossibility? The cost of one of each would be a staggering $499,950 — but cost would be only the beginning.

Achieving completeness would involve virtually insurmountable logistical problems. The Philatelic Sales Division sold the stamp only with the 29¢ denomination. Dealers who were located near the handful of PMCs offered mint stamps of other denominations, but mostly at substantial markups. Needless to say, nobody offered complete sets.

An additional complication for the hobby — and for USPS — was the aforementioned sleeve number, located on every 48th stamp on the coil roll. Specialists in plate number coils (PNCs) thus assumed a major role in the discussion of how these items should be collected.

At one point, Dr. Robert Rabinowitz, a PNC dealer of Stamford, Connecticut, and a columnist for *Stamp Collector*, suggested that "a joint meeting of USPS decision makers and representatives of the collecting, dealing and writing fraternities might be useful in attempting to define official collecting formats for the VRCs."

Some authorities on PNC collecting argued that because the sleeve number, not the denomination, was important, a PNC specialist would need only one strip of stamps for each sleeve number used by the Bureau.

The very fact that sleeve numbers existed at all created embarrassment for USPS, by giving rise to a sequence of conflicting announcements.

The Postal Service originally announced in a news release that there would be numbers at intervals on the stamps. This was corroborated by Donald M. McDowell, USPS director of stamp and philatelic marketing, in an interview with Rabinowitz.

Rabinowitz wrote in *Stamp Collector* that he had suggested to McDowell, "with tongue in cheek," that the plate numbers be burred off the plates before the stamps were printed, "since major problems could be anticipated in distributing the plate number material." McDowell replied that because the ABNC version of the coil already was printed and had plate numbers, the BEP version would have them too.

Actually, the Bureau's stamps also had been printed. BEP's plate activity reports showed that variable-rate coil sleeve 1 was canceled

September 3, 1991, after 14,000 impressions were printed August 17, 1991. (That gave a maximum of 126,000 plate number coils, the lowest "maximum PNC" total for any stamp yet reported by BEP, according to Stephen Esrati.)

A few weeks later, Rabinowitz continued, "McDowell said the BEP version had been printed without numbers, although he did not recall why they were omitted. He speculated that the BEP had asked whether plate numbers should be included and that his people had said no."

McDowell gave a similar account to *Linn's Stamp News*. "The numbers were not removed from the printing sleeves; they never existed in the first place," he said. "The Bureau of Engraving and Printing never went to press with numbers on those stamps. The press release was in error."

He added: "At some point the decision was made to leave the numbers off the BEP version, but to include them on the other (ABNC) type."

A few days elapsed, and USPS recorrected what it termed "recent information provided by the Postal Service." The BEP stamps did indeed have sleeve numbers. "The disparity is the result of a miscommunication

The sleeve number, which appears at 48-stamp intervals, is on the left side of the stamp (arrow).

between the Postal Service and the BEP," USPS said.

For all the trouble they caused, the tiny single-digit numbers were unprepossessing; in fact, they were difficult to see. They were placed at the side of the design, rather than at the bottom, which was consistent with the way the designs were laid out vis-a-vis the coil rolls. These stamps weren't true vertical coils, but rather were horizontal coils with the designs placed sideways. A true vertical coil stamp has the perforations at the top and bottom of the design, as these stamps did, but also has the narrow dimension of the stamp at the top and bottom. (The last such coil stamps issued by the United States were four Presidential series stamps in 1939, Scott 848-851.)

USPS soon found that it had undertaken an enormous job in producing variable-rate coils, and particularly sleeve-number strips, for collectors.

As mentioned, the Philatelic Sales Division offered only 29¢ variable-rate coils for sale by mail. It sold singles or strips of 30, which included a sleeve number, with a limit of five strips per order. The denominations were applied to the stamps, one at a time, on a single PMC machine at the Division offices in Kansas City, Missouri. This was "a time-consuming process," USPS acknowledged, that would produce "approximately 30 stamps per minute, or realistically, about 8,000 per shift."

(Stephen G. Esrati, editor of *The Plate Number*, noted that this speed could only be obtained without machine malfunctions. His own guess was that the Philatelic Sales Division could denominate only about two rolls of 3,000 stamps in an eight-hour day.)

Understandably, USPS declined to offer intact coils of 3,000 29¢ stamps. This would have required Postal Service workers to print a denomination on each stamp and then reroll the coil, an unworkable scenario. "Due to the highly unusual nature of this stamp and test of the PMC machines, CUSTOMERS SHOULD EXPECT IT TO TAKE SEVERAL WEEKS TO FILL MAIL ORDERS," USPS stated in its news release, using capital letters for emphasis. "All orders will be filled on a first-come, first-served basis and customers are asked to be patient."

Patience definitely was not the reaction of a number of stamp writers, collectors and dealers to the complications created by this unusual stamp issue. Rabinowitz, for one, questioned the need for stamps for the new machines in the first place. "What would have been wrong with labels of the standard Pitney-Bowes type?" he asked in *Stamp Collector*. "Could the decision to go with stamps here have been, even in the slightest, driven by the desire for philately to partially underwrite the experiment? A dated meter might have been better from a security and reuse basis."

He termed a "fiasco" the long wait and quantity limitations imposed on collectors ordering variable-rate coils from the Philatelic Sales Division, and blamed it on "those in Washington who had their hands in this experiment from the beginning."

"Don McDowell, who has taken credit for a number of USPS innovations as they pertain to philately, is on the spot here," Rabinowitz charged. "The Kansas City operation reports to him. It was his responsibility to assure that the PSD would be properly equipped to provide collectors with what they require and on a timely basis . . .

"Some of you may be lucky enough to live near the cities where the experimental machines are located. If the post offices are in areas considered safe enough to walk into with a barrel of cash and you begin feeding the machines, you'll probably get some strips.

"But what if you show up and the person in front of you also has a barrel of cash and empties the machine? After all, it only takes about two to three hours to push out 3,000 stamps. Do you expect that a clerk will be waiting with bated breath to insert the next roll? Good luck."

Ken Lawrence also was critical of the Postal Service's decision to develop and install PMCs.

"The big question," Lawrence wrote in *The Plate Number*, "is why (Assistant Postmaster General Gordon) Morison and (Donald) McDowell were trying to re-invent computerized automatic postage in the first place, when they were well aware that less expensive well-designed working machines have been available from Matsushita in Japan since 1975, from Frama in Switzerland since 1976, from Klussendorff in Germany since 1981, and from other foreign manufacturers more recently. The Postal Service has used equipment manufactured by Frama in other applications, so the reason can't be reluctance to buy abroad, or unfamiliarity with the quality available."

Esrati, also writing in *The Plate Number*, described his experience with the PMC machine in Ann Arbor, Michigan, a few days after the experiment began.

"All instructions on how to use it were shown on a small screen, about a foot across and about eight inches deep," Esrati wrote. "The instructions could be switched over into Spanish at a push of a button.

"The PMC said it could take any currency from a nickel to a $10 bill. So I put in a $10 and ordered it to print 40 1¢ stamps to find the first plate number. An ERROR message appeared on the screen. I had exceeded the maximum quantity allowed to be bought, 20 stamps. (The 20-stamp limit was not universal. The PMC at the Renaissance Center in Detroit allows a purchase of 40 stamps.) I changed my selection to 20 1¢ stamps and ordered it to begin printing.

"Another ERROR message popped up. I had exceeded the maximum allowance return of change, $4.50.

"I got my $10 bill back and inserted two nickels and a dime. One nickel kept coming back. The PMC recognized only about one nickel out of every five and rejected the rest, including the ones it gave in change.

"Finally, I printed the first 20 1¢ stamps. I did not know where the plate number should be but found none on this strip. So I inserted more change for another 20 1¢ stamps. This time, I found a plate number near the end of the strip . . .

"Eventually, after more than two hours at the PMC and after spending almost $70, I was able to print up 11 plate-numbered strips of five of the 29¢ value."

Esrati said customers "with no distraction and with deep concentration" could get a plate-numbered strip of five 29¢ stamps for only $1.88 by printing up 43 1¢ stamps and one strip of five 29¢ stamps.

"But for me the cost came to much more because the machine kept jamming up and causing me to lose count," he wrote. "I ended up at an average cost of $4 a strip and ended up with some undesired 1¢ plate-numbered strips."

Esrati passed on a tip from two dealers who had learned how to reduce machine jam-ups during a sustained purchase. Don't tear off stamps from the PMC at the slot, but hold the last two stamps that emerged and tear below them, he advised.

The Philatelic Sales Division's daily sales limit of 150 stamps created special problems for dealers who didn't have direct access to PMCs, Esrati noted. It meant they had to find a way to get the division to print up such an order on a daily basis, plus 50¢ each for postage and handling.

One dealer simply made a phone order on his credit card and ordered several thousand strips. His daily order would tie up the machine at Kansas City for about 20 minutes a day for several months, Esrati wrote.

Carrying a collector's logic to its ultimate conclusion was a *Linn's* reader, George L. Henderson of San Mateo, California. He noted that the machines made it possible to collect plate number coils in strips of five in which each stamp would be of a different value, as well as all or part of them being the same value.

"If this were the case, then there would be 9,999 possible combinations for each strip of five stamps, or a total of 9,999 to the fifth power possible combinations for strips of five," Henderson wrote. "That multiplies out to a total of some 99,950,000,000,000,000,000 combinations, at a total cost of $4,998,000,000,000,000,000,000. In English, this translates into 4 sextillion, 998 quintillion dollars . . . This amount of money would be equal to approximately 5 million times the actual value of all the real estate plus all other assets on the face of the earth.

"Now, if that seems to be a tad bit too much for most people, one can always collect the stamps in strips of three, which would cost only $50 trillion, which is much more reasonable. We are now beginning to close in on a figure that is only multiples of the U.S. national debt.

"If a machine could be developed that could print out 100 stamps a second, it would take approximately 32 billion years to print them all out. So, even if one could pay for them, it would take more than the lifetime of the earth to produce them."

A full-page notice in the August 6 *Postal Bulletin* notified post office employees that the odd-looking labels were valid for postage. Nevertheless, some didn't get the message. The philatelic press carried illustrations of various covers bearing 29¢ stamps, properly postmarked, that were marked "Returned for Postage" and sent back to the sender with the stamps X'd out, circled or handstamped "Void."

On the other hand, while letters with legitimate postage were being denied delivery, there were reports of letters bearing as little as 1¢ in

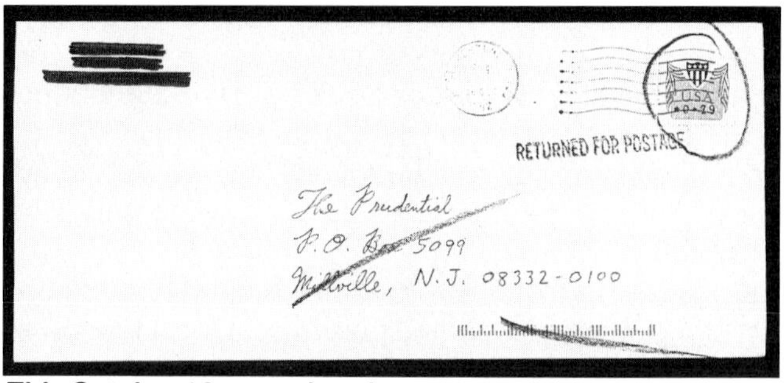

This October 16 cover, bearing a 29¢ variable-rate coil, was returned to its sender as an invalid postage item.

variable-rate coil postage that were delivered without challenge. One reason this occurred was that all variable-rate coils were, of necessity, tagged, regardless of their denomination. Tagged stamps proceed through post office facer-canceler machines without automatic rejection. For this reason, USPS policy since January 1, 1991, has been to eliminate tagging on stamps of low denomination, to block the processing of letters that are grossly underfranked.

In November, Ken Lawrence reported in *Linn's* that PMCs would be reprogrammed to produce only variable-rate coils of 19¢ or higher, and the process began the following month. This presumably would solve the Postal Service's tagging problem. It would also solve an unpublicized problem that had to be worrying USPS officials, namely, the revenue loss created by collectors who bought large quantities of 1¢ stamps to obtain sleeve numbers. However, it would create a problem for collectors, by making instant rarities of low-value (other than 1¢) variable-rate coils that had been created during the first few months of the program.

Not all the reaction to the new stamps and technology was negative, however. John F. Butkis of Los Angeles, writing in *Linn's*, reported on his own upbeat experience at the Monterey Park, California, post office on the first day of PMC use August 21. With the help of a machine technician, and with uninterrupted access to the machine for about 45 minutes, Butkis was able to produce a variety of rates, including 1¢, 2¢, 3¢, 4¢, 19¢, 29¢, 52¢, 75¢, $9.95 and $2.90. He obtained dated Monterey Park postmarks on covers, including two Express Mail envelopes.

"I've been a collector for more than 35 years, and I know I've remained one because of the fun I've had on days like this," Butkis wrote. ". . . I don't think collectors need worry about new technology. After this morning's experience, I think new technology will add a lot of new and exciting dimensions to the hobby."

As an example of Butkis' point, some collectors took advantage of their ability to juxtapose different denominations by creating strips of stamps that represented their dates of birth or other dates that were meaningful to them.

The bunting and shield on the variable-rate coil stamp were borrowed from this concept sketch that Richard Sheaff had prepared earlier for a possible definitive stamp design. The silhouettes of the* Spirit of '76 *figures were replaced by a tablet on which the PMC machine could print the stamp's denomination.

The Design

The design of the basic variable-rate coil stamp depicted at the upper center a blue and white shield with four blue stripes and four white stars. On either side of the shield, red and white striped bunting flowed out horizontally, then dropped in vertical folds from the corner. The center of the stamp held a square-shaped panel with the letters "USA" in capitals against a security background of light, wavy lines rippling down from the shield.

The machines, when activated, imprinted the denominations in five typewriterlike characters on the space beneath the engraved "USA." Denominations of less than $10 carried an asterisk, as in "* 0.29" for a 29¢ stamp. Stamps valued at more than $10 carried the actual value but without a dollar sign, as in "99.99."

The numbers were printed in black by means of a typewriterlike

On this preliminary version of the variable-rate coil stamp design by Richard Sheaff, the bunting is longer horizontally and the words "United States of America" appear across the top.

This strip of stamps, dispensed by the PMC in Ann Arbor, Michigan, contains errors and freaks caused by problems with the tension on the coil roll. On individual stamps, the denomination is printed twice, shifted and missing.

ribbon. The ink reportedly contained ingredients that made it possible for USPS to detect genuine variable-rate coils.

The design was developed by Richard Sheaff of Needham Heights, Massachusetts, a USPS design coordinator and a frequent creator of artwork for U.S. stamps and postal stationery. It was an adaptation of a design concept for a definitive stamp that Sheaff previously had worked up for use as needed. In the sketch, a similar shield and bunting hung over a silhouette treatment of the three marching figures from Archibald M. Willard's painting *The Spirit of '76*, which once had been the basis for a U.S. stamp triptych (Scott 1629-1631).

Sheaff replaced the silhouettes with a panel to receive the varying denominations, and modified the shield and bunting. He created his new design on a Macintosh computer, using graphics software.

BEP engravers Gary Chaconas and Dennis Brown created the die from which the intaglio printing sleeves were made. The engravers left a gap between the shield and bunting to prevent color contamination between the red and blue portions during printing.

Varieties

Just what constituted a legitimate variety was another question created by the variable-rate coil stamp program.

Early in the life of the machines, collectors discovered that they could manipulate an emerging strip of stamps, by exerting tension on it, or, conversely, by trying to hold the strip inside the machine, to produce double-denomination, triple-denomination and shifted-denomination prints, as well as stamps with no denomination at all. In time, the ECA GARD software was modified to foil such customer misbehavior. Thereafter, if the stamp printer module detected a change in tension, it would stop printing, adjust itself and then continue.

On the other hand, free-lance writer Ken Lawrence reported in *Linn's* that PMCs in Detroit were dispensing random errors without any outside help. At one machine, when Hahn Nguyen ordered a sequence of 34 stamps, the machine printed the denomination again and again on a single stamp, followed by a strip of 33 with no denomination. And Kurt and Joann Lenz provided a strip on which one stamp had a pair of hyphens and a number instead of the standard denomination. The number, 47, corresponded to the number of 1¢ stamps Kurt Lenz had ordered.

First-Day Facts

Because of the extraordinary amount of time it took the Philatelic Sales Division to produce variable-rate coils for collectors, USPS twice pushed back the deadline for submitting covers for the Oklahoma City August 20 first-day cancellation.

Originally USPS said it would allow 60 days, twice the normal grace period. Later, as officials began to realize the nature of the problem they had assumed in producing stamps for collectors, the cancellation deadline was extended another 60 days, to December 18. Still later, they extended the grace period to April 30, 1993, more than eight months after the actual issue date.

At Oklahoma City on the actual first day of sale, USPS limited

```
*******************************************

        UNITED STATES POSTAL SERVICE
          POSTAGE & MAILING CENTER
          DETROIT, MI         48216

ID: DET PMC 1           10-02-92     6:13PM
*******************************************

 1 @ $ 0.75 STAMP                  $  0.75
47 @ $ 0.01 STAMP                  $  0.47
                                   -------
                   Total Printed   $  1.22
                      Total Paid   $  1.25
                 Change Returned   $  0.03

*************** THANK YOU ****************
```

The stamp with two digits preceded by a pair of hyphens is an error. The adjacent 1¢ stamps are normal. The receipt for the stamps also is shown. The "47" on the error stamp may be related to the fact that the customer ordered 47 1¢ stamps in the transaction.

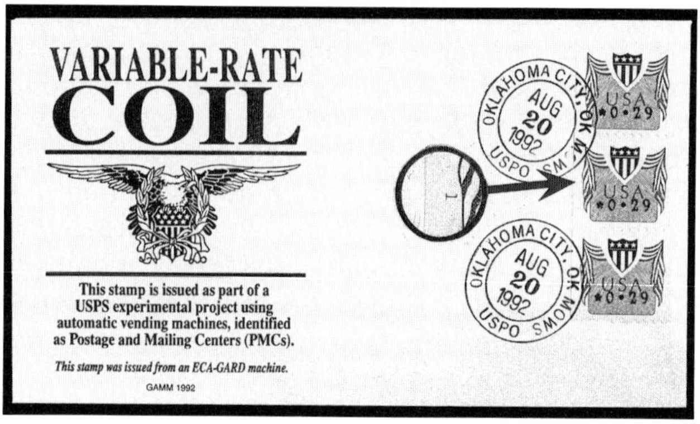

This first-day cover was prepared by Gerry Adlman and bears a sleeve 1 strip. The number is enlarged in the inset.

transactions at the machine in the main post office to one per customer from 8 a.m. to 8 p.m. After completing a transaction, customers could reenter the line to make another purchase. Post office personnel also helped customers in preparing their transactions before they reached the machine to facilitate faster processing. First-day cancellations were available on a handback basis at the post office from 8 a.m. to 8 p.m.

$2.90 AND $5.80 PLEDGE OF ALLEGIANCE BOOKLETS

Date of Issue: September 8, 1992

Catalog Numbers: Scott 2594 (single stamp); 2594a (booklet pane of 10)

Colors: red, blue, gray, black

First-Day Cancel: Rome, New York

FDCs Canceled: 61,464

Format: 1 or 2 panes of 10 vertical stamps arranged vertically 2 across by 5 down. Gravure printing cylinders of 480 subjects (20 across, 24 around).

Perf: 10.9 by 9.8 (Goebel booklet machine stroke perforator)

Selvage and Other Markings: Cylinder numbers printed on each pane binding stub.

Cover Markings: "© United States Postal Service 1992" and promotion for printed stamped envelopes on inside of front cover. Universal Product Code (UPC), information on the Pledge of Allegiance and promotion for printed stamped envelopes on outside of back cover. Coupon for information on stamped envelopes on inside of back cover. Booklet for 10 stamps has blue background on front cover; booklet for 20 stamps has white background.

Designer: Lou Nolan of McLean, Virginia

Art Director and Project Manager: Joe Brockert (USPS)

Typographer: John Boyd of New York, New York

Printing: Stamps printed by BEP on 7-color Andreotti gravure press (601). Covers printed and booklets formed on Goebel booklet machine.

Quantity Ordered: 243,966,000 in booklets of 20; 65,229,000 in booklets of 10; 4,770,000 in unfolded panes (continuing items)

Quantity Distributed: 152,754,000 in booklets of 20; 65,217,000 in booklets of 10; 4,770,000 in unfolded panes

Cylinder Number Detail: 1 group of 4 gravure cylinder numbers on each pane binding stub

Cylinder Number Combinations: 1111, 2222

Tagging: phosphor-coated paper

The Stamp

I pledge allegiance to the flag of the United States of America and to the Republic for which it stands, one Nation under God, indivisible, with liberty and justice for all.

This simple statement is recited daily in thousands of schoolrooms and at public events across the nation. Except for two minor modifications, it's the same pledge that was first printed in the September 8, 1892, issue of *The Youth's Companion*, a weekly magazine then published in Boston.

One hundred years later, on September 8, 1992, the U.S. Postal Service issued a stamp in booklet form to honor the centennial. The stamp was, however, a definitive, not a commemorative. It featured a waving American flag over the three opening words of the Pledge, "I pledge allegiance . . ."

The stamp was printed by the Bureau of Engraving and Printing and was sold in two different size booklets, one of 10 stamps (one pane) for $2.90, and another of 20 stamps (two panes) for $5.80. The Postal Service already had a Flag-stamp booklet in circulation — the $2.90 Flag with Olympic Rings booklet of 1991 — but because there was no assurance that USPS would continue as an Olympic Games sponsor after 1992, that booklet's future was uncertain.

The Pledge of Allegiance stamp was a late addition to the 1992 program, but it had a long — and unusual — history.

For half a century, admirers of Francis J. Bellamy (1855-1931), who is generally credited with authorship of the Pledge, had lobbied to have his portrait placed on a U.S. stamp. Their organizational nucleus was a non-profit patriotic and educational organization called The National Bellamy Award of Albany, New York, which was founded in 1942, the Pledge's 50th anniversary year.

On January 25, 1992, *The Rome* (New York) *Daily Sentinel*, published in the town where Bellamy was raised and where he is buried, carried a story under the headline "Pledge of Allegiance Author Francis Bellamy Gets Stamp."

According to the article, Frank P. Di Berardino, director of the National Bellamy Award, said he had been advised by the office of Rome's congressman, Representative Sherwood L. Boehlert, a Republican from Utica, New York, that the stamp would be issued in 1992 for the Pledge's centennial.

But USPS wouldn't confirm it. The Citizens' Stamp Advisory Committee had considered Bellamy and the Pledge as stamp subjects, but had made no recommendations, USPS spokeswoman Robin Minard told *Linn's Stamp News*. The Associated Press quoted Boehlert as saying:

"I thought they'd be running to embrace the idea. We were incredulous to think in terms of the Post Office issuing a commemorative stamp for someone like Elvis Presley (see The Year in Review) and ignoring the centennial of the Pledge of Allegiance. Where's our priority?" In May, however, USPS announced that there would in fact be a stamp for the anniversary, and that it would be issued September 8 in Rome. CSAC had voted at its May 7 meeting to recommend the stamp to the postmaster general, USPS spokesman Art Shealy told *Linn's*.

In late July, details were released on the design, format and denomination. The stamp would be issued in booklets, and in design it would be essentially another Flag stamp. It would carry no dates — nor would it carry any mention of Francis Bellamy. (As it turned out, however, Bellamy's name did appear on the back cover of the booklet.)

The Postal Service seldom admits to being influenced by prominent individuals, but among those who were given credit by others for successfully advocating the Pledge stamp was Matilda Raffa Cuomo, first lady of New York and chairwoman of New York's Christopher Columbus Quincentenary Commission. A September 4 news release from the commission stated that Mrs. Cuomo "was instrumental" in getting the stamp approved. She had "supported the Pledge of Allegiance stamp effort since 1985," the release said, adding that "in 1987 Mrs. Cuomo received support for the stamp from more than half of the first spouses across the country" and that as chairwoman of the Columbus commission she "last year won endorsement for the stamp from the state's congressional delegation."

Despite the fact that Bellamy wasn't pictured on the stamp, its promoters said they were very pleased. "I think the design is great — very simple, but very beautiful," Di Berardino told *The Washington Post's* Bill McAllister. "Face it, a 29¢ stamp means it's mainstream."

Jack Williams, a member of the USPS stamp staff since 1972, said a Bellamy stamp proposal had been on the agenda at the first CSAC meeting he had attended, and its advocates had never let up. Mostly, the committee was reluctant to honor Bellamy because of the lingering uncertainty that he had in fact written the Pledge — although, Williams said, the sheer persistence of the Bellamy backers also became annoying to some CSAC members.

There was no doubt, however, about the importance of the Pledge of Allegiance itself as an American institution, and so, as its centennial drew near, the committee had no objection to recognizing that event with a stamp, according to Williams.

"So there was, finally, recognition for Mr. Bellamy," he said. "But even then it was hedged; it was on the booklet cover, not the stamp."

The booklet cover itself hedged on the issue of authorship, saying: "It is generally held that it (the Pledge) was written by Francis Bellamy . . ." However, USPS was much more definite about the matter in its news release announcing details of the stamp. There, it said the Pledge was "written . . . by long-time Rome resident Francis Bellamy." And the text of the Postal Service's first-day ceremony program contained no qualifying words ("A century ago, Francis Bellamy created a 23-word verse . . .").

The fact is that the Pledge's authorship was in dispute for years. *The Youth's Companion* stated in 1917 that the original draft was written by James B. Upham, an executive of the magazine who died in 1910. A leaflet circulated by the magazine later named Upham as the originator of the draft "afterwards condensed and perfected by him and his associates of the *Companion* force."

One of those associates was Bellamy, a former Baptist preacher who was a staff writer for *The Youth's Companion* and a member of a national committee formed to carry out President Benjamin Harrison's wish for patriotic exercises in schools to mark the 400th anniversary of Christopher Columbus' first voyage to the New World. Bellamy publicly claimed authorship of the Pledge in 1923. The United States Flag Association, acting on the advice of a committee named to study the controversy, upheld in 1939 the claim of Bellamy, who had died eight years earlier. In 1957 the Library of Congress issued a report attributing authorship to Bellamy.

The Pledge as originally published was only 23 words long: "I pledge allegiance to my flag and the Republic for which it stands, one Nation indivisible, with liberty and justice for all." In 1924 the National Flag

Conference of the American Legion inserted the words "the flag of the United States of America" in place of "my flag," and in 1954 the words "under God" were added by Congress. In 1942 the Pledge was incorporated into the U.S. Flag Code.

The Pledge of Allegiance stamp wasn't the first U.S. Flag stamp to incorporate in its design words from a well-known patriotic composition. The 15¢ stamp in the Americana series (Scott 1597) bore the phrase "The Land of the Free, The Home of the Brave" from *The Star-Spangled Banner*, and the short-lived 18¢ Flag stamps of 1981 (Scott 1890-1891, 1893) included lines from *America the Beautiful.*

The Design

For the design, which had to be put together on short notice, USPS took a Flag stamp design it had in reserve. John Boyd of Anagraphics, Inc., in New York City added the first three words of the Pledge in italic type beneath.

Artist Lou Nolan of McLean, Virginia, had based his flag painting on a huge Old Glory he saw waving in front of the Christian Fellowship Church on Leesburg Pike in Fairfax, Virginia.

"I wanted to try to get away from the normal type of flag that has been shown on stamps, which is kind of flat, with a few little waves in it," Nolan said. "I had always said I wanted to try to show one that looked like a real flag — that had shadows and looked as if it was billowing."

Nolan went to the church in Fairfax on a windy day in 1991 and took several Polaroid pictures of the flag. Working from these, he developed his painting, using water-soluble designer colors. The Bureau of Engraving and Printing, in translating his painting into a gravure stamp, used a gray screen to provide the heavy shading that created the billowing effect.

First-Day Facts

Assistant Postmaster General William T. Johnstone dedicated the Pledge of Allegiance booklets in an outdoor ceremony in Rome, New York, on the grounds of Fort Stanwix National Monument. It was at Fort Stanwix, on August 6, 1777, during the Revolutionary War, that Americans raised the Stars and Stripes for the first time in history.

Representative Frank Horton, Republican from Rochester and ranking Republican member of the House Postal Operations and Services Subcommittee, delivered the principal address. Representative Horton was an old hand at successfully promoting stamp projects for his own district: These included the Chester Carlson Great Americans stamp of 1988 and the Flags on Parade stamp of 1991, which indirectly honored the town of Waterloo, New York, as the birthplace of Memorial Day. Other speakers at the ceremony were Representative Boehlert and Mrs. Cuomo.

Historical background on the Pledge was given by Frank Di Berardino, director of the National Bellamy Award. The Pledge of Allegiance was sung by the Rome Free Academy Select Choir and signed by a group from the New York State School for Deaf Students. Among the honored guests was Peter Bellamy, grandson of Francis Bellamy.

On the day of the ceremony, *CBS This Morning* opened one of its segments with its *Oh, What a Beautiful Morning* theme song performed live by a Rome elementary school choir, and followed this with a picture and announcement of the first-day ceremony coming later in the day.

Collectors were given until November 7 to submit addressed envelopes for first-day cancellations.

$5 EAGLE & SHIELD SELF-ADHESIVE PANE (STAMP VENTURERS)

Date of Issue: September 25, 1992

Catalog Number: Scott 2597 (single stamp); 2597a (pane of 17 plus label)

Colors: red, yellow, cyan, black

First-Day Cancel: Dayton, Ohio

FDCs Canceled: 65,822 (includes all three varieties)

Format: Pane of 17 stamps plus 1 message unit, horizontal, 6 across, 3 down, with vertical peel-off strip in the middle; also, coil of 5,015 stamps. Gravure printing cylinders of 380 subjects (24 across, 15 around, plus 20 coil stamps).

Perf: die cut

Front Markings: On message unit: "When addressing mail,/write clearly:/ Number and Street,/Apt. Number,/City, State and/ZIP + 4 Code." On peel-off strip: "Peel here to fold * Self-adhesive stamps * DO NOT WET *" and cylinder numbers. One-fifth of the panes will show a black dash at the left edge of the peel-off strip, one-fifth will show a dash at the right edge, and three-fifths will show a dash at both edges. On inner surface of backing paper: "Self-adhesive * DO NOT WET" in a repeat pattern.

Back Markings: Illustrated instructions on folding and stamp removal, "ExtraValue Stamps™" and "Patent Pending/© USPS 1992," Universal Product Code (UPC), all on backing paper.

Stamp Designer: Jay Haiden of Bryans Road, Maryland

Art Director: Howard Paine (CSAC)

Project Manager: Joe Brockert (USPS)

Typographer: John Boyd of New York, New York

Printing: Stamps and backing paper printed by Stamp Venturers on a Champlain gravure press in Richmond, Virginia. Laminated paper furnished by Kanzaki. Coils slit from the web in Richmond. Stamps die cut and processed into panes and coils at Stamp Venturers, Milwaukee, Wisconsin.

Quantity Ordered: 852,006,000 (50,000,000 panes and 400 coils of 5,015)

Quantity Distributed: 360,060,000

Cylinder Number Detail: Unfolded panes — 1 group of 4 cylinder numbers preceded by the letter S on vertical peel-off strip. Coils — no cylinder numbers.

Cylinder Number Combination: S1111

Tagging: phosphor-coated paper

The Stamp

Stamp Venturers printed its version of the Eagle and Shield stamp on a webfed Champlain gravure press in Richmond, Virginia, using laminated Kanzaki paper. The stamps and backing paper were printed in the same pass through the press. The coil strips were printed on the same web as the panes, with the coils positioned along the edge of the web, 20 stamps per cylinder revolution. The coils were slit from the web in Richmond. The panes and coils were then die cut and given final processing at Stamp Venturers in Milwaukee, Wisconsin.

The backing paper for this Stamp Venturers-produced Eagle and Shield pane became a booklet cover when folded.

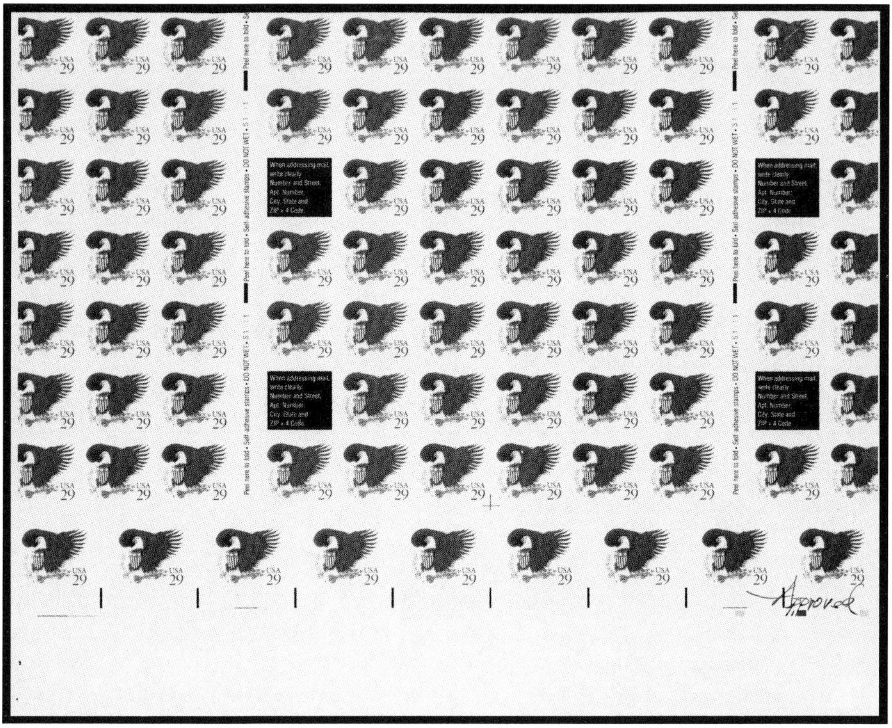

This is a portion of a plate proof of the Stamp Venturers self-adhesive. The stamps for the coil strip are arranged along the edge of the printing cylinder and are spaced more widely than the stamps in the sheetlets. They are shown here at the bottom of the proof. Note the crossed registry marks just above the coil strip. Portions of these marks are normally found on the adjacent stamps after the large sheets have been die cut and separated into panes.

The Design

In printing the backing paper, Stamp Venturers used only three colors: black, red and yellow. The blue portion of the shield was represented by a gray tone. However, even without the use of blue ink, the printer was able to create a green effect for the olive branch on the booklet cover by combining black and yellow dots.

First-Day Facts

Information on the first-day sale of the Eagle and Shield stamps can be found in the chapter on the Banknote Corporation of America version.

$5 EAGLE & SHIELD SELF-ADHESIVE PANE (DITTLER BROTHERS)

Date of Issue: September 25, 1992

Catalog Number: Scott 2596 (single stamp); 2596a (pane of 17 plus label)

Colors: magenta, yellow, cyan, black, green

First-Day Cancel: Dayton, Ohio

FDCs Canceled: 65,822 (includes all three varieties)

Format: Pane of 17 stamps plus 1 message unit, horizontal, 6 across, 3 down, with vertical peel-off strip in the middle; also, coil of 5,015 stamps. Panes printed from gravure printing cylinders of 180 subjects (6 panes across, 4 around). Coils printed from gravure printing cylinders of 126 subjects (6 stamps across, 21 around).

Perf: die cut

Front Markings: On message unit: "When addressing mail,/write clearly:/ Number and Street,/Apt. Number,/City, State and/ZIP + 4 Code." On peel-off strip: "Peel here to fold * Self-adhesive stamps * DO NOT WET *" and cylinder numbers. On inner surface of backing paper: "* SELF-ADHESIVE (A) DO NOT WET *" in a repeat pattern.

Back Markings: Illustrated instructions on folding and stamp removal, "ExtraValue Stamps™" and "Patent Pending/© USPS 1992," Universal Product Code (UPC), all on backing paper.

Stamp Designer: Jay Haiden of Bryans Road, Maryland

Art Director: Howard Paine (CSAC)

Project Manager: Joe Brockert (USPS)

Typographer: John Boyd of New York, New York

Printing: Stamps and backing paper printed by Dittler Brothers Inc., Oakwood, Georgia, on an 8-color modified Chesnut webfed gravure press. Laminated paper furnished by Fasson. Die cutting and separating into panes and coil strips by Voxcom Corporation, Peachtree City, Georgia. Finishing and shipping at Dittler Brothers.

Quantity Ordered:	1,107,006,000 (65,000,000 panes and 400 coils of 5,015)
Quantity Distributed:	722,721,000
Cylinder Number Detail:	Unfolded panes — 1 group of 5 cylinder numbers preceded by the letter D on vertical peel-off strip. Coils — no cylinder numbers.
Cylinder Number Combinations:	D11111, D21221, D22322, D32322
Tagging:	phosphor-coated paper

The Stamp

The second of the two first-time stamp printers to win a contract to produce Eagle and Shield self-adhesives was Dittler Brothers Inc. of Oakwood, Georgia, a small city northeast of Atlanta. Its contract called for the stamps to be printed by the gravure method.

Dittler Brothers undertook the work as part of a joint venture with another Georgia corporation, Voxcom, of Peachtree City, which is south of Atlanta. Dittler Brothers printed the panes, front and back, in one pass through a modified Chesnut webfed gravure press. The coils were printed separately. The printed rolls were then sent to Voxcom to be die cut and

The backing paper for the Dittler Brothers-produced Eagle and Shield pane.

separated into panes and coil rolls, which then were returned to Dittler Brothers for packaging and shipping.

Because the coils were printed on a press whose web could go from roll to roll, there was no need for splices such as those found on the sheetfed-press products of Banknote Corporation of America.

The Design

The press used by Dittler Brothers has an eight-color capability. In printing the panes, the company used five colors to print the stamps — the four standard process colors, plus green for the "USA 29" — which left three colors for the backing paper: blue, red and yellow.

First-Day Facts

Information on the first-day sale of the Eagle and Shield stamps can be found in the preceding chapter.

$5 EAGLE & SHIELD SELF-ADHESIVE PANE (BANKNOTE CORPORATION OF AMERICA)

Date of Issue: September 25, 1992

Catalog Number: Scott 2595 (single stamp); 2595a (pane of 17 plus label)

Colors: cyan, magenta, yellow, black (offset); brown (intaglio)

First-Day Cancel: Dayton, Ohio

FDCs Canceled: 65,822 (includes all three varieties)

Format: Pane of 17 stamps plus 1 message unit, horizontal, 6 across, 3 down, with vertical peel-off strip in the middle; also, coil of 5,015 stamps. Panes printed from offset printing plates of 504 subjects (28 panes — 4 across, 7 around) and intaglio printing sleeves of 504 subjects (28 panes — 4 across, 7 around). Coils printed from offset printing plates of 336 subjects (21 stamps across, 16 rows around) and intaglio printing plates of 336 subjects (21 stamps across, 16 rows around).

Perf: die cut

Front Markings: On message unit, "When addressing mail,/write clearly:/ Number and Street,/Apt. Number,/City, State and/ZIP + 4 Code." On peel-off strip, "* Peel here to fold * Self-adhesive stamps * DO NOT WET *" and plate numbers. On inner surface of backing paper: "* DO NOT WET (B) SELF ADHESIVE *" in a repeat pattern.

Back Markings: Illustrated instructions on folding and stamp removal, "ExtraValue Stamps™" and "Patent Pending/© USPS 1992," Universal Product Code (UPC), all on backing paper.

Stamp Designer: Jay Haiden of Bryans Road, Maryland

Art Director: Howard Paine (CSAC)

Project Manager: Joe Brockert (USPS)

Typographer: John Boyd of New York, New York

Engraver: Richard Baratz, BCA

Printing: Printed by Banknote Corporation of America, Suffern, New York, on sheetfed 5-color Miller offset press and sheetfed T.A. intaglio press. Backing paper printed on Miller press. Laminated paper furnished by Brown-Bridge. Stamps die cut on sheetfed rotary die-cutting equipment by Banknote Corporation of America.

Quantity Ordered: 342,006,000 (20,000,000 panes and 400 coils of 5,015)

Quantity Distributed: 342,006,000

Plate Number Detail: Unfolded panes — 1 group of 4 offset plate numbers preceded by the letter B, and 1 intaglio plate number, on vertical peel-off strip. Coils — no plate numbers.

Plate Number Combinations: B1111-1, B1111-2, B2222-1, B2222-2, B3333-1, B3333-3, B3434-1, B3434-3, B4344-1, B4444-1, B4444-3

Tagging: phosphor-coated paper

The Stamp

In 1989 the Postal Service began conducting a series of experiments to gauge the public's reaction to self-adhesive, or pressure-sensitive, stamps. That year, USPS test-marketed a sheetlet of 18 25¢ stamps that could be folded into a booklet, with the backing paper serving as the booklet cover. Post offices in 15 cities sold the sheetlets over the counter and through vending machines, charging a 50¢ premium over face value.

The following year, the Postal Service began another test program using no-lick stamps. These it sold through automatic teller machines (ATMs) in sheetlets that had the dimensions and thickness of a dollar bill. The first two varieties of ATM stamp were printed on a special polyester film. All since then have been on paper.

USPS continued its ATM stamp program on a limited basis in 1992. By now, however, it was ready to go into full production with self-adhesive stamps that would be sold in the conventional way.

On September 25, a new 29¢ self-adhesive made its debut. Like its 1989 predecessor, it was sold in small, die-cut panes with a peelable backing. The panes were foldable. Also like its predecessor, its design featured an eagle and shield, evocative of the central element of the Great Seal of the United States. In the days that followed, the stamps were available in post offices across the country.

The new self-adhesive was produced by three different private printers, under contracts awarded October 16, 1991. Although the stamps from the three printers bore the same basic design, they were readily distinguishable from each other by the color of their typography. On stamps made by Banknote Corporation of America, the color was brown;

by Dittler Brothers Inc., green; and by Stamp Venturers, red.

USPS officials ordered different colors from the printers so the stamps could be quickly told apart by postal personnel and also by stamp collectors. They realized that collectors would treat the three printers' products as different varieties anyhow, because there would inevitably be subtle differences in their appearance. Therefore, color coding them wouldn't evoke charges that USPS was deliberately creating additional varieties to increase philatelic sales. The Postal Service had used the same reasoning in 1991 when it specified that the two printers of the 29¢ Wood Duck booklet use different colors for the typography.

As it turned out, the difference in the self-adhesive stamps' basic appearance, apart from color, was more than subtle. Two different printing methods were used to produce them. Two of the contractors, Dittler Brothers and Stamp Venturers, used gravure, the process used on the 1989 experimental self-adhesive. The third, Banknote Corporation of America, opted for a combination of offset lithography and intaglio.

"We would have been satisfied if Banknote Corporation had chosen to engrave only the USA 29," said Joe Brockert of USPS, project manager for the stamps. "They said, no, we think this thing can look even better, and we'd like to go in and engrave some of the details in the feathers of

The backing paper for the Banknote Corporation of America-produced Eagle and Shield pane became a booklet cover when folded.

the eagle, to help define them better." Engraver Richard Baratz' intaglio work on the Banknote Corporation version can be seen clearly by viewing the stamp from an angle.

Why did USPS use three printers in the first place? "Quantity," Brockert said. "Especially since two of the printers (Dittler Brothers and Banknote Corporation) were brand-new to stamp production, and we were going into full nationwide distribution of the pressure-sensitives. One printer couldn't have gotten the production we required in a reasonable amount of time, which was between three and six months.

"There was a learning curve with all of them, to bring them up to speed on self-adhesive production, die cutting, front-to-back printing registration, and everything else that was involved. So this was really the only way we could get the quantity we needed. Had the stamps really caught the imagination of the mailing public, with a big demand developing, it would have been the only way we could have met that demand.

"As it was, the stamps met with average acceptance. It wasn't ho-hum, but it wasn't a groundswell of demand either. So there didn't prove to be a need to go back and reprint them on a crash basis. We'll keep them in production for a year or so, and then change designs or make other adjustments, whatever needs to be done."

The new stamps probably would have benefited from more vigorous promotion. Customers who used the self-adhesives found them to be much more convenient than conventional stamps. With larger-than-usual mailings — for example, a stack of Christmas cards — users discovered that they could complete the job with self-adhesives in a fraction of the time it would have taken to separate perforated stamps, lick them and make certain they adhered.

Moreover, the price had come down dramatically. Whereas USPS had imposed a 50¢ surcharge on its 1989 self-adhesives, these sold for $5 for a pane of 17, which made the premium over face value only 7¢. According to a USPS news release, the decision to offer the stamps at that price was based on customer responses to a survey regarding the 1989 pane of 18 25¢ stamps, which also sold for $5.

"More than one-third of the survey respondents expressed a willingness to pay a surcharge to receive the benefits of deluxe, self-adhesive stamps . . ." the release continued. "This indicated that there is a substantial segment of consumers that appreciates not having to tear stamps from a pane or coil, not having to lick them for affixing to an envelope, and not risking having stamps stick together under high-humidity conditions . . .

"The surcharge helps to defray the initial higher manufacturing costs for self-adhesive stamps which exist until larger quantities are produced for sale to customers . . . Plus, it will generate extra revenue from customers who don't mind paying a premium for extra value."

Although the surcharge was a modest one, USPS removed it effective March 1, 1993, and sold the panes at their $4.93 face value. Stamp clerks were notified of the forthcoming change in the February 18, 1993, issue of the *Postal Bulletin.*

USPS spokeswoman Robin Minard told *Linn's Stamp News* that the price was lowered because "current management doesn't believe there should be a surcharge."

Linn's went on to cite sources outside USPS as saying that Postmaster General Marvin T. Runyon Jr. "hit the ceiling" when he learned that the stamps — planned during the administration of his predecessor, Anthony M. Frank — were being sold at more than face value.

Each pane contained 17 stamps plus a label bearing a message that gave standard addressing instructions. The stamps were laid out six across by three down, with position number 10 occupied by the message label. A vertical peel-off strip bisected the pane; its removal made it easy to fold the pane. The peel-off strip carried the numbers of the gravure printing cylinders (or, in the case of Banknote Corporation, the offset printing plates and intaglio printing plate).

Because the paper used by all three printers was prephosphored, the message label was tagged. However, USPS instructed all three printers to print the label in yellow on black for total ink coverage to prevent post office sorting equipment from detecting the phosphor signal. The Postal Service hoped that this would prevent customers from successfully using the label as a stamp.

As with the 1989 self-adhesive, the printers also made coil versions. The coil stamps, which were furnished to USPS in rolls of 5,015, were spaced along a backing strip instead of being flush against each other as they were on the panes. They were created so USPS could use a label-attaching machine to affix stamps to first-day covers. Coil stamps were indistinguishable from pane stamps when they were separated from their backing. Collectors could buy them from the Philatelic Sales Division in strips of 17 — no non-postage label was included — for $5.

Banknote Corporation of America, which made the offset-intaglio version, was a spinoff of the American Bank Note Company that resulted from an antitrust action. The Suffern, New York, firm prints stock certificates, visas for passports, travelers' checks and other security documents. The Eagle and Shield contract was the company's first U.S. stamp assignment.

Banknote Corporation printed the self-adhesive stamps on laminated paper purchased from Brown-Bridge, Troy, Ohio. Three separate printing operations were required. First, the four-color backing side of the laminate was printed on a sheetfed five-color Miller offset press. Then the sheets were turned over and fed through the press again to lay down the four-color offset portion of the stamp designs. Finally, the brown intaglio portion of the stamps was printed, using a sheetfed T.A. press.

At the time, the firm had no specialized coil-making capability, although it has since acquired the necessary equipment. The coil stamps were printed in sheets on the offset and intaglio presses, after which they were sliced into strips and the strips spliced to make rolls containing 5,015 stamps each. After die cutting, workers removed the matrix — the

This was Jay Haiden's earlier eagle-and-shield design, used on the experimental self-adhesive stamp of 1989.

paper surrounding the stamps — by hand. The splices consisted of glossy yellow tape and occurred at every 21st stamp on the rolls supplied to the Postal Service. The Philatelic Sales Division routinely removed the splices as it filled collectors' orders, but acknowledged that some splices would probably get through. Specific requests by collectors for splices weren't honored.

The Design

The American eagle, fronted by a shield and clutching an olive branch and a cluster of arrows in its talons, has been one of the most frequently used icons on U.S. postage stamps. Because it is the centerpiece of the Great Seal, it has appeared on all stamps and postal stationery that have reproduced the Seal. But it has also appeared alone in various forms, as early as the 30¢ value of the 1869 series (Scott 121) and as recently as the non-denominated bulk-rate coil stamp of 1991 (Scott 2604).

The experimental self-adhesive stamp of 1989 bore an Eagle and Shield design by airbrush artist Jay Haiden of Bryans Road, Maryland, and Haiden also created the design for the 1992 full-production self-adhesives. His 1989 eagle was shown from the front, but his new design depicted the bird from the side, with dramatically larger wings.

The painting Haiden submitted to the Postal Service had no stars on the shield. The unadorned blue segment was toned, to suggest a reflection. But the finished stamps show a shield with three stars, in addition to the

This is Jay Haiden's original painting of the eagle and shield used on all three versions of the self-adhesive stamp. The stars were added during the prepress work by each printer.

13 red and white stripes Haiden had painted.

"We didn't ask him to include stars, and in fact the painting looked fine without them," said Joe Brockert. "But as we looked at it, and concluded that stars would hold up when the painting was reduced to stamp size, we decided to introduce them. We didn't go back to the artist, however. We simply told the printing contractors to add the stars electronically during the prepress work."

Although all three printers' covers carried the same design arrangement and wording, each had a distinctive look because of different printing methods and different numbers and combinations of colors. Banknote Corporation of America was the only one of the three to use four colors on its backing paper (cyan, magenta, yellow and black).

First-Day Facts

The three versions of the Eagle and Shield self-adhesive stamp were first placed on sale September 25 in Dayton, Ohio, in conjunction with Airpex XVII, the Dayton Stamp Club's annual exhibition and bourse. USPS held no first-day ceremony.

First-day cover collectors were invited to affix their own stamps to addressed envelopes and submit them for cancellation. Customers wishing USPS to affix stamps were required to send addressed envelopes, together with 87¢ per envelope, in return for which they got one stamp of each variety. USPS allowed up to 60 days after the stamps' issue date for receipt of first-day cover orders.

45¢ PUMPKINSEED SUNFISH

Date of Issue: December 2, 1992

Catalog Number: Scott 2491

Colors: black, cyan, magenta, yellow (offset); black (intaglio)

First-Day Cancel: Washington, D.C.

FDCs Canceled: final total not available

Format: Panes of 100, vertical, 10 across, 10 down. Offset printing plates of 400 subjects (20 across, 20 around) and intaglio printing sleeves of 400 subjects (20 across, 20 around).

Perf: 10.9 (L perforator)

Selvage Markings: "© United States/Postal Service 1991." "Use Correct/ZIP Code ®."

Designer: Michael R. Matherly of Cambridge City, Indiana

Art Director and Project Manager: Joe Brockert (USPS)

Typographer: John Boyd of New York, New York

Modeler: Richard Sennett, Stamp Venturers

Engraver: Yves Baril, Canadian Bank Note Company, Ottawa

Printing: Printed by Stamp Venturers. Offset printing on a 6-color Heidelberg sheetfed press at The Press, Inc., Chanhassen, Minnesota. Intaglio printing on a T.A. sheetfed press by Stamp Venturers, Ogdensburg, New York.

Quantity Ordered: 150,000,000 (continuing item)

Quantity Distributed: 150,000,000

Sleeve/Plate Number Detail: 1 intaglio sleeve number preceded by the letter S and 1 group of 4 offset plate numbers in selvage adjacent to corner stamps

Plate/Sleeve Number Combination: 1111-S1, 2222-S1, 3333-S1, 4444-S1

Tagging: phosphor-coated paper

The Stamp

On December 2, the Postal Service issued another in its de facto wildlife series of definitive stamps. The stamp, issued in sheet form, bore the 45¢ denomination and depicted a pumpkinseed sunfish in full color.

The Postal Service has acknowledged only that it is creating a wildlife series for high-value stamps. In 1990, when it issued a $2 commemorative-size stamp depicting a bobcat, USPS called it "the first issue planned in the conversion of high-value sheet stamps from the Great Americans series to the colorful, commemorative Wildlife series."

In the meantime, however, there has been a procession of lower-value definitives, in sheet and booklet form, depicting native American fauna. In 1991, for example, the 1¢ American Kestrel, 3¢ Eastern Bluebird, 19¢ Fawn and 30¢ Cardinal sheet stamps and 29¢ Wood Duck booklet joined the postal menagerie. Nevertheless, USPS officials have declined to say that these stamps are part of any planned series.

The Pumpkinseed Sunfish stamp design, with no denomination, was unveiled October 30, 1991, at the National Aquarium in Washington, D.C. Its rate, date and place of issue, and format — sheet, coil or booklet — would be announced later, the Postal Service said. Those details were disclosed in September 1992. The stamp would replace the 45¢ Great Americans stamp of 1988 that depicted Dr. Harvey Cushing, USPS said, and would pay the second half-ounce rate for international airmail as well as the one-ounce rate to Mexico. It would also pay the rate for privately produced aerograms.

Sunfish, which belong to the family Centrarchidae, are among the most popular and widespread freshwater sport fish. Their dorsal fins are joined, separated only by a notch. They have a membranous extension of the upper gill cover edge, called the "ear." In the pumpkinseed (Lepomis gibbosus) a large, blood-red blotch is found on the end of the ear flap.

The pumpkinseed is a deep, short, compressed fish. It grows to 10 inches and weighs up to a pound. It is colorful, with a back of dark greenish gold mottled with reddish orange, sides of greenish yellow, mottled orange and blue-green, a yellow-orange belly, and wavy bluish lines on the cheeks.

It is found in southeastern Canada and the Great Lakes states and upper Mississippi River states and south along the Atlantic coast to Georgia. The pumpkinseed is not sought by most experienced fishermen but is often caught by beginners. It is aggressive and will take a variety of bait.

The Design

The Pumpkinseed Sunfish was the third stamp to be designed by wildlife artist Michael R. Matherly of Cambridge City, Indiana. It resembled Matherly's first two designs, for the 1¢ American Kestrel and

After flopping Michael Matherly's original artwork so that the fish would be swimming onto the envelope rather than off it, the printer deleted one of the background plants to give a clearer view of the fish's head.

3¢ Eastern Bluebird stamps of 1991. Like them, it was vertically arranged, with the name of the depicted creature at the bottom in italics and "USA" and the denomination in the upper-right corner.

Because of their low denominations, those earlier stamps weren't considered likely candidates for counterfeiting, so they were printed by offset lithography, with no intaglio component. However, USPS felt that a 45¢ stamp needed additional security. The contractor, Stamp Venturers, had the basic design printed by offset at The Press, Inc., in Chanhassen, Minnesota, and then applied the "USA 45" by the intaglio process at its new facility in Ogdensburg, New York.

Matherly's original painting showed the sunfish swimming to the right. The Citizens' Stamp Advisory Committee prefers to have stamp subjects face left, or into the envelope when a stamp is affixed to a piece of mail. Rather than have the artist repaint his picture, "we carefully checked to make sure the markings on the left and right sides of the fish are absolutely identical, and then instructed the printers simply to reverse the image," said Joe Brockert, art director and project manager for the stamp. (The same procedure had been followed with Matherly's previous stamp paintings, the kestrel and bluebird.)

The printer also made some other, less dramatic revisions during the scanning process. An excess piece of seaweed was removed, and the colors were modified slightly to provide more contrast between the fish and the background.

First-Day Facts

The Pumpkinseed Sunfish stamp was dedicated at the National Aquarium in Washington, where its design had been unveiled more than 13 months earlier.

Karen T. Uemoto, USPS district manager for customer services, officiated. Jim Fowler, host of Mutual of Omaha's *Wild Kingdom* television show, was the principal speaker. The welcome was given by Mrs. Anthony Kennedy, secretary of the National Aquarium Society.

5¢ CIRCUS WAGON COIL (ABNC) TRANSPORTATION SERIES

Date of Issue: December 8, 1992

Catalog Number: Scott 2452B

Color: red (PMS 186)

First-Day Cancel: Cincinnati, Ohio

FDCs Canceled: figure not available

Format: Coils of 10,000. Gravure printing cylinders of 456 subjects (19 across, 24 around).

Perf: 9.8 (stroke perforator, designed and built by Guilford Gravure Division of George Schmitt and Company)

Designer: Susan Sanford of Washington, D.C.

Typographer: Bradbury Thompson (CSAC)

Art Director and Project Manager: Joe Brockert (USPS)

Modeler: Acitronics Division of George Schmitt and Company

Printing: Printed by Guilford Gravure for American Bank Note Company on an Andreotti 5-color webfed gravure press. Perforated and coiled at Guilford Gravure. Cylinders by Acitronics.

Quantity Ordered: 150,000,000

Quantity Distributed: 150,000,000

Plate Number Detail: 1 gravure cylinder number preceded by the letter A on every 24th stamp

Cylinder Numbers: A1, A2

Tagging: untagged

The Stamp

On December 8, in Cincinnati, Ohio, USPS issued a gravure-printed version of the 5¢ Circus Wagon coil definitive that had originally appeared August 31, 1990, as an intaglio-printed stamp.

The new gravure version of the Circus coil appears at top. The intaglio version is shown at bottom.

The appearance of the new variety had been predicted by stamp columnists for several months. The first public announcement of it came in the November 12 *Postal Bulletin*, a fortnightly publication of USPS. A philatelic release was sent out by USPS, but not until December 14, eight days after the first day of sale.

The gravure Circus Wagon was manufactured in coil rolls of 10,000 stamps by the American Bank Note Company. The intaglio version of the stamp was made in rolls of 500 and 3,000 by the Bureau of Engraving and Printing. Under an agreement with USPS, BEP was excused from printing coil rolls larger than 3,000, which the Bureau considered uneconomical to produce.

The Circus Wagon was the third coil definitive, and the second in the Transportation series, to be reissued as a gravure-printed stamp made in large rolls by a private printer after having been issued originally as a BEP-produced intaglio stamp. The first two were the 29¢ Mount Rushmore and 5¢ Canoe stamps of 1991 (the latter was a precanceled item for use by non-profit bulk mailers). A few months after their original appearance, both reappeared in gravure versions.

The new stamp was untagged, like the intaglio Circus Wagon that was then in production. The original intaglio Circus Wagon of 1990 had overall tagging. But USPS later decided to stop tagging low-value stamps in an effort to reduce the deliberate use of such stamps to underpay postage, and the untagged Circus Wagon made its appearance in August 1991. The gravure version had shiny gum, in contrast to the dry gum used by BEP on the intaglio stamp.

The principal demand for a 5¢ non-precanceled coil stamp in large rolls came from the Disabled American Veterans, which is headquartered in Cincinnati, the site of the new Circus Wagon stamp's first-day sale.

DAV uses up to 100 million 5¢ coil stamps a year in its direct-mail fund solicitations. Robert Rabinowitz wrote in *Stamp Collector* that the organization asked USPS for rolls of 12,000 Circus Wagons for its stamp-affixing machines, which had the capability to process from 10,000 to 11,000 envelopes per hour. In the absence of rolls larger than

3,000, DAV had been splicing four 3,000-stamp rolls together and then rewinding them so they came off the roll in the same direction as the smaller-sized rolls.

After a lapse of several months, during which DAV drew down the Postal Service's inventory of 3,000-stamp rolls, Rabinowitz wrote, USPS responded with a compromise: rolls of 10,000. "Apparently, the USPS won't provide the rolls of 12,000 because the 10,000 roll is a 'standard size' and other mailers have equipment that will accommodate 10,000 stamps," the columnist explained.

DAV sends its solicitations out at the low-cost bulk non-profit rate. But, in its mailings to people who have a record of previous contributions, it encloses stamped return envelopes to encourage fresh donations. Studies have convinced the organization that it gets the best results when it uses a combination of five 5¢ stamps and two 2¢ stamps on the return envelopes. It has been speculated that people who would find it easy to tear off and reuse a single 29¢ stamp would be less tempted to follow that procedure with two strips totaling seven stamps. On the other hand, those people would feel guilty about throwing away an envelope bearing 29¢ in live postage, and eventually, some of them probably wind up writing a check and sending it to DAV.

Use of the 2¢ Locomotive stamps of the Transportation series on DAV's return envelopes permitted the envelopes to activate postal facer-canceler machines. The 2¢ Locomotive, as of this writing, was still available in tagged form only.

The Design

The stamp used the same image of a circus wagon that was created for the 1990 stamp by artist Susan Sanford of Washington, D.C. Sanford made what USPS called a "generic composite" wagon based on a selection of picture postcards from the Circus World Museum of Baraboo, Wisconsin. The wagons shown on the cards were basically from the first decade of the 1900s, and that was the decade mentioned in the caption at the top of the stamp.

The gravure red color used by ABNC was a good match for the intaglio red that the Bureau of Engraving and Printing had used. The stamps were printed on an Andreotti press at Guilford Gravure, using a fine-line screen. At first glance, they closely resembled the intaglio version. Stephen Esrati, writing in *The Plate Number*, pointed out that in the shading at the left side of the wagon, the intaglio stamp had very fine diagonal lines, so fine in some places that the lines almost disappeared, whereas the gravure version had lines that were thick and uniform. On BEP's stamp, the top of the "W" in "Wagon" had serifs that were 0.75mm wide, while the ABNC serifs measured only 0.5mm.

A cylinder number, preceded by the letter A for American Bank Note Company, appeared on every 24th stamp of the gravure Circus Wagon. On the intaglio version, the sleeve number, without a letter prefix, appeared on every 52nd stamp. The cylinder numbers on the gravure stamps weren't centered, but could be found at the left of center, beneath the front wheel of the wagon.

The reason for this, an ABNC spokesperson told *The Plate Number*, was that the A is always in the same location. "If this had been a four-digit plate number, the number would have been centered," she said.

First-Day Facts

There was no dedication ceremony for the gravure Circus Wagon stamp. Collectors wanting first-day covers bearing the December 8 Cincinnati postmark were given 60 days to submit their addressed envelopes. For covers on which USPS affixed stamps, five Circus Wagons and one 4¢ Steam Carriage coil stamp of 1991 were used to make the 29¢ first-class rate.

In 1992 collectors continued to discover new tagging varieties of previously issued stamps. The varieties existed primarily as a result of two policies. One was the decision of the Bureau of Engraving and Printing, announced in 1990, to produce all future stamps with "full-coverage tagging," meaning by applying overall tagging or by using prephosphored paper. The other policy was the Postal Service's decision, effective in January 1991, to stop tagging stamps with a face value of 8¢ or less. That policy was amended in 1992 to raise the threshold for untagged stamps to 10¢.

3¢ Conestoga Wagon: Untagged

Sleeve 2 of the 3¢ Conestoga Wagon coil stamp (Scott 2252), with no tagging, turned up in April. Dr. Robert Rabinowitz, a dealer in plate number coils, reported finding the stamp April 28 in rolls of 3,000.

The original version of the stamp was released February 29, 1988, as a block-tagged issue. Only sleeve 1 is known for the tagged version.

10¢ Red Cloud: Untagged

The 10¢ Red Cloud sheet stamp of the Great Americans series (Scott 2176) was found in a fourth tagging variety. Red Cloud had previously been issued with block tagging (1987), overall tagging (1990) and on phosphor-coated paper (1991). In 1992, in keeping with the new policy of withholding tagging from stamps of 10¢ or less, the stamp went back to press and was left untagged. This version was first reported in late May by Stephen G. Esrati, editor of *The Plate Number*.

$5 Bret Harte: Prephosphored Paper

In 1992 USPS placed on sale a new variety of the $5 Bret Harte stamp of the Great Americans series (Scott 2196), first issued in 1987. The stamp was reprinted by BEP on its C press with sleeve number 2. It had previously been produced on the A press, which is no longer in service, with sleeve number 1.

The new stamp was printed on prephosphored paper, unlike the original version, which was block tagged.

The USPS announcement explained that the repeat lengths of the C and A presses were unequal. The top or bottom margin (depending on which part of the press sheet it came from) on a C press pane of 20 stamps was smaller than the other three margins. On an A press pane, the four margins were of the same width.

The A press panes were perforated edge-to-edge on the top and bottom horizontal lines of perforations. On C press panes, the center horizontal line of perforations (between the second and third rows of stamps) was also perforated edge-to-edge. This made it easier for postal clerks to separate the panes of 20 to obtain plate blocks of four, although they still had to tear through unperforated selvage at top and bottom.

Robin Minard, a USPS spokeswoman, told *Linn's Stamp News* that the stamps were printed in December 1991 and sent to post offices on a reorder basis. There was no first-day ceremony and no designated first day of issue. Collector Brad Arch of New Jersey informed *Linn's* that he had bought the new Harte stamp Saturday, February 29, 1992, at the Bepex stamp show station in Elmwood, New Jersey. The following

These two pictures show an example of the first printing of the $5 Bret Harte stamp in panes of 20, from sleeve number 1 on BEP's A press, and a diagram of the layout of a pane from the second printing, from sleeve number 2 on the C press. In the new version, perforations between the second and third horizontal rows of stamps extend through the selvage.

Monday, March 2, Arch was able to get a cover with the stamp postmarked to establish an earliest reported date of use.

$1 Johns Hopkins: Prephosphored Paper

Like the $5 Bret Harte stamp, the $1 Johns Hopkins Great Americans stamp (Scott 2194A), first issued in 1989, was reprinted in 1992. The original version was printed from sleeve number 1 on BEP's A press. The new printing was from sleeve number 2, on the C press.

The C press stamp was printed on prephosphored paper, making it the third tagging variety for Johns Hopkins. The stamp had block tagging when it was issued, and in 1990 it was given overall tagging.

Like the Bret Harte, the new Johns Hopkins sheets of 20 had narrower margins at the top or bottom than on the other three sides, and the center horizontal row of perforations ran edge-to-edge.

A *Linn's* reader reported finding the new variety July 7, 1992, at Christiana, Lampeter and Quarryville, three small post offices in the Lancaster, Pennsylvania, area.

Liberty Torch ATM Stamp: Overall Tagging

In 1992, USPS created a new tagging variety of the 29¢ Liberty Torch self-adhesive stamp (Scott 2531A) that it had first issued June 25, 1991, for dispensing from automatic teller machines (ATMs). At the same time that collectors learned of this variety, they also learned that there had been one other previously unpublicized variety of the stamp, which had gone into production shortly after the original version went on sale.

Wayne L. Youngblood and Charles Yeager described the three known types of Liberty Torch stamp in an article in the December 7, 1992, issue of *Linn's*. According to their account, the manufacturer of the ATM stamps, Avery Dennison, printed the first type on phosphor-coated paper, then applied a coating of lacquer to the front to keep the ink from flaking. This first type was available to collectors in time for first-day covers.

However, the lacquer coating caused the panes to curl, making it difficult to use the stamps in ATMs. The second version, produced for the banks participating in the ATM program, had no lacquer coating, and the panes lay flat. This version, which began appearing in the banks in late July 1991, was somewhat difficult to distinguish from the first. Since it didn't have a coating, the tagging was slightly brighter than on the original. It's safe to assume, Youngblood and Yeager wrote, that most first-day covers, and certainly those actually prepared on the first day, bore type I stamps.

But problems also arose with type II, and a decision was made to create the third type. In late October 1992, several collectors noticed a different kind of tagging on the Liberty Torch stamps. Stephen Esrati and collector Myron Hill brought the existence of type III to *Linn's* attention.

Instead of being printed on phosphor-coated paper, the newest version of the stamp was printed on non-phosphored paper. A lacquer coating was applied to both the front and back of the panes, neutralizing the curling effect and allowing them to lie flat in ATMs. Phosphorescent tagging was added to the lacquer for the front coating, giving it the appearance of overall tagging.

According to Youngblood and Yeager, the torch of the phosphor-coated paper types (type I and II) looked "a lot more brownish" than the torch on the phosphor-lacquer-coated type III. In addition, the paper on the first two types appeared somewhat whiter.

"Although the type I stamps were the smallest printing, the vast majority were sold to collectors, making the survival rate (particularly used) fairly high," the *Linn's* writers wrote. "The type II stamps had a much higher printing total, but were mainly sold to postal customers. They apparently are still available through many ATMs." The type IIIs were just coming into general use when the article was written.

At the same time USPS switched to the type III stamp, it also changed the design of the backing paper for the dollar-bill-sized sheetlets in which the Liberty Torch stamps were sold.

The original backing, used for types I and II, consisted of a block of text, repeated four times on each sheetlet, which bore the message "Self adhesive * DO NOT WET" and a paragraph promoting the Postal Service's stamped envelopes with preprinted return addresses. The new backing looked more like a booklet cover and, in fact, carried illustrated instructions for folding the sheetlet into a booklet. The advertisement for stamped envelopes appeared only once on the backing. An enlarged reproduction of the Liberty Torch stamp completed the design.

The Postal Service originally announced that sheetlets with the new backing would be distributed in May, but later pushed back the date of availability to July 16.

19¢ Fishing Boat Coil: New Printer

In late December 1992, 19¢ Fishing Boat coil stamps printed from cylinder combination number A5555 and issued in coils of 500 reached

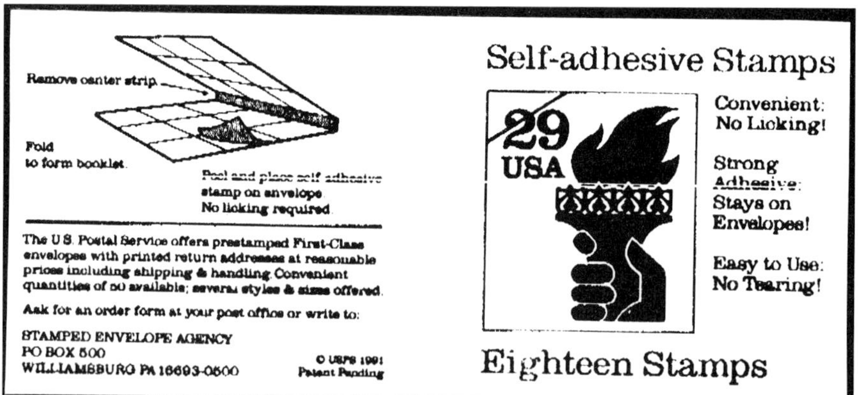

This is the revised backing design for the 29¢ Liberty Torch self-adhesive ATM stamp, showing users how to fold the sheetlet to form a booklet.

philatelic counters. The stamps printed from this cylinder combination were easily distinguishable from earlier Fishing Boat stamps. In fact, they were printed on a different press.

The original Fishing Boats, which were issued August 8, 1991, and subsequent printings of the stamp were made by Multi-Color Corporation, Scottsburg, Indiana, for American Bank Note Company on a Schiavi 10-color webfed gravure press. Solvent-based inks were used. Cylinder numbers were spaced at 36-stamp intervals. Those cylinder number combinations were A1111, A1112, A1212 and A2424.

The new version was printed by Guilford Gravure Division of George Schmitt and Company on Guilford's Andreotti five-color webfed gravure press, using water-based inks. The chemically etched cylinders contained 456 subjects, 19 across and 24 around, which meant the interval between cylinder numbers was 24 stamps. A total of 118 million stamps was ordered and delivered, according to ABNC.

As described by Ken Lawrence, who first reported the new variety in *Linn's*, the ink colors were less saturated on the new printing, causing them to be lighter overall. Under magnification, the halftone dot structure was finer. This virtually eliminated the moire effect that blurred fine details and caused the image on earlier printings to have an illusion of shimmering when examined closely. There were also paper and gum differences. When the gum side was examined under shortwave ultraviolet light, earlier printings appeared yellow or dull blue. The new version's paper glowed a much brighter blue.

After the original Fishing Boat coil appeared, ABNC shifted all its coil stamp production to Guilford Gravure, which was the sole producer of ABNC's Eagle and Shield stamps of 1991 and 23¢ First-Class Presort stamps of 1992. Multi-Color became the company's subcontractor for booklet stamps.

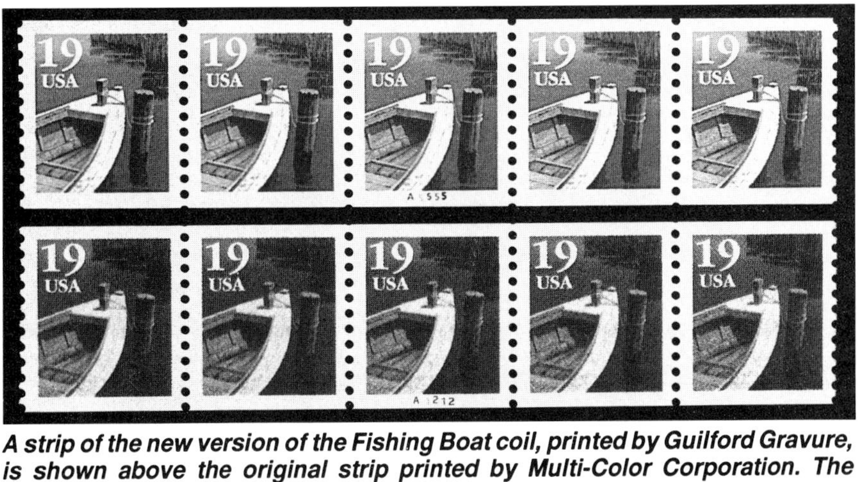

A strip of the new version of the Fishing Boat coil, printed by Guilford Gravure, is shown above the original strip printed by Multi-Color Corporation. The cylinder number of the top strip is A5555, while the number on the bottom strip is A1212.

This is the booklet cover for the 10-stamp version of the Wood Duck booklet.

Linn's reported that all Fishing Boat color separations and printing cylinders held by Multi-Color were destroyed, and Guilford Gravure started up the job again from the original artwork. The color separations for the new variety were by Image Processing and the cylinders were mechanically engraved by Acitronics.

29¢ Wood Duck: New Size Booklet

Booklets containing a single pane of 10 of the 29¢ Wood Duck stamp printed by BEP (Scott 2493) were made available nationwide after June 12, 1992. The BEP continued to produce the stamp in the 20-stamp booklets that were first issued April 12, 1991. The stamps in the smaller booklets were the same, and have not been counted as a separate variety.

USPS said the new version was made "to satisfy customer demand for booklets in the smaller size."

An informal soak test of stamps from the 10-stamp booklets showed no evidence of flaking of the printed image, even when the wet stamps were rubbed. That wasn't the case with the original Wood Duck stamps printed by BEP, on which the ink flaked readily when the stamps were soaked in water. BEP blamed the problem on the coated gravure paper it had obtained from a new supplier.

$15 MIGRATORY BIRD HUNTING (DUCK) STAMP 1992-1993

Date of Issue: June 30, 1992

Catalog Number: Scott RW59

Colors: orange (PMS 171MC), yellow (PMS 121MC), blue (PMS 291MC), gray (PMS 444MC), purple (PMS 276U), black; black (flexographic back plate)

First-Day Cancel: June 30, 1992, Washington, D.C.; July 1, 1992, Jackson, New Jersey

Format: Panes of 30, horizontal, 5 across, 6 down. Offset printing plates of 120 subjects (10 across, 12 down); intaglio printing sleeve of 240 subjects (10 across, 24 around); flexographic back plate of 120 subjects (10 across, 12 down).

Perf: 11.2 by 11.1 (Eureka off-line perforator)

Selvage Markings: sleeve number

Artist: Joe Hautman of Jackson, New Jersey

Stamp Designer and Modeler: Ronald C. Sharpe (BEP)

Engravers: Thomas Hipschen (BEP, vignette); Deborah Alexander (BEP, lettering and numerals)

Printing: printed by BEP on 6-color offset, 3-color intaglio D press (902)

Quantity Ordered: 4,000,000

Quantity Distributed: 3,997,000

Sleeve Number Detail: 1 intaglio sleeve number alongside corner stamp

Sleeve Number: 190493

Tagging: untagged

The Stamp

Two things were unusual about Joe Hautman, whose painting of a male spectacled eider in flight was the winning entry in the 1992-1993 Federal Migratory Bird Hunting and Conservation stamp design contest.

First, he was one of three gifted brothers who made names for themselves in the prestigious annual competition. Jim Hautman had won the contest two years earlier with a painting of black-bellied whistling ducks. And Robert Hautman placed fourth in the event that Joe won.

Second, until Joe Hautman's own victory at age 35, wildlife painting was only an after-hours sideline for him.

Hautman, a resident of Jackson, New Jersey, holds a Ph.D. in condensed matter physics from the University of Michigan. When he painted the spectacled eider, he was working full-time as a researcher at the University of Pennsylvania under a grant from the National Institutes of Health, tracking the dynamics of molecules through computer simulations. His published work had contributed to the understanding of a wide range of phenomena, from the shapes of water droplets and snowflakes to the microscopic structures of soap bubbles and cell membranes.

After he won the contest and was required to do some traveling to promote duck stamp sales, he cut back his research at the university to two days a week. Later, he continued on that revised schedule so he could spend more time at the easel.

Hautman's spectacled eider painting, done in acrylic on illustration board, won over 584 other entries in the 41st annual Duck Stamp Contest sponsored by the Department of the Interior and held in Washington, D.C., November 5 and 6, 1991. The contestants were required to choose their subjects from among five species of North American waterfowl that hadn't been shown on any of the 58 previous duck stamps.

Second place went to Thomas Wood of Woodbridge, New Jersey, for

This is Joe Hautman's acrylic painting of a male spectacled eider in flight that won the design competition for the 1992-1993 duck stamp.

his watercolor of a pair of Barrow's goldeneyes. Bruce Miller of Mound, Minnesota, who placed third, and the fourth-place finisher, Robert Hautman, both chose spectacled eiders as their subjects. The other species represented in the contest were red-breasted merganser, black scoter and surf scoter.

Joe Hautman was seated with his younger brothers Jim and Robert in the Interior Department auditorium when Interior Secretary Manuel Lujan announced the contest results. The winner customarily gets an opportunity to meet the president, so later in November Hautman visited President George Bush in the White House and showed him his artwork.

The three Hautman brothers, plus four other brothers and sisters, grew up in St. Louis Park, Minnesota. Both of their parents were artists and their father was a duck hunter, so they were familiar from childhood with both ducks and paints.

Joe Hautman entered the University of Minnesota as an art major, but later switched to physics. As a full-time researcher, he had little time for painting, but he did submit entries in the contests for the federal duck stamps of 1989, 1990 and 1991. His subjects were, respectively, red-breasted merganser, black-bellied whistling duck (the same species that his brother Jim chose and won with) and Barrow's goldeneye.

Science and wildlife art made "a nice combination" for him, he said.

Joe Hautman, visiting the White House, shows President George Bush a framed reproduction of his winning duck stamp painting.

"They are so different. I can come home after a day of research and be refreshed when I start painting."

However, even with a restricted schedule of research work, dividing his time between two fields meant he couldn't accomplish as much as he would like in either one. In early 1993 he said he intended to make a choice soon — and that he was "leaning toward doing the art."

The duck stamps that opened the door for Joe Hautman's expanded art career have been an important source of revenue for waterfowl conservation since 1934. To hunt ducks and geese, all hunters aged 16 and over must buy a current stamp. In addition, the stamps are purchased in large numbers by collectors and nature lovers.

The first federal duck stamp had a face value of $1. The price has reached its current $15 through a series of periodic increases. According to the Department of the Interior, 98¢ of each dollar raised through the sale of stamps goes directly to buy habitat for migratory waterfowl. To date, nearly four million wetland acres have been bought with the more than $400 million generated by the program.

For the first few years, duck stamp designs were commissioned. The first contest was held in 1949, and the design has been chosen by competition ever since. No cash prize is awarded, but the winner is free to market limited-edition prints of the design. This privilege has earned several past winners more than $1 million in royalties apiece.

Winning the federal contest also gives an artist high visibility and produces additional commissions. Hautman's works after he expanded his time for painting included ring-neck ducks, for a print sponsored by New Jersey Ducks Unlimited, and a golden eagle, for a poster marking the opening of an eagle exhibit at a wildlife park in Nashville, Tennessee. He also planned to enter some state duck stamp competitions.

Judges for the 1992 stamp contest were Jack Elrod, writer-illustrator of the "Mark Trail" comic feature; Martina Roudabush Norelli, art historian and staff member of the Smithsonian Institution's National Museum of American Art; Jeanette Rudy, conservationist and a leading promoter of duck stamps; Vin T. Sparano, outdoor writer and executive editor of *Outdoor Life* magazine; and Dr. Charles I. Wiles Jr., president of the Izaak Walton League of America.

The five waterfowl species that were eligible for the 1992 stamp were selected by the Fish and Wildlife Service from among six that had never before appeared on a federal duck stamp. The Service's original plan had been to keep working the list until, by 1997, duck stamps would have depicted all 42 species whose ranges include the contiguous United States and Alaska. Another species, Hawaii's nene goose, was shown on the 1964 stamp.

However, the plan was later changed to one of alternating lists. For the 1993 stamp competition, the five eligible species would be relatively common birds: canvasback, Canada goose, mallard, northern pintail and greater scaup. Then, for the 1994 stamp, the list would revert to the birds that hadn't been shown on stamps before: Barrow's goldeneye, surf scoter, black scoter, red-breasted merganser and mottled duck. Under this revised plan, all 42 species will have been depicted by 2002.

The spectacled eider is a large duck whose range includes coastal Alaska, the Aleutians and Siberia. The male has a pale green head with large white eye patches that are rimmed with black, giving them a spectaclelike appearance. Its body is slate black, and its throat, neck, back and folded wings are white. The female is tawny brown marked with streaks and discontinuous bars of dark brown. She can be distinguished from other female eiders by her light brown eye patches.

In May 1992 the Fish and Wildlife Service proposed the spectacled eider as a threatened species under the Endangered Species Act. The move was prompted by a 94-percent decline in breeding populations over the past two decades. The Service undertook to gather additional information on the proposal, including public comments, and was to make a final decision by May 1993.

Twenty years ago, spectacled eider numbers were estimated at 50,000 to 70,000 nesting pairs along the coast of western Alaska, in addition to 3,000 pairs on Alaska's North Slope. In 1991, however, the Service estimated that only 2,700 pairs of spectacled eiders nested on the Yukon Delta National Wildlife Refuge and a few hundred to a few thousand pairs were nesting in northern Alaska. The cause of the decline wasn't known, although one possibility cited by the Service was an alteration of the marine ecosystem in the Bering Sea, which may affect the bottom-dwelling mollusks and crustaceans on which the eiders feed.

The Design

For his 1992 contest entry, Joe Hautman wanted to try a bird he hadn't painted before. In preliminary sketches he experimented with both the spectacled eider and the surf scoter, but settled on the eider as the "most striking" in appearance.

Two years earlier, after Jim Hautman's contest victory, the three brothers had gone to Alaska to research the eligible species for the coming years' contests. Although they didn't find spectacled eiders, Joe put to good use the observations and photographs he made of the Alaska landscape. In his own winning painting, rugged mountains, heaving ocean swells and a cloud-streaked sunset sky provide the backdrop for his dramatic subject — a male spectacled eider in flight, with wings outstretched. In the distance are four other birds, including a female.

Hautman is a conscientious researcher who is determined that his work be accurate. "The extent to which a painting is good is the extent to which it really is a truthful reflection of the subject," he said. "That's a personal view, and it may come from my training as a scientist."

Unfortunately, because of the rarity of the spectacled eider, he never saw a live male specimen. He did photograph a female, however, at the Philadelphia Zoo, just a few blocks from the campus where he worked. And he traveled to Ottawa, Ontario, to examine a collection of 17 spectacled eider skins at the the Canadian National Museum.

These skins — dubbed "popsicles" because they were stiff, elongated and mounted on sticks — provided the references Hautman needed for details of feathering, even though they were quite old. One skin bore a tag noting that it had been shot in Alaska in 1914 by "Fred, an Eskimo."

To get the correct image of a duck in flight, Hautman sketched a mounted specimen from his own collection. The bird, a Barrow's goldeneye with its wings outstretched, was one of four mounted birds he kept on the top shelf of a bookcase in his studio.

After sketching the goldeneye, Hautman tried framing the sketch using a mat he had cut to the dimensions (7 by 10 inches) the contest rules prescribed. For the bird to fill the frame the way he wanted, Hautman discovered he had to crop off the tip of the right wing at the bottom of the picture. This effect — an unusual one in a wildlife painting — obviously didn't trouble the contest judges.

The lighting in the painting is dramatic, with bluish-gray shadows mottling the duck's white back and wings, and the yellow sky reflecting in the ocean swells below. Hautman found a novel way to research this aspect, he told an amused audience at the ceremony in his hometown that marked the first day of general sale of the duck stamp.

He climbed to the roof of his house at twilight with a coffee table, two of his stuffed ducks, a camera — and his wife's black nightgown.

"I was trying to get some photographs of the way the late-afternoon light falls on the birds and I had to climb onto the roof to get above the trees," Hautman told his listeners.

He needed the table, he said, to provide a flat surface on the slanted roof, and the camera and ducks for the photographs. The nightgown, he explained, provided "a piece of dark cloth to cut down the glare."

Noting that he wouldn't be eligible to enter the duck stamp contest for another three years, Hautman joked: "If my neighbors see me climbing around my roof this year, they should call the police."

The stamp was printed by a combination of offset and intaglio on the Bureau of Engraving and Printing's D press. The vignette engraver was BEP's top intaglio craftsman, Thomas Hipschen, who provided more engraving detail than had been included on some other recent duck stamps. This was partly because the nature of the artwork called for it and partly because in 1992, with no postal rate change, more engraving time was available at the Bureau, according to Leonard Buckley, BEP's foreman of design. When possible, Buckley said, "We like to have an intaglio stamp with offset support rather than an offset stamp with intaglio support."

First-Day Facts

Each year the new duck stamp is the focus of three ceremonies.

First comes the signing of the first sheets as they come off the presses of the BEP. A number of federal officials and the artist take part in this event. The signed sheets are then sent to the Smithsonian Institution's National Philatelic Collection. Among the participants on May 5, 1992,

Artist Joe Hautman autographs a program at the first-day ceremony at the Department of Interior auditorium. James Bruns, director of the National Postal Museum, is at left.

were Interior Secretary Lujan; Catalina Vasquez Villalpando, treasurer of the United States; John Turner, director of the Fish and Wildlife Service; and Joe Hautman.

The first day of sale ceremony follows, held at the Department of the Interior auditorium, the same room where the annual contest takes place. Attendees at the June 30, 1992, event included Interior Secretary Lujan; Christopher Koss, president of the J.N. "Ding" Darling Foundation; J. Michael Hayden, assistant secretary for fish and wildlife and parks; and James Bruns, director of the National Postal History Museum. On this date the only place the public could buy the stamps was at Washington's National Museum of American History.

The second day of sale — which is the first day the stamps are available nationwide — is celebrated in the artist's hometown. For the 1992 stamp, the ceremony was held on July 1 at Six Flags/Great Adventure theme park in Jackson, New Jersey. Joe Hautman was the principal speaker, and

The U.S. Postal Service offered these two special pictorial cancellations in conjunction with the 1992 duck stamp, at Washington, D.C., June 30 and at Jackson, New Jersey, July 1.

Secretary Hayden and several other federal and state officials participated. In the evening, some 150 people attended a banquet and auction hosted by New Jersey Ducks Unlimited to raise funds for wetlands projects in New Jersey.

On display at each of the three ceremonies in Washington and Jackson was the first federal duck stamp sold in 1934. The original buyer was its designer, J.N. "Ding" Darling, an Iowa editorial cartoonist and vigorous promoter of wildlife conservation. The stamp is now owned by Jeanette Rudy, one of the contest judges, who lent it for the occasion.

USPS furnished two pictorial postmarks for the two special sale dates, in Washington ("Duck Stamp Station") June 30 and in Jackson ("Spectacled Eider Station") July 1. First-day cover collectors were allowed 30 days to send their addressed envelopes, with duck stamps and 29¢ postage affixed, to the appropriate post offices for canceling.

POSTAL STATIONERY

The total number of postal stationery items issued in 1992 was greatly inflated by the Postal Service's decision to reissue 18 stamped envelopes from 1991 and early 1992 on recycled paper.

In the past, the *Yearbook* hasn't counted stamped-envelope paper, window and size varieties in annual totals. But for 1992, we're counting the recycled-paper envelopes — as well as a 1991 envelope, Country Geese, that was issued in a new size — because the Postal Service chose to treat them as new issues by providing first-day postmarks for them. This made them collectible varieties, not only for postal-stationery specialists but for first-day cover fanciers as well.

There were also seven all-new stamped envelopes, including a new version, at the current first-class rate, of the popular Space Station hologram envelope of 1989. To meet the State Department's needs in mailing passports, USPS provided two new Official Mail envelopes, in 52¢ (two-ounce) and 75¢ (three-ounce) denominations. These served the additional function of commemorating the 200th anniversary of the Consular Service.

No new ground was broken with the seven new postal cards that appeared in 1992. Four were in the Historic Preservation series, one was in the America the Beautiful series, one was a picture postal card (for the America's Cup races) and one was a new and more visually interesting Postal Buddy card.

29¢ SPACE STATION HOLOGRAM ENVELOPE

Date of Issue: January 21, 1992

Catalog Number: Scott U625

Colors: green; hologram

First-Day Cancel: Virginia Beach, Virginia

FDCs Canceled: 37,646

Size: number 10, no window

Watermark: none

Markings: "© USPS 1989" under flap

Stamp Art: Ken Hodges of Los Alamitos, California

Designer and Typographer: Richard Sheaff of Needham Heights, Massachusetts

Project Manager: Joe Brockert (USPS)

Printing: Westvaco-USEnvelope Division used VH machine to print envelopes by flexography, die-cut windows, affix holograms and form envelopes. Holograms printed in rolls on foil by American Bank Note Holographics.

Quantity Ordered: 19,652,900

Quantity Distributed: 19,652,900

Tagging: vertical bar at right

The Envelope

On January 21, USPS issued a new version of the Space Station Hologram envelope that it had produced with a 25¢ denomination in 1989. The new envelope's denomination was 29¢, which covered the current first-class rate.

This envelope, like the 1989 original, had a die-cut window containing a film patch that bore a type of hologram — a three-dimensional picture with elements that shifted their relative position depending on the horizontal angle at which it was held, and colors that changed depending on the vertical angle.

The hologram, based on art by Ken Hodges, showed a futuristic space scene. A space station orbited a cratered planetary body, with another planet visible over the horizon. A space shuttle was about to dock in one of the eight berths radiating out from the domed control area; seven other shuttles were already docked. Two astronauts free-floated nearby, and planets and stars filled the dark void in the background.

"The first Space Station envelope was so popular that we wanted to keep a hologram envelope in inventory," said Joe Brockert, the project manager. "Holograms take a long time to develop, so we decided to reissue the Space Station envelope at 29¢." The Space Station was chosen over the only other hologram envelope available — the Football envelope of 1990 — because it had a broader appeal, and its futuristic theme was more appropriate to the use of hologram technology, Brockert said.

Two different kinds of materials were used to make the holograms for the 29¢ Space Station envelope. The first was an acetate film that met Postal Service standards for biodegradability. However, somewhere past the midway point in the manufacturing process — no precise records were kept —Westvaco-USEnvelope was forced to begin patching into its envelopes the same kind of non-biodegradable polyester film that USPS had used with its first two hologram envelopes.

The Postal Service's intentions had been admirable. Its stamp procurement officials had been stung by previous accusations from environmental purists that they were marketing non-recyclable products. So they asked the hologram maker, American Bank Note Holographics, to develop a more biodegradable film, and the company complied by furnishing the first batch of holograms for the new envelope on acetate.

However, the manufacturer of the acetate "ran into problems with a processing chemical that was determined to be a carcinogen," according to Richard Salois of Westvaco-USEnvelope. As a result, the remainder of the manufacturing run was made with the polyester film.

Could a collector tell the two varieties apart? "Not unless you're an expert in the field of films," Salois said.

The new envelope was made in the number 10 size, whereas the original was a number 9. It sold for 34¢ each, or in boxes of 500 for $157 (31.4¢ each). The Stamped Envelope Unit of USPS also offered envelopes with the customer's return address printed on them, in boxes of 50 for $17.40 per box (34.8¢ each) or in boxes of 500 for $161 (32.2¢ each).

USPS promoted the new envelope in an unusual way. Various post offices nationwide distributed free samples of the old 25¢ Space Station Hologram envelope overprinted in blue with an advertisement for the 29¢ envelope and an order blank. The sample envelopes were demonetized by a bar through the flexo-printed "25" denomination. The advertisement, under the heading "Make an Impression/Buy Space Hologram Envelopes," stretched over most of the envelope's front. The order blank for personalized envelopes in batches of 50 or 500 was on the back side.

Although the promotional envelopes had no postal value, they were considered collectibles by postal stationery fanciers. The Philatelic Sales Division offered them for sale at 30¢ apiece.

The Design

The "USA 29," like the denomination logo on the 25¢ envelope, was in a typeface that simulated light-emitting diodes (LEDs) on a digital clock. However, the typography this time was smaller than on the original, and was green rather than blue. The horizontal line over the hologram was shifted more to the right on the new envelope.

Back when the original Space Station envelope was developed, USPS had made color proofs of the typography in both green and orange, on the theory that these were the colors most commonly identified with LEDs. However, these brighter colors were "too overpowering" with the large-size letters and numbers that were used on that envelope, Brockert said, so the color that was finally selected was blue.

"This time, we went back to the original concept of using a more luminescent color," Brockert said. "To make it work, we reduced the size of the typography."

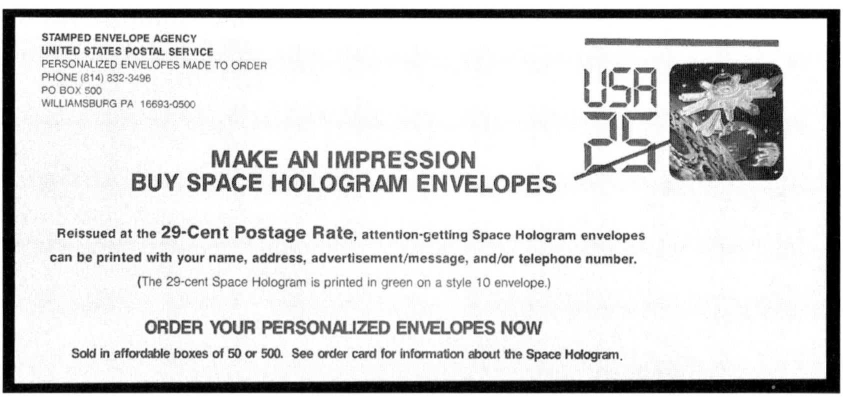

The front of a demonetized 25¢ Space Station hologram envelope, overprinted with an advertisement promoting similar 29¢ envelopes with the buyer's return address printed on them. The overprinted envelope samples, which for a time were available free at many post offices, were offered for sale to collectors.

First-Day Facts

The 29¢ Space Station Hologram envelope, along with a number 10 size version of the 29¢ Country Geese envelope of 1991, had first-day sale in Virginia Beach, Virginia. There was no dedication ceremony. Collectors were originally given 30 days to send their addressed envelopes or their addressed pressure-sensitive labels plus remittance for first-day postmarks. Later the deadline was extended to April 17.

29¢ WESTERN AMERICANA ENVELOPE

Date of Issue: April 10, 1992

Catalog Number: Scott U626

Colors: magenta, cyan, yellow, black (window patch); red, brown (lettering)

First-Day Cancel: Dodge City, Kansas

FDCs Canceled: 34,268

Size: number 10, no window

Watermark: none

Markings: "© USPS 1992" and "recycled" symbol under flap

Designer: Harry Zelenko of New York, New York

Art Director and Project Manager: Elizabeth A. Altobell (USPS)

Typographer: John Boyd, Anagraphics Inc., New York, New York

Printing: Westvaco-USEnvelope Division used VH machine to print envelopes by flexography, die-cut windows, affix stamps and form envelopes. Stamps printed in rolls by offset lithography by Amgraph Packaging Inc., Versailles, Connecticut. Recycled paper used.

Quantity Ordered: 9,772,150

Quantity Distributed: 9,772,150

Tagging: vertical bar at right

The Envelope

On April 10, USPS issued a stamped envelope with the theme of Western Americana. The envelope's indicium was another example of the patch-in-the-window type that originated with the 25¢ Space Station hologram envelope of 1989. Instead of a hologram, however, the picture on the patch was a four-color offset reproduction of a fancy saddle, riding blanket and stirrup.

The envelope had an unusual evolution. As USPS officials reconstructed it, the sequence began with a discussion within the Citizens' Stamp Advisory Committee of a stamp to mark the 1992 centennial of Ellis Island, the entry point in New York Harbor for immigrants from Europe. It was suggested that the stamp focus on immigrants themselves rather than the site, and Howard Paine, a CSAC design coordinator, signed up an artist with previous stamp-design experience to make some sketches of immigrants on shipboard. "They were pretty grim and lacked color," Paine admitted.

At some point the proposal changed again, from immigration to the internal Westward migration of the 19th century. That, in turn, metamorphosed into a Western Americana project, with the committee undecided whether the emphasis should be on the Wild West or the more domesticated West. More stamp sketches were commissioned, and Howard Paine made some drawings for a block of four stamps in which "The Wild West," in poster-style type, would be a dominant part of the design.

Citizens' Stamp Advisory Committee design coordinator Howard Paine sketched these ideas for a multiple stamp issue in which the poster-style typography would be a dominant element.

Finally, Peggy Grant, a USPS staff member who specialized in developing marketing tie-ins for philatelic products, saw an opportunity for a joint promotion with MCA/Universal Home Video, which was about to release a home-video cassette of the full-length animated cartoon *An American Tail: Fievel Goes West.*

The decision was made to make the issue a stamped envelope rather than a stamp or series of stamps, and to focus on some kind of "icon" — a favorite CSAC word — that was emblematic of the West. Meanwhile, Ellis Island, the subject with which the project originated, was approved for a postal card in the Historic Preservation series (see separate chapter on the Ellis Island postal card).

On January 13, Postmaster General Anthony M. Frank unveiled the design of the Western Americana envelope at the Gene Autry Western Heritage Museum in Los Angeles, California. Joining him was Robert Blattner, president of MCA/Universal, who announced plans to release *Fievel* in mid-March.

Frank, speaking at the event, said USPS was pleased to join the home-video company "to promote and commemorate our nation's heritage through an appreciation of the American Old West."

The joint promotional campaign included posters and order forms for the envelopes in post office lobbies, video stores and other retail outlets with tag lines promoting the envelope and video cassette.

This campaign was the third cooperative project involving USPS and MCA/Universal. In 1989 the two agencies joined forces to promote the block of four Prehistoric Animals stamps and MCA Home Video's video cassette of the movie *The Land Before Time*. And in 1991 the merchandise that was promoted was the Postal Service's Comedians by Hirschfeld booklet and two new Abbott and Costello video cassette films. On each previous occasion, Postmaster General Frank had flown west to join MCA's Blattner in announcing the joint venture.

In addition, USPS and Paramount Studios had jointly promoted the Space Exploration stamp booklet of 1991 and Paramount's celebration of the 25th anniversary of its TV and movie series, *Star Trek.*

The Western Americana envelopes sold for 34¢ apiece. Personalized envelopes with a preprinted return address were available in boxes of 50 for $17.40 and boxes of 500 for $161.

The Design

Harry Zelenko, a New York City artist, painted the saddle that was used on the window-patch indicium. He had been instructed to "do something in the way of a Western artifact, but no guns, no animal trophies, no saloons," said Elizabeth A. Altobell, the art director and project manager. "We wanted to be politically safe!"

Zelenko was also told that the Postal Service wanted a simple, bright image against a white background. Among the icons considered were a sheriff's badge, a blacksmith's anvil and a pair of tall Western boots. The ultimate choice was a saddle, but the artist's first color sketch, showing

This was Harry Zelenko's concept sketch of a saddle and blanket. The Citizens' Stamp Advisory Committee told him to brighten it up, make it more Hollywood.

a rather drab example with a gray blanket decorated with brown and black, was too realistic, and not bright enough, for the committee's taste.

"We told him to take the art and brighten it, make it more Hollywood — more show business — and add silver," Altobell said. Zelenko returned with the picture CSAC wanted: a stylish saddle with a silver horn and silver spangles, over a deep blue blanket with horizontal red and yellow stripes.

For the red "Western Americana" and the brown "USA 29," which were printed by flexography on the envelope next to the indicium window, typographer John Boyd used a Western-looking typeface called Crenshaw Outlaw.

Window patches allow USPS to use a paper for the stamp portion of an envelope that is of much higher quality than the envelopes themselves, and thus more receptive to fine printing techniques. A patch was first used for an envelope image other than a hologram on the 29¢ Magazine Industry envelope of 1991.

The patches for the Western Americana envelope were printed by offset lithography by Amgraph Packaging, Inc., of Versailles, Connecticut, and delivered in rolls to the envelope maker, Westvaco-USEnvelope Division, where they were glued into the windows during the envelope-making process. Each patch had a black dash at the lower-left corner, below the window line, but visible when the envelopes are held up to the light. This marking was used to guide the machinery that cut the individual patches from the rolls.

First-Day Facts

The envelope had its first-day sale April 10 in Dodge City, Kansas, a key point on the old Western Trail that brought cattle north from Texas. There was no dedication ceremony, but first-day postmarks were available at the Dodge City Post Office and by mail order. Collectors were given 60 days from the date of issue to submit their addressed envelopes, or their addressed labels and remittance, for the postmarks.

29¢ PROTECT THE ENVIRONMENT ENVELOPE

Date of Issue: April 22, 1992

Catalog Number: Scott U627

Colors: yellow, magenta, cyan, black (window patch); black (lettering)

First-Day Cancel: Chicago, Illinois

FDCs Canceled: 29,432

Size: number 10, no window

Watermark: none

Markings: "© USPS 1992" and recycled symbol under flap

Designer: Joseph Brockert (USPS)

Art Director and Project Manager: Elizabeth A. Altobell (USPS)

Typographer: John Boyd of Anagraphics, Inc., New York, New York

Printing: Westvaco-USEnvelope Division used VH machine to print envelopes by flexography, die-cut windows, affix stamps and form envelopes. Stamps printed in rolls by offset by Amgraph Packaging Inc., Versailles, Connecticut.

Quantity Ordered: 7,854,350

Quantity Distributed: 7,854,350

Tagging: vertical bar to right of stamp

The Envelope

The Postal Service took part in the Earth Day 1992 celebration by issuing a recyclable envelope urging users to "Protect the Environment" and "Save the Rain Forests." The envelope was dedicated during Earth Day festivities in Chicago, Illinois, April 22.

Mitchell Gordon, senior assistant postmaster general, unveiled the envelope's design March 16 at the opening of "Caring for Earth," an environmental exhibit, at the United Nations in New York City. The exhibit was sponsored by the U.N. Environmental Program, the U.N. Education, Science and Cultural Organization (UNESCO) and the U.S. Department of State and Environmental Protection Agency (EPA).

The envelope was issued in the number 10 size without window. It met all EPA recyclability standards for paper, inks and adhesives, USPS said in a news release. It was the latest in a number of environmental initiatives that had won recognition for the Postal Service from EPA and other regulatory agencies, the release continued.

Among the initiatives listed were the use of alternative-fuel vehicles; replacement of underground storage tanks; development of environmental assessments and impact statements; and the abatement of PCBs, asbestos and lead in postal facilities. In addition, EPA had cited as a model the USPS program for recycling waste paper, cardboard, pallets and plastics, the news release said.

The "Save the Rain Forests" line was added to the envelope as the result of a joint promotion worked out between USPS and Fox Video Inc., a subdivision of the Twentieth Century Fox Film Corporation. Fox Video was bringing out a home video cassette of *FernGully: The Last Rain Forest*, a full-length animated movie. The arrangement was similar to the one USPS had entered into with movie and home video companies in the past, most recently in connection with the Western Americana envelope.

Buyers of *FernGully* video cassettes found order forms for the Protect the Environment envelopes inside. Posters in post offices depicted the fairy sprite Crysta and other characters from the movie, pleading to "help us save the tropical rain forests!" "Use the envelope that sends an important environmental message!" said the accompanying text. "This pre-stamped envelope from the U.S. Postal Service is made from recycled paper, and is available at participating post offices."

The envelope was the latest in a series of stamps and stationery items

This 1974 stamp (Scott 1527), designed by pop artist Peter Max, bore virtually the same wording as the 1992 Protect the Environment envelope.

These two flowers were among those considered by the committee for the Protect the Environment stamped envelope. The round blossom, which is red, is the hibiscus, the state flower of Hawaii. The graceful winged flower, which is orange, is the bird of paradise.

over the years that bore environmental messages. As early as the 1950s, stamps were publicizing Wildlife Conservation, Forest Conservation, Soil Conservation and Water Conservation. In 1970, the year of the first Earth Day, an Anti-Pollution block of four stamps urged users to "Save Our Soil," "Save Our Cities," "Save Our Water" and "Save Our Air" (Scott 1410-1413). And the Expo 74 commemorative stamp (Scott 1527), designed by artist Peter Max, bore virtually the same wording ("Preserve the Environment") that would be used on the 1992 envelope.

The Design

This envelope, like the Western Americana, was of the patch-in-the-window kind, in which a stamp-sized patch of high-quality paper bearing an offset-printed image in four colors is affixed inside the envelope so that it shows through a cut-out window in the upper-right corner.

The image on the patch was a branch of nodding pink Hillebrandia blossoms against a black background. Hillebrandia is a member of the Begonia family and grows only in the rain forests of Hawaii, where its native name is Pua Maka Nui, meaning "large-eyed flower." The stamp

This yellow flower, mocked up for CSAC's consideration, is an imaginary plant. It was drawn by a Fox cartoonist for the animated cartoon film FernGully.

picture was a detail from a larger photograph made by Warren L. Wagner, curator of Pacific botany for the Smithsonian Institution's National Museum of Natural History.

Design credit was assigned to Joe Brockert, Design Section manager, although Brockert said: "Essentially, the only designing I did was to take an existing image and put it into the context of an envelope."

In fact, several images were tried out and shown to the Citizens' Stamp Advisory Committee. As Elizabeth A. Altobell, the project manager, explained, "Originally, we had other, more generic-type flowers. When we started getting wind of a potential cross-promotion, with *FernGully*, we decided we wanted something that was representative of a rain forest, rather than just a delicate plant."

Among the alternatives considered were some flower photographs obtained from Allstock Inc., a stock photo house in Seattle, Washington. These included a Hawaiian pond lily, a hibiscus, and a flower called bird of paradise. The Design Section even created some sample designs using imaginary flowers, whose images were borrowed from advance promotional material for *FernGully*. Brockert admitted that one of these — a

CSAC originally chose this photograph of a Hawaiian pond lily, a lavender flower with an orange center, for the indicium of the Protect the Environment envelope. However, the pond lily is not a rain forest flower, so it was dropped in favor of Hillebrandia. The Hawaiian pond lily photo was taken by Christopher Arend of Allstock Inc.

This is Warren L. Wagner's photograph of Hillebrandia from which the center section was taken for the envelope.

yellow blossom — was among his favorites.

"The committee insists on realism," he said. "There might have been other problems, as well, with using actual stills from the film, but I still think it might have made a more interesting envelope."

From the Allstock flower group, CSAC selected the Hawaiian pond lily for use on the indicium. But experts who were consulted thought the flower would be inappropriate as a representative of rain-forest botany. At this point, the Smithsonian's Warren Wagner offered Altobell the use of his photograph of Hillebrandia.

"We don't have a tropical rain forest in the United States," she said. "We have a temperate rain forest, in the Pacific Northwest, and a subtropical rain forest, in Hawaii. Warren Wagner said the Hillebrandia was very representative of flowers of the subtropical rain forest."

Using the entire photograph would have produced an image with too much black background and too little flower, so the photo was cropped tightly to focus on a group of the moisture-beaded blossoms themselves.

A seemingly minor problem, but a time-consuming one, was determining whether "rain forest" was one word or two. "We went through Lexis/Nexis (a computerized library) to determine usage," Altobell said. "We found about a 40-60 split on whether it was used as one or two words. Some publications, from institutions more grand than the Postal Service, had it both ways in one paragraph!

"We called the American Heritage and Random House dictionary editors and asked them about it; whether they would be giving an optional spelling. They said 'It's two words.' So that's what we stuck with. Half the paperwork in the file on this project relates to that problem!"

First-Day Facts

Mitchell Gordon, the USPS official who had unveiled the envelope's design, dedicated the envelope during Earth Day Chicago festivities, which got under way at 7:30 a.m. April 22 at the intersection of Washington and Dearborn streets in downtown Chicago. Earth Day Chicago's day-long, 22nd annual event included speakers, entertainment and educational exhibits, all aimed at raising the public's consciousness about environmental issues.

19.8¢ STAR BULK RATE ENVELOPE

Date of Issue: May 19, 1992

Catalog Number: Scott U628

Colors: red (PMS 186) and blue (PMS 288)

First-Day Cancel: Las Vegas, Nevada

FDCs Canceled: 18,478

Size: number 10, no window

Watermark: none

Markings: "© USPS 1992" and recycled symbol under flap

Designer: Joe Brockert (USPS)

Art Director and Project Manager: Elizabeth Altobell (USPS)

Typographer: John Boyd of Anagraphics, Inc., New York, New York

Printing: printed by Westvaco-USEnvelope Division by flexography and embossing on a VH machine

Quantity Ordered: 2,837,000 (continuing item)

Quantity Distributed: 2,837,000

Tagging: untagged

The Envelope

Until 1991, the Postal Rate Commission allowed USPS to issue stamped envelopes for only two purposes: first-class mail at the basic one-ounce rate, and non-profit bulk mail. (Official mail, being covered by federal interagency agreements, wasn't subject to PRC oversight.)

In PRC's 1990 rate-case finding, however, it relaxed its restrictions on stamped envelopes. Since then, USPS has assumed that it has the authority to sell envelopes of any denomination up to the basic first-class rate — and, possibly, multiple-ounce and priority-mail rates as well.

The first product of this new flexibility was a 19.8¢ envelope for bulk mail that was issued at the 25th National Postal Forum in Las Vegas, Nevada, May 19. It was the first decimal-denominated stamped envelope intended for bulk mail generated by for-profit organizations. The item appeared with little advance notice, and USPS didn't release its design to the philatelic press until well after its issue date.

The 19.8¢ rate was chosen because it was the highest rate for presorted bulk mail and required the lowest level of sorting, said Joe Brockert, the envelope's designer and its original project manager. "Most of the users will be small businesses whose mailings barely make the cutoff to qualify for bulk rates," Brockert said. "They would get the 19.8¢ rate." The same reasoning was applied when USPS put an 11.1¢ denomination on its current non-profit bulk mail envelope, issued in 1991, he added.

In theory, businesses that sorted to five digits, or by carrier route, could use the envelopes and obtain a credit at the time of mailing for the difference between 19.8¢ and the lower rate for which they qualified, a procedure known as false franking. However, it was unlikely that many mailers would do this, Brockert said. Normally, false franking is used when the actual rate is higher than the face value of the postage on the envelopes; the mailer pays the difference at the time of mailing. When a mailer overpays and applies for a credit, the paperwork is much more complicated. Also, mailers following this practice would find their money tied up in postage that they didn't need.

USPS doesn't plan to issue any more fractional-rate envelopes, Brockert said. Instead, it may take the same approach with bulk-rate envelopes that it has taken with stamps. Officials have discussed whether to issue an envelope bearing a round-number denomination below the lowest available rate, e.g. 15¢, or even a non-denominated envelope that would sell for a predetermined low price. In either case, mailers, at the time of mailing, would pay the difference between the face value of each envelope and the higher actual rate per piece.

The 19.8¢ envelope was made only in the number 10 size, without window. It was sold in local post offices in boxes of 500 for $110, making the per-piece price 22¢. Collectors buying individual envelopes from the Philatelic Sales Division were charged 25¢.

Because USPS considered the envelope a precancel, it bore no phosphor tagging. Collectors wishing to use the envelope for mailing purposes were required to obtain a permit to use precanceled stamps and stationery. They also had to add sufficient postage to each envelope to meet the 29¢ first-class rate.

The Design

Joe Brockert, section leader of the USPS Design Section, was credited with the design of the envelope's indicium. It consisted of a blue rectangle enclosing a blue star with a white outline. Three horizontal parallel white lines ran behind the star. These suggested a cancellation strike and constituted the envelope's precanceling. The white portions were embossed. The words "USA 19.8 Bulk Rate," in three lines of red type, were printed by flexography to the left of the blue rectangle.

This particular design had been on the shelf at USPS since 1988. Brockert had made a concept sketch of it in late 1987, in anticipation of the pending change of rates. The intention had been to create a 21.5¢ envelope for first-class mail presorted to three or five digits, as a companion piece to the 25¢ Circle of Stars first-class rate envelope — also designed by Brockert — that was then in preparation.

To make the presort envelope different enough to be distinct, Brockert suggested a different color scheme: rust for the indicium and violet-blue for the external typography. John Boyd of Anagraphics, Inc., created a finished design from Brockert's sketch, reversing the star and lines out of a solid background and moving the "USA" from the center of the star, where Brockert had put it, to a point between the star's lower points.

But the Rate Commission's 1988 decision didn't include authorization to create additional stamped-envelope denominations, and the design was put aside. In 1992, with that authorization now in hand, USPS retrieved the design — this time, for use on a third-class bulk-rate envelope — and put it into service, with some revisions made by John Boyd in consultation with Westvaco, the envelope manufacturer.

The indicium portion could have been reproduced by either embossing or flexography, Brockert said. "Because we're doing more exotic designs, and patch-in designs, on stamped envelopes for our household markets, we thought this would be a good candidate for old-fashioned embossing," he explained.

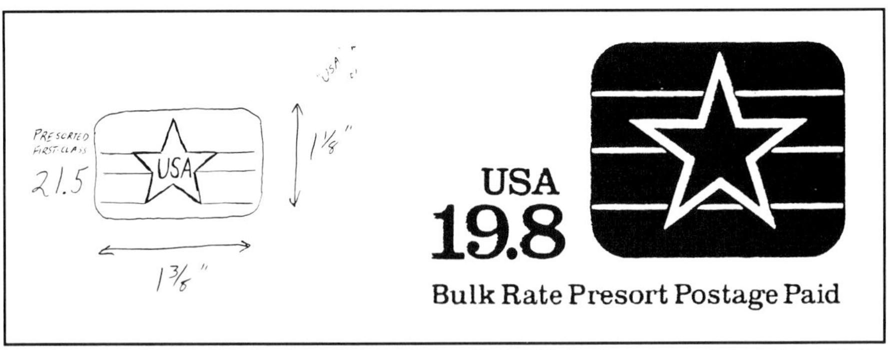

This is John Boyd's first version of the 19.8¢ Bulk Rate envelope. Boyd later simplified his design by shortening and relocating the wording, removing a piece of canceling bar between the two lower points of the star, and placing spaces between the bars and the star and the indicium border.

This is Joe Brockert's sketch and the finished design that John Boyd prepared in 1988 for a 21.5¢ first-class presort stamped envelope. The envelope was never issued.

First-Day Facts

There was no first-day ceremony for the envelope. Collectors wishing first-day covers could purchase them, already canceled with the Las Vegas May 19 postmark, by sending 25¢ and an addressed, pressure-sensitive label for each cover desired to the Philatelic Sales Division. They were given 60 days from the date of issue to order the covers. Later the grace period was extended to 90 days.

52¢ CONSULAR SERVICE BICENTENNIAL OFFICIAL ENVELOPE

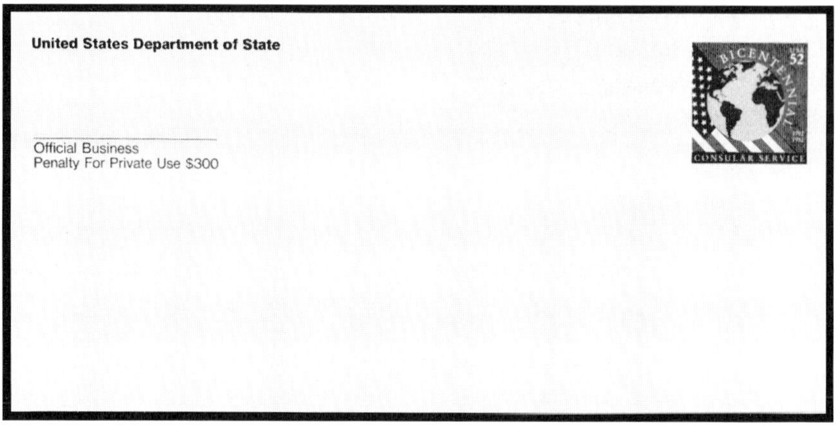

Date of Issue: July 10, 1992

Catalog Number: Scott UO86

Colors: red (PMS 032), blue (PMS 072)

First-Day Cancel: Washington, D.C.

FDCs Canceled: 30,374

Size: special size (4⅜ by 8⅞ inches), no window

Watermark: none

Markings: "United States Department of State/Official Business/Penalty For Private Use $300" in upper-left corner. "© USPS 1992" under flap. " 'You can't appreciate home 'til you've left it,/..nor old glory 'til you see it hanging on a/broomstick on the shanty of a consul in a/foreign town.'/O.HENRY" on outside of flap.

Designer and typographer: Zebulon Rogerson of Washington, D.C.

Art Director: Terrence McCaffrey (USPS)

Project Manager: Joe Brockert (USPS)

Printing: Manufactured by Westvaco-USEnvelope Division, Springfield, Massachusetts, where inscriptions on reverse were applied by flexography. Stamped image and corner card were then applied by offset lithography on a 2-color Jet press at Westvaco's Williamsburg, Pennsylvania, plant.

Quantity Ordered: 2,210,000

Quantity Distributed: 2,210,000

Tagging: square block left of indicium

The Envelope

The U.S. Postal Service issued its first commemorative Official Mail postage items July 10 with a set of two envelopes, of identical design, to mark the 200th anniversary of the U.S. Consular Service.

The 52¢ and 75¢ envelopes covered the first-class rate for two-ounce and three-ounce mail, respectively. These overweight-denomination items were made for the Department of State for mailing passports.

The moving force behind the project was John M. Hotchner, a State Department employee who is also a prominent stamp collector and stamp writer. Hotchner, of Falls Church, Virginia, serves as director of internal controls and compliance programs for Passport Services, within the department's Bureau of Consular Affairs.

He set things in motion October 19, 1990, by drafting a letter for Ivan Selin, undersecretary of state for management, to Postmaster General Anthony M. Frank, requesting a stamp for the upcoming bicentennial of the Consular Service. The letter explained the significance of the event.

"On April 14, 1792, the Congress established a Consular Service distinct from our young republic's fledgling Diplomatic Service," the letter said. "Today both services are combined in the Foreign Service of the United States of America. The consular function continues, as it has for almost 200 years, to focus on providing assistance and protection to millions of Americans who reside in or travel to foreign lands . . .

"Whether during the worst earthquake to devastate Mexico City (1988), in Tiananmen Square when the bullets began to fly (1989), in the streets of Liberia as the civil war raged (1990), or in Iraq where Americans are being held under armed guard as 'guests' of the Iraqi government, U.S. consuls have and continue to risk their own lives to lead Americans to safety, help them to evacuate troubled areas and sustain their morale when they are in distress. Stories of consular heroism and going beyond the call of duty are legion . . .

"In more normal times, consular personnel in the United States and abroad issue over 4 million passports each year, arrange for and distribute over 3 million federal benefits checks to American citizens residing abroad, help Americans abroad register to vote, and issue visas to foreigners coming to visit or live in our country.

"Since the passage of the Rogers Act of 1924, most of our Foreign Service officers have served at least one tour abroad as a consular officer, and most career consular officers have served in jobs that go beyond the traditional limits of consular work. Indeed, it is crucial to have broadly experienced officers doing consular work since nearly all of the political, economic, development and cultural issues that we deal with in bilateral and multilateral relationships have a consular facet.

"As the world becomes seemingly smaller and smaller because of technological advances in transportation and communication, the importance of a high-quality consular service to Americans abroad is immeasurable. I believe that a U.S. postage stamp to honor the 200th anniversary of the establishment of the Consular Service is warranted. It would recognize and honor those who established, and have worked to build, the proud traditions of the best and most caring Consular Service in the world."

As sometimes happens, the Postal Service honored the stamp request not with a stamp, but with postal stationery. In this case, with a rate increase scheduled to take effect early the following year, the Citizens' Stamp Advisory Committee and USPS staff knew they would need to replace the 45¢ and 65¢ stamped envelopes the State Department was then using to mail passports. So it was decided to wait and issue the new-rate envelopes as commemoratives for the Consular Service anniversary.

The State Department was so informed. In July 1991 the department notified its personnel that the Consular Officers' Association (of which Hotchner was vice president) would sponsor a contest to develop a suitable envelope design to submit to USPS. All American-citizen employees of the department were eligible. Entries, which were due August 15, could be in sketch form, but all artwork had to incorporate the words "Consular Service Bicentennial, 1792-1992," "Official Mail" and the denomination and "USA."

Joe Brockert, section leader of the USPS Design Section and project manager for the envelopes, helped the association judge the entries. Several drawings prominently featured the emblem of the Consular Service, a large block C in a circle of 13 stars. They were turned down because the emblem was unfamiliar to the general public. Other drawings were rejected because of the color-registration problems they would create in the printing process.

On September 19, 1991, the department sent USPS its winning entry. It was the work of Darren T. Roots, a college student working as a summer employee in the department's graphic arts section. Arranged in a horizontal rectangle, the design incorporated the colors of the U.S. flag, showing a blue globe at the center of a large white star set against a red background. Roots received a $50 prize from the association.

This is the contest-winning design submitted by State Department employee Darren T. Roots for a stamp to mark the 200th anniversary of the Consular Service.

The State Department chose this basic design for the two envelopes. Department officials originally wanted the envelopes to show two different sides of the globe, but changed their minds after USPS demonstrated with this graphic that one of the views would show mostly empty ocean.

The department's covering letter from John Adams, acting assistant secretary for consular affairs, included some suggested revisions in the design. It also requested that the Postal Service include somewhere on the envelope a relevant quotation from a short story, *The Fourth in Salvador*, written in 1903 by William Sidney Porter (O. Henry) and later included in the collection *Roads of Destiny*:

"You can't appreciate home 'til you've left it, . . . nor old glory 'til you see it hanging on a broomstick on the shanty of a consul in a foreign town.'' The quotation, in blue, appears on the back flaps of the finished envelopes of both denominations.

The envelopes were self-sealing, with wallet flaps that bore grip-seal adhesive and silicone-coated release paper. USPS provided this feature at the request of the State Department, which had found that self-sealing envelopes — which USPS had furnished for experimental purposes in 1990 — speeded up the mailing of passports.

The Springfield, Massachusetts, plant of the USEnvelope Division of Westvaco manufactured the envelopes and applied the copyright line and the O. Henry quotation to the reverse side by flexography. The envelopes then were sent to Westvaco's plant in Williamsburg, Pennsylvania, where the stamped images and the Department of State corner cards were

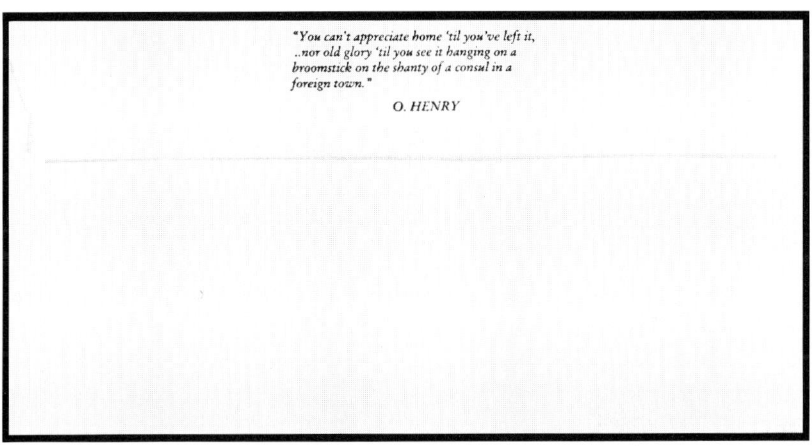

A quotation attributed to William Sidney Porter (O. Henry) appears on the back flap of the Consular Service envelopes.

applied in two colors on a Jet offset press.

Collectors could obtain mint envelopes only by mail order from the Philatelic Sales Division or in person at the philatelic center at USPS headquarters in Washington. Each envelope cost 5¢ over face value.

The Design

Terrence McCaffrey of USPS, the art director for the project, gave Roots' design and the State Department's suggestions for modifications to Zebulon Rogerson, a Washington, D.C., computer graphics specialist who had designed pictorial cancellations for the Olympic games and other events.

In addition to all the wording and other typographical elements on Roots' sketch, the department wanted to incorporate the phrase "Proud to Serve'' in the design. "They had a whole laundry list of things they wanted in there,'' McCaffrey said. "We just said, 'Whoa, this is too much. There are too many things going on here for such a small area.' ''

Rogerson prepared several designs on his Macintosh computer, each of them in the square format appropriate for a stamped envelope. Each design had as its central element a map or a globe, but otherwise they differed from Roots' sketch. The artist also changed the background color — at the State Department's suggestion — from red to blue.

The Citizens' Stamp Advisory Committee narrowed Rogerson's designs down to two and gave the State Department the final choice. One showed two views of the globe from opposite sides with a red and white striped ribbon flowing between and around them; the other placed a single large globe against a diagonal section of the American flag. Department officials picked this second alternative.

Among the requests made by the department was that an Atlantic Ocean projection of the globe be used on the 52¢ envelope and a Pacific Ocean projection be used on the 75¢ envelope. "We told them we didn't think it was going to work,'' Terrence McCaffrey said. "We actually made up a design to show them that when you show the far side of the globe, you have nothing — just the Pacific Ocean, Australia and a number of islands.'' The department agreed to settle for the projection

These are some of the design concepts for an envelope indicium developed by Zebulon Rogerson on his Macintosh computer.

centered on the Atlantic Ocean, which showed all of South America and Africa and most of North America and Europe.

The designs were unveiled at a Consular Service awards ceremony at the State Department April 13, one day before the actual 200th anniversary of the Service. Deputy Postmaster General Michael S. Coughlin, who was serving as acting postmaster general, attended.

First-Day Facts

No first-day ceremony was held.

Because the envelopes couldn't be purchased at post offices and required an official return address, first-day cover collectors couldn't prepare their own envelopes for cancellation. They were instructed to send an addressed, pressure-sensitive label and 57¢ for each 52¢ Consular Service envelope or 80¢ for each 75¢ envelope to the postmaster in Washington, D.C. The Postal Service affixed the labels, applied the first-day postmarks and returned the envelopes through the mail.

The original deadline for submitting requests was August 10. It was later moved back to September 9.

75¢ CONSULAR SERVICE BICENTENNIAL OFFICIAL ENVELOPE

Date of Issue: July 10, 1992

Catalog Number: Scott UO87

Colors: red (PMS 032), blue (PMS 072)

First-Day Cancel: Washington, D.C.

FDCs Canceled: 25,995

Size: special size (4⅜ by 8⅞ inches), no window

Watermark: none

Markings: "United States Department of State/Official Business/Penalty For Private Use $300" in upper-left corner. "© USPS 1992" under flap. " 'You can't appreciate home 'til you've left it,/.. nor old glory 'til you see it hanging on a/broomstick on the shanty of a consul in a/foreign town.'/O.HENRY" on outside of flap.

Designer and typographer: Zebulon Rogerson of Washington, D.C.

Art Director: Terrence McCaffrey (USPS)

Project Manager: Joe Brockert (USPS)

Printing: Manufactured by Westvaco-USEnvelope Division, Springfield, Massachusetts, where inscriptions on reverse were applied by flexography. Stamped image and corner card were then applied by offset lithography on a 2-color Jet press at Westvaco's Williamsburg, Pennsylvania, plant.

Quantity Ordered: 1,840,000

Quantity Distributed: 1,840,000

Tagging: square block left of indicium

The Envelope

The 75¢ stamped envelope commemorating the 200th anniversary of the U.S. Consular Service was created by USPS for use by the U.S. Department of State in passport mailings weighing between two and three ounces. It was issued with the 52¢ envelope of identical design on July 10 in Washington, D.C. Details on these two issues can be found in the preceding chapter.

29¢ AMERICANS WITH DISABILITIES ENVELOPE

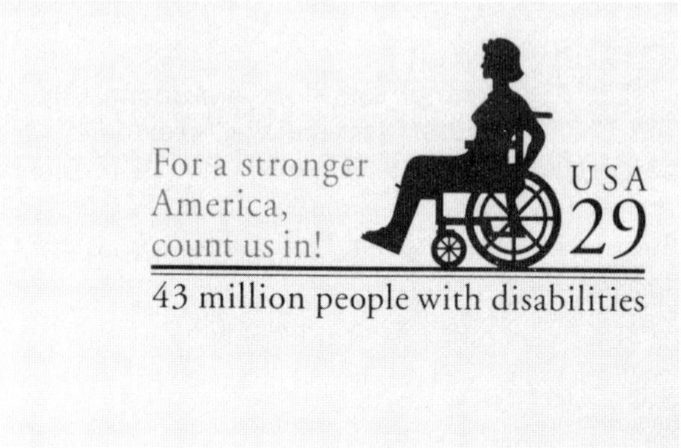

Date of Issue: July 22, 1992

Catalog Number: Scott U629

Colors: red, blue

First-Day Cancel: Washington, D.C.

FDCs Canceled: 28,218

Size: number 6¾ and number 10, no window

Watermark: none

Markings: "© USPS 1992" and recycled logo under flap

Designer and Typographer: Richard Sheaff of Needham Heights, Massachusetts

Project Manager and Art Director: Elizabeth Altobell (USPS)

Printing: Westvaco-USEnvelope Division by flexography on a VH press

Quantity Ordered: 3,734,000

Quantity Distributed: 3,734,000

Tagging: square block to left of figure

The Envelope

The stamped envelope that was issued July 22 in honor of America's citizens with disabilities was the product of a networking process among three alumni of Dartmouth College. The process began in June 1991 with Alan A. Reich, Dartmouth '52, president of the National Organization on Disability (NOD), and John W. Patten, Dartmouth '53, the publisher of *Business Week* magazine and a NOD director.

Reich and Patten were discussing ways to publicize the effort to bring disabled Americans into the economic, social and cultural mainstream. The subject was particularly timely. Businesses were looking forward — some with apprehension — to the implementation in little more than a year of the Americans With Disabilities Act, a measure designed to offer the nation's 43 million disabled persons new job opportunities and greater access to public accommodations and transit and communications systems.

"I said, let's call Tony and see if we can get a stamp," recalled Patten. "Tony" was Anthony M. Frank, also Dartmouth '52 — and the U.S. postmaster general. "My thought was that there hadn't been a stamp for the disabled in 10 years: Let's do something about it!" Patten said.

On June 28, Patten and Reich had lunch with Frank at USPS headquarters in Washington, D.C., and made their pitch. "Tony brought in a couple of his people, and they said it would take years to get a stamp designed and produced," Patten said. "Tony said, 'Let's do a stamped envelope instead. We can do that quickly.' " The advocates accepted the offer, and planning began for the Americans With Disabilities envelope.

On May 28, 1992, 11 months after the luncheon meeting, Joseph J. Mahon, senior assistant postmaster general, unveiled the design of the envelope during the annual meeting of the President's Committee on Employment of People With Disabilities in Washington. He was assisted by Alan Reich and Justin Dart, chairman of the President's Committee. And on July 22 — four days before the Americans With Disabilities Act would go into effect on the second anniversary of its signing by President George Bush — the 29¢ envelope was dedicated in the nation's capital.

The image area depicted a silhouetted woman in a wheelchair, with the slogan "For a stronger America, count us in!" and the caption, "43 million people with disabilities." Printed in two-color flexography on recycled paper, it was available in two sizes, number 6¾ and number 10, at a price of 34¢ per envelope. It was also sold in boxes of 500 for $154 and $157, respectively. Personalized envelopes, with a name and return address printed in the upper left corner, were offered in boxes of 50 ($17.20 and $17.40) and boxes of 500 ($158 and $161).

Several previous stamps and stamped envelopes had also called attention to disabled Americans. Three of them, like the 1992 envelope, had designs featuring people in wheelchairs: the 4¢ stamp of 1960 urging businesses to "Employ the Handicapped" (Scott 1155), the 6¢ Hope for the Crippled stamp of 1969 (Scott 1385) and the 18¢ International Year of the Disabled commemorative of 1981 (Scott 1925), which carried the slogan: "Disabled doesn't mean Unable."

Other items on this topic were:

• The 10¢ "Retarded Children Can Be Helped" commemorative of 1974 (Scott 1549).

• The 15¢ "Seeing For Me" stamp of 1979 that marked the 50th anniversary of the first guide dog program in America (Scott 1787).

• The 15¢ commemorative of the same year for the Special Olympics in Brockport, New York (Scott 1788).

• The 22¢ Social Security Act anniversary stamp of 1985, picturing a group of Social Security beneficiaries, including a woman in a wheelchair and a man on crutches (Scott 2153).

• The 18¢ "Remember the Blinded Veteran" stamped envelope of 1981, with the inscription embossed in Braille (Scott U600).

• The "Remember Our Paralyzed Veterans" envelope of 1983, depicting an empty wheelchair (Scott U605).

• The 8.4¢ Transportation coil stamp of 1988, showing a wheelchair of 1920s vintage (Scott 2256).

The Americans With Disabilities Act of 1990 was termed the most sweeping federal civil rights measure in more than 25 years. Before it took effect, handicapped men and women were protected by only a patchwork of state and local laws.

The new law prohibited firms with more than 25 employees from discriminating in hiring or promotion against workers with physical or mental impairments, including those with AIDS. The law banned tests that tend to screen out handicapped job applicants. Employers would be allowed, however, to inquire about a worker's ability to perform a job.

Under other provisions, companies were required to make "reasonable accommodations" for disabled employees, such as providing readers for blind workers and arranging part-time or modified work schedules. Restaurants, stores and other public accommodations were forced to widen doorways and provide ramps for people in wheelchairs (or use alternatives, if such modifications would pose an "undue burden"), and inner-city bus companies were required to make their vehicles accessible to the handicapped.

Though the act was widely praised by advocates of the disabled and by political leaders of both parties, it had many critics, particularly among small businesses. Some said the cost of compliance would be prohibitive in many cases. One columnist, citing the statute's ambiguity, called it "more an effective make-work project for lawyers than an effective way to help the disabled." On the other hand, a *U.S. News & World Report* survey reported that "business owners find that compliance can prove cheap and easy."

The Design

The design and wording of the envelope grew out of what Elizabeth A. Altobell, the envelope's designated art director, called "brainstorming" sessions at Alan Reich's office at NOD in Washington. Altobell, who took part in the sessions for USPS, relayed ideas to Richard D. Sheaff of Needham Heights, Massachusetts, the designer, and brought Sheaff's sketches back to Reich and his associates for their scrutiny.

The NOD officials, Altobell recalled, wanted the envelope to express the idea that the disabled are actually "differently abled." They felt it should focus on what people can do rather than what they cannot. At the outset, the group sought designs other than the conventional wheelchair image, such as a person speaking from a podium or speaking on the telephone. The problem was that these images didn't in themselves convey the idea of disability. Eventually, the group settled on a woman in a wheelchair because the visual message "was so internationally recognizable at a glance," Altobell said.

Once that was settled, "the important thing then became the wording," she said. "We worked back and forth to make it say exactly what they wanted it to say. We ended up with a pretty good, positive statement."

In the process, the group considered and turned down such phrases as "Americans with disabilities are Willing & Able" ("It sounded too much like a law firm," Altobell said), "America's hidden strength" and "All Americans have abilities to contribute." The final inscription was printed in two colors. "For a stronger America, count us in!" was in red, and "43

Designer Richard Sheaff and CSAC tried several combinations of picture and message before the final indicium design was chosen.

million people with disabilities" was in blue.

The design was unusually wordy, even for a so-called "message" stamp or envelope. "It isn't a rectangle with a picture and the denomination; it's almost like a little editorial presentation," said Sheaff. "That's actually one of the most interesting things about it."

Sheaff based the silhouette of the woman in the wheelchair on a sketch in a brochure supplied by NOD. Originally, he had her facing right, but the Postal Service prefers to have images looking into rather than off the envelope, so he reversed it. "I never bought that theory much," Sheaff confessed. "I can make an equal case, at least in certain designs, that it's more interesting and gives more momentum to the envelope as a whole if the image is going the other way."

For the typography, the designer used a Garamond uppercase and lowercase typeface. "Given that it was a kind of text presentation, I wanted it to be something traditional, something with serifs; not Helvetica, or machine-looking," Sheaff said. Although the wording itself was the product of group effort, Sheaff took credit for the exclamation point ("I thought it would give it a little life").

Altobell found it personally satisfying to be involved in the project. "I was very proud to work on this and meet the people at NOD," she said.

First-Day Facts

Senior Assistant Postmaster General Mahon dedicated the envelope in a public ceremony in the Great Hall of the Department of Justice in Washington, D.C., July 22. Attendees were asked to provide personal identification and to allow sufficient time before the 10 a.m. ceremony to receive an entrance pass.

Speakers included the two men whose advocacy had brought about the envelope, Alan A. Reich and John W. Patten, as well as Evan Kemp Jr., chairman of the Equal Employment Opportunities Commission. The welcome was extended by John R. Dunne, assistant U.S. attorney general for civil rights. An honored guest was James S. Brady, vice chairman of the National Organization on Disability, who was President Ronald Reagan's White House press secretary and who was shot in the head during the assassination attempt on President Reagan in 1981.

The first-day cancellation was available at specified times at the main post office in Washington and in a Department of Justice conference room. A telecommunications device (TDD) phone line was available to facilitate inquiries from the hearing impaired.

Country Geese: Number 10 Size

On January 21, 1992, USPS issued its 29¢ Country Geese envelope in a number 10 size. The size of the original envelope, which had been issued November 8, 1991, was the smaller number 6¾.

The design of the stamped portion, created by Marc Zaref of New York City, was the same: It showed an adult goose, wearing a blue bow, leading three goslings on a stroll. The outline of the geese, the patterned row of flowers beneath them, and "USA 29" were in blue, and the bills and feet of the birds were yellow.

The new envelope was issued in Virginia Beach, Virginia, the site of the original version's first-day sale. On the earlier occasion, the Vapex 91 stamp show was in progress. This time there was no such event to provide a launchpad for the item. Also on January 21 in Virginia Beach, USPS issued a new 29¢ version of the Space Station hologram envelope (see separate chapter). No first-day ceremony was held for either item, but first-day postmarks were provided. Collectors were given 30 days, to February 20, to submit their envelopes or addressed, pressure-sensitive labels plus remittance for first-day covers. Later the deadline was extended to April 17.

Recycled Envelopes

On May 1, to enhance its reputation for environmental responsibility and to appeal to environment-conscious consumers, USPS reissued 18 stamped envelopes on recycled paper. The set comprised 16 envelopes that had originally been issued in 1991 and two that had been in use less than four months: the 29¢ Space Station hologram and 29¢ Country Geese number 10 size (see above).

The envelopes were of the same design as their predecessors. They were distinguishable from the earlier versions by the presence of the three-arrow recycling symbol, printed on the back side under the flap.

The 16 envelopes of 1991 that were reissued were: 29¢ Official Mail regular and window; 29¢ Savings Bond; 29¢ Star number 10 regular and window and number 6¾ regular and window; 11.1¢ Non-profit number 10 regular and window and number 6 3/4 regular and window; 29¢ Love number 10 and number 6¾; 29¢ Security regular and window; and 29¢ Country Geese number 6¾.

Mike Fanning, an environmental programs specialist for the Postal Service, told *Linn's* that the new envelopes met the Environmental Protection Agency's standard for the "recycled paper" designation and included "10 percent post-consumer waste, 40 percent preconsumer waste and 50 percent virgin fiber."

Collectors could buy individual envelopes or a complete set for $5.44 (14 29¢ envelopes at 34¢ each and four 11.1¢ envelopes at 17¢ each).

This is the reverse of a reissued 29¢ Star envelope, with the flap pulled back to show the three-arrow recycling symbol.

The first-day sale of the envelopes was in Kansas City, Missouri, home of the Philatelic Sales Division. First-day postmarks were available at the Kansas City main post office and by mail order. Cover collectors were invited to buy the new envelopes, address them and send them to the Kansas City postmaster for first-day postmarks, making sure to add at least 18¢ postage to the Non-profit envelopes to meet the 29¢ first-class rate. USPS also offered for sale complete sets of the recycled envelopes with first-day postmarks for $6.20 per set. The cost included four 19¢ Fawn stamps that were affixed to the four 11.1¢ Non-profit envelopes to provide adequate first-class postage.

19¢ WADSWORTH ATHENEUM POSTAL CARD HISTORIC PRESERVATION SERIES

Date of Issue: January 16, 1992

Catalog Number: Scott UX160

Colors: yellow, magenta, cyan, black

First-Day Cancel: Hartford, Connecticut

FDCs Canceled: 41,499

Format: Printed in 80-card sheets, but available only in single cards. Printing plates of 80 subjects (8 across, 10 around).

Size: 5½ by 3½ inches

Markings: "Wadsworth Atheneum/Hartford, Connecticut/150th Anniversary/ 1842-1992/© USPS 1991."

Designer: Frank Costantino of Winthrop, Massachusetts

Art Director and Typographer: Richard Sheaff

Project Manager: Joe Brockert (USPS)

Printing: U.S. Government Printing Office (GPO) on a 5-color Roland Man 800 sheetfed offset press

Quantity Ordered: 20,000,000

Quantity Distributed: 11,667,000

Tagging: vertical bar to right of stamp

The Postal Card

The first U.S. postal issue of 1992 was a postal card marking the 150th anniversary of the Wadsworth Atheneum, an art museum in Hartford, Connecticut. The card was dedicated at the museum January 16.

By the Postal Service's count, the postal card was the 22nd in the Historic Preservation series since the series began in 1977, and the third to honor a building in New England. The second was the card's immediate predecessor, an October 1991 issue that showed the Old Mill at the University of Vermont.

The project originated in 1989 when staff members of the Wadsworth Atheneum began making plans to celebrate the museum's anniversary. The idea of a commemorative stamp was raised, and Linda Ayres, who had just been hired as deputy director, telephoned a knowledgeable ex-associate in Washington to discuss the idea. He was C. Douglas Lewis, vice chairman of the Citizens' Stamp Advisory Committee and curator of sculpture at the National Gallery, where Ayres had once worked.

Lewis told her the museum would stand a much better chance of getting a Historic Preservation postal card than a stamp. At his suggestion, Ayres and other Wadsworth staffers sent a formal request to CSAC, along with supporting data. In due course, the card was approved.

The Wadsworth Atheneum (rhymes with "museum"), founded in 1842 by Hartford philanthropist Daniel Wadsworth, has been open to the public longer than any other American art gallery. Its nearly 50,000 works of art are housed in five connected buildings, erected between 1842 and 1969, each representing a distinct architectural style.

The first of these five buildings, the Gothic-Revival Wadsworth building pictured on the postal card, was designed by the New York architects Ithiel Town and Alexander Jackson Davis. The Wadsworth

This is one of the photographs of the Wadsworth Atheneum in downtown Hartford on which artist Frank Costantino modeled his postal card design.

building is a castlelike structure, with towers, battlements and lead windows and a facade of rough-hewn, cream-colored granite. It stands at 600 Main Street in downtown Hartford.

The museum's collection includes Hudson River School paintings, Impressionist paintings, American furniture (particularly the Nutting collection of Pilgrim-century furniture, the largest of its kind in the United States), costumes and textiles, the J. Pierpont Morgan collection of European decorative art, Renaissance and Baroque paintings, contemporary and modern art, and the Amistad Foundation's collection of African-American art.

The Design

When the museum staff submitted information to CSAC to support its request for a card, it sent along, for possible use as a design, a transparency of a 19th-century color lithograph of the Atheneum by E.B. and E.C. Kellogg, published by Case, Tiffany and Burnham.

However, the committee chose to have an up-to-date painting made, to make the card consistent with previous cards in the series. To do the job, art director Richard Sheaff enlisted Frank Costantino, a Winthrop, Massachusetts, watercolor artist specializing in architectural illustration.

Costantino, who had previously designed the Isaac Royall House postal card of 1990 and the Main Building at the University of Notre Dame card of 1991, photographed the Atheneum in the spring of 1991 and made color sketches based on these pictures. For his final version, at CSAC's suggestion, he "idealized" the scene, adding beds of red flowers between the building and the sidewalk and a tree on the right to conceal

The Wadsworth Atheneum staff offered CSAC this 19th-century lithograph of the museum as a possible image for the postal card. The committee decided to commission a modern-day painting instead.

This color sketch by Frank Costantino was modified for the final design by the addition of beds of red flowers between the building and the sidewalk and the enlargement of the tree foliage to conceal neighboring buildings.

a next-door building. The legend on the building over the main entrance, "1842/Wadsworth Atheneum," was visible in Costantino's painting, but emerged as only a blur in the offset-printed stamp image.

First-Day Facts

The first-day ceremony, by invitation only, was held in the museum's Aetna Theater.

Postmaster General Anthony M. Frank dedicated the card. The featured speaker was Mrs. Barbara Bush, first lady of the United States. She had no particular connection to the museum, but "somebody suggested that we invite her, and we figured, what can we lose?" recalled Linda Ayres. "We were delighted that she accepted." Patrick McCaughey, director of the Wadsworth Atheneum, also spoke, and Robert H. Smith Jr., the Atheneum's president, gave the welcome. The pictorial first-day handstamped postmark included an outline drawing of two towers flanking the Atheneum's entrance.

The postal card's dedication kicked off a year-long celebration of the Atheneum's anniversary, which included a gala ball for the museum's top donors, publication of a book on the art collection, a family day in the fall attended by 6,000 children, a distinguished lecture series, and renovation of several old galleries and the opening of two new ones.

19¢ COBB HALL POSTAL CARD HISTORIC PRESERVATION SERIES

Date of Issue: January 23, 1992

Catalog Number: Scott UX161

Colors: yellow, magenta, cyan, black

First-Day Cancel: Chicago, Illinois

FDCs Canceled: 27,150

Format: Printed in 80-card sheets, but available only in single cards. Printing plates of 80 subjects (8 across, 10 around).

Size: 5½ by 3½ inches

Markings: "Cobb Hall/The University of Chicago/Centennial Year, 1991-1992/ © USPS 1991."

Designer: Michael P. Hagel of Arlington Heights, Illinois

Art Director: Derry Noyes (CSAC)

Project Manager: Joe Brockert (USPS)

Typographer: Bradbury Thompson (CSAC)

Printing: U.S. Government Printing Office (GPO) on a 5-color Roland Man 800 sheetfed offset press

Quantity Ordered: 20,000,000

Quantity Distributed: 12,184,000

Tagging: vertical bar to right of stamp

The Postal Card

In 1992 the Postal Service continued its policy of commemorating significant anniversaries of colleges and universities with postal cards in the Historic Preservation series. The first of two such cards was issued January 23 to honor the University of Chicago on its centennial. It depicted the university's first building, Cobb Hall.

More than four years earlier, the planners of the centennial celebration had begun discussing the possibility of obtaining postal recognition. Kineret Jaffe, who became director of the university's Centennial Office in the fall of 1987, consulted individuals at other institutions who had tackled similar projects. Particularly helpful was a Chicago alumnus, Hugh Cloke, an associate dean at Georgetown University and a stamp collector, who told her how Georgetown had gotten a Historic Preservation postal card to help mark the university's bicentennial. That card, depicting a campus landmark, Healy Hall, was issued in January 1989.

Because the entire University of Chicago campus is on the National Register of Historic Places, the planners had several possibilities to offer as subject matter. They chose Cobb Hall and made a formal application for a postal card to the Citizens' Stamp Advisory Committee, supplementing it with documentation, pictures of the building and letters of support from members of the Illinois delegation to Congress.

"Then came the fingernail-biting," Jaffe said. Finally, late in 1991, the Chicagoans learned that their card had been approved and was scheduled for issue early the next year.

The University of Chicago was founded by a group of Chicago civic leaders led by William Rainey Harper, who one writer described as "the most prodigious young overachiever of the 19th century." Harper was a high-school graduate at age 9, a college graduate at 13, a college teacher at 16, a Ph.D. and the principal of a Tennessee college at 19. Before he was 30, he had become the country's leading instructor of Hebrew. He was 36 when, as president of the University of Chicago, he opened the new institution in the city's Hyde Park section October 1, 1892. The major contributor of start-up funds for the new university was oil magnate John D. Rockefeller. He would ultimately give $35 million to the school, and the Rockefeller Foundation would later contribute another $45 million.

Cobb Hall was built with funds donated by Silas B. Cobb. One of the original Chicagoans, Cobb had arrived as a poor youth at the settlement in 1833, the year of its incorporation as a town. Over the next 60 years he amassed a fortune, and he shared his wealth with city and university.

Harper and his board of trustees hired another Cobb — architect Henry Ives Cobb, no relation to Silas — to prepare a plan for the campus and to design the first buildings. Henry Cobb was a prominent institutional architect in Chicago. Some of his other design contributions included the Chicago Opera House, Chicago Athletic Club, Newberry Library and the Chicago Historical Society.

He built Cobb Hall of blue Bedford limestone and roofed it with copper-crested, flat red tiling. Cobb used a few elements of the Gothic style: steep-roof gables, deep-set rectangular windows and slender towers flanking the main entrance. The building originally contained the offices of the president and the university press, the registrar, examiner, dean of graduate students and university extension, as well as a main lecture hall and classrooms.

Since Cobb Hall was the beginning and center of the university, and because of its architectural significance, it has been preserved on campus, even as other, more modern buildings have grown up around it. Extensive interior renovations began in 1963, but the outer shell has remained essentially the same as Henry Cobb conceived it.

One hundred years after its founding, the University of Chicago ranks among the top educational institutions in the United States. On its faculty are dozens of Nobel Prize winners. The University of Chicago Press, its publishing concern, is the largest scholarly press in the country. Also renowned are its Oriental Institute, libraries, nuclear studies, medical and law schools, and undergraduate college. Among William Harper's well-known successors as president have been Robert Maynard Hutchins and the present incumbent, Hanna Holborn Gray.

The Design

To paint the image of Cobb Hall that would be used in the postal card's stamp area, USPS hired Michael P. Hagel of Arlington Heights, Illinois. Hagel had designed two previous Historic Preservation cards with Chicago subjects: Hull House (1989) and Orchestra Hall (1990).

With Cobb Hall, Hagel encountered the same problem he had had to deal with at Hull House: The building, which originally stood in the open, is now hemmed in closely by newer, bigger structures. He solved it the same way — by restoring the open setting while depicting the building, in a full frontal view, as it looks today.

"The view you're seeing on the card really doesn't exist now, in the sense that to see it you would have to be standing inside the building (Swift Hall) that's about 25 yards in front of it," Hagel said. "I photographed Cobb Hall in stages, to make sure I got all the architectural nuances, and then 'built' the finished picture."

In his painting, Hagel eliminated all extraneous features except one tree on each side of the building. He eliminated a building that is now

This is designer Michael Hagel's original color sketch of the view of Cobb Hall that was ultimately used on the postal card. In the final version, the trees at the sides have been changed, the trees and lamp post in front of the building have been removed, and the sky is cloudless.

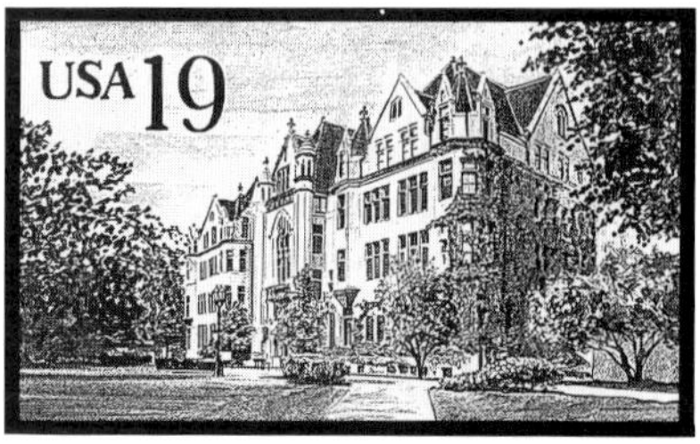

Michael Hagel offered CSAC this color sketch of a three-quarters front view of Cobb Hall, showing the ivy clinging to the side of the building.

connected to Cobb Hall, as well as buildings in the background and trees and a lamp post that stand between the front facade and the viewing point.

Before CSAC finally settled on this view, Hagel also made a color sketch showing a three-quarter front view of Cobb Hall. He personally liked this angle, but CSAC members thought it didn't show enough of the building, so he did a finished version of the straight-on view. He painted the building in its natural colors, but tinted the windows blue to suggest the reflection of the sky.

Imprinted in the postal card's cachet area, in the lower left corner, was the inscription: "Cobb Hall/The University of Chicago/Centennial Year, 1991-1992." USPS frequently uses this corner for information about the subject of Historic Preservation cards, despite recurring fears that printing in this location will confuse the optical address-scanning machines used to sort mail.

As it turned out, the inscription on the Cobb Hall card did cause a certain amount of confusion. Kineret Jaffe said a few cards deemed undeliverable because of wrong or outdated addresses had been returned to the University of Chicago instead of to their actual senders because an optical scanner (or possibly a live postal worker) had mistaken the inscription for a return address.

First-Day Facts

The public first-day ceremony was held in the Swift Lecture Hall on the third floor of the university's Swift Hall, with Cobb Hall visible through the room's windows.

Gordon C. Morison, assistant postmaster general, dedicated the card. Speakers included Hanna Holborn Gray, president of the university, and Walter Blum, chairman of the Faculty Centennial Committee.

"When we were getting ready for the ceremony," said Kineret Jaffe, "we tried to see if there was a descendant of either Henry Ives Cobb or Silas Cobb to join us, and we drew a blank on both Cobbs. Henry Ives Cobb moved East, and Silas Cobb — we traced his family tree as far as we could, and then it just went nowhere."

USPS made available an oval pictorial first-day handstamp for canceling covers. It reproduced, in outline form, the drawing of the building shown in the card's design.

19¢ WALLER HALL POSTAL CARD HISTORIC PRESERVATION SERIES

Date of Issue: February 1, 1992

Catalog Number: Scott UX162

Colors: yellow, magenta, cyan, black

First-Day Cancel: Salem, Oregon

FDCs Canceled: 28,463

Format: Printed in 80-card sheets, but available only in single cards. Printing plates of 80 subjects (8 across, 10 around).

Size: 5½ by 3½ inches

Markings: "Waller Hall/Salem, Oregon/Willamette University/Sesquicentennial/1842-1992/© USPS 1991."

Designer, Typographer and Art Director: Bradbury Thompson (CSAC)

Project Manager: Jack Williams (USPS)

Printing: U.S. Government Printing Office (GPO) on a 5-color Roland Man 800 sheetfed offset press

Quantity Ordered: 20,000,000

Quantity Distributed: 12,381,000

Tagging: vertical bar to right of stamp

The Postal Card

On February 1, USPS issued a 19¢ postal card in the Historic Preservation series to honor the 150th anniversary of the oldest university in the

West, Willamette University of Salem, Oregon. The design of the card featured the university's oldest building, Waller Hall.

The card was the third in the series to be issued in 16 days. And it was the seventh Historic Preservation card to commemorate the anniversary of an American university since USPS began using the series for that purpose with the Healy Hall (Georgetown University) issue of 1989.

One of the most influential advocates of the card was U.S. Senator Mark Hatfield, Republican of Oregon, who had attended Willamette as an undergraduate and later returned to serve as a professor of political science and dean of students. It was during his tenure as dean that Hatfield began his political career by winning a seat in the Oregon legislature.

Hatfield wrote to Postmaster General Anthony M. Frank on behalf of the project. On March 15, 1991, the Citizens' Stamp Advisory Committee met and recommended a card for Willamette, to be issued in 1992. Frank notified Hatfield of the decision by phone, and, on April 9, followed up with a letter to the senator promising to keep him informed on further plans. The postmaster general added a postscript in handwriting: "150 years, west of the Rockies, is a very genuine milestone."

On May 7, Hatfield distributed a press release announcing the news, and disclosing that the card would depict Waller Hall. USPS issued its own announcement of the card May 31.

The card was the second in the Historic Preservation series to feature an Oregon landmark. The first, in 1987, depicted Timberline Lodge at Mount Hood (Scott UX119).

Willamette (the accent is on the second syllable) is independent and coeducational. In 1992 it had 2,410 students enrolled in a college of liberal arts and graduate programs of law, management and teaching.

The institution was founded by Methodist pioneers in 1842, 17 years before Oregon became a state, and was named for the nearby Willamette River. Salem, the capital city, grew around the university. The state capitol was built across the street from the campus.

In 1860 the trustees decided that Willamette's survival depended on construction of a new building. The result was the Georgian-style Waller Hall, then known as University Hall. It was designed without the benefit of architects and built with brick fired from clay at the building site.

Begun in 1864 and officially opened October 21, 1867, the building, with its lantern cupola, dominated the campus and Salem, housing the entire university in its four floors. For four decades, University Hall was Willamette. In the 1880s the university allowed a few men students to room on the fourth floor. The heating appliances used in these garret rooms caused two catastrophic fires, one in 1891 that burned the upper floors and a second in 1919 that gutted the entire building.

After the second fire, architect Fred Legge restored the building's classical appearance (which had been altered with a mansard-style roof and gothic-style bell tower after the 1891 blaze) and remodeled the interior, putting a full-floor library above the main floor chapel.

In 1912 the building was renamed Waller Hall after the Reverend

Alvan F. Waller, who raised funds for and supervised its original construction. Waller Hall was listed on the National Register of Historic Places in 1975. A $2.6 million renovation was begun in 1988 and completed the following year. The structure now houses administrative offices, exhibits and archives, and the Cone Chapel.

The building is celebrated in the *Ode to Willamette*, with this quatrain, written by a student in 1915: "There's an old historic temple/Rising grandly through the years,/Where the oaken hearted fathers/Drew their strength for strong careers . . ." The Waller cupola is featured on the university's logo.

The Design

The design of the Waller Hall postal card was unusual in that it was taken from a painting that was already in existence. Many stamps have reproduced existing paintings, but virtually all modern postal card designs before this one had been based on artwork specifically commissioned by the Postal Service. In this case, however, USPS officials decided there was no need to have a new picture made.

The available piece was a watercolor done in 1989 by George Custer Warner, a Eugene, Oregon, artist who specializes in buildings. It was commissioned by June Cone of Eugene as a Christmas gift for her husband, Edwin E. Cone, the retired president of Cone Lumber Company and a former mayor of Eugene. The Cones are alumni of Willamette, and the refurbished chapel of Waller Hall bears their name.

The couple lent the painting to the university, which had it photo-

After a fire in 1891, Waller Hall (right) was rebuilt with a mansard roof and bell tower. The classic roofline and cupola of the original building were restored after a second fire, in 1919, gutted the building. The old Oregon state capitol is in the background.

graphed. From the slides furnished by Willamette, the Government Printing Office made the color separations for the postal card. The image required only minor cropping at the top to fit in the indicium space.

The fact that the piece of art on which the Postal Service based its design was privately owned was highly unusual in itself. In recent years USPS has avoided using privately held artwork as a basis for stamp designs, on the theory that to do so would automatically enhance the work's value. In 1990 a painting owned by Jack Rosenthal, who was then chairman of CSAC, was reproduced on the Wyoming Statehood Centennial stamp — but the decision was contingent on Rosenthal's arranging to donate the painting to the Nicolaysen Art Museum in Casper, Wyoming. Asked about the use of the Cones' painting of Waller Hall on the postal card, Rosenthal said he had no recollection that the matter had been discussed by CSAC.

The Waller Hall painting was approximately 22 inches wide by 15 inches deep. It showed the building with some of its windows open. This dated it as prior to the completion of the 1989 rehabilitation, according to Michael W. Bennett, director of planned giving at Willamette. As part of that project, non-opening windows were installed.

As a token of gratitude to Edwin and June Cone for lending the painting, the university presented them with a framed piece that included a lithograph of the Warner painting and a copy of the USPS first-day ceremony program. At last report, the display was hanging beside the painting itself in the Cones' bedroom in Eugene.

First-Day Facts

The first-day ceremony, which was open to the public, was held in

This is George Custer Warner's 1989 painting of Waller Hall, which Edwin and June Cone made available for reproduction on the postal card.

Waller Hall's Cone Chapel. William T. Johnstone, assistant postmaster general, dedicated the card, substituting for Postmaster General Anthony M. Frank. Jerry E. Hudson, president of Willamette University, gave the welcome, and the principal speaker was Wallace P. Carson, chief justice of the Oregon Supreme Court.

The pictorial handstamped first-day postmark featured an outline drawing of Waller Hall seen from the same angle as the building as shown in the card's indicium.

19¢ AMERICA'S CUP PICTURE POSTAL CARD

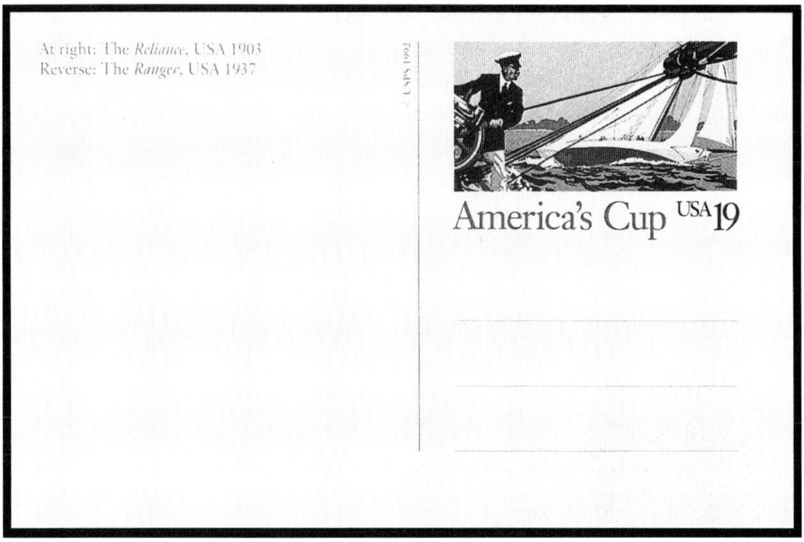

Date of Issue: May 6, 1992

Catalog Number: Scott UX163

Colors: yellow, magenta, cyan, black

First-Day Cancel: San Diego, California

FDCs Canceled: 19,944

Format: Printed on Krome Coat paper in 72-card sheets but available only in single cards. Printing plates of 72 subjects (8 across, 9 around).

Size: 5½ by 3½ inches

Markings: "At Right: The Reliance, USA 1903/Reverse: The Ranger, USA 1937." "© USPS 1992."

Designer: Dennis Simon of Sparks, Maryland

Art Director, Project Manager and Typographer: Terrence McCaffrey (USPS)

Printing: U.S. Government Printing Office (GPO) on a 5-color Roland Man 800 sheetfed offset press

Quantity Ordered: 3,500,000

Quantity Distributed: 3,496,000

Tagging: vertical bar to right of stamp

The Postal Card

On May 6, in San Diego, California, USPS issued a picture postal card to honor the America's Cup yacht competition, which would begin three days later in the Pacific Ocean off San Diego.

The card was the fifth in the Postal Service's series of premium-priced "EXTRAordinary View Cards." Like a conventional picture postcard, it had a glossy, full-color picture on one side. On the address/message side, however, was a colorful indicium indicating prepayment of postage. The indicium bore a 19¢ denomination, corresponding to the postcard rate, and the card sold for 50¢.

Previous EXTRAordinary View Cards (the name is trademarked) had shown buildings in Washington, D.C. (the White House, the Jefferson Memorial, and Constitution Hall/Memorial Continental Hall), and a painting by American artist George Caleb Bingham, *Fur Traders Descending the Missouri*. This one depicted yachts: one on the picture side, a second and portion of a third in the stamp image.

The card was originally conceived by the Citizens' Stamp Advisory Committee as a standard commemorative postal card. According to Terrence McCaffrey of USPS, the project manager and art director, it wasn't issued in response to any of the usual forces that produce a stamp or postal stationery.

There was no campaign from the outside. "The America's Cup people were surprised to learn that we were doing the card," McCaffrey said. "They hadn't lobbied for it." No request came from Postmaster General Anthony M. Frank, who hailed from California, where the Cup was being held: "Mr. Frank didn't know anything about the card until he saw the artwork." Finally, none of the CSAC members was particularly absorbed by the sport of sailing.

"It was one of those things," said McCaffrey. "We wanted to do something action-oriented. Ships seemed to be popular. And the America's

This stamped envelope honoring the America's Cup (Scott U598) was issued in 1980.

Cup is a big event."

Added Jack Williams of the USPS Design Section: "The committee is always talking about things that are pretty, that are nice, that are topical, that are current, that might have some selling value."

Once before, in 1980, USPS had honored the America's Cup with postal stationery. It was a 15¢ stamped envelope (Scott U598) bearing an embossed image of a racing yacht. The impetus for that issue, Williams recalled, came from the then-postmaster general, the late William Bolger, who was from New England and had friends associated with the Newport, Rhode Island, yachting community.

The America's Cup was first offered in 1851 by the Royal Yacht Squadron of Great Britain for a 53-mile race around the Isle of Wight. The race was won by the 100-foot schooner *America* against a large fleet of British yachts. Six years later the syndicate that had built *America* gave the cup to the New York Yacht Club as a perpetual challenge trophy to be raced for by yachts of foreign countries. The first challenge was made in 1870, with *Magic*, a U.S. yacht, successfully defending against the British *Cambria*.

The 1992 competition was the 28th in the 141-year series. Only once, in 1983, had a non-American boat won the cup. That year, the Australian yacht *Australia II* defeated the American yacht *Liberty*. On May 10, 1992, *Il Moro di Venezia*, the first Italian boat ever to reach the final round, began a best-of-seven-races match against *America3* (America Cubed), skippered by oil executive Bill Koch. *America3* captured the fifth and decisive race May 16 to retain the cup for the United States by a four-to-one score. The Italians won only the second race, by three seconds — the smallest margin of victory in America's Cup history.

To win the cup, Koch built four boats and spent $64 million. The Italian syndicate spent an estimated $100 million in its losing effort.

Dennis Simon submitted these pencil sketches to the Citizens' Stamp Advisory Committee for consideration as subjects for an America's Cup postal card indicium.

The Design

Dennis Simon of Sparks, Maryland, is an artist who specializes in poster work, with flat colors and hard edges. A one-time creator of historical paintings for the National Park Service and the National Geographic Society, he has concentrated in recent years on automotive subjects, creating deco-revival style images of classic sports and racing cars for posters and automobile magazines.

He submitted a portfolio of his paintings to USPS at the suggestion of an artist friend from Baltimore, Jerry Dadds, who had designed the 1986 set of Presidential miniature sheets honoring Ameripex 86. Dadds was a partner of another of Simon's friends, Richard Waldrep, who designed the five Summer Olympics commemorative stamps of 1992.

Among the samples Simon sent to USPS were some sailing vessels he had done for American Bank Stationery's series of illustrated checks. He described these as among the more "obscure" items in his portfolio. But when USPS officials were looking for an artist for the America's Cup card, they thought of Simon's boat pictures and asked him to submit some sketches for that purpose.

Simon made four pencil drawings of racing yachts from past America's Cup races, based on photographs he had found in books at his local library. "The committee really liked the sketches," said McCaffrey. "They liked the light, loose, free feel to them."

CSAC's design subcommittee suggested that Simon proceed to finished art with two of his drawings, which he did, in acrylic on illustration board. The full committee was so pleased with the paintings that it

Terrence McCaffrey experimented with using both of Dennis Simon's finished paintings for the indicium of the card before settling on the picture that included the helmsman in the foreground. The other painting was Simon's original picture of the dark-hulled British yacht Endeavour II, *which the artist later replaced with a painting of the U.S. yacht* Ranger *for use on the picture side.*

The helmsman in the indicium was based on this photograph of Charles Nicholson, a well-known yacht designer, at the wheel of* Candida. *The picture was made some time after World War I.

decided to make the card a picture postal card and use both. One of the paintings showed a side view of a yacht cutting through the water, under full sail. The other showed a yacht racing in the middle distance; in the left foreground was a helmsman at the wheel of a second boat, natty in yachting cap, blazer, white shirt, club tie and white flannels.

McCaffrey chose the latter painting as the subject of the indicium after trying both of them in that position. The vessels were identified, in two lines of type on the corner of the postal card, as "The Reliance, USA 1903" (indicium) and "The Ranger, USA 1937" (picture side). The USPS news release on the card stated that the indicium featured "the Reliance, winner of the 1903 America's Cup, in a race against the Shamrock III of England" — the yacht defeated by *Reliance* in that year's challenge.

In painting the image for the indicium, Simon referred to two different photographs he had found in his library books. Neither of them, as it happened, was of the 1903 America's Cup race.

The helmsman at the left was based on a photograph of Charles Nicholson, a well-known British yacht designer, at the wheel of a yacht named *Candida*, some time after World War I. That photograph was from the Beken of Cowes, Ltd., collection in England. The vessel that USPS described as *Reliance* was based on a photograph belonging to the Rosenfeld Collection at Mystic Seaport, Connecticut. But, according to Rosenfeld Collection officials (who supplied *The Yearbook* with a photocopy), the photograph showed, not *Reliance,* but a yacht named *Resolute*, which won the America's Cup in 1920.

Ranger, on the picture side of the postal card, wasn't the yacht Simon had originally painted. Sara Day, a USPS fact-checker, reviewed Simon's finished artwork and reported that he had actually reproduced the British

This is Dennis Simon's original painting for the picture side of the postal card. When a researcher pointed out that the yacht was a British vessel,* **Endeavour II**, *Simon made another painting, from the same perspective, showing* **Ranger**, *the American yacht that had defeated* **Endeavour II** *in the 1937 Cup races.

vessel that had lost the 1937 challenge series to *Ranger*, a yacht named *Endeavour II*. A British boat wouldn't do for a U.S. postal card celebrating the America's Cup, so Simon was asked to repaint the picture.

The artist made a new painting, replacing the dark-hulled *Endeavour II* with the light-hulled *Ranger*. His new picture was very similar to the old one. "I didn't want to go back and start from zero again," Simon said, so he used the same perspective, working from photographs and actual schematic drawings of *Ranger's* deck.

The new painting was then shown to experts at Sparkman and Stephens, the New York City firm whose founder, Olin Stephens, had designed *Ranger*, to make certain the technical details of the yacht's sails, lines and

This photocopy of Simon's painting of* **Ranger** *was annotated on the basis of experts' recommendations and then returned to the artist for changes.

This is the picture side of the America's Cup card as it was issued.

hardware were correct. "They nitpicked it to perfection," McCaffrey said. On the basis of the experts' comments, a color photocopy of Simon's painting was annotated and returned to the artist for corrections.

The marginal notes included comments like these: "Snaphooks too far apart." "Straight lines — no sway." "Never have loose sheet on jib — should be taut." "Angle of wheel is wrong." "Deck does not slope up at stern; stern deck is flat and straight — clean line." "Are these running back stays? If so, they're wrongly placed."

Simon made the recommended changes, but he also simplified his picture and removed some of the detail. "We kept emphasizing that we were after a poster effect, that this wasn't a literal rendering, and that we had to have some artistic license," McCaffrey said.

First-Day Facts

No first-day ceremony was held on May 6. However, two days later Deputy Postmaster General Michael S. Coughlin took part in the opening ceremony for America's Cup XXVIII in San Diego. Principals at the event were Maureen O'Connor, mayor of San Diego; Clifford Graves, chairman of the San Diego Unified Port commission; and Malin Burnham, president of the America's Cup Organizing Committee.

A first-day postmark was offered May 6 at the San Diego main post office, and a special pictorial postmark was available May 8 at the USPS booth on the Broadway Pier.

19¢ COLUMBIA RIVER GORGE POSTAL CARD AMERICA THE BEAUTIFUL SERIES

Date of Issue: May 9, 1992

Catalog Number: Scott UX164

Colors: yellow, magenta, cyan, black

First-Day Cancel: Stevenson, Washington

FDCs Canceled: 32,344

Format: Printed in 80-card sheets, but available only in single cards. Printing plates of 80 subjects (8 across, 10 around).

Size: 5½ by 3½ inches

Markings: "© USPS 1992."

Designer: Ken Hodges of Los Alamitos, California

Art Director and Typographer: Richard Sheaff (CSAC)

Project Manager: Joe Brockert (USPS)

Printing: U.S. Government Printing Office (GPO) on a 5-color Roland Man 800 sheetfed offset press

Quantity Ordered: 7,500,000

Quantity Distributed: 7,500,000

Tagging: vertical bar to right of stamp

The Postal Card

On May 9, USPS issued the 12th postal card in its America the Beautiful series. It depicted a scene in the Columbia River Gorge, between Oregon and Washington, where the great river cuts through the Cascade Mountains.

The America the Beautiful series has had three identifiable phases. The series began in 1988 with a prairie scene, which was followed in 1989 by five cards showing other scenes representative of different types of landscape: desert, wetlands, mountains, seashore and woodlands. Like the first card, these all showed generic rather than specific places.

Then, late in 1989, USPS issued four cityscape cards in the series, each showing a specific city: Philadelphia, Baltimore, New York and Washington. These were produced in connection with the USPS-sponsored World Stamp Expo, held in Washington in December 1989, and their common theme was cities that visitors to the stamp show might conveniently visit while they were on the U.S. East Coast.

The third phase of the America the Beautiful series has focused on identifiable non-urban places. It began in 1991 with a postal card depicting Niagara Falls. The Columbia River Gorge card of 1992 was the second in this group.

The Columbia River Gorge card was also the second postal card of 1992 to depict a scene in Oregon. A card in the Historic Preservation series, issued February 1, showed Waller Hall on the campus of Willamette University in Salem.

Coincidentally, the new card was issued in the year of the 200th anniversary of the discovery of the Columbia River, but the Postal Service made no attempt at a commemorative tie-in. Members of the Beta Sigma Phi Sorority of Astoria, Oregon, had led a campaign to win Citizens' Stamp Advisory Committee approval of a stamp for the anniversary, but their efforts were unsuccessful.

The river's discoverer was Captain Robert Gray, a Boston trader. Ship captains of several nations who had probed the Pacific Northwest coast before him were deceived by a sandbar that sealed the mouth of the river. Gray, in 1792, crossed the bar in his vessel, the *Columbia Rediviva*, and named the river in honor of his ship. Later Sacagawea, the Indian guide, led Lewis and Clark to the Columbia, and they explored it in 1805-06.

At 1,210 miles in length, the Columbia is the longest river flowing into the Pacific Ocean from North America. It originates in British Columbia and flows through Washington state, with its lower course forming the border between Washington and Oregon.

The Columbia River Gorge extends for some 60 miles, from Troutdale, Oregon, just east of Portland, to The Dalles. The most mountainous portion is about 20 miles long. Roughly halfway through the Gorge is the Bonneville Dam, completed in 1937 for navigation, flood control and power at a cost of $40 million. The dam is famous for its fish ladders that permit salmon to travel upstream to their spawning grounds.

The Gorge is a recreational playground, extensively used for fishing, boating and water skiing. The topography of the Gorge, which creates strong winds in some stretches, makes it a popular area for wind surfers.

The Design

The indicium design by Ken Hodges features a panoramic view of the gorge, looking eastward from the Oregon side of the river. Vista House, in Oregon's Crown Point State Park, can be seen on top of a high cliff, overlooking the gorge. Crown Point is below Bonneville Dam, a few miles upstream from Portland.

Art director Richard Sheaff had first brought to the Citizens' Stamp Advisory Committee some samples from another artist, a commercial illustrator. (His name was withheld under USPS policy of not disclosing the names of artists who submit proposed stamp or postal stationery designs but aren't chosen.) "He's a really interesting man, and does beautiful work," Sheaff said. "He has a fairly realistic style, slightly abstract, but he has a little surrealistic twist to what he does. He might have a green country landscape, verdant hills and trees, and there's a shark fin cutting through the fields."

Sheaff assured him that what CSAC wanted was not surrealism but straight illustration, and the artist produced a sketch, based on the same view that can be seen on the postal card as issued. "The committee loved the sketch," Sheaff said. "But when he went to final art, oil on canvas, it was pretty monochromatic. It wasn't rich and bright and with a long color range; it was all sort of medium gray green. When you looked at it it was just sort of blah, and the committee said to me, we liked the sketch, but . . . get another artist.

"So I went to Ken Hodges, who has done a number of things for us in the past and done them very well, and asked him if he'd be interested, and he was, and he very quickly did the final piece. He did it in oil on artist's board. The committee already knew they liked the scene OK, they just

Another artist made this pencil sketch and later painted a finished picture of the same scene. The committee members thought the result was too monochromatic, however, and the assignment was given to Ken Hodges.

wanted it in brighter colors."

The reference material Sheaff supplied to the artists consisted of photographs from various sources, taken at different times of day and with coloration that varied accordingly. The scene as painted by Hodges was based on an aerial photograph and showed the gorge in the afternoon, with sunlight shining full on the golden cliffs and touching the ridges of the distant mountains.

Previous cards in the America the Beautiful series carried the series name below and outside the indicium. This one didn't. In fact, all the card's typography was inside the indicium, including the "19 USA" in dropout white Futura in the lower-left corner, and "Columbia River Gorge" in a single line of small black Futura in the upper-left corner.

Some CSAC members complained about the inclusion of the identifying line inside the indicium, saying it cluttered the design. But postal officials had specified that postal-card designs be limited in depth so as not to encroach on the address area and possibly confuse the optical address-reading equipment. To meet that requirement, the decision was made to keep the typography internal, Sheaff said.

Dropping out letters and numbers from a process-color background can present tough registration problems, but the Government Printing Office seems to have mastered the technique. The Columbia River Gorge card was the third to display dropout typography since the GPO installed its five-color, sheetfed, offset Roland Man 800 press in 1987. The others were the Isaac Royall House card of 1990 and the Carnegie Hall card of 1991, both of them part of the Historic Preservation series.

This is one of several stock color photographs of the Columbia River Gorge, seen from the Oregon side, that Ken Hodges used as reference in painting the picture used in the indicium.

First Day Facts

Astoria, Oregon, was originally announced as the site of the first-day ceremony. This struck Oregonians as strange, inasmuch as Astoria is located near the mouth of the Columbia, far from the gorge that the postal card depicts. Later, USPS changed the site to the Rock Creek Center in Stevenson, Washington, which is situated on the river just above the Bonneville Dam, in the heart of the Columbia River Gorge.

Associate Postmaster General Edward E. Horgan Jr. dedicated the card, and Bill Lange of the Center for Columbia River History was the principal speaker. Various other community events were held in conjunction with the issuance of the postal card. The first-day handstamped postmark featured an outline drawing of a wind surfer.

19¢ ELLIS ISLAND POSTAL CARD
HISTORIC PRESERVATION SERIES

Date of Issue: May 11, 1992

Catalog Number: Scott UX165

Colors: yellow, magenta, cyan, black

First-Day Cancel: New York (Ellis Island), New York

FDCs Canceled: 38,482

Format: Printed in 80-card sheets, but available only in single cards. Printing plates of 80 subjects (8 across, 10 around).

Size: 5½ by 3½ inches

Markings: "Ellis Island/Centennial 1992/© USPS 1991"

Designer: Howard Koslow of East Norwich, New York

Art Director: Derry Noyes (CSAC)

Project Manager: Joe Brockert (USPS)

Typographer: Bradbury Thompson (CSAC)

Printing: U.S. Government Printing Office (GPO) on a 5-color Roland Man 800 sheetfed offset press

Quantity Ordered: 20,000,000

Quantity Distributed: 14,086,000

Tagging: vertical bar to right of stamp

The Postal Card

The Postal Service marked the 100th anniversary of Ellis Island, the processing center for immigrants arriving from Europe, with a Historic Preservation postal card issued May 11. It depicted the former Main Building, which was restored and reopened in 1990 as the Ellis Island Immigration Museum.

The anniversary, and the building, were obvious subjects for postal recognition, and the Citizens' Stamp Advisory Committee approved the card "fairly routinely," according to Joe Brockert, the project manager.

However, the committee's discussion of the immigrant experience and how, or whether, it should be commemorated led, by an indirect route, to a second piece of postal stationery that was issued in 1992: the Western Americana envelope. Details can be found in the chapter on that item.

Ellis Island is a 27.5-acre island in the shadow of the Statue of Liberty. It is located off the New Jersey shoreline in upper New York Harbor. Between January 1, 1892, and 1924, when Congress sharply reduced immigration with restrictive quotas, some 12 million immigrants entered America, and a new life, through its doors. In its busiest year, 1907, more than 1.2 million people came through. Today, nearly half the nation's population — an estimated 140 million of us — can trace an ancestor's passage through this tiny gateway.

Europe's so-called great migration was entering a final phase in 1900, the year the Main Building was completed at a cost of $1.5 million. Described as a beaux arts structure with French Renaissance trappings, the Main Building was designed by the New York City firm of Boring & Tilton and was erected to replace a wood-frame terminal that had burned to the ground 3½ years earlier. Above its brick-and-limestone walls rose four exotic turrets with domes and finials, shiny in ornamental copper. In its immense, vaulted Registry Room on the second floor, medical examinations and interviews determined whether the new arrivals would be accepted or — in a small percentage of cases — denied entry, usually for ill health or radical politics.

By 1954 the immigration station had been abandoned and the building was deteriorating badly. Revival was in its future, however. In 1965, by proclamation of President Lyndon B. Johnson, Ellis Island became part of the Statue of Liberty National Monument under the administration of the National Park Service. The date of the proclamation was May 11 (which is the significance of the May 11 date on which the postal card was dedicated). The Statue of Liberty-Ellis Island Foundation raised money from private and corporate sources, and work was begun in the 1980s.

The job took seven years and cost $156 million — 100 times the original construction cost — making it the most expensive single restoration in the nation's history. The Main Building was transformed into what *Time* called "a monument to the majesty and pain of the immigrant experience." While many of the rooms were restored as the bare examination chambers they once were, about half the structure became the Museum of Immigration, housing films, artifacts, oral histories and 1,500 photographs. The museum, which opened in September 1990, was designed to tell the story of not only the mostly European arrivals who passed through Ellis Island but also the millions who came during other eras, from other places and through other entry points.

The Design

To prepare the artwork, USPS called on Howard Koslow, who had frequently created stamp designs in the past. Koslow had also designed the Carnegie Hall postal card of 1991, which was the most recent Historic Preservation card that showed a New York City landmark.

Derry Noyes, the card's art director, contacted the National Park Service, which had staff photographer Brian Feeney make some color pictures of the museum building for the Postal Service. Feeney furnished two or three color transparencies, and Koslow supplemented these with some reference pictures he had found himself.

Feeney's photographs showed the building from a slight angle. However, Noyes and Koslow had decided that the view on the postal card should be head-on, so the artist, working with his pictorial reference material, created an image with the perspective they wanted. He did a detailed pencil sketch first, then made his painting, in acrylic on illustration board, with no significant changes.

Koslow was obliged to omit from his picture many of the building's ornate visual attractions. "You're doing a seven-inch painting which is then going to be reduced to a couple of inches," he said. "So you have to cut out detail that just isn't going to reproduce."

His completed painting showed the museum as one would see it from a point across a ferry channel on the island. He had included a portion of

National Park Service photographer Brian Feeney furnished this color photograph for Howard Koslow to use as a visual reference. It was taken from a slight angle, so Koslow had to make adjustments to create the head-on view of the building that was needed for the postal card.

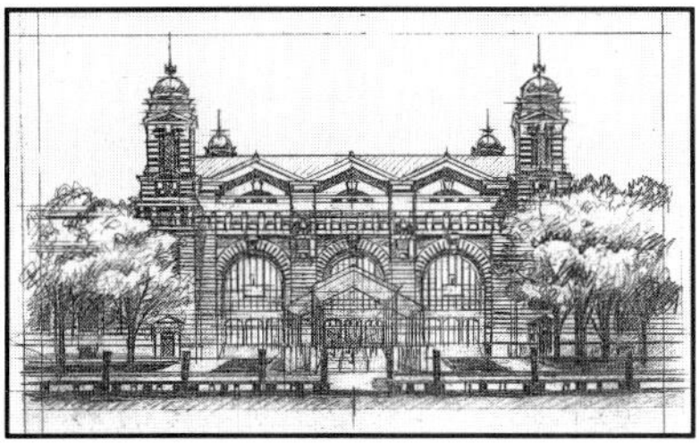

This is Howard Koslow's preliminary pencil sketch of the restored Main Building on Ellis Island. He made the sketch before painting the finished artwork in acrylic.

the channel in the foreground, but this was cropped out during the prepress work at the Government Printing Office. In Koslow's picture, the two front towers rise above the trees on either side of the entrance, and the tops of the rear towers peep over the red roof. Immediately behind a row of piers at the bottom is the latticed-roof arcade through which visitors approach the museum entrance. Traces of clouds float in the blue

Artist Howard Koslow is shown with an enlargement of his postal card design at the first-day ceremony on Ellis Island. The ceremony was held against a backdrop of the Manhattan skyline. Note that the design on the finished postal card is cropped slightly on all four sides so that no water shows in the foreground.

sky overhead.

The "19 USA" logo could have gone in either corner of the perfectly balanced picture, but Koslow and Noyes placed it in the upper right. "That's the outside corner of the card, and it makes a better pattern to have it there," Koslow explained. "It makes a fence and holds the eye in."

First-Day Facts

The public first-day ceremony was held May 11 just outside the Immigration Museum, with the skyline of Lower Manhattan as a backdrop. "It was a marvelous day. The sun came out right on schedule," said Koslow, who was on the program as an honored guest.

John F. Kelly, general manager and postmaster of the New York Division, dedicated the card, substituting for Assistant Postmaster General William T. Johnstone, who had been scheduled to do it. Herbert S. Cables Jr., deputy director of the National Park Service, was the principal speaker, and the welcome was given by M. Ann Belkov, superintendent of the Statue of Liberty/Ellis Island National Monument.

The pictorial handstamped first-day postmark furnished by USPS contained an outline drawing of the same view of the Great Hall that was depicted on the postal card.

19¢ POSTAL BUDDY POSTAL CARD

92117-001-30106-004

Date of Issue: November 13, 1992

Catalog Number: Scott 3 (under heading Computer Vended Postage/Postal Cards)

Colors: black (address side); blue, red, gray, (message side)

First-Day Cancel: none

FDCs Canceled: none

Format: sheets of four

Size: 5⅝ by 4¼ inches

Perf: extremely fine

Markings: On front, 16-digit control number and "© 1992, U.S.P.S." near stamped image. On message side, at top and bottom, "postal (SM)/ buddy" and "POSTAL BUDDY (SM)/AUTHORIZED BY THE/UNITED STATES POSTAL SERVICE" with USPS logo; at side, arrow and stock lot number.

Designer and Typographer: Steff Geissbuhler of Chermayeff & Geismar Inc., New York, New York

Printing: computerized laser printing by Postal Buddy vending machine

Tagging: 6½-millimeter square at center of stamped design

The Postal Card

On November 13, 1992, the second generation of Postal Buddy, a high-tech vending-machine system that processed changes of address and printed postal cards and other products, went on line in two Northern Virginia post offices.

The installations were the forerunners of a nationwide network of 10,000 machines planned by USPS and its private-sector partner in the venture, the Postal Buddy Corporation of San Diego, California.

Postal Buddy had made its debut in 1990 when USPS and the company began a market test with machines in 30 locations in Northern Virginia.

The machines offered numerous services and products, but of principal interest to stamp collectors was the 15¢ postal card they dispensed. The card, with a simple stamped design featuring the USPS eagle logo in black, was the first U.S. postage item with a fixed denomination to be printed on demand by a laser printer.

Using a computer keyboard, customers could also print their change-of-address information, meeting notices or other messages onto the front of the cards. (Collectors had the option of obtaining cards without messages.) Once a card was obtained from the machine, it could be mailed anywhere at any time.

On February 3, 1991, when the postcard rate was increased to 19¢, the Postal Buddy Corporation changed the software in its machines to create a new version of the card that was identical to the original except for its higher denomination.

USPS ultimately deemed the experiment a success, and in January 1992 signed an 8½-year license agreement with the company authorizing it to produce, deploy and service 10,000 or more Postal Buddy machines. Under the agreement, the company would assume all costs and pay USPS a commission on products sold.

Of greatest potential value to USPS, however, was the Postal Buddy's change-of-address function. Each year the Postal Service deals with 41.5 million address changes, spending an estimated $1.3 billion annually to forward some 2.3 billion pieces of mail. Postal Buddy, in time, was

This is a Postal Buddy machine, which the company terms "a revolutionary, new, interactive one-stop convenience kiosk that offers customers and businesses a variety of convenient services and customized laser-printed products in seconds."

The small tagging block at center, photographed under shortwave ultraviolet light, is the new type of tagging for Postal Buddy postal cards.

expected to handle a significant number of these address changes — up to half of them, USPS predicted — resulting in a large cost savings. Postal Buddy also helped promote wider use of ZIP+4 because its access to a database of more than 120 million addresses enabled it to provide the correct nine-digit ZIP code for each new address.

On August 30, at the Postal Forum in Washington, a new generation of the machines was unveiled, along with an updated Postal Buddy postal card. On the new card, the Postal Service eagle was replaced by a stylized design suggestive of the American flag, with simulated perforations.

Unlike the first two cards, the new one was tagged, with a 6½-millimeter square at the center of the design that was visible under shortwave ultraviolet light. This change made the cards compatible with automated post office equipment, and prevented the haphazard facing and misplaced or missing cancellations that had been reported with the earlier ones. The cards were dispensed by the machine in sheets of four, with microscopic perforations. The card stock was pretagged and preperforated and bore a preprinted design on the back or message side.

The new cards were the same depth as the old ones, 4¼ inches, but were slightly wider, 5⅝ inches instead of 5½. (Postal cards produced by USPS for post office sale are 5½ inches wide but only 3½ inches deep.)

Each of the new cards bore a set of small numbers that recorded details of the transaction that produced it. The control numbers on the new cards were somewhat different from those on the old ones, however.

There were 16 digits, separated by dashes, designating the ZIP code of the machine (5 digits), the machine number (3 digits), the date (5 digits), and the transaction number (3 digits). An example of the 5-digit date number would be "21113," which represented the day the machines and cards first went into use in the Reston and Chantilly, Virginia, post offices. The 2 was the last digit of the year (1992), the 11 was the month (November) and the 13 was the day of the month.

Although the cards carried the 19¢ denomination, they sold for 39¢ each with their custom-printed messages. The previous 19¢ Postal Buddy card had sold for 37¢. Sidney R. Goodman, inventor of Postal Buddy and chief executive officer of the corporation, said the 2¢ price increase helped cover the increased cost of the card stock, which was tagged and of a non-standard size (8½ by 11¼ inches). The previous cards had used 8½- by 11-inch stock.

USPS listed the cards for sale in its *Stamps etc. Catalog* for January-

March 1993. However, the listing was dropped in the April-June issue after the Philatelic Fulfillment Service decided not to handle the cards.

Besides postal cards, these services and products were available from the machines at a touch of the video screen:

• Free electronic change-of-address notification to the Postal Service and many major magazines and catalogs (with follow-up confirmation as a security check).

• For persons contemplating moving, data sheets on most major cities of the United States, followed by mailed information packets.

• Personalized self-adhesive labels for return address or other purposes, in more than 100 variations and styles.

• Business cards in dozens of business and personal styles.

• Personal stationery or business letterheads with the customer's choice of logo or monogram, produced in a camera-ready master suitable for quantity production by a quick printer or on a photocopy machine.

• Postage stamps, available at face value in self-adhesive sheetlets, rolls of 100 or individually.

• OpinionGrams, promised for early 1993. These were Postal Buddy

Sidney Goodman of the Postal Buddy Corporation stands next to a kiosk November 13, the first day the new machines went into operation. He is holding a first-day sheet of four souvenir Postal Buddy postal cards created by the company. (Photo by Rollin Berger)

postal cards printed with messages supporting or opposing pending legislation, for mailing to state or federal representatives.

• A receipt for each transaction.

Collectors could obtain Postal Buddy cards that were blank on the address side except for the stamped image and ruled lines for an address or, if they preferred, could get cards with the Postal Buddy logo applied as a cachet by the machine.

For payment, customers could use cash, credit cards, bank cards and a new prepaid, reusable Postal Buddy money card. When cash was used, the machine issued in lieu of change a money card with the appropriate amount of credit recorded on its magnetic strip. When the credit was depleted, the same card could be reprogrammed or a new one purchased.

The machines, or "kiosks," as Postal Buddy called them, were designed by Frog Design. Postal Buddy's technology partner was EDS of Herndon, Virginia, which integrated all the software and hardware used in the system. The kiosks were touted as user-friendly. Wheelchair accessible, they featured, in addition to touch-interactive screens, full-color graphics, stereo sound, animation and full-motion video.

By early January 1993, some 80 kiosks had been installed in the Washington and San Diego, California, areas, with another 110 scheduled to be in place in those markets a few weeks thereafter. Beginning in July 1993 they would be deployed nationwide at a rate of about 500 a month, Goodman said. They would be placed in post office lobbies, shopping malls, transportation centers and other high-traffic areas.

The Design

For his new cards, Goodman wanted a stamp design that was more creative than the simple USPS logo that the Postal Service had produced for the prototypes. He asked and was granted permission to commission his own design.

In May 1992, Goodman contacted the New York City design firm of Chermayeff and Geismar, Inc., one of whose partners, Steff Geissbuhler, had created the logo used by the Postal Buddy Corporation. Because the Postal Service had told him that postal customers liked patriotic subjects, Goodman instructed Geissbuhler that the black and white stamp design had to "look patriotic." He also told the artist he wanted "perforations to show, to make it look like a stamp."

Using a Macintosh computer, Geissbuhler produced several alternative designs that depicted or suggested the American flag. Goodman chose one and showed it to Postal Service officials, who approved it, purchased it from the design firm and copyrighted it.

The design consisted of a single dominant white star, with solid black on the left and 13 straight horizontal stripes flowing off the star to the right. Seven of the stripes were shaded with horizontal lines to give the impression of gray. A large black "USA 19" was superimposed on the stripes. Geissbuhler described the design as a "sort of abbreviated flag," with a single star representing a field of stars.

"The design had to be one that could be easily reproduced in low-resolution printing. It couldn't be very intricate," Geissbuhler said. "We have a low-resolution laser printer here that we normally use just to check design content. In this case we used it to check the final art."

Chermayeff and Geismar specializes in graphic design, corporate identification programs, architectural sign systems and exhibition design. As a partner in the firm, Geissbuhler had designed logos for, among others, NBC (the well-known peacock), Time Warner, Crane Business Papers, ConEdison and the Alvin Ailey American Dance Theater. He was familiar with stamp design requirements. As a young art-school graduate in his native Switzerland in the 1960s, he entered competitions to design Swiss stamps. "We specialize in identification design in our firm, and stamps are very much in that vein," he said.

The reverse, or message side, of the new Postal Buddy cards was also different from the previous cards. The new cards bore the red, blue and gray Postal Buddy logo and an inscription: "Postal Buddy/Authorized by the/United States Postal Service." These devices appeared at the top and bottom, in inverted relationship to each other. On the previous cards, the blank space was surrounded by a set of inscriptions in a repeat pattern.

First-Day Facts

No first-day ceremony or first-day service was provided by USPS at the Reston and Chantilly post offices where the first new Postal Buddy machines and cards went on line November 13. As a result, cards bearing a first-day postmark are quite scarce.

Rollin Berger, a collector, and Postal Buddy CEO Sidney Goodman told *Linn's Stamp News* that between 775 and 900 sheets of four cards

The Postal Buddy Corporation considered these five alternative designs by Steff Geissbuhler before choosing the star-and-stripes design used on its new postal card.

This is the reverse, or message side, of the 1992 Postal Buddy postal card. The arrow at the side of the card indicates to the person servicing the machine which way to place the stack of unprinted card stock.

were created at the Chantilly post office the first day. About two-thirds that number, or 600 cards, were created in Reston, Goodman said.

However, since the Reston machine was only in operation for a short period before the window closed — and was non-functional for a time — only about four cards were actually serviced with a Reston postmark. Other first-day covers exist bearing a Merrifield, Virginia, postmark.

An exact count of the number of cards created from the Chantilly and Reston machines couldn't be determined, since the total number of cards

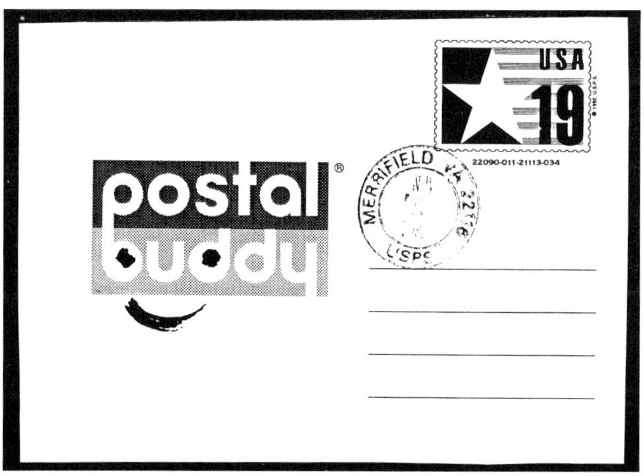

This Postal Buddy card bears a special logo cachet that can be applied by the machine. It was canceled November 13, making it one of a relatively few first-day covers.

reported by the machine included all test items run while it was set up.

Another Northern Virginia location, the Fair Oaks Mall, had been scheduled to be the first new Postal Buddy installation site, but technical problems kept the machine from going into service November 15. After a technician worked with the new machine at Fair Oaks for several hours without success, a decision was made to install machines at Reston and Chantilly, Berger said.

The Chantilly post office was the first new Postal Buddy location to be operational, going on line at about 3:30 p.m. This gave collectors an opportunity to create and service a number of cards, with the additional help of a clerk who agreed to stay later than 5 p.m.

Fair Oaks had had the last of the original Postal Buddy machines. It was removed November 12. All other first-generation Postal Buddy machines had been taken from their sites in the preceding few weeks.

WORLD COLUMBIAN STAMP EXPO 92
SOUVENIR CARD (BEP)

Date of Issue: May 22, 1992

Catalog Number: Scott 132

First-Day Release: Rosemont, Illinois (World Columbian Stamp Expo 92) and Washington, D.C. (BEP Visitors Center)

Colors: black, gray (offset); brown, blue (intaglio); metallic silver (letterpress)

Size: 10 by 8 inches

Conceptual Design: Steve Manset (BEP)

Designer: Steve Manset (BEP)

Modeler: Peter Cocci (BEP)

Engraver of Frame for Invert: Chris Madden (BEP)

Paper Stock: artificial parchment, 100-percent rag

Printing: 6-color Miller offset sheetfed press; foil stamping on Kluge letterpress; intaglio die stamper

Quantity: 8,750

The Card

On May 22, the Bureau of Engraving and Printing issued a souvenir card for World Columbian Stamp Expo 92 in Rosemont, Illinois, near Chicago. It was the first of two philatelic cards that BEP created in 1992.

The theme of the philatelic and numismatic souvenir cards and intaglio prints issued by BEP during the year was the 500th anniversary of the first voyage of Christopher Columbus to America.

The World Columbian Stamp Expo card reproduced a classic U.S. bicolored stamp of 1869, the 15¢ Landing of Columbus, in two variations: normal and inverted center. A portion of the design of the 15¢ 1869 had also been used for the 29¢ commemorative stamp issued by USPS for World Columbian Stamp Expo (see the World Columbian Stamp Expo stamp chapter). Each of the two stamp reproductions on the souvenir card bore the customary diagonal black canceling line across the corner, applied by offset lithography, and each was framed in black.

The text on the back of the card read as follows:

"This souvenir card features two 15¢ 'Landing of Columbus' postage stamps. The vignettes in both stamps are based on the painting by John Vanderlyn which hangs in the U.S. Capitol Rotunda. These stamps have the distinction of being some of the first to be issued with a vignette as the central theme, rather than featuring the portrait of statesman (sic). They are also set apart from their predecessors by the use of two colors, one for the frame and one for the vignette, in a regular issue.

"The stamp on the left has been classified as a Type I stamp (Scott United States Stamp Catalogue, Specialized 1991) which was issued in 1869. The one on the right is a reproduction of the inverted version of a Type II stamp, a very rare collectible. The distinction between the two is very subtle. The Type I may be distinguished from the Type II by the 'single line which crosses the top of the picture in a straight line.' The Type I is also described as the 'picture unframed' or is more commonly referred to as the one 'without the diamond.' The first stamp was created using P.O. die #341 for the frame and P.O. die #342 for the vignette. The spectacular invert on the right is a combination of a recreated die for the Type II frame and P.O. die #342 for the vignette. Both intaglio impressions have been die-stamped onto the souvenir card. The foil-stamped figure and border on the card are from the World's Columbian Exposition Diploma. The Diploma was an engraved print which was presented to international exhibitors at the Columbian Exposition held in Chicago, Illinois, in 1893. Each Diploma was individualized with the exhibitor's name and contribution using 'surface printing.' "

The latter figure and border, as well as the inscription, "The Historic Voyage/1492-1992," were common elements on all the BEP philatelic and numismatic souvenir cards of 1992.

George Brett, one of philately's foremost authorities on U.S. stamp printing, found the information on the back of the card wanting in some respects. Writing in *The United States Specialist* for October 1992, he offered to try to "clarify things."

"Three types (of the 15¢ 1869) are listed in our catalogs, but only the first two were regularly issued," Brett wrote. "Type I, as listed, only exists as a stamp, not as a die. So while in 1992 the Bureau used the best die they had for the Type I, the 1869 stamps differ from this card die print because every subject on the printing plate was changed individually, both the subjects on the frame plate and those on the vignette plate. Thus the BEP has inadvertently wound up with essentially a Type III rendition instead of Type I in terms of the stamps."

(Type III was a new border plate that was made for the 1875 sale to collectors of special printings of obsolete stamps. It was similar to Type I, but without the horizontal border vignetting lines.)

"The BEP's explanation is that they used P.O. Die #341 for the frame and P.O. Die #342 for the vignette. Well, those two dies were created in 1903 (when they were making up the Roosevelt albums) to simulate dies they hadn't received from the Post Office Department. So when the BEP at this time again used the same two dies for their Type I simulation as they had back in 1903, they unknowingly made something that we've not been able to differentiate from the Type III's.

"If they had used P.O. Die #121, a complete design die, which they had, and which was an original as received from the Post Office Department in 1897, they wouldn't have been any closer, as they would have had to separate the vignette from the frame, the same as was done in making Die #341 and #342 originally, and then run into more trouble because of the changes that were made on the plates."

(At the time Brett wrote the preceding paragraph, he wouldn't have known that BEP was preparing to use die number 121 for its second philatelic souvenir card of 1992. See the chapter on the card issued for the American Philatelic Society Stampshow 92).

"Now we go to the simulated Type II invert on the card," Brett continued. "Here the BEP says that they used a recreated die for the Type II frame — in other words, they made up a new frame die — and then used Die #342 for the vignette, the latter being the same die as for their Type I simulation. Well, the BEP had a die — according to our records — that was the correct original Type II frame die: P.O. Die #120, and that could have been used without any change whatever in making their second simulation. As it is, their newly made frame die makes a new type which we could designate as Type IV, depending on whether a careful check of the 1903 combination of dies #120 (frame) and #342 (center) and #341 (frame) and #342 (center) had created a Type IV or even a Type V already. But we don't know the answer to that, so we leave this unsettled for the present.

"Of course, if we had known of the BEP plans for the card, we could have helped out, or maybe just helped to confuse things further, because the 1869 issue presents some peculiar actions that have not been performed before or since, and we can sympathize with anyone trying to figure them out. Still, on the plus side, the BEP card provides the student with some cheap examples of prints from Dies #341 and #342, so that is a gain that is welcome."

BEP sold the World Stamp Expo card at the show for $4 mint and $4.25 canceled. By mail, the prices were $5 and $5.75.

As part of BEP's exhibit at World Columbian Stamp Expo, a plate printer demonstrated intaglio printing on an antique, hand-operated press, an engraver explained his trade and a collection of stamps with a Columbian theme was placed on display.

The Bureau's numismatic cards of 1992 reproduced four different images from currency. These were: an unfinished engraving of the Vanderlyn *Landing of Columbus* painting that was intended for a $1 United States Note in 1869 (Florida United Numismatists show); the back of a $5 Bank Note, Series of 1875, that also reproduced the Vanderlyn painting (AmericANA Coin show); the back of a $5 Federal Reserve Bank Note of the series 1915-1918 that showed "Columbus in Sight of Land" (International Paper Money Show); and the face of a $1,000 United States Note in the Series of 1878 showing Columbus in his study (Central States Numismatic Society show).

AMERICAN PHILATELIC SOCIETY STAMPSHOW 92 SOUVENIR CARD (BEP)

Date of Issue: August 27, 1992

Catalog Number: Scott 133

First-Day Release: Oakland, California (Stampshow 92) and Washington, D.C. (BEP Visitors Center)

Colors: black, gray (offset); black (intaglio); metallic silver (letterpress)

Size: 10 by 8 inches

Conceptual Design: Steve Manset (BEP)

Designer: Steve Manset (BEP)

Modeler: Peter Cocci (BEP)

Paper Stock: artificial parchment, 100-percent rag, ivory

Printing: 6-color Miller offset sheetfed press; foil stamping on Kluge letterpress; intaglio die stamper

Quantity: 8,750

The Card

The Bureau of Engraving and Printing issued its second and final philatelic exhibition souvenir card of 1992 on August 27 in Oakland, California. The occasion was Stampshow 92, the annual show of the American Philatelic Society.

Like the first card, issued for World Columbian Stamp Expo, the APS card featured the 15¢ stamp of the 1869 series, with its engraved reproduction of the John Vanderlyn painting *The Landing of Columbus*. This card, however, displayed a block of four die imprints, printed in one color — black —instead of the brown and blue of the original stamp.

The explanatory text on the back of the card read as follows:

"The stamps featured on this souvenir card are believed to be representative of a die essay, Type III variety, of the 1869 'Landing of Columbus' postage stamp. Type I and II were featured on the World Columbian Stamp Expo souvenir card. The Bureau representation of a Type II postage stamp was presented as an invert.

"This block of four stamps has bccn fcaturcd in a single color created from the die-stamped impression of P.O. die #121. Unlike the Type I and II which were printed using two separate dies, one for the frame and one for the vignette, the essay on this souvenir card was created from a single die of both the vignette and frame. Interestingly, the die number for this block of stamps indicates that it might have predated both the Type I and II varieties and that some consideration may have been given to issuing this stamp in a single color. Type III is almost identical to the Type I, except for fringe (sic) of shading lines around the vignette.

"The engraved vignette is based on a John Vanderlyn painting, representative of the first landing of Columbus. The painting was installed in the Capitol Rotunda in 1846. The foil-stamped figure and border on the card are from the World's Columbian Exposition Diploma. The Diploma was an engraved print which was presented to international exhibitors at the Columbian Exposition held in Chicago, Illinois, in 1893. Each Diploma was individualized with the exhibitor's name and contribution using 'surface printing.' "

As George Brett pointed out in articles in *The United States Specialist* in May and October 1992 (see chapter on the World Columbian Stamp Expo souvenir card), P.O. die number 121 was received by BEP from the Post Office Department in 1897, and was used in making simulated proofs of the 15¢ 1869 stamp, Types I and II, for the so-called Roosevelt presentation albums of 1903. Two transfers were made from this complete die, the frame was cut away from one and the picture from the other, and from these two transfers two new dies were made so the Type I and II proofs could be printed in the appropriate two colors.

BEP sold the cards by mail for $5.50 mint and $5.75 canceled.

1992 SAVINGS BOND COMMEMORATIVE SOUVENIR CARD (BEP)

Date of Issue: June 15, 1992

Catalog Number: Scott 132

First-Day Release: Washington, D.C. (BEP Visitors Center)

Colors: green (PMS 3385), red (PMS 186), black (offset); red (PMS 200), black (intaglio)

Size: 10 by 8 inches

Conceptual Design: Steve Manset (BEP)

Designer: Steve Manset (BEP)

Modeler: Ron Sharpe (BEP)

Paper Stock: artificial parchment, 100-percent rag, ivory

Printing: 6-color Miller offset sheetfed press; intaglio die stamper

Quantity: 8,500

The Card

In 1992, for the second year, the Bureau of Engraving and Printing created a souvenir card to give to employees who signed up for its Savings Bond payroll savings program or increased their deduction. But this card, unlike the previous one, was also offered for sale to the public.

The card, which BEP described as "a tribute to employees . . . both past and present who have lent support to the program," was made available for purchase June 15. The cost was $4 at the BEP Visitors Center and $5.50 if ordered through the mail.

The action headed off any complaints like those registered by collectors and the philatelic press in 1991, when BEP printed — for employees only — a handsome souvenir card to mark the 50th anniversary of E Series Savings Bonds. That card bore an intaglio die imprint of the 10¢ Minute Man Postal Savings stamp of 1941 (Scott PS11) in red ink.

Reportedly, 2,000 cards were made, of which 1,400 were given to qualified BEP workers and the rest destroyed. A few copies reached collectors' hands at $300 apiccc. "It's unfair for the Bureau to create desirable collectibles and then not make them available to collectors," *Linn's Stamp News* Editor Michael Laurence wrote. "BEP should rethink its policies here before it creates another privately distributed card." BEP took the advice.

The new card reproduced, from original BEP dies and plates, two intaglio products of the World War II E bond program. One was a $25 War Savings Bond, with the Gilbert Stuart portrait of George Washington — the same one that appears on the $1 bill. The other was a 10¢ red War Savings stamp (Scott WS7), issued by the Treasury Department October 29, 1942.

Like the Postal Savings stamp that had been shown on the previous year's card, this stamp depicted Daniel Chester French's statue, *The Minute Man*, at Concord, Massachusetts. The stamp was designed by William A. Roach of BEP.

The engraving was by two old-time Bureau craftsmen, Charles A. Brooks (vignette) and Axel W. Christensen (frame, lettering and numerals). The master die, number 15434, was completed in May 1942. The engraved portions of the card were printed on a green-toned background featuring an enlarged offset-printed reproduction of the George Washington portrait on the War Bond. The card contained this text above the signatures of Peter H. Daly, BEP director, and Catalina Vasquez Villalpando, treasurer of the United States:

"BEP Employees are Making Dreams a Reality by Investing in U.S. Savings Bonds. This beautiful 10 cent United States War Savings Stamp, Series 1942, was collected by schoolchildren during World War II 'a dime at a time.' After saving $18.75 worth of stamps, they were then redeemed for a $25.00 War Savings Bond. Both the bond and the stamp were printed, by the intaglio process, at the BEP. Thrift education helped these young children to be financially secure citizens in future years. Today, BEP Employees make their dreams a reality through U.S.

Savings Bonds payroll allotments."

During World War II, War Savings stamps were also offered in denominations of 25¢, 50¢ and $1, and later $5. The two lowest values were also sold in coil and booklet as well as sheet form. Stamp albums in which to paste the stamps were distributed through post offices and schools. More than 25 million students purchased some $2 billion worth of War Savings Stamps and Savings Bonds from the beginning of the school program through December 1945.

1992-93 DUCK STAMP SOUVENIR CARD (FISH AND WILDLIFE SERVICE)

Date of Issue: June 30, 1992

Catalog Number: none

First-Day Release: June 30, Washington, D.C.; July 1, Jackson, New Jersey

Colors: yellow, magenta, cyan, black, maroon, gray (offset); gold foil (letterpress)

Size: 10 by 8 inches

Designer: Peter Cocci (BEP)

Typographer: Howard Brown (BEP)

Modeler: Peter Cocci (BEP)

Paper Stock: white Poseidon perfect

Printing: 6-color Miller offset sheetfed press (4-subject plates); Kluge letterpress for gold foil stamping

Quantity: 10,000, of which 750 are numbered in gold

The Card

For the sixth consecutive year, the National Fish and Wildlife Foundation, a non-profit organization chartered by Congress to support wildlife conservation projects, sponsored a duck stamp souvenir card to help fund its programs.

The card, offset-printed by the Bureau of Engraving and Printing, bore an enlarged full-color replica of the 1992 duck stamp, with simulated perforations around the stamp's edges, against a maroon background. The stamp's design was based on Joe Hautman's contest-winning acrylic painting of a spectacled eider in flight over an Alaska seascape.

The card carried the signatures and the agency seals or logos of Manuel Lujan Jr., secretary of the Interior; John Turner, director of the U.S. Fish and Wildlife Service; Johnny Morris, chairman of the National Fish and Wildlife Foundation; and artist Joe Hautman of Jackson, New Jersey.

Ten thousand cards were printed. These cards, along with a copy of the $15 duck stamp itself, were sold by the Fish and Wildlife Service for varying prices. The least expensive were 8,250 cards without serial numbers or cancellations, which cost $20. (BEP also sold these plain cards by mail order, but for $22.50).

The remaining 1,750 cards had first-day cancellations from Washington, D.C., where the cards went on sale June 30, and Jackson, New Jersey, where they were first sold July 1. Of these canceled cards, 1,000 bore no serial numbers and sold for $25 each, and 750 were numbered in gold and sold for $150 each (numbers 1 through 10), $75 (11 through 100) or $50 (101 through 750). The gold numbers were applied by letterpress.

The $15 cost of the stamp was deducted from the proceeds of each card, and the Washington-based National Fish and Wildlife Foundation kept the balance. After paying BEP for the printing costs, the Foundation used the funds in its conservation projects.

Postal Service, Stamps Operation Reorganized

In 1992 the Postal Service Board of Governors named Marvin T. Runyon Jr. to be postmaster general, succeeding Anthony M. Frank, who resigned after four years in office to return to private industry. During a brief interim period, Deputy Postmaster General Michael S. Coughlin served as acting PMG.

The governors instructed Runyon, a former auto executive who had earned the nickname "Carvin' Marvin" as a cost-cutting chairman of the Tennessee Valley Authority, to slash expenses at USPS. Runyon took his mandate seriously.

On July 6, Runyon's first day on the job, he and the Board of Governors announced that the Postal Service wouldn't renew its controversial sponsorship of the Olympic Games. (He would later express skepticism over previous claims that the Olympic program would net the Postal Service $55 million in profits.) That was only the beginning.

Early in August, the new postal chief launched a massive reorganization and retrenchment, with the stated aim of trimming an anticipated $2.2 billion deficit and delaying a postal rate hike that had been expected in 1994. Retirement incentives were offered to senior employees in an effort to reduce management positions by a net 30,000. More than 46,000 individuals reportedly accepted the incentives. Runyon eliminated the 42

Postmaster General Marvin Runyon during an August 7 press conference at which he announced his intention to cut many management positions from USPS.

assistant postmaster generals' positions and created vice presidencies in their place, 12 of them to report directly to him.

For philatelists, the New Postal Order had far-reaching consequences.

At least half the staff positions in what had been the Department of Philatelic and Retail Services were eliminated. The stamp program was split up. Stamp acquisition and distribution, with Michael Spates as manager, became one of eight divisions under the new vice president for customer service and support, Patricia M. Gilbert. Stamp management, headed by James Tolbert, became one of six divisions reporting to the vice president for marketing and sales. Stamp publicity was placed under the new vice president for communications, Deborah K. Bowker.

As new people moved in and up, others moved out. In a single year, 1992, because of the reorganization and for other reasons, the U.S. stamp program lost a startlingly large number of the people who had made it what it is today.

One of them, of course, was Anthony M. Frank.

Although he headed the Postal Service for only a relatively short time, Frank wielded a greater influence on stamp policy than any postmaster general since James A. Farley, who was postmaster general under Franklin D. Roosevelt. Frank clearly saw the significance of the philatelic program as a way of publicizing America — and as a profitable sideline for USPS. He personally reviewed and critiqued each new-issue proposal, presided at dozens of first-day ceremonies, and functioned as a customer advocate when he insisted that stamp designs and stamp selvage offer more information on the people and events the stamps depicted. The hoopla over the Elvis Presley stamp that Frank conceived and choreographed (see next section) was a promotional masterstroke, and caused the public to pay more sustained attention to stamps and stamp collecting than any other event in U.S. postal history had done.

Other familiar figures who departed in the 1992 exodus included:

Gordon C. Morison. Morison took the early retirement option. A former public relations executive with the General Dynamics Corporation and a stamp collector himself, he had been with USPS since the agency's creation January 1, 1971. Under his leadership, first as director of the Office of Stamps, then through several other job titles ending with assistant postmaster general in charge of Philatelic and Retail Services, the stamp program changed dramatically.

The number of annual issues exploded, with a proliferation of topicals with popular themes such as space and wildlife. USPS switched from total reliance on the Bureau of Engraving and Printing for stamps to diversified procurement in which a growing number of private companies competed for contracts. Consignment and vending-machine sales were expanded, which helped swell the demand for booklet stamps. A stream of innovations pleased — and sometimes frustrated — collectors.

Multicolor printing quality was improved. Single-digit plate numbers supplanted multidigits, eliminating the extra-large plate number blocks that collectors hated. Cylinder and sleeve numbers were added to coil stamps and booklet pane tabs. Non-denominated stamps appeared, to help smooth rate-change transitions and simplify stamp use in bulk mailings. Self-adhesive stamps, easy to use and with collector-friendly water-soluble adhesives, were marketed in booklets and through automatic teller machines.

The 50-variety commemorative stamp pane was introduced. So were full-color postal card designs; picture postal cards; patch-and-window stamped envelopes that allowed the use of multicolor fine-screen printing and holograms; computer-vended stamps and postal cards; coils in sticks and with slit perforations; and many other innovations.

Donald M. McDowell. In October, McDowell left the Postal Service's stamp program, and as of this writing, he was awaiting reassignment. An ex-journalist from Texas, McDowell joined USPS in 1973 as manager of the Stamp Development Branch and, in the course of various reorganizations, became general manager of the Stamps Division, acting director of the Office of Stamps and Philatelic Marketing, and, in 1990, director of the slightly renamed Office of Stamp and Philatelic Marketing. Over the years he was closely associated with most of the developments mentioned above, and personally responsible for many of them. Perhaps his most dramatic impact on the hobby of stamp collecting was as "father of the PNC," or plate number coil.

W.L. (Pete) Davidson. Davidson, director of the Office of Licensing, took the early retirement option in 1992. Since the birth of the Postal Service, Davidson was a major shaper of the stamp program and particularly of marketing strategies. As a brand-new law-school graduate in 1970, he worked on the transition team that converted the old cabinet-level Post Office Department into an autonomous public corporation, USPS. He was later hired by Gordon Morison to be general manager of the new Philatelic Sales Division. In 1975 he became general manager of the Stamps Division, in 1980 he was promoted to director of the Office of Stamps and Philatelic Marketing, and in 1989 he became the Office of Olympic Marketing's first director.

Jack Williams. Williams was another charter member of USPS who took the early retirement option. From 1972 to 1983, he was official spokesman for the stamp office. Since 1983, as manager, stamp design, he managed an average of 13 stamp and stamp-design projects each year, including the selection of artists, art directors and researchers. He played a major role in developing and implementing the five-year World War II souvenir sheet series, and personally designed the 29¢ Operation Desert Storm stamp of 1991.

Belmont Faries. Faries was the long-time news editor and stamp columnist for *The Washington Star* and in recent years has been a free-lance writer. He served a two-year term on the Citizens' Stamp Advisory Committee from 1967-1969, was reappointed in 1971 and was a member from that time until his resignation in 1992. From 1975 until 1990, when he moved from the Washington, D.C., area to Montana, he served as chairman of CSAC.

Jack Rosenthal. A Casper, Wyoming, broadcast executive, Rosenthal resigned as chairman and member of CSAC in 1992. He had been a member of the committee since 1985 and chairman since 1990. A strong advocate within CSAC of stamps with Western themes, Rosenthal personally designed three such stamps, the 15¢ Buffalo Bill definitive of 1988, the 25¢ Wyoming statehood commemorative of 1990 and the 29¢ Oregon Trail commemorative, scheduled for issue in 1993. As a stamp collector, Rosenthal amassed one of the hobby's finest collections of 19th-century U.S. stamps, proofs and essays.

Bradbury Thompson. Thompson resigned as a CSAC design coordinator after more than 14 years' service. Before that, from 1969 to 1978, he had been a voting member of CSAC. A long-time instructor at the Yale University School of Art and Architecture, he designed his first U.S. stamp in 1958 — it was the 3¢ Brussels Exhibition commemorative — and since then had designed dozens more, including the current series of Official Mail stamps and most of the traditional Christmas stamps of the past two decades. Thompson, an authority on typefaces, also created the typography for the majority of stamps in recent years.

USPS Stirs Up Elvismania

It started as a long, sustained tease by the postmaster general. It ended as the most highly publicized event in the history of U.S. postage stamps.

Ever since the death at age 42 of rock 'n' roll idol Elvis Presley August 16, 1977, his fans had urged the Postal Service to memorialize him on a postage stamp. When the 10th anniversary of his death passed, and Presley actually became eligible for postal commemoration under the Postal Service's guidelines, the intensity of the Elvis stamp campaign took a sudden surge upward.

Many people who were familiar with U.S. stamp traditions refused to take the idea seriously. Elvis Presley, although a pop-culture icon, just didn't seem to have the historic importance, the weight, the gravitas to fit comfortably into the U.S. postal pantheon. Besides, he was a substance abuser whose death was attributed to an overdose of prescription drugs. It seemed unlikely, they thought, that the Citizens' Stamp Advisory Committee would take a long time turning down this proposal.

But Anthony M. Frank was a new breed of postmaster general, one who saw promotional possibilities in stamps that even the veterans of CSAC didn't recognize. Not long after he took office in 1988, he began throwing out hints that he might eventually approve an Elvis stamp.

For a time it seemed, from his bantering tone, that he was joking. Supermarket tabloids insisted that Elvis was still alive, he pointed out, which would make the singer ineligible to be on a stamp. Some critics, though, took him at his word and attacked the idea of honoring a person of such disreputable personal habits. All this made news. The controversy, as Frank would later remark, "has taught a lot of people about stamp collecting who never thought about stamp collecting before."

It became increasingly clear from Frank's public statements that he intended to have an Elvis stamp. He kept the uncertainty bubbling, however, by suggesting, implausibly, that philatelic conservatives on CSAC might block the project. CSAC was "wrestling," he said, with the "difficult question" of whether the manner of Presley's death sent a message that was "inappropriate." Even so, it was his "guess" that there would in time be a series of stamps on popular American music, "and that Elvis will be represented in this series."

Finally, on January 7, 1992 — the same day he revealed his own plan to resign as postmaster general — Frank announced that there would be, in fact, an Elvis Presley stamp, and that it would be the forerunner of a Legends of American Music series. Even if Presley had drug problems, Frank said, "he was a genuine American musical giant, and for sure he won't be the first famous flawed American to show up on a stamp."

The kicker to the announcement was this P.R. masterstroke: USPS would take the unprecedented step of letting the American public help choose the design.

First, a large number of designs prepared by artists under contract to USPS would be winnowed down to two, one representing Presley as a young man early in his career, the other showing him in maturity. "Then we will reproduce them on a postcard and have them available in post offices and let people vote" by mailing the cards in, Frank said.

"It's important to have fun," Frank explained. "The American people are not having a lot of fun right now" — the reference was to the economic recession — "so if this adds to the fun, that's good."

Elvis fans were delighted. None was more so than Pat Geiger, 71, of North Springfield, Vermont, who had written more than 60 letters to CSAC herself and gathered more than 10,000 petition signatures. ("She really stayed on our case," Anthony Frank told *The New York Times*.) Geiger said she had "fallen in love" with Presley, 16 years her junior, after watching him perform in a black leather suit in 1968.

At CSAC's meeting January 10, 1992, the committee chose the two designs that would be finalists — although some CSAC members later said publicly that they had opposed the whole idea to the end. The design the public would select would be used on a sheet stamp in 1993, and would also be part of a booklet featuring other popular musicians.

The announcement failed to end the controversy. "Nothin' but a Hound Dog Idea," Ralph Schoenstein wrote on *The New York Times'* Op-Ed page. *The Washington Post's* Jonathan Yardley took a similarly dim view. These and other columns drew heavy reader mail, pro and con.

And two Republican members of Congress squared off. Representative Marge Roukema, R-New Jersey, wrote to Frank to denounce both the plan to honor Presley and the design-selection scheme. "I believe it is highly inappropriate for the USPS to commemorate individuals who engaged in illegal and blatantly unhealthy behavior during their lifetime," she wrote. In reply, Representative Don Sundquist, R-Tennessee, who represented part of Presley's hometown of Memphis, wrote: "If personal righteousness is to be the standard for deciding who appears on a postage stamp, the only fit subjects are likely to be birds, bunnies, flowers and flags." He said Memphis people knew Presley as a caring, charitable individual.

On February 24, two weeks before Frank left office, he unveiled the two competing designs on the Showroom stage of the Las Vegas Hilton Hotel, with USPS providing satellite coverage to the nation's television stations. Frank was assisted by actor Milton Berle, who had given Presley his TV debut, and actress Barbara Eden, who had starred in several films with the singer.

As *Stamp Collector* observed, the unveiling was a "fitting coda" for Frank's term: "He entered office being questioned about an Elvis stamp and will leave office with those questions answered."

The two designs showed "a slick-haired Elvis the younger" and "a rhinestone-encrusted Elvis the elder," in the words of *The Washington Post's* Bill McAllister. As McAllister noted, "both designs are flattering and about as non-controversial as an Elvis stamp could be; no gyrating hips and no black velvet backgrounds; head shots only. Even Elvis the elder shows none of the weight that (he) had gained in his final years."

The "young Elvis" portrait was the work of Mark Stutzman, 33, of Mountain Lake Park, Maryland, who had never designed a U.S. stamp before. John C. Berkey, 59, of Excelsior, Minnesota, painted the "old Elvis." Berkey had previously designed Christmas stamps, including the five-design Santa Claus booklet of 1991, and the Hubert Humphrey Great Americans stamp.

Commentators, comics and cartoonists had a field day. For example, *The New York Times'* Arts & Leisure section ran a picture feature titled "Sticky Questions in Stamp Land," which offered possible "young" and "old" stamp designs for actors Marlon Brando and Elizabeth Taylor, and showed TV weatherman Willard Scott with and without a toupee, and Madonna as a blonde or brunette.

"If the stamp represented the post office correctly," joked the *Tonight* show's Jay Leno, "it would show the young Elvis when you mailed it and the old Elvis when it was delivered." Columnist David Sarasohn suggested that the first-ever national balloting for a stamp design was "a warm-up for next year's vote to select the Missouri Indoor Plumbing Commemorative Postcard."

USPS printed 5 million preaddressed and barcoded ballot cards and distributed them to post offices. In addition, *People* magazine's April 13 issue, on the newsstands April 6, contained 4.5 million official tearout ballots. The Postal Service said it would also accept ordinary postcards or letters. Frank invited Americans to vote "early and often" between April 4 and April 26, the balloting period, taking care to put a 19¢ stamp on each card, of course.

Before the official vote was tallied, several news organizations conducted their own polls. Virtually all, if not all, of them showed the "young Elvis" to be the winner, including those run by *The Washington Post*, *USA Today*, the *Akron Beacon Journal* and the *Long Beach, California,*

Press Telegram. Dozens of newspapers printed feature stories on spot reaction from people at their local post offices.

Even the presidential candidates were called on to take a stand. Governor Bill Clinton, a Presley fan who happened to be seeking the Democratic presidential nomination, told reporters he preferred the younger Elvis because "I think he'd want to be remembered that way." Republican candidate Patrick Buchanan also backed the younger version. President George Bush said through a spokesman that he would "leave it up to the American people to decide," which drew this blast from a Buchanan spokesman: "(Bush) waffled on taxes, he waffled on the quota bill . . . and now he waffles on Elvis. This is the last straw!"

More seriously, consumer activist Ralph Nader, a frequent critic of USPS, weighed in with an attack on the "wasteful spending" to promote the Presley stamp. Nader said the nearly $300,000 spent by USPS on the Elvis poll — which didn't include worktime devoted to it by postal employees — would have been better spent on improved service. "The question in American communities today," Nader said, "is no longer whether or not citizens have seen Elvis, but whether or not citizens have seen their neighborhood collection box, on-time mail delivery, affordable postage rates, or a post office without lines."

The New Jersey firm of Bruskin-Goldring Research was hired to make the official tabulation of the ballots, which totaled 1,128,923. At 6:36 a.m. Central Standard Time on June 4, at Graceland, the Elvis Presley mansion in Memphis, actress Priscilla Presley, who was once married to the singer, opened the envelope containing the results, and Anthony M. Frank — now a private citizen — announced: "It is the young Elvis!" The early hour was chosen to enable the network morning television shows to carry the event live.

At the same ceremony, the Postal Service announced that the sheet stamp would be issued in Memphis January 8, 1993, on what would have been Presley's 58th birthday. The booklet stamps bearing his picture would be issued later in 1993, USPS said.

"Elvis loved his fans very, very much and I think that he would have just been totally overwhelmed by all of your support," Priscilla Presley told the audience.

The postmaster-general designate, Marvin Runyon, didn't attend the ceremony, but some time after he had taken office, he made it clear that he endorsed the Elvis stamp.

"I'll tell you what, if I could find another one like Elvis, I'd do it in a minute," Runyon told an audience at the Washington's National Press Club in November. "I'd like to find 20 like Elvis, as a matter of fact. It would be a wonderful thing."

ASDA Postal Connection is Introduced

The American Stamp Dealers Association and the Postal Service announced in March 1992 that they had reached a consignment agreement that would allow dealers to be able to provide their customers with

U.S. postal issues on their date of nationwide availability, namely, the day after the official dedication.

The new service, called the ASDA Postal Connection, was introduced with the Columbian souvenir sheets that were released May 22 at World Columbian Stamp Expo 92. Under the previous system, USPS wouldn't fill new-issue orders until after the first-day date.

Once the Postal Connection was fully operational, USPS said, the Philatelic Sales Division would no longer affix stamps to customer-submitted envelopes for first-day covers, a costly and time-consuming process, and would no longer accept 29¢ checks. However, the division

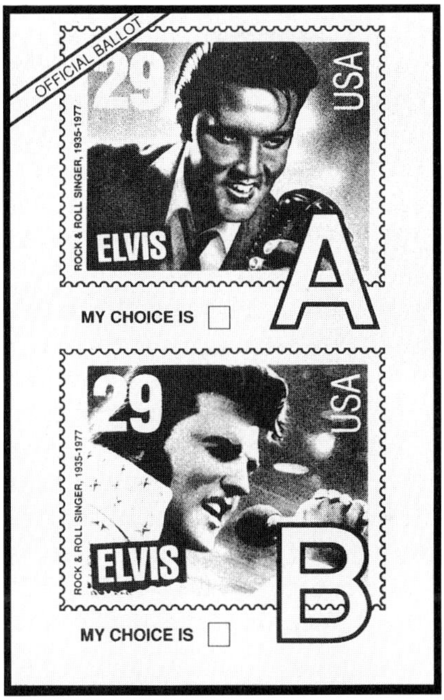

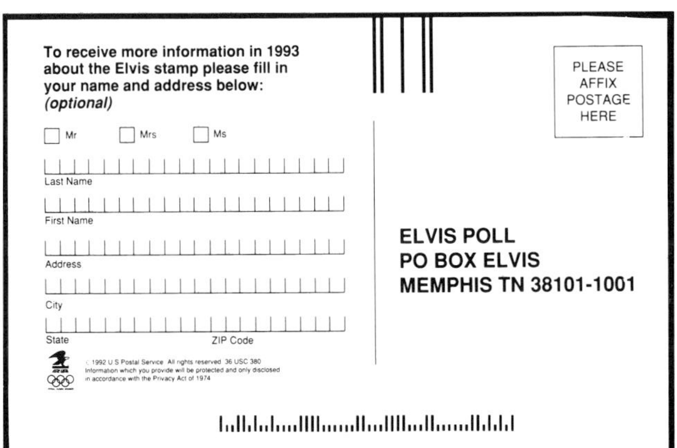

This is the front and back of the Elvis poll postcard that USPS distributed in post offices.

would begin offering customers the opportunity to purchase plain envelopes, without cachets, to which new stamps had been affixed and given the first-day postmark, USPS said. As of this writing, however, early in 1993, the division was still affixing stamps.

GAO Issues Report on Postal Service Matters

Two General Accounting Office reports in 1992 dealt with issues of importance to the Postal Service.

The first report, titled *Pricing Postal Services in a Competitive Environment*, noted that USPS "has not been an effective competitor" in carrying parcel post or Express Mail, and warned that it may lose second-class and third-class business, as well, to private delivery firms. Even the Postal Service's statutory monopoly on first-class mail could soon be threatened by electronic technologies, such as computer-to-computer exchanges, fax, telephone, direct deposit of payrolls and so-called wire transfers by banks and businesses.

As a partial remedy, the GAO suggested that there be a review of the pricing system, now controlled by the Postal Rate Commission. The agency sided with the Postal Service in arguing for what it called "demand pricing." That theory had been behind the Postal Service's 1991 attempt, rejected by the PRC, to raise the letter rate to 30¢, while increasing third-class rates less sharply.

The second GAO report confirmed assertions by USPS that it could economize by diversifying stamp production into the private sector. The study, titled *Postage Stamp Production: Private Sector Can Be a Lower Cost Optional Source*, was ordered after a 1991 congressional hearing on stamp procurement. It found that private printers produced seven stamps similar to those made by the Bureau of Engraving and Printing at prices from 6.8 percent to 62.4 percent lower than BEP's. In only one of GAO's price comparisons did government printers produce a cheaper stamp, 16.4 percent below the price charged by a private printer. The GAO said it could detect no difference in the quality of stamps printed by private and government printers.

However, the report cautioned that the comparisons of the eight pairs of stamps couldn't be extrapolated to the whole of the stamp-printing program, and recommended that the Postal Service should continue to rely on BEP as its major supplier, inasmuch as the Bureau was a stable provider of stamps that was immune to strikes, bankruptcy and other problems that occur within private industry. Postmaster General Runyon said the findings "validated" the Postal Service's use of private printers, but said USPS "will continue to rely upon the Bureau to balance the relative youth and inexperience of the private sector."

Peter M. Daly, BEP director, wrote to the GAO that BEP faces numerous fixed costs that a private printer filling a single stamp order doesn't face. At the time of writing, he said, BEP was using only half its stamp production capacity, but still had to pay fixed costs. He objected to the stamps the GAO compared, saying they presented "a snapshot of price comparability . . . for a very small portion of the stamp program."

World War II Sheet Wins Popularity Polls

The World War II souvenir sheet of 1991 swept the two major popularity polls, those of *Linn's Stamp News* and *Stamp Collector*. The sheet won the most important and best designed commemorative titles in both polls, and was the overall favorite of *Stamp Collector* readers.

In the *Linn's* poll, the Operation Desert Storm stamp and booklet and Space Exploration booklet were runners-up in the most important commemorative category, and the Space Exploration and Fishing Flies booklets were runners-up for best commemorative design. Voted least necessary among commemoratives were Fishing Flies, the Comedians by Hirschfeld booklet and Jan Matzeliger stamp, and voted worst-designed commemoratives were Comedians, the Vermont Statehood stamp and the Desert Storm issue.

Among definitives, the top three places in each *Linn's* category were: best design, $2.90 Priority Mail, $14 Express Mail and 19¢ Fawn; most important, 29¢ Mount Rushmore (engraved), 52¢ Hubert Humphrey and 29¢ Flags on Parade; worst design, non-denominated (4¢) Makeup Rate, $1 Olympics and non-denominated (29¢) "F" Flower; least necessary, $1 Olympics, $14 Express Mail and non-denominated Makeup Rate. The postal stationery winners and losers were: best design, 40¢ Yankee Clipper postal card, 30¢ Niagara Falls card and 11.1¢ Birds on a Wire envelope; most important, 19¢ Bill of Rights postal card, 29¢ Love envelope and 40¢ Yankee Clipper card; worst design, 29¢ Star envelope, 29¢ Magazine Industry envelope and 29¢ Country Geese envelope; least necessary, Country Geese, Magazine Industry and Love envelopes.

Voters in the *Stamp Collector* poll picked the Desert Storm stamp as the year's second most important commemorative. The Hubert Humphrey stamp was picked as the most important definitive, followed by the Mount Rushmore and the Flags on Parade. In postal stationery, the Bill of Rights postal card was chosen the most important subject and the Yankee Clipper airmail was voted the best-designed postal card.

On the negative side, the Comedians by Hirschfeld booklet was chosen least important and worst-designed among commemoratives. The Makeup Rate definitive and the 19¢ Postal Buddy postal card were chosen as the worst-designed in their respective categories. The Fishing Flies booklet pane, Postal Buddy card and Country Geese envelope were termed the least important commemorative, postal card and envelope issues.

Penalty Mail Will End for Federal Agencies

Effective October 1, 1993, the system of official U.S. government correspondence called penalty mail will end. After that date, every government agency except USPS itself will be required to pay actual postage with appropriate stamps, meters or permit imprints. Under the present system, federal offices frank their mail with imprint endorsements that read "Official Business, Penalty for Private Use $300."

Instead of collecting the actual postal value of the mail, USPS assesses each agency's postage based on averages projected from infrequent samples of outgoing mail. Although Official Mail stamps and postal stationery have been available since 1983, going off the penalty mail system has been voluntary up to now. That will change October 1.

USPS Promotes Privately Produced Stamp Replicas

The Postal Service drew strong criticism from some sectors of the collecting community when it promoted The American Dream Collection, an expensive collection of gold-plated sterling silver stamp replicas offered for sale by Philatelic Engravers and Diemakers Inc., a private firm doing business internationally under the name Hallmark Group Ltd.

The promotional offer, sent out on USPS letterhead stationery over the signature of Assistant Postmaster General Gordon C. Morison, went to collectors on the Postal Service mailing list and urged them to buy these products from its authorized licensee. The collection consisted of 25 stamp replicas costing $79 each, for a total cost of $1,975.

Linn's Stamp News, in an editorial denouncing the Postal Service's involvement in the plan, said it had the potential to "drain nearly $100 million out of the stamp hobby into the wasteland of Sunday-supplement kitsch collectibles that invariably end up as flea-market bargains a few years down the road."

National Postal Museum Set to Open

The National Postal Museum, run by the Smithsonian Institution and housed in the former Washington City Post Office building next door to Union Station on Capitol Hill in Washington, is scheduled to open to the public July 30, 1993.

Under the directorship of James H. Bruns, the museum will house the Smithsonian's philatelic and postal history collections, described as the largest and most comprehensive of its kind in the world. The collections comprise more than 16 million stamps, covers and artifacts, including vintage postal vehicles. They were previously housed in inadequate quarters at the National Museum of American History.

Using a wide range of sophisticated exhibitions, interactive displays and permanent galleries, the 75,000-square-foot museum will tell the story of America's mail service. Its 40,000-plus volume Library Research Center will be an invaluable resource for scholars and researchers.

The museum was made possible by an agreement between the Smithsonian and USPS, which provided $15.4 million for renovation and construction costs. In addition, a $6 million goal was set for private fund raising. One of the largest gifts announced to date was a $200,000 grant from Hallmark Cards Inc. to develop and install a gallery to be called "The Art of Cards and Letters."

Stamps for Missions Program Discontinued

The Board for Mission Services of the Lutheran Church — Missouri

Synod announced that it would discontinue its Stamps for Missions program January 1, 1993. The program was at one time one of the largest sources of used stamps for collectors.

In place of the program, the church said, it would encourage local churches to develop their own Stamps for Missions programs, emphasizing the participant involvement aspect. Part of its encouragement would be in providing outlets for the stamps collected by churches, including the names and addresses of dealers who buy stamp mixtures.

The Lutheran Stamps for Missions program, which had operated for many years, was severely cut back in 1990, when U.S. postal inspectors asked that the program stop saving common used stamps. This request was based on the premise that stamps originating with the Lutherans were being illegally washed of their cancellations and reused.

The Missouri Synod signed an agreement to discontinue the practice. Since then, the annual revenues from the program dwindled, from $12,900 in 1989 to $722 in 1992.

The drying up of this source of supply made it difficult for many collectors to keep up to date on new used commemoratives and PNCs (plate number coils), according to *Linn's Stamp News*. And although the situation had eased somewhat by the end of 1992, *Linn's* said, many mixture dealers reported having difficulty obtaining fresh U.S. mixtures.

The discontinuance of Stamps for Missions did have a positive side for collectors, however. It left local churches free to sell and save whatever they wished, without the fear of postal inspectors knocking at their doors. No agreement with the inspectors was signed at the local level.

"Although the U.S. Postal Service is rightly concerned with the amount of revenue lost each year to stamp washing, its tactics of shutting down primarily legitimate stamp outlets is unjust," wrote Wayne Youngblood of *Linn's*. "Most individuals who wash and reuse stamps prefer large numbers of one type of stamp, rather than the variety present in most mixtures. As a result, many stamp washers don't bother with mixtures.

"The unspoken fear of USPS, however, may actually be that of skips, or those stamps that were not canceled when they were first used. Technically, reusing uncanceled skips is illegal. However, there is no way to prove the reuse of skips, and many people regard the practice as found money. If USPS did its job correctly the first time, they reason, the skips would not present themselves for reuse."

Essay-Proof Society to Cease Operations

The final 1992 issue of *The Essay-Proof Journal*, quarterly publication of the Essay-Proof Society, announced that the organization would cease operations in mid-1993, its 50th anniversary year.

In an article titled "Coming Attraction: A Golden Anniversary for EPS & EPJ and a Look at Their Future," editor Barbara R. Mueller wrote:

"Although there is always more to learn and there are always new developments, it seems that the time has come for the Society as presently constituted to end its existence, at least in its present form. A stagnant and aging membership can't continue to fund its activities any longer.''

At midyear, the EPS planned to ask to go on inactive status as an American Philatelic Society affiliate.

Mueller was the sixth editor of the *Essay-Proof Journal.* Clarence Brazer was the founding father, bringing out Volume I, Number 1 in 1944. He was followed by Julian Blanchard, Prescott Holden Thorp, Edith Faulstich, David Lidman and Mueller.

The magazine's thrust "has always been the study of the artistic and historical background of stamps,'' Mueller wrote in *The Philatelic Communicator.* "Paper currency was added to the mix almost from the start because of common connections between the two by virtue of shared designs and producers. All this has been carried out by a dedicated group that never approached the thousand mark but usually numbered half that membership.''

VARIETIES

$1 Seaplane, Imperforate

An imperforate strip of nine of the $1 blue and red Seaplane coil of 1990 (Scott 2468) turned up on a non-philatelic Express Mail cover. The cover also bore two normal 45¢ Harvey Cushing and one 5¢ Hugo Black stamp to make the $9.95 Express Mail rate. The cover is in the collection of imperforate plate number coils of California collector John Greenwood, Ken Lawrence reported in *Linn's Stamp News*.

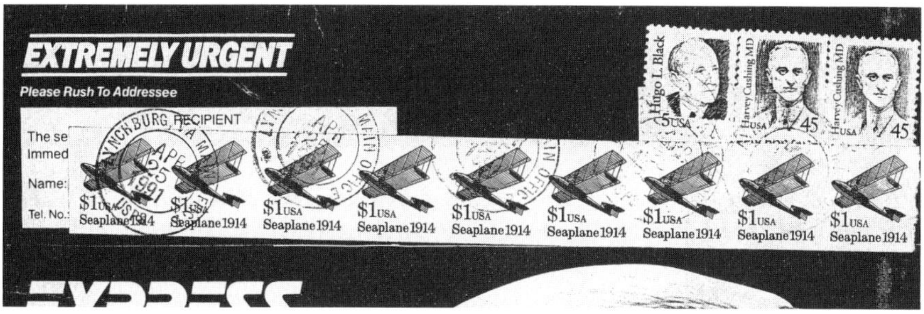

This remarkable error, a strip of nine imperforate $1 Seaplane coil stamps, was found on a non-philatelic Express Mail cover.

Other Imperforate Coils

Imperforate varieties of coil stamps issued in 1991 were reported in 1992. These included the 5¢ Canoe, intaglio version (Scott 2453), the 10¢ Tractor Trailer (Scott 2457) and the non-denominated Eagle and Shield

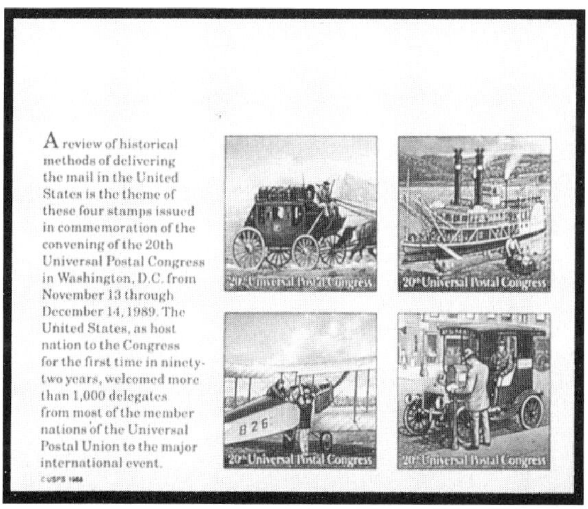

This Universal Postal Congress souvenir sheet of 1989 is missing its intaglio blue (stamp denominations) and offset gray ("20th Universal Postal Congress") inscriptions.

This is the only known copy of the 25¢ Wyoming Statehood Centennial commemorative of 1990 with the black intaglio missing. On a normal stamp, the intaglio portion constituted a row of pine trees between the meadow and mountains.

bulk-rate stamp (Scott 2604).

Souvenir Sheet With Colors Omitted

A 1989 Universal Postal Congress souvenir sheet (Scott 2438) with the intaglio blue and offset gray colors omitted was auctioned at World Columbian Stamp Expo 92 May 28 by Jacques C. Schiff Inc. for $9,500. This was a previously unreported error. The sheet bore replicas of the four 25¢ Traditional Mail Delivery commemoratives that were also issued for the UPU Congress. The intaglio portion that was missing was the "USA 25" in the upper-left corner of each stamp. The missing offset portion was the inscription "20th Universal Postal Congress" and UPU logo across the top of the sheet.

Wyoming Stamp With Intaglio Black Omitted

At the same May 28 auction, Schiff sold a single copy of the 25¢ Wyoming Statehood commemorative of 1990 (Scott 2444) with the black intaglio portion — a row of evergreen trees — omitted from the design. The specimen was on a postcard with a May 1990 machine cancellation from San Francisco, California. The only known example, it sold for $1,700.

1991 Christmas Stamp With Intaglio Omitted

Also at the WCSE auction, Schiff sold a 1991 Christmas Madonna

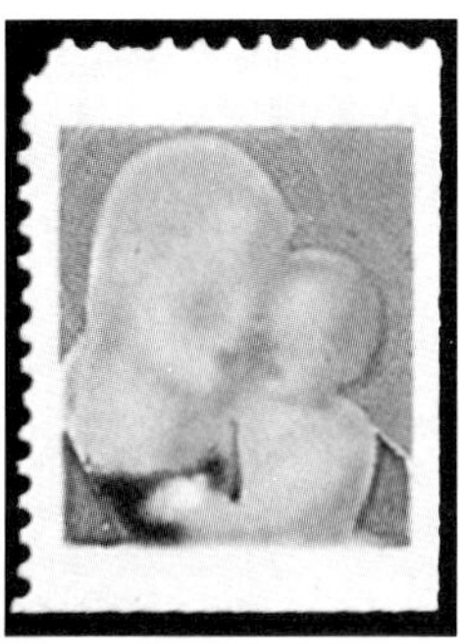

This is a single, damaged in removal, from a booklet pane of 10 of the non-denominated Christmas Madonna stamps of 1991 on which the intaglio portion that provides design detail and typography is missing.

stamp booklet (Scott 2578a), containing the bottom pane only with one stamp detached and damaged, with the intaglio portion of the stamps omitted. Only the offset background colors were present. The item was knocked down for $3,000.

Desert Storm, Imperforate Horizontally

About a year after the 29¢ Desert Shield/Desert Storm commemorative sheet stamp (Scott 2551) was issued July 2, 1991, a collector

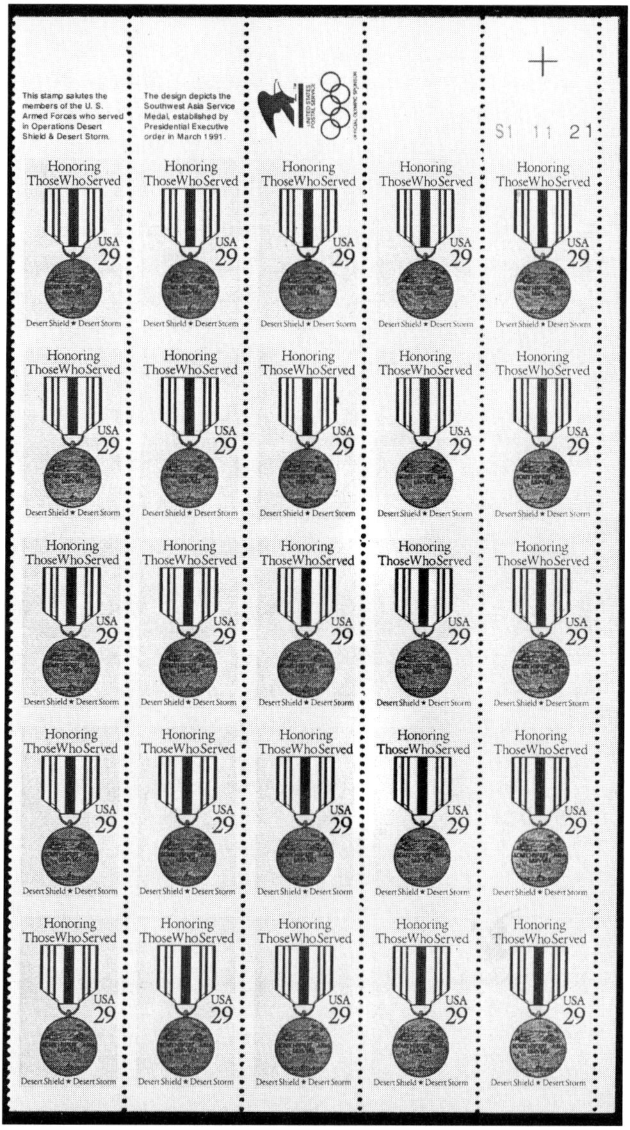

This half-pane of 29¢ Desert Shield/Desert Storm sheet stamps with missing horizontal perforations was purchased nearly a year after the stamps were issued.

This block of four Christmas Santa sheet stamps with missing horizontal perforations has cylinder-number selvage attached but no bottom selvage.

purchased a half pane of 25 with the horizontal perforations missing. The collector, who wished to remain anonymous, bought the stamps in a small northwestern New Jersey post office. He was assured by the postal clerk that the other half of the pane had been used as postage, according to Ross Weissmann, a New Jersey stamp dealer, who purchased the stamps and notified *Linn's* of the find.

The error stamps bore the cylinder numbers S111121 and were from the upper-right quadrant of a 200-stamp printing sheet.

Weissmann told *Linn's* that after purchasing the errors, he initialed and numbered each stamp to mark the find. The entire half pane was privately placed by Lowell S. Newman & Co. of Weehawken, New Jersey.

Santa Claus, Imperforate Between

In September Jacques C. Schiff Jr. Inc. auctioned a block of four of the 1991 Christmas Santa Claus sheet stamp (Scott 2579) that was imperforate vertically for $700. The block was a plate number block, but without bottom selvage.

Makeup Rate Stamp With Double Frameline

A single unused non-denominated 4¢ Makeup Rate stamp of 1991 (Scott 2521) with a strongly doubled frameline was found on a postal card and confirmed by the American Bank Note Company, its printer, as a true double-printing error.

The error was found by Dan Malan, who deals in Illustrated Classics comics and publishes a regular newsletter on the subject. He discovered the error, uncanceled, on a stamped, addressed postal card from one of his readers. The reader had purchased a single copy of the stamp to add to a non-denominated 14¢ postal card he already possessed (thereby creating a card underfranked by 1¢).

When Malan contacted the reader and sent him back to the post office, the remainder of the 100-stamp error pane had already been sold. Since the Makeup Rate stamps were printed in six-pane printing sheets, at least 600 error stamps like Malan's existed at one time.

The stamp was offset printed in two colors on a Harris sheetfed offset press at ABNC, Bedford Park, Illinois. The lettering that comprised the vignette was red, and the frameline was gold. The frameline images on the error stamp were misaligned both vertically and horizontally, with the vertical misregistration more severe. The text contained within the frame was aligned with the misaligned frame.

In a letter to Malan quoted in *Linn's*, Thomas C. Harris, vice president of government sales for ABNC, confirmed the error. His letter said, in part: "... The stamps undoubtedly passed through the press a second time when the borders were being printed. While it is difficult to determine with certainty why this occurred, our postage stamp program manager opines that the sheet at interest was probably used for press set up at which time it should have been discarded. However, it was inadvertently included in the 'good' ready for press lot and run through the press a second time."

Duck Stamp With Intaglio Omitted

A single copy of the 1991 Migratory Bird Hunting and Conservation stamp (Scott RW58) was found without its black intaglio portion.

According to Bob Dumaine, Duck Stamp columnist for *Linn's*, the error was purchased by an art dealer at a San Francisco area post office shortly after it was issued. It was placed with the dealer's print of the stamp art. Almost a year later, he sold the print and stamp to Dan Harshman of Sport'en Art in Sullivan, Illinois. Harshman questioned the stamp's unusual appearance and sent it to Dumaine for examination.

The engraved area of the stamp, which depicts a pair of resting king eiders, was much smaller than on other combination-process duck stamps. Only the lower breast of the drake and the front and top of the hen

The single double-printed non-denominated 4¢ Makeup Rate stamp shown affixed to this postal card (along with a normal stamp for comparison) was verified by the American Bank Note Company as a legitimate double-impression error.

The 1991 duck stamp was discovered with missing black intaglio. An enlargement of a section of the error stamp (left) shows lack of detail on the ducks' bodies. The normal stamp and its enlargement is at right.

bore BEP Engraver Gary Chaconas' intaglio lines.

According to Dumaine, the absence of the black created a mauve shade on the drake's breast, and the hen appeared as a much lighter brown than on a normal stamp.

Dumaine, who is a stamp dealer, said the error stamp had been "placed with an advanced duck stamp collector."

Mount Rushmore Color Error Confirmed

The line-engraved Flag Over Mount Rushmore coil stamp of 1991 with the Mount Rushmore image printed in brown instead of maroon was confirmed as a color error by the Bureau of Engraving and Printing. BEP had examined specimens of the stamps at the request of *Linn's*, which first discovered the variety on a piece of mail from the Toledo, Ohio, area. The Scott Publishing Company assigned the variety the number 2523c in its stamp catalogs.

PLATE NUMBERS

Transportation Coils (not precanceled)

Scott number	Stamp	Plate number	Tagging type
1897	1¢ Omnibus (1983)	1,2,3,4,5,6	overall
2225	1¢ Omnibus (1986)	1,2	block
2225a	1¢ Omnibus (1991)	2	untagged
1897A	2¢ Locomotive (1982)	2,3,4,6,8,10	overall
2226	2¢ Locomotive (1987)	1	block
1898	3¢ Handcar (1983)	1,2,3,4	overall
2252	3¢ Conestoga Wagon (1988)	1	block
2252a	3¢ Conestoga Wagon (1988)	2	untagged
2123	3.4¢ School Bus (1985)	1,2	overall
1898A	4¢ Stagecoach (1982)	1,2,3,4,5,6	overall
2228	4¢ Stagecoach (1986)	1	block
2228a	4¢ Stagecoach (1990)	1	overall
2451	4¢ Steam Carriage (1991)	1	overall
2451b	4¢ Steam Carriage (1991)	1	untagged
2124	4.9¢ Buckboard (1985)	3,4	overall
1899	5¢ Motorcycle (1983)	1,2,3,4	overall
2253	5¢ Milk Wagon (1987)	1	block
2452	5¢ Circus Wagon (1990)	1	overall
2452a	5¢ Circus Wagon (1991)	1	untagged
2452B	5¢ Circus Wagon (1992)	A1,A2 (gravure)	untagged
1900	5.2¢ Sleigh (1983)	1,2,3,5	overall
2125	5.5¢ Star Route Truck (1986)	1	block
1901	5.9¢ Bicycle (1982)	3,4	overall
2126	6¢ Tricycle (1985)	1	block
2127	7.1¢ Tractor (1987)	1	block
1902	7.4¢ Baby Buggy (1984)	2	block
2128	8.3¢ Ambulance (1985)	1,2	overall
2129	8.5¢ Tow Truck (1987)	1	block
1903	9.3¢ Mail Wagon (1981)	1,2,3,4,5,6	overall
2257	10¢ Canal Boat (1987)	1	block
not yet assigned	10¢ Canal Boat (1987)	1	overall
2130	10.1¢ Oil Wagon (1985)	1	block
1904	10.9¢ Hansom Cab (1982)	1,2	overall
1905	11¢ Caboose (1984)	1	block
2131	11¢ Stutz Bearcat (1985)	1,2,3,4	overall
2132	12¢ Stanley Steamer (1985)	1,2	overall
2133	12.5¢ Pushcart (1985)	1,2	block
2134	14¢ Iceboat (1985)	1,2,3,4	overall
2134b	14¢ Iceboat (1986)	2	block
2260	15¢ Tugboat (1988)	1, 2	block
2260a	15¢ Tugboat (1988)	2	overall
1906	17¢ Electric Auto (1981)	1-7	overall
2135	17¢ Dog Sled (1986)	2	block

Scott number	Stamp	Plate number	Tagging type
2262	17.5¢ Racing Car (1987)	1	block
1907	18¢ Surrey (1981)	1 through 18 complete	overall
1908	20¢ Fire Pumper (1981)	1 through 16 complete	overall
2263	20¢ Cable Car (1988)	1,2	block
2263b	20¢ Cable Car (1990)	2	overall
2464	23¢ Lunch Wagon (1991)	2,3	phosphor-coated paper
2136	25¢ Bread Wagon (1986)	1 through 5 complete	block
2468	$1 Seaplane (1990)	1	overall

Transportation Coils (precanceled)

Scott number	Stamp	Plate number	Tagging type
2123	3.4¢ School Bus (1985)	1,2	untagged
1898A	4¢ Stagecoach (1982)	3,4,5,6	untagged
2124	4.9¢ Buckboard (1985)	1,2,3,4,5,6	untagged
2453	5¢ Canoe (1991)	1,2	untagged
2454	5¢ Canoe (gravure) (1991)	S11	untagged
1900	5.2¢ Sleigh (1983)	1,2,3,4,5,6	untagged
2254	5.3¢ Elevator (1988)	1	untagged
2125	5.5¢ Star Route Truck (1986)	1,2	untagged
1901	5.9¢ Bicycle (1982)	3,4,5,6	untagged
2126	6¢ Tricycle (1985)	1,2	untagged
2127a	7.1¢ Tractor (1987)	1	untagged
2127a	7.1¢ Tractor (1989)	1	untagged
1902	7.4¢ Buggy (1984)	2	untagged
2255	7.6¢ Carreta (1988)	1,2,3	untagged
2128	8.3¢ Ambulance (1985)	1,2,3,4	untagged
2231	8.3¢ Ambulance (1986)	1,2	untagged
2256	8.4¢ Wheel Chair (1988)	1,2,3	untagged
2129	8.5¢ Tow Truck (1987)	1,2	untagged
1903	9.3¢ Mail Wagon (1981)	1,2,3,4,5,6,8	untagged
2457	10¢ Tractor Trailer (1991)	1	untagged
2130a	10.1¢ Oil Wagon (1985)	1,2	untagged
2130a	10.1¢ Oil Wagon (1988)	2,3	untagged
1904	10.9¢ Hansom Cab (1982)	1,2,3,4	untagged
1905	11¢ Caboose (1984)	1	untagged
not yet assigned	11¢ Caboose (1991)	2	untagged
2132	12¢ Stanley Steamer (1985)	1,2	untagged
2132b	12¢ Stanley Steamer (1987)	1	untagged
2133	12.5¢ Pushcart (1985)	1,2	untagged
2258	13¢ Patrol Wagon (1988)	1	untagged
2259	13.2¢ Coal Car (1988)	1,2	untagged
2261	16.7¢ Popcorn Wagon (1988)	1,2	untagged
1906	17¢ Electric Auto (1981)	1,2,3,4,5,6,7	untagged
2262	17.5¢ Racing Car (1987)	1	untagged
2264	20.5¢ Fire Engine (1988)	1	untagged
2265	21¢ Railroad Mail Car (1988)	1,2	untagged
2266	24.1¢ Tandem Bicycle (1988)	1	untagged

Great Americans Sheet Stamps

Scott number	Stamp	Plate number	Perf type	Tagging type
1844	1¢ Dix	1 floating	bull's-eye	block
1844c	1¢ Dix	1,2 floating	L perf	block
2168	1¢ Mitchell	1	bull's-eye	block
1845	2¢ Stravinsky	1,2,3,4,5,6	electric-eye	overall
2169	2¢ Lyon	1,2	bull's-eye	block
1846	3¢ Clay	1,2	electric-eye	overall
2170	3¢ White	1,2,3	bull's-eye	block
1847	4¢ Schurz	1,2,3,4	electric-eye	overall
2171	4¢ Flanagan	1	bull's-eye	block
2171a	4¢ Flanagan	1	bull's-eye	untagged
1848	5¢ Buck	1,2,3,4	electric-eye	overall
2172	5¢ Black	1,2	bull's-eye	block
2173	5¢ Munoz	1	bull's-eye	overall
		2	bull's-eye	untagged
1849	6¢ Lippmann	1 floating	L perf	block
1850	7¢ Baldwin	1 floating	L perf	block
1851	8¢ Knox	3,4,5,6	L perf	overall
1852	9¢ Thayer	1 floating	L perf	block
1853	10¢ Russell	1 floating	L perf	block
2176	10¢ Red Cloud	1	bull's-eye	block
2176a	10¢ Red Cloud	1,2	bull's-eye	overall
		2	bull's-eye	phosphor-coated
1854	11¢ Partridge	2,3,4,5	L perf	overall
1855	13¢ Crazy Horse	1,2,3,4	electric-eye	overall
1856	14¢ Lewis	1 floating	L perf	block
2177	14¢ Howe	1,2	bull's-eye	block
2178	15¢ Cody	1,3	bull's-eye	block
2178a	15¢ Cody	1,2,3	bull's-eye	overall
1857	17¢ Carson	1,2,3,4,13,14,15,16	electric-eye	overall
2179	17¢ Lockwood	1,2	bull's-eye	block
1858	18¢ Mason	1,2,3,4,5,6	electric-eye	overall
1859	19¢ Sequoyah	39529, 39530	electric-eye	overall
1860	20¢ Bunche	1,2,3,4,5,6,7,8,10,11,13	electric-eye	overall
1861	20¢ Gallaudet	1,2,5,6,8,9	electric-eye	overall
1862	20¢ Truman	1 floating	L perf	block
1862a	20¢ Truman	2	bull's-eye	block
1862b	20¢ Truman	3	bull's-eye	overall
2180	21¢ Carlson	1	bull's-eye	block
1863	22¢ Audubon	1 floating	L perf	block
1863d	22¢ Audubon	3	bull's-eye	block
2182	23¢ Cassatt	1	bull's-eye	block
		1,2	bull's-eye	overall
2182a	23¢ Cassatt	2	bull's-eye	phosphor-coated
2183	25¢ London	1,2	bull's-eye	block
2184	28¢ Sitting Bull	1	bull's-eye	block
2184A	29¢ Warren	S1,S2 (six positions)	bull's-eye	prephosphored

Scott number	Stamp	Plate number	Perf type	Tagging type
1864	30¢ Laubach	1 floating	L perf	block
1864a	30¢ Laubach	2	bull's-eye	block
		2	bull's-eye	overall
1865	35¢ Drew	1,2,3,4	electric-eye	overall
2185	35¢ Chavez	S1,S2 (six positions)	L perf	prephosphored
1866	37¢ Millikan	1,2,3,4	electric-eye	overall
1867	39¢ Clark	1 floating	L perf	block
1867c	39¢ Clark	2	bull's-eye	block
1868	40¢ Gilbreth	1 floating	L perf	block
1868a	40¢ Gilbreth	2	bull's-eye	block
2186	40¢ Chennault	1	bull's-eye	overall
		2	bull's-eye	phosphor-coated
2188	45¢ Cushing	1	bull's-eye	block
2188a	45¢ Cushing	1	bull's-eye	overall
1869	50¢ Nimitz	1,2,3,4	L perf	overall
1869a	50¢ Nimitz	1,2	bull's-eye	block
		2,3	bull's-eye	overall
		3	bull's-eye	prephosphored
2190	52¢ Humphrey	1	bull's-eye	phosphor-coated
2191	56¢ Harvard	1	bull's-eye	block
2192	65¢ Arnold	1	bull's-eye	block
2193	75¢ Willkie	1	bull's-eye	phosphor-coated
		1	bull's-eye	prephosphored
2194	$1 Revel	1	bull's-eye	block
2194A	$1 Hopkins	1	bull's-eye	block
2194Ab	$1 Hopkins	1	bull's-eye	overall
		2	bull's-eye	phosphor-coated
2195	$2 Bryan	2	bull's-eye	block
2196	$5 Bret Harte	1	bull's-eye	block
		2	bull's-eye	prephosphored

Notes:

Plate positions: ***Floating plate number positions are left or right, either blocks of six or strips of 20 (number must be centered in selvage in a block of six). All other plate number positions consist of upper left, upper right, lower left and lower right, with the following exceptions: 29¢ Warren and 35¢ Chavez, which has positions of upper left, center upper right, upper right, lower left, center lower right and lower right. (Traditional corners have plate numbers to the side of the stamps; center positions have plate numbers above or below stamps.)***

Tagging types:

Block: tagging block centered over design of stamp; no tagging in selvage.

Overall: tagging applied to entire pane, often leaving an untagged strip at outer edge of large margin selvage.

Phosphor-coated: paper with coating of phosphor applied before stamps are printed. The phosphor coating is added by the paper finisher rather than the printer.

Prephosphored: paper with phosphor built into structure of paper.

ITEMS WITHDRAWN FROM SALE IN 1992

Commemoratives: 50¢ Switzerland (6/30)
29¢ Vermont (6/30)
29¢ Savings Bonds (8/31)
29¢ William Saroyan (8/31)
$5.80 Fishing Flies booklet (10/31)
$1.45 Fishing Flies booklet pane (10/31)
29¢ Cole Porter (10/31)
29¢ Desert Storm (8/31)
$5.80 Desert Storm booklet (8/31)
$1.45 Desert Storm booklet pane (8/31)
29¢ Numismatics (10/31)
29¢ Basketball (10/31)
29¢ District of Columbia (10/31)
$16.34 Columbian souvenir sheets (9/27)

Special Stamps: 29¢ Love 1991, bull's-eye perf (12/31)
29¢ Love 1991, L perf (12/31)
Non-denominated (29¢) Christmas Madonna, 1991 *
Non-denominated ($5.80) Christmas Madonna, 1991, booklet *
Non-denominated ($2.90) Christmas Madonna, 1991, booklet pane*
Non-denominated (29¢) Christmas Santa, 1991 *
Non-denominated ($5.80) Christmas Santa, 1991, booklet *
Non-denominated ($5.80) Christmas Santa, 1991, 5 booklet panes of 5 designs *

* — No off-sale announcement was made for these items, but they were last listed in the July-August catalog of the Philatelic Sales Division.

Definitives: 7¢ Abraham Baldwin (2/28)
39¢ Grenville Clark (8/31)
9¢ Sylvanus Thayer (2/28)
8¢ Henry Knox (6/30)
17¢ Dog Sled coils of 100 (6/30)
$5 Bret Harte, original issue (4/30)
5¢ Milk Wagon coils of 100 (6/30)
$3 U.S. Flag sheetlet, ATM (2/28)
F (29¢) (8/31)
F (29¢) coils of 100 (6/30)
F (29¢) coils of 500 (6/30)
F ($2.90) booklet, KCS (8/31)
F ($2.90) booklet, BEP (8/31)
F ($5.80) booklet, BEP (8/31)
F ($3.48) U.S. flag sheetlet, ATM (10/31)
Makeup Rate (4¢) (10/31)

$5.80 Flower booklet (10/31)
$2.90 Flower booklet pane (10/31)
$5.80 Wood Duck booklet, BEP (8/31)
$2.90 Wood Duck booklet pane, BEP (10/31)
$5.80 Wood Duck booklet, KCS (8/31)
$2.90 Wood Duck booklet pane, KCS (10/31)

Airmail and Expedited Mail: 45¢ America, 1990 (6/30)

Duck Stamps: $12.50 Lesser Scaup, 1989 (8/31)

Stamped Envelopes: F (29¢) Official Mail (6/30)
29¢ Security, "Arizona" variety (12/31)
29¢ Magazine Industry (12/31)
75¢ Consular Service Official Mail (11/10)

Postal Cards: 15¢ White House (8/31)
15¢ Jefferson Memorial (6/30)
19¢ Carnegie Hall (2/28)
19¢ Old Red (12/31)
19¢ Bill of Rights (12/31)
19¢ Notre Dame (12/31)
19¢ Old Mill (12/31)